An
Historical Introduction
to Moral Philosophy

An
Historical Introduction
to Moral Philosophy

MICHAEL F. WAGNER
The University of San Diego

Prentice Hall
Englewood Cliffs, New Jersey 07632

Library of Congress Cataloging-in-Publication Data

An Historical introduction to moral philosophy / [selected and edited
by] MICHAEL F. WAGNER.
   p. cm.
  Includes index.
  ISBN 0-13-601451-8
  1. Ethics—History. 2. Ethics. I. Wagner, Michael F.
BJ71.H57   1991   90-46813
170'.9—dc20

Editorial/production supervision
  and interior design: *Edith Riker/Chris Nassauer*
Cover design: *20/20 Services*
Prepress buyer: *Herb Klein*
Manufacturing buyer: *Dave Dickey*

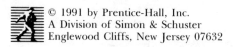

Printed in the United States of America

10 9 8 7 6 5 4 3 2 1

ISBN   0-13-601451-8

Prentice-Hall International (UK) Limited, *London*
Prentice-Hall of Australia Pty. Limited, *Sydney*
Prentice-Hall Canada Inc., *Toronto*
Prentice-Hall Hispanoamericana, S.A., *Mexico*
Prentice-Hall of India Private Limited, *New Delhi*
Prentice-Hall of Japan, Inc., *Tokyo*
Simon & Schuster Asia Pte. Ltd., *Singapore*
Editora Prentice-Hall do Brasil, Ltda., *Rio de Janeiro*

Contents

Chapter Three

Classical Developments

Chapter Four

Medieval Developments

Chapter Five

Modern Developments

Chapter Six

Contemporary Perspectives

Preface

A free and democratic society demands as much from its citizens as it permits of them. A sense of individual responsibility and a capacity for prudent judgment are crucial if such a society is to survive and flourish. How should I live? How should I act? Such questions are fundamental expressions of our desire for liberty; and commitment to answering them is essential to meeting liberty's demands. They are also among the most basic questions of moral philosophy. Indeed, moral philosophy consists, in large part, of the attempt to answer such questions.

This text is titled *An Historical Introduction to Moral Philosophy* because it approaches moral philosophy as a connected, living tradition which is best understood by studying its great ideas and thinkers, past as well as present. It does not pretend to be a "complete" history of moral philosophy. It does, however, see much in every major period of Western thought that is still worth studying, for its own sake as well as to deepen your understanding of current thought by appreciating its antecedents and origins. Examining its readings will allow you to observe the origination of ideas and to experience the adventure of our intellectual heritage. Its historical approach also exposes you to a wider variety of approaches and ideas within moral philosophy than is possible in more parochial approaches to the subject.

In selecting and compiling the readings in this text, the desire to present a diversity of approaches and ideas was weighed against the equally important desire to expose you to significant chunks of material from individual philosophers—and in a reasonably sized textbook. The twenty-five readings in this text were chosen for their diversity, historical significance, and their attention to the topics or questions which have been most fundamental in the history of moral philosophy overall. They include significant chunks of uninterrupted philosophical discourse; however, most are also judiciously edited to introduce you to main elements in the author's moral philosophy while maintaining an intelligible sense of the narrative and logical development of the longer work. Each reading is introduced by a brief biography of its author—and in Plato's case, of his teacher, Socrates—to give you some sense of the man or woman who generated such a work.

This text also pays serious attention to the way philosophers and philosophy teachers tend to approach moral philosophy today. The general introduction introduces you to main concepts and distinctions in contemporary metaethics, for example; and the importance of reasoned analysis and critique is emphasized—especially in the general introduction's discussion of logical technique, in the Study/Discussion Forms, and in the five "Themes and Ideas" chapter introductions, which highlight some of the reasoning behind certain features of the readings.

The Study/Discussion Forms, in effect, outline how you should approach philosophical works to fully understand them and in critically reflecting on their ideas. They are fairly detailed but are easily modified by paraphrasing or omitting certain parts (or subparts). They can also all be answered narratively, as raising points for you to consider in an essay or narrative form; or you may answer some of them by reconstructing pertinent ideas from the readings in concise, logically related terms—for example, when identifying the justifying reasons or arguments that are explicitly or implicitly contained in the readings. The analytic, critical approach emphasized in the Study/Discussion Forms will also enhance your own intellectual skills and stimulate your own search for answers to the fundamentally human questions addressed in moral philosophy.

I thank my editors and the anonymous readers employed by Prentice Hall for their comments and suggestions, and the publishers and living authors of the protected works used in this text for their cooperation. I especially thank Monica Wagner and Pat Bodin for their immense skill and patience in preparing the various drafts of the manuscript. Early work was aided by a research grant and a research sabbatical from the University of San Diego, for which I am truly grateful. In many ways, however, it is my philosophy teachers at Texas A & M University and Ohio State University and my students at the University of San Diego who have made composing this text possible.

An
Historical Introduction
to Moral Philosophy

Chapter One

Introduction:
What is Moral Philosophy?

This text includes readings from some of the most important thinkers in the history of moral philosophy. Moral philosophy is a living tradition which can best be understood and appreciated by studying its major figures. Here, as in other areas of philosophy, careful study of perennial themes and diverse approaches also develops one's own philosophical acumen. Continual reexamination of our philosophical heritage remains a major force in intellectual progress. Finally, many of our own ideas and beliefs are products of that heritage. Understanding it deepens our understanding of our own day and time, and even of ourselves.

The readings in this text are divided into five chapters, corresponding to five stages or eras in the development of moral philosophy. Each chapter begins with a brief introduction ("Themes and Ideas"). These introductions outline main features of each era and discuss some main ideas and concerns of the philosophers in the chapter. In this way, they should help organize and clarify your encounter with the readings. However, they do not capture the full philosophical content of the readings. They in no way substitute for careful reading (and rereading) of each selection.

The remainder of this general introduction will orient you to the study of moral philosophy. First, it will discuss the motivations for moral philosophy and state a general definition of it. It will then discuss the

1

central place of reason and tradition in philosophy generally and the distinctive, normative nature of moral philosophy in particular. Special attention will be paid next to philosophical reasoning and how to critically assess it. Finally, it will introduce main topics and concepts in metaethics.

DEFINING MORAL PHILOSOPHY

Human beings are faced with numerous choices, day in and day out, throughout life. We choose what clothes to wear, whether to go to work (or to school) today, what to eat for lunch, how to spend our leisure time, what career to pursue, how to conduct ourselves around others, what political candidate to support, whether to donate money to charity, whether to consume alcohol, and so on, and so on. Sometimes our choices seem unimportant; there is nothing earthshaking about them. Other times they can have profound effects—on our own lives and on the lives of others. We make some choices quite readily, with little or no forethought. Other times we deliberate long and arduously before deciding what to do. But, whatever their significance or difficulty, we are responsible for all of our actions, at least insofar as we choose them or are their agents.

We can also be responsible for our actions in a more important way: insofar as we take responsibility for their consequences or significance, or for the quality of choices we make. We can take our agency seriously and attend to how well we perform as agents. Rather than doing just the first thing that comes to mind, for example, we can reflect on our options, evaluate them, and choose our actions accordingly. Moral philosophy is motivated by the fact that people generally do strive to be responsible agents. In particular, we often want not merely to make some choice or other but to make a (perhaps *the*) right, good, or correct choice. We try to determine which among our options would be the (or at least *a*) right, good, or correct choice, and then try to act accordingly. What career shall I choose? Well, what career would be the right one (at least for me)? Shall I support a policy of nuclear deterrence or one of nuclear disarmament? Well, which would be the right (or at least better) way to proceed? And so on. Thus, we do not wish simply to live our lives and get them over with, but to make our way through life's complexities and myriad choices with some degree of success, perhaps even excellence. We do not wish simply to live, but to live well, or in a good way.

But how, as we evaluate our options, can we determine which ones are right or good—and, conversely, which ones are wrong or bad? This question takes us from motivations for moral philosophy to the activity of moral philosophy itself. Moral philosophy is the search for something to guide us in determining what is right or good, wrong or bad. Insofar as we characterize this "something" as a kind of wisdom, we can define moral philosophy as the search for wisdom to guide us in determining what is right or good and what is wrong or bad. This definition also reflects the literal meaning of "moral philosophy." *Philosophy* comes from the Greek word *philosophia*, meaning love of wisdom; and *moral* comes from the Latin word *mos*, which means conduct or ways of acting—as does the Greek word *ethos*, from which we get *ethical* and *ethics*. Moral philosophy (or ethics) literally refers to a love of wisdom pertaining to our conduct or (chosen) actions.

The search for moral wisdom has led philosophers to investigate many related (and interrelated) topics and issues. However, most of these center on certain distinctions we rely upon to evaluate things, especially those between right and wrong, and good and bad. Exploring these distinctions, or the concepts they employ, will be the dominant theme of this text. Two related themes will also emerge as special, perennial concerns of moral philosophers. One is the relationship between right action, or the pursuit of goodness, and quality of life. Right action, according to many moral philosophers, pays: A well-lived life is a happy life. Right action promotes human happiness. The second theme is the social nature of morality. Humans are social beings, and our actions often affect those around us and even the general quality of life in our society. Many moral philosophers view moral conduct and civility, or socially right action, as inseparable. Some even view morality and civility as one and the same thing.

REASON AND TRADITION IN MORAL PHILOSOPHY

Philosophy students sometimes ask: What is the *practical* value of philosophy, anyway? Students often expect each of their courses to deal with some single, narrowly defined aspect of life; and they assume that a course is "practical" only if it relates directly to a particular job or career. However, "practical" means applicable to our conduct, actions, or choices. Viewed in this light, no course is more practical than moral philosophy. For moral philosophy does not deal just with some particular aspect of human life but with human conduct in general. It pertains to everything we do in life, not just to what we do while at work or while engaging in this or that activity.

Many students also expect each of their courses to supply them with definitive answers, with a preestablished body of knowledge; but philosophy courses are not like that. To be sure, philosophy instructors require students to study and understand lecture and text materials, but they also emphasize the reasoning behind philosophers' views and critically discuss them. Philosophy instructors present their material, not as a fixed body of knowledge, but as ideas or viewpoints to be understood, analyzed, and critically discussed. But this only enhances the practical value of philosophy. Analytic and critical skills are essential to success in life, as well as to the moral goal of living well.

Philosophy courses do not just teach about philosophy. They try to teach the activity of philosophy itself. In this course, for example, students are expected not merely to learn something about moral philosophy but to become moral philosophers. The ability to understand diverse viewpoints, to analyze the reasoning behind them, and to critically assess them is essential to being a philosopher, or to doing philosophy.

Philosophy is a rational activity. Philosophers seek wisdom as the outcome of rational investigation. They do not accept blindly what other people believe or say, nor what is commonplace, or "common sense," in a given society. Nor do they merely rationalize their own prephilosophical beliefs. Every philosopher must accept responsibility for what he or she ultimately will believe and for the reasoning which led to that belief.

In philosophy, no single person's ideas or viewpoints carry any special weight or authority. A philosopher must examine everyone's ideas—his or her own, as well as those of other people. At the same time, he or she must be open to the possibility that his or her own or someone else's ideas might in fact turn out to be correct. A philosophical investigation *might* result in some completely novel idea. However, a philosopher cannot anticipate any particular result at the outset of an investigation, but must remain open to going wherever the investigation will lead.

Philosophical open-mindedness should not be confused with the following viewpoints:

1. An open-minded person never believes anything at all; he or she never accepts any idea as true.
2. An open-minded person believes that anything that anyone believes to be true thereby is in fact true.
3. An open-minded person believes that nothing is ever really true, even that no idea is ever any better than any other idea.
4. An open-minded person never critically assesses other people's ideas or beliefs.

Each of these viewpoints expresses a particular philosophical position, a possible result of philosophical investigation; but none of them captures the sense in which a philosopher must be open-minded at the outset of an investigation. The first expresses a position known as Pyrrhonian Skepticism. The second is a version of a position called relativism, while the third is a type of nihilism. The fourth viewpoint is sometimes inferred from one of the previous three and is an extreme form of tolerance.

A philosopher must be open to going wherever an investigation will lead. This does not mean that he or she will (or should) never believe anything at all (position [1]), but only that he or she must not be prejudiced toward (or against) any particular idea or possible outcome from the outset. A philosopher must also be willing to reopen an investigation when new evidence or a new idea presents itself, but this also does not mean that he or she should not actually believe the results of the investigation. Moreover, philosophical open-mindedness embraces the possibility—contrary to (2)—that an investigation might conclude that some things people believe to be true are not true at all, as well as the possibility—contrary to (3)—that some things people believe to be true are indeed true after all.

Philosophical investigation involves critically assessing ideas, and a philosopher certainly must never rule out the possibility that he or she had made a mistake somewhere in the investigation. Moreover, concluding that someone else's ideas are in fact false certainly does not imply that he or she should be shot, exiled, denied freedom of speech, or the like. But this does not mean, as viewpoint (4) claims, that a philosopher should not critically assess other peoples' ideas at all, or that he or she should not proclaim that certain of their ideas are false if the investigation leads to that conclusion.

The rational activity of philosophy originated in classical Greece. The classical Greeks' belief in the power and dignity of human reason prompted them to adopt a critical attitude toward one another's (and also toward their own) ideas. This attitude requires, however, that one seriously considers other peoples' ideas. Rational debate among philosophers has been an essential feature of philosophy ever since. As a result, philosophy is not a collection of unrelated investigations by solitary thinkers, but a connected, living tradition.

Although every philosopher must take up the search for wisdom anew, he or she does not somehow start from scratch, but seeks to learn from his or her predecessors and contemporaries. The search for moral wisdom is usually traced to Socrates, whose own search was continued by his students and by moral philosophers in each succeeding generation; and it still continues today. By making ourselves part of this tradition, we avail ourselves of its insights, ideas, and reasoning, while honing our own capacities to live responsibly and well.

THE NORMATIVE NATURE OF MORAL PHILOSOPHY

Philosophy is the oldest of what came to be known as the liberal arts. The term *liberal arts* refers to disciplines or courses of study which seek to liberate us from ignorance and free us from the particular forces and prejudices which influence our beliefs and threaten to control our lives, allowing us to achieve our own human excellence. Historically, philosophy has been the source of all other liberal arts. Mathematics, theology, physics, psychology, and the rest are branches on the tree of philosophy, the results of certain thinkers deciding to focus on particular topics and, in some cases, to develop special methods of investigation.

The idea that philosophy in general, and so moral philosophy in particular, liberates the best features of our humanity may seem opposed to many people's concept of morality. Many view morality as a repressive institution, as a set of rules which society, religion, parents, or the like impose on us to prevent us from living as we see fit. Indeed, moral philosophy does seek to impose something on us, since its goal is to discern standards or principles which determine what is right or good, wrong or bad, and so which shape our moral deliberations and conduct. This wisdom is not imposed on us by other people, however, but by ourselves, insofar as we are genuinely committed to attaining it. The idea that moral wisdom does seek to impose itself on us in this way is sometimes expressed by saying that moral philosophy is a normative discipline. *Normative,* and its root *norm,* come from the Latin word *norma,* meaning a rule or standard. To better understand the normative nature of moral philosophy, consider two different, though not always unrelated, sorts of rules or standards.

Sometimes a rule or standard refers to what is usual or average. (The Latin word *norma* is also the source of our word *normal.*) Thus, we might say that as a rule it is sunny in southern California, meaning that it usually is sunny in southern California or that on an average day it (probably) will be sunny in southern California. Or we might say that it is standard practice to make an appointment before going to the doctor, meaning that people usually do this, or that in average (normal) situations people make an appointment before going to the doctor. This first sort of rule or standard does not "impose" anything on our moral deliberations; it simply summarizes or states certain facts—viz., what is usual or average.

A rule or standard may also determine how we are to evaluate something. When we say, for example, that a doctor meets the norms of the medical profession, we might be saying just that he or she is an average doctor. However, we might have something more in mind: That there exist certain standards which determine when someone is a good doctor, and this doctor meets those standards. This sort of standard (or rule) does not merely state some fact about doctors—say, what an "average" doctor is like. Its primary function is evaluative, telling us when a doctor is to be deemed a good doctor. It also establishes a goal for doctors to strive for, insofar as one wishes to be deemed a good doctor.

An evaluative standard may, of course, derive from what is usual or average. Sometimes the two sorts of standards may even be one and the same, especially when applied to professions or activities that demand a special proficiency to begin with. Being an average professional basketball player, for example, should suffice for being deemed a good professional basketball player. An evaluative standard may also require a higher level of achievement than just being average. When we say that someone is a good doctor, or a good teacher, or perhaps a good person, this may mean that he or she has achieved more than just an average level of performance, that his or her performance is superior in some way. In such cases, the evaluative standard may still derive from facts about average doctors, teachers, or persons—say, by observing what is usually the case and simply demanding more of it. Or it might derive from certain characteristics observed in a special, select group of individuals. Or, finally, it might somehow derive from somewhere or something other than observations of individuals and their activities or accomplishments. Its source might lie elsewhere in nature, for example, perhaps even outside of the natural world altogether, or at least in part. But whatever its source, an evaluative standard's primary function is to determine when something merits a positive evaluation; and, insofar as it functions in this way, an evaluative standard is not concerned with the way things are, but with the way they should or ought to be (if they are to be deemed good). If the (evaluative) standard for being a good doctor is X, then someone is a good doctor just in case he or she attains or satisfies X, whether or not he or she or any other doctor in fact satisfies or has ever satisfied X.

The distinctive, "normative" nature of moral philosophy lies in its attempt to discern evaluative standards for human conduct. The "wisdom" sought by moral philosophers is evaluative standards—an understanding of what determines when something is good or right, or bad or wrong. It seeks to impose itself on us by telling us what human conduct should or ought to be like, if it is to merit a positive evaluation.

Moral philosophers do not all present the wisdom that they believe they have attained in the same way. Some explicitly state normative rules or principles. Other moral philosophers, in fact the majority in this text, do not canonize their moral wisdom so succinctly. They try to develop and communicate an understanding of goodness and moral conduct which cannot always be easily captured in a single rule, or even an exact set of rules. This does not, however, diminish the normative intent of their moral philosophies.

Much of the moral wisdom purported in this text is very general and, sometimes, abstract. Once again, the classical Greeks set the tone. They believed that wisdom or knowledge begins with understanding. Before one can articulate, much less "know," detailed, specific standards or principles—whether moral, scientific, or whatever—he or she must first understand the general nature of the subject matter. Let us call an evaluative standard which states exactly what ought to be the case or how one ought to act at a particular time or in a particular situation a first-order standard, and one which expresses how we ought to behave or live generally a second-order standard. In these terms, we can say that the readings in this text are more concerned with discerning and expressing second-order standards, rather than first-order standards. They presume that the first, and perhaps the most important, step to attaining moral wisdom is the second-order one of understanding the nature of rightness, goodness, or of moral conduct and living well.

THE RATIONAL NATURE OF PHILOSOPHY

Many philosophers have argued that rationality is unique to human beings—that our ability to reason sets us apart from all other creatures and gives us the unique capacity to attain wisdom or knowledge. Some contend, however, that some nonhuman creatures are also rational, or at least that they are capable of certain behaviors usually associated with rationality— for example, symbolic communication (language), or solving practical problems. But, despite this contention, the idea of rationality remains central to our conception of philosophical activity. This is especially true insofar as rationality is associated with logical thinking. This section will focus on two characteristics of logical (hence, rational) thought: (1) it is systematic, and (2) it moves and results are based on justifying reasons.

(1) Rational Thought Is Systematic. One of Greek philosophy's most enduring achievements is mathematics. A mathematician investigates a topic (or problem) by breaking it down into main parts or steps, examining each part in sequence, and synthesizing the results of examining each part into a coherent whole—for example, into a "proof." In this way, mathematics is a systematic, or logically structured, activity. A mathematical investigation moves systematically through a number of logically ordered steps to arrive at a final solution to some problem.

Philosophical investigations are systematic in a similar way: A philosopher breaks a topic down into main parts or subtopics, investigates each part in sequence, and arrives at a synthesis and final resolution of the topic. Thus, every philosophical investigation has a logical structure and systematically achieved results. This might not always seem obvious, especially on a first reading of many selections in this text. In every case, however, you should try to identify the main point, or final result, of a philosopher's investigation and the main subtopics or steps which lead to that result. One way to do this is to analyze and outline each reading's basic structure: What (sub)topics are discussed, what are the main things that are said about each one, and how do they all fit together to lead to a final result, or to develop the main point of the reading? You should keep an especially sharp eye out for points and discussions which can be rendered or reconstructed as arguments. This brings us to the second general characteristic of logical thought, and to how one critically assesses a philosopher's ideas.

(2) Rational Thought Is Based on Justifying Reasons.   We have said that a philosopher must adopt an open-minded attitude toward an investigation. Another way of saying this is that a philosopher must remain objective and not allow personal feelings, preconceived ideas, or prejudices to influence the investigation—insofar as this is humanly possible. One way in which philosophers try to do this is to search for *reasons* which would *justify* an investigation's moving in one direction rather than another, ending in one particular result.

A philosophical investigation can be viewed as a set of statements—of ideas which can be expressed in subject-predicate sentences. Now, let us define a justifying reason as a statement which seeks to establish the truth of another statement. Justifying reasons are not rationalizations. Rationalizations attempt to avoid determining whether or not an idea or belief is in fact true. They are excuses for believing something, whether or not it is in fact true. In seeking wisdom, however, a philosopher seeks the truth regarding some topic. Searching for justifying reasons is the primary way in which philosophers try to determine what the truth is on a given topic. The logical complexity of a philosophical investigation depends on the number of justifying reasons included among its statements and the number of different statements which it seeks to establish. Thus, every philosophical investigation includes one or more (usually more) subsets of statements related to one another in a very special way: such that one (perhaps more) of the statements in each subset is intended as a justifying reason(s) for the remaining statement in the subset. Such subsets of statements are called arguments. An argument, in this sense, is not a fight or a verbal free-for-all but a structured activity in which one (or more) statement(s) is meant to establish the truth of another statement. In an argument, the statement whose truth is purportedly established by the justifying reason(s) is called the *conclusion,* and the justifying reason(s) is (are) called the *premise(s).* Thus, an argument is composed of a premise (or premises) and a conclusion; and the ways in which an investigation's arguments build on or relate to one another determine its logical structure. Finally, to critically assess an investigation, we must examine its arguments. Arguments are the backbone of any philosophical investigation. Whether or not we should accept its final conclusion(s) depends on how strong a case has been made for it (or them), and this can be determined only by assessing its arguments.

(Keep in mind that this section is discussing the nature of philosophical investigation, as conceived in the rationalistic tradition which has dominated Western thought at least since Socrates proclaimed that he always searches for and follows the "best argument" in deciding what to believe on any topic. In the case of moral philosophers, accordingly, this discussion concerns their conclusions *about* morality, not necessarily their, or anyone else's, morality or values as such. We shall see later, in a section on so-called metaethics, that there are serious philosophical issues regarding whether moral judgments, beliefs, or values are themselves capable of justification in the sense of being shown to be "true" or "false"; and we shall also see that a philosopher may hold both that philosophical conclusions *about* morality or values may be true or false and yet that morality itself is not likewise a rational enterprise capable of containing truths or falsehoods.)

An argument succeeds in justifying, or establishing the truth of, its conclusion when it satisfies two conditions. First, its premises must be the sort of premises that would establish the truth of the conclusion if they were themselves true. Second, the premises must in fact be true. Only true premises can establish the actual truth of a conclusion. A false beginning (premise) cannot lead us to the truth. However, before true premises can actually establish the truth of the conclusion, they must first point us toward that conclusion as the one which they would establish if they were true. To invoke a crude analogy, a rocket needs fuel in order to reach the moon; if it is empty, it cannot reach the moon. But, it must first be the right sort of rocket—viz., the sort of rocket that would reach the moon if it were fueled up. Arguments satisfying the first condition are termed *valid,* while arguments that also satisfy the second condition are termed *sound.*

You may still wonder, our rocket analogy aside, why the first, more complicated condition is introduced as prior to the second, simpler-sounding condition. For one thing, determining whether an argument's premises are themselves true is often a more difficult task than assessing validity, and it is a task which becomes unnecessary if the argument is not valid anyway. Moreover, the critical acumen developed by assessing the logical structures, or the purported validity, of arguments is often essential to assessing the truth of premises. Indeed, determining whether a given premise is itself true often requires looking for additional justifying reasons, ones which would establish the truth of that premise when taken as itself the conclusion of some previous argument. If nothing else, a practiced, highly developed understanding of validity can help us figure out where we might look to assess the truth of a premise.

Suppose I want to know what day of the week today is and, after some reflection, I come up with the following argument: Today is Wednesday because yesterday was Tuesday. This argument contains two statements, expressed in two subject-predicate sentence structures: "Today is Wednesday" and "yesterday was Tuesday." The use of *because* in composing this argument indicates that the statement expressed in "yesterday was Tuesday" is meant to justify the one expressed in "Today is Wednesday." Hence, "yesterday was Tuesday" expresses a premise—a justifying reason—and "Today is Wednesday" expresses the conclusion of this argument.

Does this argument provide me with the knowledge I seek? Do I now know what day of the week today is? To be sure, this argument *claims* to provide me with this knowledge. It concludes that today is Wednesday, and it tells me why I should accept this conclusion as true. But merely concluding that today is Wednesday and offering a (justifying) reason for this conclusion does not, by itself, establish that today is Wednesday. For this to occur, these statements or allegations must constitute a sound argument. The premise expressed in "yesterday was Tuesday" must be the sort of premise which would establish that today is Wednesday if it were itself true—in other words, the argument must be valid—and it must in fact be true that yesterday was Tuesday. Is this the case? Does this argument satisfy our two conditions?

Earlier we noted that figuring out whether a premise is itself true can be more difficult than determining whether an argument is at least valid. Thus, our present example certainly appears to be at least a valid argument: Yesterday's being Tuesday would seem to point to today's being Wednesday; or, conversely, today's being Wednesday would seem to follow from yesterday's being Tuesday. Always keep in mind, though, that appearances can be deceiving. Strictly speaking, yesterday's being Tuesday would not, by itself, lead to today's being Wednesday. Additional premises are needed for this argument to be indisputably valid—say, "The day after Tuesday is always Wednesday" and "Today is the day after yesterday." Nevertheless, an important point emerges: Determining validity does not require knowing whether its premise(s) is (are) in fact true. No matter what day of the week yesterday in fact was, it would still be the case that today would be Wednesday if it were true that yesterday was Tuesday.

For contrast, suppose I argued instead: Today is Wednesday because yesterday was Monday. In this case, even if the premise was in fact true, the argument would still fail to establish the truth of its conclusion. Today's being Wednesday simply does not follow from yesterday's being Monday. Thus, the question to ask when determining validity is, "If the premise(s) were true, would this establish that the conclusion must also be true?" If the answer to this hypothetical question is yes, then the argument is valid, whether its premise(s) is (are) in fact true or not; and if the answer is no, then the argument is simply not valid, regardless of the actual truth-status of its premise(s). Indeed, if you think that an argument is valid, you could also suppose that its premise(s) is (are) in fact false and ask, "But does the conclusion at least follow from the premise? Would it have to be true if the premise had been true?" If the argument is valid, you should be able to answer yes to these questions.

Recall, however, that even our original argument was clearly valid only because we supposed that it contained certain suppressed premises. Similarly, although our second argument appears not to be valid, we could turn it into a valid argument by adding certain premises. Thus, the following argument is valid: Today is Wednesday because yesterday was Monday, because the day after Monday is always Wednesday, and because today is the day after yesterday. A special area of philosophy, Logic, studies more objective ways to determine once and for all whether an argument is valid. For now, however, remember to keep a sharp eye out for ways in which a philosopher's reasoning might rely on suppressed, unstated premises. Being a stickler about always demanding a full accounting of every last bit of information that is needed to show clearly why a given conclusion supposedly follows from given premises, or continually asking yourself what it would take to make an argument valid, can reveal much about a philosopher's views—and your own as well.

When critically assessing an argument, you should also keep in mind that, actually, there are two main types of arguments: deductive arguments and inductive arguments. Some arguments may intend to justify their conclusions more strongly than others. Strictly speaking, validity and soundness apply only to deductive arguments—arguments which try to establish the truth of their conclusions absolutely, once and for all time. A sound deductive argument leaves no room whatsoever for its conclusion even possibly failing to be true. Thus, in a valid (deductive) argument it is impossible that its conclusion might fail to be true if its premises were to turn out to be true. This suggests yet another way to critically assess a deductive argument. Suppose (for the sake of argument) that the premise(s) is (are) in fact true, and ask, "Is there any way whatsoever that its conclusion could fail to be true under these conditions?" If the (deductive) argument is valid, the answer must be "Absolutely not!" Conversely, if the answer is, "Yes, there is!" then the argument is not valid. Searching for ways in which a conclusion might fail to be true, even when its premise(s) is (are) presumed to be true, is also an excellent way to identify suppressed or unstated premises.

Deductively valid arguments are philosophers' ultimate goal. As a seeker of truth, a philosopher should like nothing better than to find arguments which are absolutely conclusive. It can sometimes be very difficult, however, to find justifying reasons which both can serve as premises in a (deductively) valid argument and which are also themselves clearly true. Sometimes the best, or most arguably true, justifying reasons one can find are not sufficient to yield a (deductively) valid argument. Moreover, suppose that an argument is not (deductively) valid. Does this mean that it is simply no good, that it does not provide us with any reason at all to believe its conclusion? Not necessarily. An argument can fail to be absolutely conclusive and still justify its conclusion to some degree. It might establish that its conclusion is probably, though not definitively, true. This is the intent of inductive arguments.

The strength of an inductive argument depends on how likely it is that its conclusion might fail to be true even if its premise(s) were in fact true. Precisely how strong an inductive argument must be before a rational person should accept its conclusion varies, depending on the nature of its topic, on the relative strengths of opposing arguments, and perhaps even on how frustrated we became at trying to find sound (deductive) arguments. Nevertheless, keep in mind that an argument should not be simply disregarded just because it is not (deductively) valid. For, considered as an inductive argument, it may still be rationally convincing. Moreover, when comparing the arguments of different philosophers, even if none of them is absolutely conclusive, some might at least be (inductively) stronger than others.

THEORY AND METATHEORY IN MORAL PHILOSOPHY

The capacity to discriminate right and wrong, or good and bad, is central to moral agency. Indeed, we normally exempt creatures which lack this capacity from moral considerations. A lion killing its prey, a bear ravaging a campsite, a gerbil cannibalizing its young—such behaviors may elicit disapproval, even disgust from us. We do not, however, debate the morality of these behaviors. Animal behaviors are not "immoral" (nor "moral"). Morality, we might say, is human centered. Among creatures, human beings alone are capable of moral discrimination and deliberation, and so of moral agency.

Morality is also very much a social activity. If you were stranded on a desert island, you could continue adhering to moral standards if you so desire; but the very idea of morality would lose much of its meaning. Arguably, anything you might do would be permissible in such a solitary context. At the very least, you would have much greater "moral" latitude. The social nature of morality also demands that we be able to communicate the results of our moral deliberations, that those results be capable of linguistic expression. Accordingly, moral judgments are sometimes characterized as beliefs, thoughts, or deliberative conclusions about what is right or wrong, or good or bad, which can be expressed in sentences of the form "X is F," where X refers to the object of the judgment and F expresses a moral concept—e.g., right, wrong, good, or bad.

Normative ethics—the primary subject matter of this text—searches for standards of moral conduct. Metaethics, in contrast, investigates moral philosophy itself—its methods, basic concepts, and the natures of various moral philosophies. Metaethics as distinct, or at least distinguishable, from normative ethics is largely a twentieth-century development. Three main topics in metaethics are the natures of main (normative) theories, or of the moral standards they propose; the nature of moral judgments; and the nature or function of moral concepts.

(1). The Natures of Ethical Theories.   Metaethicists distinguish two main classes of ethical theories: consequentialist theories and deontological theo-

ries. The basic idea in consequentialism is that an action's rightness or wrongness depends upon its consequences. To determine whether an action is right or wrong, consequentialism maintains, we must examine its consequences. All moral philosophers recognize that, obviously, our actions have consequences; and most would agree that right actions aim at, or result in, goodness in some way. Consequentialism insists, however, that right actions do not merely result in goodness, but that this is what makes them right. Rightness is solely a function of producing goodness, or of having good consequences. Particular consequentialist theories differ, however, in their conception of goodness—over precisely what sorts of consequences are good, right-making consequences. Some examples of consequentialist theories include the following:

Hedonism—the rightness of an action depends upon the amount and/or the quality of pleasure it produces.

Epicureanism—right action promotes pleasure while minimizing pain.

Egoism—an action is right insofar as it promotes the self-interests of its agent.

Classic or Generic Utilitarianism—the rightness of an action depends upon how useful or beneficial it is, as opposed to how disuseful or harmful it is.

Act Utilitarianism—the right action (in a given situation) is the one which would promote the greatest amount of happiness for the greatest number of persons (in that situation); or, right action promotes the common good, the general welfare, or interests common to all persons.

Rule Utilitarianism—an action is right if consistently acting on a rule or law sanctioning that sort of action would promote the common good, the greatest happiness, or etc.

Instrumentalism (or Pragmatism)—an action is right if it improves the existing situation, remedies some deficiency in it, or resolves a specific problem.

(These, and also our later, examples of theory types and metatheoretic definitions of them are gross simplifications of highly complex moral philosophies. They obscure a number of differences and variations among the individual moral philosophies they attempt to encapsulate. Such general characterizations of main theory types are also not always mutually exclusive. A philosopher's actual moral theory might resemble more than one of them in certain of its aspects, and some theory types may be further defined in such a way that they become subtypes of other theory types. Moreover, these, and also later, definitions of main theory types are not necessarily the only ones possible. As in most areas of philosophy, meta-ethicists do not universally agree upon a single, absolutely best way to define various types of ethical theories.)

In deontology, in contrast, the rightness or wrongness of actions is not solely a function of their consequences. The fact that right actions produce goodness is not what makes them right. The metaethical term *deontology* comes from the Greek word *deon*, meaning what is binding, right, or proper. For deontologists, once we judge an action to be right, we are morally bound to do it, regardless of its actual ensuing consequences. The contrast here with consequentialism is subtle, but important. In a way, consequentalism requires a wait-and-see attitude. We must first see, or somehow determine, the actual consequences of an action before we can determine whether it is right or not. But what if things turn out differently than expected? How can a moral agent ever be "morally certain" about what action to choose, if he or she must always wait to see whether his or her expectations were accurate? Accordingly, deontologists insist that the rightness or wrongness of an action must have priority over its actual consequences. Thus, while a deontological theory may require us to consider an action's potential consequences, it would not make the rightness (or wrongness) of the action a function of what would in fact happen were someone to do it. Deontologists differ, however, over what does make an action right (or wrong)— and so morally binds us to (or prohibits us from) doing it. Some main types of deontological theories include the following:

Natural Law Theories—moral standards exist in the very fabric or nature of our universe; an action is right just in case it conforms to these natural moral laws.

Natural Rights Theories—human beings share certain basic rights which obligate us to treat one another in certain ways, or at least to refrain from treating one another in certain ways.

Divine Command Theories—rightness is established by God, who either establishes general moral laws and standards or prescribes and prohibits particular actions (or both); and an action is right just in case it conforms to these laws, prescriptions, or prohibitions.

Social Contract Theories—rightness is a function of rules and institutions established in a society and implicitly or explicitly agreed to by its members.

Formalist Theories—correct moral reasoning exemplifies a certain form or logic; and the rightness of an action is a consequence of that form or of some special "right-making" feature of it. An action is right, in other words, just in case correct moral reasoning—reasoning having this "right-making" form or feature—would judge it to be right.

Virtue Theories—an action is right insofar as it would be judged to be right by one who possesses certain moral characteristics or "virtues."

(2) The Nature of Moral Judgments. Philosophy, we have said, is a rational activity. It is systematic, and it relies on rational argument or justifying reasons. But, what about morality itself—as opposed to a philo-sophical study of morality. Is it also a rational activity? In particular, is it a deliberate search for justifying reasons—for reasons which, if they were themselves true, would establish true moral judgments? This presupposes, however, that moral judgments (and also "moral reasons") are capable of being true in the first place. Are moral judgments capable of being true?

Judgments that are capable of being true are termed cognitive—from the Latin word *cognitio*, referring to knowledge or a recognition of the truth about something. Ethical or metaethical theories which presuppose or maintain that moral judgments can be true are termed cognitivist. Conversely, ethical (or metaethical) theories which presuppose (or maintain) that moral judgments are incapable of being true are termed noncognitivist. To clarify this distinction, let us consider what makes cognitive judgments cognitive. Our discussion will rely upon a common, though by no means universally accepted, account of cognitive judgment.

Cognitive judgments are expressible in subject-predicate sentences whose predicates, let us suppose, refer to properties and whose subjects refer to objects. Cognitive judgments purport to describe objects by ascribing properties to them; and a cognitive judgment is *true* just in case the object it refers to does in fact possess the property being ascribed to it. Accordingly, cognitivist ethical theories view moral judgments as attempts to ascribe properties of some sort to objects—for example, to actions or to things. Noncognitivist ethical theories, in contrast, deny that this is the purpose or function of moral judgments. Moral judgments do not purport to describe objects, or to ascribe properties to them. They are, for this reason, incapable of being true.

Consequentialism and deontology can be construed as variations on the cognitivist theme. Both can be interpreted as claiming that judging an action to be right is a matter of ascribing some "right-making" property to it. In consequentialism, this will be the property of having certain (good) consequences. In deontology, this might be just rightness itself, perhaps as discerned by some (nonconsequentialist) moral principle or standard, or it might be some other nonconsequentialist "right-making" property—for example, conformity to the natural law, or to God's will. Two examples of noncognitivist theories are

> Emotivism—moral judgments do not purport to describe objects; instead, they express our feelings or emotional reactions to objects.
>
> Prescriptivism—moral judgments prescribe how people are to react to objects; or they are meant to make other people react to objects the way we react to them, thereby influencing their behavior.

Metaethicists sometimes distinguish a third, intermediate view called quasi-cognitivism. This view, like noncognitivism, maintains that moral judgments are incapable of being true. It argues, however, that moral judgments are tied to certain cognitive judgments such that we are rationally committed to accepting a given moral judgment if its cognitive basis turns out to be true. This additional distinction allows us to describe some otherwise cognitivist theories as, more accurately, quasi-cognitivist. Some classic utilitarians, for example, view moral judgments in much the same way as twentieth-century emotivists; yet, they hold that an action is right just in case it has useful or beneficial consequences—say, because human beings always react favorably toward useful or beneficial things.

(3) The Nature of Moral Concepts. The cognitivist/noncognitivist debate strikes at the very heart of moral philosophy. Traditionally, searching for wisdom has been viewed as a cognitive activity. For, to possess wisdom or knowledge a person must, at the very least, be capable of formulating true judgments. One who believes, and so judges, that Columbus discovered America in 1274 lacks historical knowledge. Believing, and so judging, that the earth is flat indicates a lack of scientific wisdom. Similarly, the traditional view of moral philosophy as a search for moral wisdom presumes that moral judgments are cognitive, or at least that they are "quasi-cognitive." Noncognitivism challenges this traditional view. Indeed, it challenges anyone who supposes that morality has anything whatsoever to do with truth or "the truth." Conversely, cognitivism forces us to consider precisely how the moral sphere fits into the wider universe of nonmoral cognitive judgment—most especially, how the properties ascribed to objects in moral judgment relate to the natural, material universe in which we live. When one human being kills another, the physical act of killing as such does not differ in kind from similar acts of violence found elsewhere in the animal kingdom. What cognitive grounds could we possibly have for passing moral judgment on human violence, especially since we normally do not pass moral judgment on similar acts by nonhuman animals? What are these "right- (or wrong-) making" properties that human actions alone seem to possess, and how do they relate to the "nonmoral" properties of human actions and, indeed, of physical things and processes generally?

Metaethically, what is at stake here is the nature of moral concepts and their purpose or function. Moral judgments are distinguished by their use of certain concepts—right, wrong, good, and bad, for example; and cognitivism claims that these concepts refer to certain properties which moral judgments ascribe to actions or things. To this extent, at least, moral concepts are similar to the many other concepts used in cognitive judgment. How, then, do they also differ from these other concepts? Or do they? Historically, these questions were first raised by cognitivists—though noncognitivists also discuss the nature and function of so-called moral concepts. Accordingly, the two main metaethical approaches to answering these questions can best be viewed, in effect, as versions of cognitivism. These views are called naturalism and nonnaturalism.

Naturalism and nonnaturalism both begin with the idea that nonmoral cognitive judgments ascribe natural properties to objects, where this notion of "natural" properties is to be closely associated with natural science: A property is "natural" if natural science would ascribe it to objects or, at the very least, if it is compatible with the way natural science views our world. Oftentimes, this notion is associated with observation or sense experience as well: A property is "natural" just in case we do or could observe it through one or more of our five physical senses—sight, hearing, taste, touch, and smell. Given these two associations, clear examples of natural properties thus include colors, shapes, textures, movements, sounds, spatial extension and location, inertia, and so forth. As a metaethical view, however, naturalism maintains that so-called moral concepts also refer just to certain natural properties, or that the properties ascribed to objects in moral judgment are in fact just certain natural properties. Alternatively, naturalism is sometimes described as the view that every moral concept can be defined in terms of some natural property or set of natural properties. Regarding the apparent human-centeredness of morality, a naturalist has three options:

(a) He or she can argue that human actions do indeed possess certain natural properties not found in the behaviors of other animals.

(b) He or she can explain it in a way that does not rely upon the (naturalistic) nature of moral concepts themselves—for example, by arguing that moral judgment is a species-relative activity. It is human-centered for us simply because we are humans.

(c) He or she can argue that morality is in fact not (just) a human-centered activity.

Nonnaturalism is the denial of naturalism. It maintains that moral concepts differ from other, "natural" concepts because they refer to special, "nonnatural" properties. Typically, nonnaturalism sets up a one-to-one relationship between moral concepts and these nonnatural properties, insisting that the concept of goodness, for example, refers just to the property of being good, or to goodness itself. Thus, insofar as morality is indeed a human-centered activity, nonnaturalism can explain that it is simply the case that human actions alone possess these nonnatural, moral properties.

Nonnaturalism can be broadened, however, to include noncognitivism. Since noncognitivism denies that moral judgments ascribe properties to actions or things in the first place, it agrees with the basic idea of nonnaturalism: its denial of naturalism. Many noncognitivists would balk at being characterized as nonnaturalists, however, because they consider the whole issue of the nature of moral concepts to be misguided. So-called moral concepts, they argue, are not really concepts at all; terms like *right, wrong, good,* and *bad* do not express concepts at all but something else— feelings or emotional reactions, for instance.

Two intermediate positions between naturalism and nonnaturalism are noteworthy. The first, quasi-naturalism, parallels quasi-cognitivism in many ways. Like nonnaturalism, quasi-naturalism denies that moral concepts refer (directly) to natural properties, but it also rejects the notion of special, nonnatural properties that objects may possess independently of their natural properties. Instead, quasi-naturalism argues, moral concepts refer to natural properties indirectly. Moral concepts are logically tied somehow to certain natural properties, although these natural properties do not actually define them. Alternatively, quasi-naturalism might claim that moral concepts, though not themselves referential at all, are logically tied somehow to other concepts which do refer to natural properties.

A second intermediate position is supernaturalism. If quasi-naturalism is closer to nonnaturalism, supernaturalism is closer to naturalism. Indeed, insofar as we consider moral concepts as they function in moral judgments about objects in the natural universe, supernaturalism may be indistinguishable from naturalism. Supernaturalism insists, however, that moral concepts somehow derive their (naturalistic) meanings from some supernatural—normally divine—source, whose own properties are nonnatural or supernatural. Thus, moral concepts have a double meaning or reference. In moral judgments about objects in the natural universe, their meanings are naturalistic; yet, they also have a supernatural meaning and reference.

Twentieth-century metaethics has uncovered a number of new and interesting issues and has resulted in new and sometimes fruitful ways to approach certain traditional issues in ethics. Its distinctions and concepts may also help you to understand the basic thrust of various moral philosophies included in this text. Keep in mind, however, that individual moral philosophies are often much richer and more subtle than metaethics typically recognizes, or is able to capture in its taxonomies and distinctions.

STUDY/DISCUSSION FORMS

These eleven Forms are phrased for use at the end of each of the five chapters of readings, with Forms 1 and 2 referring to the terms and theses listed in the Elements at the end of each chapter. They—or portions of them—may be used for class discussion, as exam questions, or for essay topics. They are also study guides. Working through them will enhance your understanding of the readings, sharpen your critical skills, and they emphasize the sorts of things you should be thinking about as you read the selections. You should read them now, before you begin the readings, and reflect on what they are asking you to consider about the readings.

If your instructor does not assign all of the readings in this text, references to "the readings/philosophers in this chapter" can be taken to mean the ones assigned in your course. Indeed, these Forms can be used at any time, in reference to the readings covered to that point, or to however your syllabus has sectioned the course.

1. For each term listed in this section's Study/Discussion Elements, identify the

reading or readings in this chapter which use it. If you have not covered all of the readings in this chapter, you must first determine whether the term relates to any of your assigned readings. In each case,

   (i) define or explain its meaning as used in that reading; and
   (ii) explain its significance and function in the moral philosophy presented in that reading, and its relationship to other terms in the list which relate to the same reading.
   (iii) If it is used in more than one reading or (beginning with chapter 3) in previous chapters, compare and contrast its meanings and functions in those various readings.
   (iv) Identify, compare, and contrast any pairs (or sets) of terms, whether from the same or different readings, which seem especially close to one another in meaning or function.

2. For each thesis listed in this chapter's Study/Discussion Elements, identify the reading or readings in this chapter which advance it, and precisely where in the reading(s) it is advanced. If you have not covered all of the readings in this chapter, you must first determine whether the thesis relates to any of your assigned readings. (NOTE: Most of the theses are fairly literal expressions of statements found in the readings. Some are more literal than others, however; and a thesis may be literal to one reading, or to a statement made at one place in a reading, yet also capture a similar conclusion found in other readings or elsewhere in the same reading. Moreover, a few will summarize more than one conclusion or line of argument found in a single reading, and some might include one or more of the other theses listed among its justifying reasons. Allow for these things when identifying the thesis and its justifying reason or reasons in the readings.) In each case,

   (i) discuss precisely what the thesis is asserting, paying special attention to defining its key terms and any philosophical jargon; and explain its role or significance in the reading.
   (ii) identify the justifying reason or reasons given in the reading to support it; and
   (iii) critically assess the resulting argument, beginning with its validity.
       (a) If the argument is valid, explain why or how the conclusion follows from the premise(s), and for each premise discuss
           (1) why this philosopher believes that it is true; and
           (2) whether you believe that it is true, and why or why not. (If you cannot decide, discuss how we could determine whether the premise is true.)
       (b) If the argument is not valid, explain why its conclusion (the thesis) does not follow from its premise(s), and discuss the following:
           (1) Is the argument rationally convincing nevertheless—in other words, is it a reasonable inductive argument? Why, or why not?
           (2) What additional premise or premises would be needed for it to be a valid argument?
   (iv) If the thesis is explicitly or implicitly advanced in more than one reading, or if a reading argues for it in more than one way, compare the various arguments in terms of their validity and soundness, or their inductive strength.

Which argument is strongest or best, and why? Which is weakest or worst, and why?

(v) For each thesis, discuss how the remaining philosophers in this chapter and (beginning with chapter 3) how philosophers in previous chapters might critically assess the thesis and the argument(s) given for it. Would they agree? Could they agree? Why, or why not?

(vi) Beginning with chapter 3, go back to the theses listed in earlier Study/ Discussion Elements and discuss how philosophers in this chapter would critically assess them and the argument(s) given for them. Would they agree? Could they agree? Why, or why not?

3. Four recurring issues or themes in this text are

The nature of right action;

The nature of goodness;

The nature of moral deliberation (or, how to determine whether something is right or good); and

The relationship between individual action and social conduct (or civility).

For each of these four, discuss

(i) how the philosophers in this chapter address, or would address, it;

(ii) how their viewpoints compare and contrast with one another's and (beginning with chapter 3) with those of philosophers in previous chapters; and

(iii) why you would, or would not, agree with each of their viewpoints.

4. Reflecting on the readings in this chapter, individually and then collectively, identify other important issues or themes that emerge in the course of their investigations.

(i) How does, or would, each philosopher in this chapter address these issues or themes?

(ii) In each case, do you agree or disagree with the philosopher's viewpoint? Why, or why not?

(iii) Beginning with chapter 3, go back to the issues or themes you identified in previous chapters and compare them with the ones you identified in this chapter:

(a) Where they have changed, why has this occurred? How would the philosophers in this chapter address those earlier issues or themes? How would earlier philosophers address the ones in this chapter?

(b) Where they remain the same or reoccur, compare and contrast the viewpoints of philosophers in this chapter with those in previous chapters: Have they changed? If so, how and why? If not, why not?

5. For each philosopher in this chapter, summarize, explain, and critically discuss the essential characteristics—the bottom line, as it were—of his or her moral philosophy. Or, compose a thesis for each philosopher which captures the most basic or final conclusion of his or her moral investigation and critically assess it as outlined in Form 2.

6. Identify a particular decision you have made, action you have taken, or problem you have grappled with (or are grappling with) which you consider distinctly moral or ethical in character.

(i) Why do you see it as a question of morality or ethics?

(ii) For each philosopher in this chapter, how might his or her moral philosophy apply to it? How would he or she evaluate your decision or action, or try to resolve your problem, and why? (If a particular philosopher's ideas appear simply irrelevant or inapplicable to your example, explain why.) Compare and contrast your answers for the various philosophers in this chapter.

(iii) How would *you* evaluate your decision or action, or try to resolve your problem? Which philosopher in this chapter comes closest to your own approach? Why, or in what way? Which one is the farthest from your approach? Why, or in what way?

(iv) Beginning with chapter 3, compare and contrast your discussion of (ii) and (iii) for this chapter with your discussion of Form 6 for previous chapters.

7. For each philosopher in this chapter (beginning with chapter 3), compare and contrast his or her moral philosophy with those in previous chapters.

(i) Explain specific ways in which his or her moral philosophy appears to be influenced by or to build upon the work of philosophers in earlier chapters and

(ii) Explain specific ways in which his or her moral philosophy is novel or distinctively different from previous ones studied in this text.

8. Reflecting on the readings in this chapter, identify one idea or line of thought that seems especially insightful or interesting.

(i) Explain what is so insightful or interesting about it; and

(ii) discuss how it might relate or apply to your own life and what impact, if any, studying it has had on your own ethical outlook.

9. Reflecting on the readings in this chapter, identify any ideas or lines of thought which seem especially unusual, different, perhaps even bizarre or absurd. For each one, discuss

(i) why is strikes you this way;

(ii) why the philosopher who proposed it would believe or propose such an idea; and

(iii) whether it at least expresses some insight or raises some relevant and interesting issue about morality and human conduct.

10. Relativism—roughly, the idea that there are no universal moral truths or that moral truth is relative in some important way—is mentioned in the general introduction and discussed in the "Themes and Ideas" introductions to chapters 2 and 6.

(i) Discuss how each philosopher in this chapter would address the idea of relativism: Would he or she agree with it, and why or why not?

(ii) Compare and contrast the philosophers in this chapter and (beginning with chapter 3) this chapter's philosophers with previous philosophers on the idea of relativism. Discuss how and why their views on relativism differ or are the same, and what *you* think about their views and about relativism itself.

11. The final section of the general introduction ("What is Moral Philosophy?") discussed three main topics in metaethics and some main approaches to those topics. For each philosopher in this chapter,

(i) discuss how he or she would approach those topics and how he or she might argue for his or her position; and

(ii) identify the metaethical approach described in the general introduction that would most closely match his or her position.

Chapter Two

Classical Foundations

THEMES AND IDEAS

Why philosophy originated in classical Greece continues to fascinate historians. Factors probably include the Greek character, environment, and language. Individual initiative and heroism, tempered with a capacity to work together when facing a common enemy or in pursuit of larger goals, are central themes, for example, in Homer's *Iliad* and *Odyssey*. The mountainous, largely infertile terrain of Greece, together with early advances in metallurgy, pottery, and other manufactures, led to an emphasis on expert craftsmanship and trade. The Greeks were also an inquisitive people, and they established a number of colonies, especially on the Italian peninsula and in Asia Minor. They remained, however, a politically diverse people. Greece was never united under a single ruler or monarch. The city-state was the center of Greek life, their love of freedom and independence finding its ultimate expression in the establishment of the world's first democracy in the city-state of Athens. Also, the Greek language was the first language with a complete alphabet, one containing both consonants and vowels. (The word *alphabet*, in fact, comes from its first two characters, alpha and beta.) This allowed Greek thinkers to symbolize their ideas precisely and unambiguously so that any literate person—including, of course, philosphers—may read and reflect upon them.

The beginnings of Greek philosophy are usually traced to Thales (c. 580), and the notion of philosophy itself was first articulated by Pythagoras (580–497 B.C.). The earliest Greek philosophers are known mainly for their reasoned speculations on the nature of the material universe, though some also reflected on the nature of right action and the well-lived life; but it remained for a fifth-century B.C. Athenian, Socrates, to make the pursuit of moral wisdom a central concern of philosophers.

Socrates wrote nothing. His student, Plato, and Plato's student, Aristotle, defined many of the basic concepts and issues in moral philosophy. For both, the primary object of moral wisdom is goodness. Standards of right action depend upon understanding the nature of goodness. Moreover, Plato and Aristotle both considered moral wisdom to be an intensely practical pursuit. Everyone wishes to live well, which they equated with being happy, and a person lives well by acting rightly. Previous writers, especially the Greek tragedians, considered happiness to be outside our own control—to be determined by fate, destiny, or the gods. Plato and Aristotle insisted, however, that moral wisdom gives us power over the quality of our actions and lives. Moral wisdom, not fate or the gods, is the source of human happiness. They also believed that civilization—in Plato's case, the city-state—is necessary to living well or to achieving happiness. Hence, right action is inseparable from social responsibility, or from civilized (or "civil") behavior. Indeed, the Greek concept of rightness (*dikaios*) encompasses justice, a concept closely associated with social and political conduct, institutions, and rights.

Plato

Our first reading is taken from two of Plato's dialogues: *Euthydemus* and *Republic*. Both have Plato's teacher, Socrates, pursuing moral wisdom in dialogue with various philosophical opponents as well as friends. The extent to which the dramatic figure of Socrates reflects Socrates' actual teachings is unknown. Let us simply ascribe them to their literary author, Plato. Among the themes introduced in those dialogues are the relationship between right action and living well (or happiness), the importance of wisdom or knowledge to living well, Plato's concepts of goodness and virtue, and the identity of moral action with civility, or of individual virtue with "political" virtue. All of these themes depend, moreover, on Plato's notion of art or excellence (in Greek, *arete*).

Art, for Plato, does not refer just to the so-called fine arts—painting, music, sculpture, and the like. Rather, it refers to any sort of activity in which we can distinguish between a right way and a wrong way of doing things and where training and knowledge enable us to do it rightly or well.

Medicine and shoemaking are arts, in this sense. The art of medicine—that is, the knowledge and practice of medicine—enables a doctor to treat illnesses in the right way. Similarly, shoemaking is not just throwing together pieces of leather. Rather, a shoemaker is someone who has learned how to make shoes, and knows how to make them in the right way. Plato believes that living well is also an art. He believes that there is also a right way to live, and he equates living rightly with living well—especially insofar as living wrongly may likewise be equated with living badly, or with doing a bad job at living. Finally, Plato maintains, living rightly, like other arts, requires training and knowledge. People may disagree over the importance of such things as health, good looks, and power to living well, but everyone agrees that a person must be living well insofar as he or she is fortunate, or is experiencing good fortune; and good fortune normally follows upon wise action, as illustrated by the fact that people who are wise or knowledgeable at piloting ships are normally the most fortunate seafarers. Moreover, such things as health, wealth, and power contribute to living well only when they are used rightly; and the ability to use something rightly requires wisdom or knowledge.

Plato encountered a number of objections to his linking right action with knowledge. Genuine knowledge, Plato believed, must be fixed and objective. To know that two plus two equals four, for example, is to know a truth which is the same for everyone who knows arithmetic, and no amount of wishing that two plus two did not equal four can alter this truth. Some philosophers insisted, however, that morality is very different, say, from arithmetic in this regard. One and the same action can be right to one person and wrong to another person. Moral rightness is a matter of opinion, not knowledge, and it depends especially on the opinions or "conventions" that prevail in a given society. In our reading, Plato addresses a variant of this conventionalist view when he examines Thrasymachus' claim that might make right—more precisely, that rightness is relative to the interests and dictates of whomever is in power.

Thrasymachus' claim also contains an element of egoism, which ties rightness to self-interest. This allows Socrates to turn the tables on Thrasymachus and get him to agree that morality is an art, or that rightness depends upon knowledge or wisdom. Thrasymachus admits that a person can be mistaken about what is, in fact, in his or her own best interest. For example, suppose some despot, whose primary interest is to stay in power, commands his or her followers to torture dissidents; but suppose as well that this leads to revolution. Torturing dissidents did not serve the interests of the despot, even though he or she obviously thought that it would, and so had commanded it. Thrasymachus reacts by agreeing that even his might makes right view of morality presupposes some kind of knowledge. The true ruler, he claims, is never mistaken about what, in fact, will serve his or her own interests. Ruling, even for the despot, is a kind of art. Socrates argues, however, that the object of any art—medicine, for example—is always the interests of its subjects or "patients," rather than of its practitioners.

Thrasymachus' conventionalism also links rightness to how a person acts as a citizen of his or her society or state. (For this reason, our reading translates the Greek word for rightness, *dikaios*, as justice.) Likewise, for Plato, the "virtue" (art, or excellence) of right action (or justice) manifests itself primarily in individuals but also, when its citizens are just, in the society or state itself. Justice is thus a social virtue as much as an individual character trait, and it is intimately related to three other virtues: wisdom (or knowledge), courage, and temperance (or moderation). We have already seen, of course, that the link between justice and knowledge is most important: Justice (or rightness) requires knowledge. So do courage and temperance. But knowledge of what? Or, what kind of knowledge?

Plato's answer is based on the relationship between art and goodness. Learning an art enables a person to act rightly in some sphere of human conduct—in medicine, shoemaking, seafaring, ruling, or citizenship, for example. The right way to act, however, is always the way that produces goodness of an appropriate sort. Treating illnesses in the right way, for example, produces good health. Making shoes in the right way results in good shoes. Likewise, ruling a society in the right way yields a good society; and acting rightly results in a good (well-lived, and so happy) life. The primary or "highest" object of knowledge for the practitioner of any art, Plato believes, is always the nature of the appropriate sort of goodness. Above all else, a doctor must understand the nature of good health, a shoemaker must know what makes for a good shoe, and so on. The art of living, of always acting rightly, also requires knowledge of the appropriate sort of goodness. However, this special art permeates or underlies all of our activities, and so also all of the other arts. Its "appropriate sort" of goodness, in fact, is not a specific goodness at all but is just goodness itself. The primary object of knowledge for practitioners of the art of living is just goodness itself, and this is also the "highest" object of all knowledge whatsoever. Plato's investigation of the nature of "goodness itself" leads him to conclude that it must be a real, objectively existing "thing" (since it is an object of knowledge) yet that it cannot be any particular physical thing or a property of physical things (since it is the source of any and every instance of physical goodness and is presupposed by any knowledge of physical things or their properties).

Undaunted by Plato's claim that he cannot say anything more about "goodness itself," scholars have scoured his writings for clues to his "real" views about its nature. Over the centuries, two main interpretations of Plato have emerged. One argues that Plato cannot say anything more about "goodness itself" because there simply is nothing more to be said about it. It just *is* the highest possible object of knowledge and the source of any and every instance of goodness. Asking for more precise information about it simply reveals that one has not attained this knowledge. The second interpretation observes that Plato repeatedly associates goodness and knowledge with a certain family of concepts, including harmony, order, proportion, and coherence or consistency. Perhaps no one of these concepts captures the full meaning of "goodness itself," but they do convey its essential nature. At the very least, "goodness itself" is the cause of things (and knowledge) possessing these sorts of characteristics, such that something is good just insofar as it possesses these sorts of characteristics.

Aristotle

For Aristotle, like Plato, moral conduct is inseparable from civility—from proper action in a society or state. Indeed, Aristotle claims that the "highest" of all human arts—which for Plato we termed the art of living—is politics. By *politics*, Aristotle does not mean what we normally mean by this term—or at least not just that. We associate politics mainly with the game—the "art," perhaps—of pursuing elected office and with related processes of legislation and governance. For Aristotle, politics includes everything that transpires within a society or state. The lives and actions of civilized beings are inextricably intertwined. Everything we do has, or can have, a social significance. Every sphere of human conduct contributes to, or detracts from, life in one's society. Politics, Aristotle thus claims, is the universal art. It encompasses and coordinates all other arts to a single, ultimate goal or end. For Aristotle, like Plato, this ultimate goal is happiness. Insofar as politics also has a distinctive goal and requires a special skill all its own, this lies in its legislative function, whose purpose is to establish conditions conducive to the moral or "artistic" education of all citizens.

Though deeply influenced by Plato, Aristotle's moral philosophy does depart from Plato's in significant ways. Plato held that the primary object of moral wisdom is "goodness itself." Aristotle thus begins his investigation with the concept of goodness, but he immediately states a definition of it: Goodness is the end or goal of every art and every activity; it is that at which all things aim. Moreover, this definition depicts goodness as a goal or an end, as something to be brought into existence through action, instead of as some already existing "thing" or object. Aristotle rejects Plato's claim that goodness itself exists apart from all instances of goodness. The goal or end of any art or activity is always a particular instance of goodness. A medical doctor, for example, does not aim merely to produce "goodness" but to promote good health—indeed, good health in a particular patient—and a shoemaker always tries to manufacture particular (pairs of) good shoes. Accordingly, to know the precise nature of goodness one must examine the natures of the particular arts or activities which yield instances of goodness.

Aristotle's claim that every action aims at goodness seems to go way beyond Plato's association of goodness just with artistic activity. Clearly, Aristotle does have a broader conception of goodness than Plato, but he might not really mean that any action or activity whatsoever aims at goodness. He is concerned that since art requires knowledge, Plato's conception implies that only creatures capable of acting from knowledge can aim at goodness. Aristotle, in contrast, associates goodness with natural activity—actions and processes that express growth, movement, or activities directed toward some end implicit in a thing's nature. Every thing possesses a nature, which determines the kind of thing it is and which also sets a certain ideal or mature state for it to attain if it is to be a good specimen of its kind. All trees, for example, have something in common (a "nature") which makes them all trees and which directs their natural processes toward some mature, ideal condition—some condition shared by all "good trees." A good tree, let us suppose, is free from blights or other diseases, is as tall and sturdy as possible for a tree of its sort, and is laden with leaves during certain times of the year. These same characteristics would not make for a good rabbit, however—nor for a good human being.

Despite his biological rather than artistic model of goodness, Aristotle still relies heavily on Plato's concept of art in his moral philosophy. Three features of art were especially important to Plato's conception of morality: its goal or purpose (to produce an appropriate sort of goodness), its basis (knowledge or wisdom), and its high standards (of excellence or virtuosity). The first and third of these features are still evident within Aristotle's own biological approach: Each thing's nature directs it toward a particular end, an appropriate sort of goodness. Moreover, each nature is distinguished by a capacity to act in some distinctive way, and each thing will reach the goal (goodness) appropriate to its nature just in case it achieves excellence or "virtuosity" in that distinctive capacity. If we suppose that the distinctive capacity of trees (or at least of plants) is photosynthesis—though this would be an alien concept to Aristotle—we can say that a good tree is one that has achieved an excellent capacity for photosynthetic activity. The second feature of art, its dependence on knowledge, remains central just to Aristotle's concept of *human* goodness.

Aristotle's biological model leads to a narrower, perhaps a more precise, concept of moral philosophy. Trees, for example, are not moral beings; their natural or appropriate goal is not a kind of *moral* goodness. Morality is the province of human action, of human goals or ends. Accordingly, the ultimate object of moral philosophy is just the natural goal (or goodness) of human nature and to understand the meaning of excellence or virtuosity just in the case of distinctively human activities. Examining this object also leads Aristotle to a more precise characterization of the content of "moral wisdom" than Plato gave us. The natural goal of human nature, Aristotle argues, is happiness; and our distinctive capacity is reason or rationality. Aristotle's investigation into the nature of human (or rational) excellence and, in particular, of moral (rational) excellence—that excellence which results in our attaining happiness—leads to the so-called Principle of the Golden Mean: Right action always lies on a mean between two extremes, one excessive and the other deficient with respect to the sort of conduct appropriate to a given activity, as determined by the sort of end or positive result intended by that activity. For example, if the positive result intended by warfare is victory, defeat being a failure rather than an achievement in warfare, then the right way for a soldier to act in battle would be intermediate between the excessive pursuit of victory ("victory at all costs," or rashness) and the deficient pursuit of victory ("victory only if at no cost," or cowardice). Or, if the positive result intended by stating or asserting something is truth, falsity being a failure rather than an achievement in this sort of speech activity, then the right way to state or assert things would be intermediate between the excessive pursuit of truth (say, bragging or overstatement) and the deficient pursuit of truth (understating the facts, if not outright lying). Specific capacities to act moderately with respect to specific sorts of conduct are termed virtues, and capacities to act in either excessive or deficient ways that "destroy virtue" are termed vices.

Plato
(427–347 B.C)

Socrate's life spanned the Age of Pericles—the "golden age" of Athens—and the disastrous Peloponnesian War with Sparta. The son of Sophronicus, a sculpture, and Phaenarete, a midwife, Socrates inspired philosophers throughout the classical era through his life and teachings. As a hoplite in the Athenian army, Socrates distinguished himself by his bravery and physical endurance. He lived a simple, ascetic life, wearing a single garment year-round and always going barefoot, even during winter military campaigns. He became notorious, however, for constantly interrogating his fellow Athenians and self-proclaimed wise men (or Sophists) in his search for truth. Refusing any payment for his "teaching," Socrates died a pauper despite having been close to some of the richest and most powerful figures in Athens. Legend traces Socrates' single-minded search for truth to a claim by the Delphic Oracle that no one was wiser than Socrates. This perplexed Socrates since he alleged that he was not wise at all. His interrogations led him to conclude that the oracle meant that while others think that they are wise when they are not, he at least knew that he knew nothing. Socrates' cult status, especially among younger Athenians, was heightened by the presence of his *daimonion*—a kind of inner voice or personal oracle—and his propensity to sudden trances or fits of rapture. Following the Athenian defeat by Sparta—attributed by many to Alcibiades, a follower of Socrates—he was charged with introducing new deities, not worshipping the gods of the city, and corrupting the young. Led by Anytus, whose son Socrates had persuaded to pursue philosophy rather than continue in his father's business, Socrates' prosecutors managed to convict him by a handful of votes. Given the choice between exile from Athens and death, Socrates chose death.

Plato, whose early life had been devoted to poetry, was a disciple of Socrates during the final eight years of Socrates' life. Plato was born into a wealthy and aristocratic Athenian family. His father, Ariston, traced his lineage to Codrus, the last king of Athens; and his mother, Perictione, was a descendant of Solon, the great lawgiver who laid the foundation for the Athenian democracy. Dubbed Aristocles at birth, he was nicknamed Plato in reference to his broad physique. After Socrates' death, Plato traveled for a number of years. He studied with Euclid, Pythagoreans, and finally ended up in Sicily, where the tyrant Dionysius, tired of his preachments about justice and wisdom, sold him into slavery. After a friend purchased his freedom, Plato returned to Athens and established his Academy, named after its location on a sight dedicated to the Athenian hero Academus. Its library solemnly proclaimed: Let no one enter who does not know geometry.

*Euthydemus**

And now, O son of Axiochus, let me put a question to you: Do not all men desire happiness? And yet, perhaps, this is one of those ridiculous questions which I am afraid to ask, and which ought not to be asked by a sensible man: for what human being is there who does not desire happiness?

There is no one, said Cleinias, who does not.

Well, then, I said, since we all of us desire happiness, how can we be happy?—that is the next question. Shall we not be happy if we have many good things? And this perhaps, is even a more simple question than the first, for there can be no doubt of the answer.

He assented.

And what things do we esteem good? No solemn sage is required to tell us this, which may be easily answered; for every one will say that wealth is a good.

Certainly, he said.

And are not health and beauty goods, and other personal gifts?

He agreed.

Can there be any doubt that good birth, and power, and honours in one's own land, are goods?

He assented.

And what other goods are there? I said. What do you say of temperance, justice, courage: do you not verily and indeed think, Cleinias, that we shall be more right in ranking them as goods than in not ranking them as goods? For a dispute might possibly arise about this. What then do you say?

They are goods, said Cleinias.

Very well, I said; and where in the company shall we find a place for wisdom—among the goods or not?

Among the goods.

And now, I said, think whether we have left out any considerable goods.

I do not think that we have, said Cleinias.

Upon recollection, I said, indeed I am afraid that we have left out the greatest of them all.

What is that? he asked.

Fortune, Cleinias, I replied; which all, even the most foolish, admit to be the greatest of goods.

From Plato, "Euthydemus" in *The Dialogues of Plato*, vol. I, translated by Benjamin Jowett (New York: Oxford University Press, American Branch, and Macmillan and Co., 1892).

True, he said.

On second thoughts, I added, how narrowly, O son of Axiochus, have you and I escaped making a laughing-stock of ourselves to the strangers.

Why do you say so?

Why, because we have already spoken of good-fortune, and are but repeating ourselves.

What do you mean?

I mean that there is something ridiculous in again putting forward good-fortune, which has a place in the list already, and saying the same thing twice over.

He asked what was the meaning of this, and I replied: Surely wisdom is good-fortune; even a child may know that.

The simple-minded youth was amazed; and, observing his surprise, I said to him: Do you not know, Cleinias, that flute-players are most fortunate and successful in performing on the flute?

He assented.

And are not the scribes most fortunate in writing and reading letters?

Certainly.

Amid the dangers of the sea, again, are any more fortunate on the whole than wise pilots?

None, certainly.

And if you were engaged in war, in whose company would you rather take the risk—in company with a wise general, or with a foolish one?

With a wise one.

And if you were ill, whom would you rather have as a companion in a dangerous illness—a wise physician, or an ignorant one?

A wise one.

You think, I said, that to act with a wise man is more fortunate than to act with an ignorant one?

He assented.

Then wisdom always makes men fortunate: for by wisdom no man would ever err, and therefore he must act rightly and succeed, or his wisdom would be wisdom no longer.

We contrived at last, somehow or other, to agree in a general conclusion, that he who had wisdom had no need of fortune. I then recalled to his mind the previous state of the question. You remember, I said, our making the admission that we should be happy and fortunate if many good things were present with us?

He assented.

And should we be happy by reason of the presence of good things, if they profited us not, or if they profited us?

If they profited us, he said.

And would they profit us, if we only had them and did not use them? For example, if we had a great deal of food and did not eat, or a great deal of drink and did not drink, should we be profited?

Certainly not, he said.

Or would an artisan, who had all the implements necessary for his work, and did not use them, be any the better for the possession of them? For example, would a carpenter be any the better for having all his tools and plenty of wood, if he never worked?

Certainly not, he said.

And if a person had wealth and all the goods of which we were just now speaking, and did not use them, would he be happy because he possessed them?

No indeed, Socrates.

Then, I said, a man who would be happy must not only have the good things, but he must also use them; there is no advantage in merely having them?

True.

Well, Cleinias, but if you have the use as well as the possession of good things, is that sufficient to confer happiness?

Yes, in my opinion.

And may a person use them either rightly or wrongly?

He must use them rightly.

That is quite true, I said. And the wrong use of a thing is far worse than the non-use; for the one is an evil, and the other is neither a good nor an evil. Do we not say so?

He assented.

Now in the working and use of wood, is not that which gives the right use simply the knowledge of the carpenter?

Nothing else, he said.

And surely, in the manufacture of vessels, knowledge is that which gives the right way of making them?

He agreed.

And in the use of the goods of which we spoke at first—wealth and health and beauty, is not knowledge that which directs us to the right use of them, and regulates our practice about them?

He assented.

Then in every possession and every use of a thing, knowledge is that which gives a man not only good-fortune but success?

He again assented.

And tell me, I said, O tell me, what do possessions profit a man, if he have neither good sense nor wisdom? Would a man be better off, having and doing many things without wisdom, or a few things with wisdom? Look at the matter thus: If he did fewer things would he not make fewer mistakes? if he made fewer mistakes would he not have fewer misfortunes? and if he had fewer misfortunes would he not be less miserable?

Certainly, he said.

And who would do least—a poor man or a rich man?

A poor man.

A weak man or a strong man?

A weak man.

A noble man or a mean man?

A mean man.

And a coward would do less than a courageous and temperate man?

Yes.

And a indolent man less than an active man?

He assented.

And a slow man less than a quick; and one who had dull perceptions of seeing and hearing less than one who had keen ones?

All this was mutually allowed by us.

Then, I said, Cleinias, the sum of the matter appears to be that the goods of which we spoke before are not to be regarded as goods in themselves, but the degree of good and evil in them depends on whether they are or are not under the guidance of knowledge: under the guidance of ignorance, they are greater evils than their opposites, inasmuch as they are more able to minister to the evil principle which rules them; and when under the guidance of wisdom and prudence, they are greater goods: but in themselves they are nothing?

That, he replied, is obvious.

What then is the result of what has been said? Is not this the result—that other things are indifferent, and that wisdom is the only good, and ignorance the only evil? He assented.

Let us consider a further point, I said: Seeing that all men desire happiness, and happiness, as has been shown, is gained by a use, and a right use, of the things of life, and the right use of them, and good-fortune in the use of them, is given by knowledge,—the inference is that everybody ought by all means to try and make himself as wise as he can?

Yes, he said.

Republic[*]

. . .Listen, then, he said; I proclaim that might is right, justice the interest of the stronger. But why don't you praise me?

Let me first understand you, I replied. Justice, as you say, is the interest of the stronger. Now what, Thrasymachus, is the meaning of this? You cannot mean to say that because Polydamas, the pancratiast, who is stronger than we are, finds the eating of beef for his interest, that this is equally for our interest who are weaker than he is?

That's abominable of you, Socrates; why you are just taking the words in the way which is most damaging to the argument.

Not all, my good sir, I said; I am trying to understand them; and I wish that you would be a little clearer.

Well, he said, I suppose you know that forms of government differ; there are tyrannies, and there are democracies, and there are aristocracies?

Yes, I know that.

And the government is that which has power in each State?

Certainly.

And the different forms of government make laws democratical, aristocratical, tyrannical, with a view to their several interests; and these laws, which are made by them for their interests, they deliver to their subjects as justice, and punish him who transgresses them as a breaker of the law, and unjust. And that is what I mean when I say that in all States there is the same principle of justice, which is neither more nor less than the interest of the government; and as the government must be supposed

From Plato, "Republic" in *The Dialogues of Plato*, vol. II, translated by Benjamin Jowett (New York: The Jefferson Press, 1871).

to have power, the reasonable conclusion is, that everywhere there is one principle of justice, which is the interest of the stronger.

Now I understand you, I said; and whether you are right or not I will try to learn. But let me first remark, that you have yourself said "interest," although you forbade me to use that word in answer. I do not, however, deny that in your definition the words are added "of the stronger."

A slight addition, that you must allow, he said.

Great or small, never mind that; the simple question is, whether what you are saying is the truth. Now we are both agreed that justice is interest of some sort, but we are not agreed as to the additional words "of the stronger;" and this is the point which I will now examine.

Proceed.

That I will; and first tell me, Do you admit that it is just for subjects to obey their rulers?

I do.

But are the rulers of States absolutely infallible, or are they sometimes liable to err?

To be sure, he replied; they are liable to err.

Then in making their laws they may sometimes make them rightly, but they are not always right?

True.

When they make them rightly, they make them agreeably to their interests; when they are mistaken, contrary to their interests,—that is what you would say?

Yes.

And the laws which they make must be obeyed by their subjects,—and that is what you call justice?

Doubtless.

Then justice, according to your argument, is not only the interest of the stronger but the reverse?

What are you saying? he asked flurriedly.

I am only saying what you were saying, I believe. But let us consider. Have we not admitted that the rulers may be mistaken about their own interests in what they command, and also that to obey them is justice? Has not that been admitted?

Yes.

Then you must also have acknowledged that justice is not the interest of the stronger, when the rulers who are stronger unintentionally command that which is to their own injury. For if, as you say, justice is the obedience which the subject renders to their commands, then in the case supposed, O thou wisest of men, is there any escape from the conclusion that justice is the injury and not the interest of the stronger, which is imposed on the weaker?

Nothing can be clearer, Socrates, said Polemarchus.

Yes, said Cleitophon, interposing, if you are admitted as his witness.

But there is no need of any witness, said Polemarchus, for Thrasymachus himself acknowledges that rulers command what is not for their own interest, and that to obey them is justice.

Yes, Polemarchus,—Thrasymachus said that for subjects to do what was commanded by the rulers was just.

Yes, but he also said that justice was the interest of the stronger, and, while admitting both these propositions, he further admitted that the stronger commands what is not for his own interest; whence follows that justice is the injury quite as much as the interest of the stronger.

But, said Cleitophon, he meant by the interest of the stronger what the stronger thought to be for his interest.

That was not the statement, said Polemarchus.

Never mind, I said; let us accept the new statement, if Thrasymachus has changed his opinion.

Tell me then, I said, Thrasymachus, did you mean by justice what the stronger thought to be his interest, whether really so or not?

Certainly not, he said. Do you suppose that I call him who is mistaken the stronger at the time when he is mistaken?

Yes, I said, that I supposed to be your meaning when you admitted that the ruler was not infallible and might be mistaken.

You are a sharper, Socrates, in argument. Pray do you imagine that he who is mistaken about the sick is a physician in that he is mistaken and at the time that he is mistaken? or that he who errs in arithmetic or grammar is an arithmetician or grammarian in that he is mistaken and at the time that he is mistaken? True, we say that the arithmetician or grammarian or physician has made a mistake, but this is only a way of speaking; for the fact is that neither the grammarian nor any other person of skill ever makes a mistake in as far as he is what his name implies: they all of them err only when their skill fails them. No craftsman or sage or ruler errs at the time when he is what he is called, though he is commonly said to err; and after this manner I answered you. But the more precise expression, since you will have precision, is that the ruler, as ruler, is unerring, and, being unerring, always commands that which is for his own interest; and the subject is required to execute this: and therefore, as I said at first and now repeat, justice is the interest of the stronger.

Indeed, Thrasymachus, and do you really think that I am a sharper?

Certainly, he replied.

And do you think that I ask these questions with any special design of injuring you?

Nay, he replied, I am quite sure of it; and your dishonesty shall do you no good, for I shall detect you, and in a fair argument you will not be able to overthrow me.

I shall certainly not attempt that; but to avoid anything of the kind occurring between us again, please to say, when you speak of a ruler or stronger whose interest the weaker is required to execute, do you speak of a ruler in the popular or in the strict sense of the term?

The ruler in the strictest of all senses, he said. And now cheat and deceive if you can; I ask no quarter at your hands. But you won't be able.

And do you imagine, I said, that I am such a madman as to try and cheat Thrasymachus? I might as well try to shave a lion.

Why, he said, you made the attempt a minute ago, although you failed, as you will again.

Well, I said, I will not continue these civilities. I would rather ask you a question: Is the physician, in that strict sense of which you are speaking, a healer of the sick or a maker of money? And remember that I am now speaking of the true physician.

A healer of the sick, he replied.

And the pilot—that is to say, the true pilot—is he a captain of sailors or a mere sailor?

A captain of sailors.

The circumstance that he sails in the ship is not to be reckoned; this is an accident only, and has nothing to do with the name pilot, which is significant of his skill and of his authority.

Very true, he said.

Now, I said, each of these has an interest?

Certainly.

And the art has to find and provide for this interest?

Yes that is the aim of the art.

And the interest of each of the arts is the perfection of each of them; nothing but that?

What do you mean?

I mean that I may illustrate negatively by the example of the body. Suppose you were to ask me whether the body is self-sufficing or has wants, I should reply: Certainly the body has wants; for the body may be ill and require to be cured, and has therefore interests to which the art of medicine ministers; and this is the origin and intention of medicine, as you will acknowledge. Am I not right in saying that?

Quite right, he replied.

But is the art of medicine or any other art faulty or deficient in any quality in the same way that the eye may be deficient in sight or the ear fail of hearing, and, in consequence of this defect, require another art to provide for the interest of seeing and hearing? Has art, I say, any similar liability to fault or defect, and does every art require another supplementary art to provide for its interests, and that another and another without end? Or may the arts be said to look after their own interests? Or have they no need of either?—having no faults or defects, they have no need to correct them, either by the exercise of their own art of any other—that is not required of them for the preservation of their interests; they have only to consider the interest of their subject-matter, for every art remains pure and faultless while remaining true—that is to say, while perfect and unimpaired? Is not all this clear? And I would have you take the words in your precise manner.

Yes, that is clear?

Then medicine does not consider the interest of medicine, but the interest of the body?

True, he said.

Nor does farriery consider the interests of farriery, but the interests of the horse; neither do any other arts care for themselves, for they have no needs, but they care only for that which is the subject of their art?

True, he said.

But surely, I added, the arts are the superiors and rulers of their own subjects; you will admit that, Thrasymachus?

To this he assented with a good deal of reluctance.

Then, I said, no science or art considers or enjoins the interest of the stronger or superior, but only the interest of the subject and weaker?

He acquiesced in this after a feint of resistance.

Then, I continued, no physician, in as far as he is a physician, considers his own good but the good of the patient; for the true physician is also a ruler having the human body as a subject, and is not a mere money-maker; that has been admitted?

Yes.

And the pilot likewise, in the strict sense of the term, is a ruler of sailors and not a mere sailor?

That has been admitted.

And such a pilot and ruler will provide and prescribe for the interest of the sailor who is under him, and not for his own or the ruler's interest?

He gave a very reluctant "Yes."

Then, I said, Thrasymachus, there is no one in any rule who, in as far as he is a ruler, considers or enjoins that which is for his own interest, but always that which is for the interest of his subject and of his art; to that he looks, and that alone he considers in everything which he says and does. . .

. . .Glaucon and the rest entreated me by all means not to let the question drop, but to proceed in the investigation. They wanted to arrive at the truth, first, about the nature of justice and injustice, and secondly, about their relative advantages. I told them, what I really thought, that the search would be no easy one, and would require very good eyes. Seeing then, I said, we are not great wits, I think that we had better adopt a method which might be recommended to those who are shortsighted, and are bidden by some one to read small letters a long way off; one of the party recollects that he has seen the very same letters elsewhere written larger and on a larger scale—if they were the same and we could read the larger letters first, and then proceed to the lesser—that would be thought a rare piece of good fortune.

Very true, said Adeimantus, but how does this apply to our present inquiry?

I will tell you, I replied; justice, which is the subject of our inquiry, is, as you know, sometimes spoken of as a virtue of an individual, and sometimes as the virtue of a State.

True, he replied.

And is not a State larger than an individual?

It is.

Then in the larger the quantity of justice will be larger and more easily discernible. I propose therefore that we inquire into the nature of justice and injustice as appearing in the State first, and secondly in the individual, proceeding from the greater to the lesser and comparing them.

That, he said, is an excellent proposal.

And suppose we imagine the State as in a process of creation, and then we shall see the justice and injustice of the State in process of creation also.

Very likely.

When the State is completed there may be a hope that the object of our search will be more easily discovered.

Yes, more easily.

And shall we make the attempt? I said; although I cannot promise you as an inducement that the task will be a light one. Reflect therefore.

I have reflected, said Adeimantus, and am anxious that you should proceed.

A State, I said, arises, as I conceive, out of the needs of mankind; no one is self-sufficing, but all of us have many wants. Can any other origin of a State be imagined?

None, he replied.

Then, as we have many wants, and many persons are needed to supply them, one takes a helper for one purpose and another for another; and when these helpers and partners are gathered together in one habitation, the body of inhabitants is termed a State.

True, he said.

And they exchange with one another, and one gives, and another receives, under the idea that the exchange will be for their good.

Very true.

Then, I said, let us begin and create a State; and yet the true creator is necessity, who is the mother of our invention.

True, he replied.

Now the first and greatest of necessities is food, which is the condition of life and existence.

Certainly.

The second is a dwelling, and the third clothing and that sort of thing.

True.

And now let us see how our city will be able to supply this great demand. We may suppose that one man is a husbandman, another a builder, some one else a weaver: shall we add to them a shoemaker, or perhaps some other purveyor to our bodily wants?

Quite right.

The barest notion of a State must include four or five men.

Clearly.

And how then will they proceed? Will each give the result of his labors to all?— the husbandman, for example, producing, for four, and laboring in the production of food for himself and others four times as long and as much as he needs to labor; or shall he leave others and not be at the trouble of producing for them, but produce a fourth for himself in a fourth of the time, and in the remaining three fourths of his time be employed in making a house or a coat or a pair of shoes?

Adeimantus thought that the former would be the better way.

I dare say that you are right, I replied, for I am reminded as you speak that we are not all alike; there are diversities of natures among us which are adapted to different occupations.

Very true.

And will you have a work better done when the workman has many occupations, or when he has only one?

When he has only one.

Further, there can be no doubt that a work is spoilt when not done at the right time?

No doubt of that.

For business is not disposed to wait until the doer of the business is at leisure; but the doer must be at command, and make the business his first object.

He must.

Thus then all things are produced more plentifully and easily and of a better quality when one man does one thing which is natural to him and is done at the right time, and leaves other things.

Undoubtedly.

Then more than four citizens will be required, for the husbandman will not make his own plough or mattock, or other implements of agriculture, if they are to be good for anything. Neither will the builder make his tools—and he, too, needs many; and the same may be said of the weaver and shoemaker.

True.

Then carpenters, and smiths, and other artisans, will be sharers in our little State, which is already beginning to grow.

True.

Yet even if we add neatherds, shepherds, and other herdsmen, in order that our husbandmen may have oxen to plough with, and builders as well as husbandmen have the use of beasts of burden for their carrying, and weavers and curriers of their fleeces and skins,—still our State will not be very large.

That is true; yet neither will that be a very small State which contains all these.

Further, I said, to place the city on a spot where no imports are required is wellnigh impossible.

Impossible.

Then there must be another class of citizens who will bring the required supply from another city?

There must.

But if the trader goes empty-handed, taking nothing which those who are to supply the need want, he will come back empty-handed.

That is certain.

And therefore what they produce at home must be not only enough for themselves, but such both in quantity and quality as to accommodate those from whom their wants are supplied.

That is true.

Then more husbandmen and more artisans will be required?

They will.

Not to mention the importers and exporters, who are called merchants.

Yes.

Then we shall want merchants?

We shall.

And if merchandise is to be carried over the sea, skillful sailors will be needed, and in considerable numbers?

Yes, in considerable numbers.

Then, again, within the city, how will they exchange their productions? and this, as you may remember, was the object of our society.

The way will be, that they will buy and sell.

Then they will need a market place, and a money-token for purposes of exchange.

Certainly.

Suppose now that a husbandman, or possibly an artisan, brings some production to market, and he comes at a time when there is no one to exchange with him,—is he to leave his work and sit idle in the market-place?

Not at all; he will find people there who, seeing this want, take upon themselves the duty of sale. In well-ordered States they are commonly those who are the weakest in bodily strength, and therefore unable to do anything else; for all they have to do is to be in the market, and take money of those who desire to buy goods, and in exchange for goods to give money to those who desire to sell.

This want, then, will introduce retailers into our State. Is not "retailer" the term which is applied to those who sit in the market-place buying and selling, while those who wander from one city to another are called merchants?

Yes, he said.

And there is another class of servants, who are intellectually hardly on the level of companionship; still they have plenty of bodily strength for labor, which accordingly they sell, and are called, if I do not mistake, hirelings, hire being the name which is given to the price of their labor.

True.

Then hirelings will help to make our population.

And now, Adeimantus, is our State matured and perfected?

Surely.

Where, then, is justice, and where is injustice, and in which part of the State are they to be found?

Probably in the relations of these citizens with one another. I cannot imagine any other place in which they are more likely to be found.

I dare say that you are right in that suggestion, I said; still, we had better consider the matter further, and not shrink from the task.

First, then, let us consider what will be their way of life, now that we have thus established them. Will they not produce corn, and wine, and clothes, and shoes, and build houses for themselves? And when they are housed, they will work in summer commonly stripped and barefoot, but in winter substantially clothed and shod. They will feed on barley and wheat, baking the wheat and kneading the flour, making noble puddings and loaves; these they will serve up on a mat of reeds or clean leaves, themselves reclining the while upon beds of yew or myrtle boughs. And they and their children will feast, drinking of the wine which they have made, wearing garlands on their heads, and having the praises of the gods on their lips, living in sweet society, and having a care that their families do no exceed their means; for they will have an eye to poverty or war.

But, said Glaucon, interposing, you have not given them a relish to their meal.

True, I replied, I had forgotten that; of course they will have a relish,—salt, and olives, and cheese, and onions, and cabbages or other country herbs which are fit for boiling; and we shall give them a dessert of figs, and pulse, and beans, and myrtle-berries, and beech-nuts, which they will roast at the fire, drinking in moderation. And with such a diet they may be expected to live in peace to a good old age, and bequeath a similar life to their children after them.

Yes, Socrates, he said, and if you were making a city of pigs, how else would you feed the beasts?

But what would you have, Glaucon? I replied.

Why, he said, you should give them the properties of life. People who are to be comfortable are accustomed to lie on sofas, and dine off tables, and they should have dainties and dessert in the modern fashion.

Yes, said I, now I understand; the question which you would have me consider is, not only how a State, but how a luxurious State is to be created; and possibly there is no harm in this, for in such a State we shall be more likely to see how justice and injustice grow up. I am certainly of opinion that the true State, and that which may be said to be a healthy constitution, is the one which I have described. But if you would like to see the inflamed constitution there is no objection to this. For I suppose that many will be dissatisfied with the simpler way of life. They will be for adding sofas, and tables, and other furniture; also dainties, and perfumes, and incense, and courtesans, and cakes, not of one sort only, but in profusion and variety; our imagination must not be limited to the necessaries of which I was at first speaking, such as houses, and clothes, and shoes; but the art of the painter and embroiderer will have to be set in motion, and gold and ivory and other materials of art will be required.

True, he said.

Then we must enlarge our borders; for the original healthy State is too small. Now will the city have to fill and swell with a multitude of callings which go beyond what is required by any natural want; such as the whole tribe of hunters and actors, of which one large class have to do with figures and colors, another are musicians; there will be poets and their attendant train of rhapsodists, players, dancers, contractors; also makers of divers kinds of utensils, not forgetting women's ornaments. And we shall want more servants. Will not tutors be also in request, and nurses wet and dry, tirewomen and barbers, as well as confectioners and cooks; and swineherds, too, who were not needed and therefore not included in the former edition of our State, but needed in this? They must not be forgotten: and there will be hosts of animals, if people are to eat them.

Certainly.

And living in this way we shall have much greater need of physicians than before?

Much greater.

And the country which was enough to support the original inhabitants will be too small now, and not enough?

Quite true.

Then a slice of our neighbor's land will be wanted by us for pasture and tillage, and they will want a slice of ours, if, like ourselves, they exceed the limit of necessity, and give themselves up to the unlimited accumulation of wealth?

That, Socrates, will be unavoidable.

And then we shall go to war, Glaucon,—that will be the next thing.

So we shall, he replied.

Then, without determining as yet whether war does good or harm, thus much we may affirm, that now we have discovered war to be derived from causes which are also the causes of almost all the evils in States, private as well as public.

Undoubtedly.

Then our state must once more enlarge; and this time the enlargement will be nothing short of a whole army, which will have to go out and fight with the invaders for all that we have, as well as for the precious souls whom we were describing above.

Why? he said; are they not capable of defending themselves?

No, I said; not if you and all of us were right in the principle which was acknowledged at the first creation of the State: that principle was, as you will remember, that one man could not practice many arts.

Very true, he said.

But is not war an art?

Certainly.

And an art requiring as much attention as shoemaking?

Quite true.

And the shoemaker was not allowed to be a husbandman, or a weaver, or a builder—in order that we might have our shoes well made: but to him and to every other worker one work was assigned by us for which he was fitted by nature, and he was to continue working all his life long at that and at no other, and not to let opportunities slip, and then he would become a good workman. And is there any more important work than to be a good soldier? But is war an art so easily acquired that a man may be a warrior who is also a husbandman, or shoemaker, or other artisan; although no one in the world would be a good dice or draught player who merely took up the game as a recreation, and had not from his earliest years devoted himself to this and nothing else? The mere handling of tools will not make a man a skilled workman, or master of defense, nor be of any use to him who knows not the nature of each, and has never bestowed any attention upon them. How then will he who takes up a shield or other implement of war all in a day become a good fighter, whether with heavy-armed or any other kind of troops?

Yes, he said, the tools which would teach their own use would be of rare value.

And the greater the business of the guardian is, I said, the more time, and art, and skill will be needed by him?

That is what I should suppose, he replied.

Will he not also require natural gifts?

Certainly.

We shall have to select natures which are suited to their task of guarding the city?

That will be our duty.

And anything but an easy duty, I said; but still we must endeavor to do our best as far as we can?

We must. . . .

Very well, I said; and what is the next question? Must we not ask who are to be rulers and who subjects?

Certainly.

There can be no doubt that the elder sort must rule the younger.

Clearly.

And that the best of the elder sort must rule.

That is also clear.

Now, are not the best husbandmen those who are most devoted to husbandry?

Yes.

And as we must have the best guardians of our city, must they not be those who have most the character of guardians?

Yes.

And to this end they ought to be wise and efficient, and to have a special interest about the State?

True.

And a man will most likely to care about that which he happens to love?

That may be truly inferred.

And he will be most likely to love that which he regards as having the same interests with himself, and anything the good or evil fortune of which he imagines to involve as a result his own good or evil fortune, and to be proportionably careless when he is less concerned?

Very true, he replied.

Then there must be a selection. Let us note among the guardians those who in their whole life show the greatest desire to do what is for the good of their country, and will not do what is against her interests.

Those are the right men.

They will have to be watched at every turn of their lives, in order that we may see whether they preserve this resolution, and never, under the influence either of force or enchantment, forget or let go their duty to the State.

I do not understand, he said, the meaning of the latter words.

I will explain them to you, I replied. A resolution may go out of a man's mind either with his will or against his will; with his will when he gets rid of a falsehood, against his will whenever he is deprived of a truth.

I understand, he said, the willing loss of a resolution; the meaning of the unwilling I have yet to learn.

Why, I said, do you not see that men are unwillingly deprived of good, and willingly of evil? Is not to have lost the truth an evil, and to have the truth a good? and you would allow that to conceive things as they are is to have the truth?

Yes, he replied; I agree with you in thinking that mankind are deprived of truth against their will.

And do they not experience this involuntary effect owing either to theft, or force, or enchantment?

Still, he replied, I do not understand you.

I fear that I must have been talking darkly, like the tragedians. All that I mean is that some men change and others forget; persuasion steals away the hearts of the one class, and time of the other; and this I call theft. Now you understand me?

Yes.

Those again who are forced, are those whom the violence of some pain or grief compels to change their opinion.

That, he said, I understand, and you are quite right.

And you would also acknowledge with me that those are enchanted who change their minds either under the softer influence of pleasure, or the sterner influence of fear?

Yes, he said; everything that deceives may be said to enchant.

Therefore, as I was just now saying, we must inquire who are the best guardians of their own conviction that the interest of the State is to be the rule of all their actions. We must watch them from their youth upwards, and propose deeds for them to perform in which they are most likely to forget or to be deceived, and he who remembers and is not deceived is to be selected, and he who fails in the trial is to be rejected. That will be the way.

Yes.

And there should also be toils and pains and conflicts prescribed for them, in which they will give further proof of the same qualities.

Very right, he replied.

And then, I said, we must try them with enchantments—that is the third sort of test—and see what will be their behavior: like those who take colts amid noises and cries to see if they are of a timid nature, so must we take our youth amid terrors of some kind, and again pass them into pleasures, and try them more thoroughly than gold is tried in the fire, in order to discover whether they are armed against all enchantments, and of a noble bearing always, good guardians of themselves and of the music which they have learned, and retain under all circumstances a rhythmical and harmonious nature, such as will be most serviceable to the man himself and to the State. And he who at every age, as boy and youth and in mature life, has come out of the trial victorious and pure, shall be appointed a ruler and guardian of the State; he shall be honored in life and death, and shall receive sepulture and other memorials of honor, the greatest that we have to give. And as he is chosen his opposite is rejected. I am inclined to think that this is the sort of way in which our rulers and guardians should be chosen. I speak generally, and not with any pretension to exactness.

And, speaking generally, I agree with you, he said.

And perhaps the word "guardian" in the fullest sense ought to be applied to this class only who are our warriors abroad and our peacemakers at home, and who save us from those who might have the will or the power to injure us. The young men whom we before called guardians may be more properly designated auxiliaries and allies of the principles of the rulers.

In that I agree with you, he said. . . .

But where, amid all this, is justice? Son of Ariston, tell me where. Now that our city has been made habitable, light a candle and search, and get your brother and Polemarchus, and the rest of our friends, to help, and let us see whether we can discover the place of justice and injustice, and discern the difference between them, and find out which of them the man who would be happy should have as his portion, whether perceived or unperceived by gods and men.

Nonsense, said Glaucon; did you not promise to search yourself, saying that to desert justice in her need would be an impiety?

Very true, I said; and as you remind me, I will be as good as my word; but you must join.

That we will, he replied.

Well, then, I hope to make the discovery in this way. I mean to proceed by a method of residues, beginning with the assumption that our State, if rightly ordered, is perfect.

That is most certain.

And being perfect, our State is wise and valiant and temperate and just.

That is also clear.

And of whatever is known, that which is unknown will be the residue; this is the next step.

Very good.

Suppose the number of terms to be four, and we were searching for one of them, that one might be known to us at first, and there would be no further trouble; or, if we knew the other three first, and could eliminate them, then the fourth would clearly be the remainder.

Very true, he said.

And is not this the method to be pursued about the virtues, which are also four in number?

Clearly.

First among the virtues found in the State wisdom comes into view, and in this I detect a certain peculiarity.

What is that?

The State that we have been describing is said to be wise as being good in counsel: that is true?

Yes.

And good counsel is clearly a kind of knowledge, for not by ignorance, but by knowledge, do men counsel well?

Clearly.

And the kinds of knowledge in a State are many and diverse?

Of course.

There is the knowledge of the carpenter; but is that the sort of knowledge which gives a city the title of wise and good in counsel?

Certainly not; that would only give a city the reputation of skill in carpentering.

Then a city is not to be called wise because possessed of knowledge which counsels for the best about wooden implements?

Certainly not.

Nor by reason of a knowledge which advises about brazen implements, I said, nor as possessing any other similar knowledge?

Not by reason of any of them, he said.

Nor by reason of agricultural knowledge; that would give the city the name of agriculture?

Yes, that is what I should suppose.

Well, I said, and is there any knowledge in our recently-founded State among any of the citizens which advises, not about any particular thing in the State, but about the whole State, and considers what may be regarded as the best policy, both internal and external?

There certainly is.

And what is this knowledge, and among whom found? I asked.

This is the knowledge of the guardians, he replied, and is found among those whom we were just now describing as perfect guardians.

And is there any name which the city derives from the possession of this sort of knowledge?

The name of good in counsel and truly wise.

And do you suppose that there will be as many of these true guardians as there are blacksmiths in a city?

No, he replied, the blacksmiths will be far more numerous.

Will they not be the smallest of all the classes who receive a name for the profession of some kind of knowledge?

Much the smallest.

And by reason of this smallest part or class of a State, which is the governing and presiding class, and of the knowledge which resides in them, the whole State, being in the order of nature, will be called wise; and nature appears to have ordained that this, which has the only knowledge worthy to be called knowledge, should be the smallest of all classes.

Most true, he said.

Thus, then, I said, the nature and place in the State of one of the four virtues has somehow been discovered.

I am sure, he said, that the discovery is to my mind quite satisfactory.

Again, I said, there is no difficulty in seeing the nature of courage, and in what part that quality resides which gives the name of courageous to the State.

How do you mean?

Why, I said, every one who calls any State courageous or cowardly, will be thinking of that part which fights and goes to battle on the State's behalf.

No one, he replied, would ever think of any other.

The rest of the citizens may be courageous or may be cowardly, but that, as I conceive, will not have the effect of making the city either one or the other.

Certainly not.

The city will be courageous in virtue of a portion of the city in which there resides a never-failing quality preservative of the opinion which the legislator inculcated about the right sort of fear; and this is what you term courage.

I should like to hear what you are saying once more, for I do not think that I perfectly understand you.

I mean, I said, that courage is a kind of preservation.

What kind of preservation?

The preservation, I said, of the opinion about the nature and manner of dangers which the law implants through education; and I mean by the word "never-failing," to intimate that in pleasure or in pain, or under the influence of desire or fear, a man preserves, and does not lose this opinion. . . .

Two virtues remain to be discovered in the State,—first, temperance, and then justice, which is the great object of our search.

Very true.

Now, can we find justice without troubling ourselves about temperance?

I do not know how that can be accomplished, he said, nor do I desire that justice should be brought to light, and temperance lost sight of; and therefore I wish you would do me the favor of considering temperance first.

Certainly, I replied, I cannot be wrong in granting you a favor.

Then do as I ask, he said.

Yes, I replied, I will do as you ask, and next consider temperance; this, as far as I can see at present, has more of the nature of symphony and harmony than the preceding.

How is that? he asked.

Temperance, I replied, is, as I conceive, a sort of order and control of certain pleasures and desires; this is implied in the saying of a man being his own master; and there are other traces of the same notion.

No doubt, he said.

There is something ridiculous in the expression "master of himself;" for the master is also the slave and the slave the master; and in all these modes of speaking the same person is predicated.

Certainly.

But the real meaning of the expression, I believe, is that the human soul has a better principle, and has also a worse principle; and when the better principle controls the worse, then a man is said to be master of himself; and this is certainly a term of praise: but when, owing to evil education or association, the better principle, which is less, is overcome by the worse principle, which is greater, this is censured; and he who is in this case is called the slave of self and unprincipled.

Yes, he said, there is reason in that.

And now, I said, look at our newly-created State, and there you will find one of these two conditions realized; for the State, as you will acknowledge, may be justly called master of self, if the words temperance and self-mastery truly express the rule of the better over the worse.

Yes, he said, I have looked, and perceive the truth of what you say.

Moreover, I said, the pleasures and desires and pains, which are many and various, are found in children and women and servants, and in the lower classes of the free citizens.

Certainly, he said.

Whereas the simple and moderate desires which follow reason, and are under the guidance of mind and true opinion, are confined to a few, being those who are the best born and the best educated.

Very true, he said.

And these also, I said, as you may perceive, have a place in our State, but the meaner desires of the many are held down by the virtuous desires and wisdom of the few.

That I perceive, he said.

Then if there be any city which may be described as master of pleasures and desires, and master of self, ours may claim that designation?

Certainly, he replied.

And also that of temperate, and for the same reasons?

Yes, he said.

And if there be any State in which rulers and subjects will be agreed about the question who are to rule, that again will be our State?

No doubt at all of that.

And the citizens being thus agreed among themselves, in which class will temperance be found,—in the rulers or in the subjects?

In both, as I should imagine, he replied.

Do you observe, I said, that we are pretty right in our anticipation that temperance was a sort of harmony?

Why do you say that?

Why, because temperance is unlike courage and wisdom, each of which resides in a portion of the State only, which the one makes wise and the other valiant; but that is not the way with temperance, which extends to the whole, and runs through the notes of the scale, and produces a harmony of the weaker and the stronger and the middle class, whether you suppose them to be stronger or weaker in wisdom or strength or numbers or wealth, or whatever else may be the measure of them. Most truly, then, do we describe temperance as the natural harmony of master and slaves, both in States and individuals, in which the subjects are as willing to obey as the governors are to rule.

I entirely agree with you.

And so, I said, three of the virtues have been discovered in our State, and this is the form in which they appear. There remains the last element of virtue in a State, which must be justice, if we only knew what that was.

That, he said, is obvious.

The time then has arrived, Glaucon, when, like huntsmen, we should surround the cover, and look sharp that justice does not slip away, and pass out of sight, and get lost; for there can be no doubt that we are in the right direction; only try and get a sight of her, and if you come within view first, let me know.

I wish that there were any chance of that, he said; but I believe that you will find in me a follower who has just eyes enough to see what you show him; that is as much as I am good for.

Offer up a prayer, I said, and follow.

I will follow, he said, but you must show me the way.

Here is no path, I said, and the wood is dark and perplexing; still we must push on. Let us push on then.

Halloo! I said, I begin to perceive indications of a track, and I believe that the quarry will not escape.

That's good news, he said.

Truly, I said, we are very stupid.

Why so?

Why, my good sir, I said, when we first began, ages ago, there lay justice rolling at our feet, and we, fools that we were, failed to see her, like people who go about looking for what they have in their hands: And that was the way with us; we looked away into the far distance, and I suspect this to have been the reason why we missed her.

What do you mean?

I mean to say that we have already had her on our lips and in our ears, and failed to recognize her.

I get impatient at the length of your exordium.

Well, then, say whether I am right or not; you will remember the original principle of which we spoke at the foundation of the State, that every man, as we often insisted, should practice one thing only, that being the thing to which his nature was most perfectly adapted; now justice is either this or a part of this.

Yes, that was often repeated by us.

Further, we affirmed that justice was doing one's own business, and not being a busybody; that was often said by us, and many others have said the same.

Yes, that was said by us.

Then this doing one's own business in a certain way may be assumed to be justice. Do you know why I say this?

I do not, and should like to be told.

Because I think that this alone remains in the State when the other virtues of temperance and courage and wisdom are abstracted; and this is the ultimate cause and condition of the existence of all of them, and while remaining in them is also their preservative; and we were saying that if the three were discovered by us, justice would be the fourth or remaining one.

That follows of necessity. . . .

I proceeded to ask: When two things, a greater and less, are called by the same name, are they like or unlike in so far as they are called the same?

Like, he replied.

The just man then, in being just, and in reference to the mere principle of justice, will be like the just State?

He will.

And a State was thought by us to be just when the three classes in the State did their own business; and also thought to be temperate and valiant and wise by reason of certain other affections and qualities of these same classes?

True, he said.

And so of the individual; we shall be right in arguing that he has these same principles in his own soul, and may fairly receive the same appellations as possessing the affections which correspond to them?

Certainly, he said. . . .

Can I be wrong, I said, in acknowledging that in the individual there are the same principles and habits which there are in the State? for if they did not pass from one to the other, whence did they come? Take the quality of spirit or passion; there would be something ridiculous in thinking that this quality, which is characteristic of the Thracians, Scythians, and in general of the northern nations, when found in States, does not originate in the individuals who compose them; and the same may be said of the love of knowledge, which is the special characteristic of our part of the world, or the love of money, which may, with equal truth, be attributed to the Phoenicians and Egyptians.

Exactly, he said.

There is no difficulty in understanding this.

And now, after much tossing in the argument, we have reached land, and are fairly agreed that the principles which exist in the State, like those in the individual, are three in number, and the same with them.

Exactly.

And must we not infer that the individual is wise in the same way, and in virtue of the same quality which makes the State wise?

Certainly.

And the same quality which constitutes bravery in the State constitutes bravery in the individual, and the same is true of all the other virtues?

Assuredly.

And the individual will be acknowledged by us to be just in the same way that the State was just?

That will also follow of course.

And the justice of the State consisted, as we very well remember, in each of the three classes doing the work of that class?

We are not very likely to forget that, he said.

And we must also remember that the individual whose several principles do their own work will be just, and will do his own work?

Yes, he said, we must remember that.

And ought not the rational principle, which is wise, and has the care of the whole soul, to rule, and the passionate or spirited principle to be the subject and ally?

Certainly.

And, as you were saying, the harmonizing influence of music and gymnastic will bring them into accord, nerving and educating the reason with noble words and lessons, and softening and consoling and civilizing the wildness of passion with harmony and rhythm?

Quite true, he said.

And these two, thus nurtured and educated, and having learned truly to know their own functions, will set a rule over the concupiscent part of every man, which is the largest and most insatiable; over this they will set a guard, lest, waxing great with the fullness of bodily pleasures, as they are termed, and no longer confined to her own sphere, the concupiscent soul should attempt to enslave and rule those who are not her natural-born subjects, and overturn the whole life of man?

Very true, he said.

The two will be the defenders of the whole soul and the whole body against attacks from without; the one counseling, and the other fighting under the command of their leader, and courageously executing his counsels.

True.

And he is to be deemed courageous who, having the element of passion working in him, preserves, in the midst of pain and pleasure, the notion of danger which reason prescribes?

Right, he replied.

And he is wise who has in him that little part which rules and gives orders; that part being supposed to have a knowledge of what is for the interest of each and all of the three other parts?

Assuredly.

And would you not say that he is temperate who has these same elements in friendly harmony, in whom the one ruling principle of reason, and the two subject ones of spirit and desire are equally agreed that reason ought to rule, and do not rebel?

Certainly, he said, that is the true account of temperance whether in the State or individual.

And surely, I said, a man will be just in the manner of which we have several times already spoken and no other?

That is very certain.

And is the edge of justice blunted in the individual, or is there any reason why our definition of justice should not apply equally to the individual and to the State?

None in my judgment, he said. . . .

[Y]ou have been often told that the idea of good is the highest knowledge, and that all other things become useful and advantageous only by their use of this. And you must be quite aware that of this I am about to speak, concerning which, as I shall say, we know so little; and, wanting which, any other knowledge or possession of any kind will profit us nothing. Do you think that the possession of the whole world is of any value without the good? or of all wisdom, without the beautiful and good?

No, indeed, he said.

You are doubtless aware that most people call pleasure good, and the finer sort of wits say wisdom? And you are aware that the latter cannot explain the nature of wisdom, but are obliged after all to say that wisdom is of the good?

That is very ridiculous, he said.

Yes, I said, that they should begin by reproaching us with our ignorance, and then presume our knowledge of good—for wisdom, as they say, is of the good, which implies that we understand them when they use the term "good"—is certainly ridiculous.

Most true, he said.

And those who make pleasure their good are in equal perplexity; for they are compelled to admit that there are bad pleasures as well as good.

Certainly.

And therefore to acknowledge that bad and good are the same?

True.

There can be no doubt about the numerous difficulties in which this question is involved.

There can be none.

Well, and is not this an obvious fact, that many are willing to possess, or to do, or to wear the appearance of the just and honorable without the reality; but no one is satisfied to possess the appearance of good—the reality is what they seek; the appearance in the case of the good is despised by every one.

Very true, he said.

This, then, which every man pursues and makes his end, having a presentiment that there is such an end, and yet hesitating because neither knowing the nature nor having the same sure proof of this as of other things, and therefore having no profit in other things,—is this, I would ask, a principle about which those who are called the best men in the State, and to whom everything is to be entrusted, ought to be in such darkness?

Certainly not, he said.

I am sure, I said, that he who does not know how the beautiful and the just are likewise good will not be worth much as a guardian of them: and I suspect that no one will have a true knowledge of them without this knowledge.

That, he said, is a shrewd suspicion of yours.

And if we only have a guardian who has this knowledge our State will be perfectly ordered?

Of course, he replied; but I wish you would tell me whether you conceive of this supreme principle of the good to be knowledge or pleasure, or different from either?

Aye, I said, I knew quite well that a fine gentleman like you would not be contented with the thoughts of other men.

True, Socrates; and I must say that you have no right to be always repeating the opinions of others, and never to tell your own, and this after having passed a lifetime in the study of philosophy.

Well, but has any one a right to say, positively, what he does not know?

Not, he said, with the positiveness of knowledge; he has no right to do that: but he ought to say what he thinks, as a matter of opinion.

But do you not know, I said, that opinions are bad all, and the best of them blind? You would not deny that those who have any true notion without intelligence are only like blind men finding their way along a straight road?

Very true.

And do you wish to behold what is blind and crooked and base, when brightness and beauty are within your reach?

Still, I must implore you, Socrates, said Glaucon, not to turn away just as you are reaching the goal; if you will only give such an explanation of the good as you have already given about justice and temperance and the other virtues, that will satisfy us.

Yes, my friend, I said, and that will satisfy me too, extremely well, but I cannot help fearing that I shall fail, and that in my zeal I shall make a fool of myself. No, sweet sirs, let us not at present ask what is the actual nature of the good, for to reach what is in my thoughts now is too much for me in my present mood. But of the child of the good who is likest him, I would fain speak, if I could be sure that you wished to hear—otherwise, not.

Nay, he said, speak; the child shall be the interest, and you shall remain in our debt for an account of the parent or principal.

I do indeed wish, I replied, that I could pay, and you receive, the parent or principal account, and not, as now, the interest or child only; take, however, the child, which is the interest, and at the same time have a care that I do not render a false account, although I have no intention of deceiving you.

Yes, we will take all the care that we can: proceed.

Yes, I said, but I must first come to an understanding with you, and remind you of what I have mentioned in the course of this discussion, and at many other times.

What is that? he said.

The old story, that there is a many beautiful and a many good, and so of other things which we describe and define; to all of them the term "many" is applied.

True, he said.

And there is an absolute beauty and an absolute good, and so of other things to which the term "many" is applied; they may be brought under a single idea, which is called the essence of each.

That is true.

The many, as we say, are seen but not known, and the ideas are known but not seen.

Exactly.

And what is the organ with which we see the visible things?

The sight, he said.

And with the hearing, I said, we hear, and with the other senses perceive the other objects of sense?

True.

But have you remarked that sight is by far the most costly and complex piece of workmanship which the aritificer of the senses ever contrived?

No, I never have, he said.

Then reflect: does the ear hear, and is the voice heard by virtue of some other nature which is required as a third condition before they can meet?

Nothing of the sort.

No, indeed, I replied; and the same is true of most, if not all, the other senses: you would not regard any of them as requiring such an addition?

Indeed not. But you see that without such an addition there is no seeing or being seen?

How do you mean?

Sight being, as I conceive, in the eyes, and the possessor making use of his vision, and color being also present in them, unless there is a third nature at hand designed for this special purpose, you know that the sight will see nothing and the colors will be invisible?

And of what nature are you speaking?

Of that which you term light, I replied.

True, he said.

Noble, then, is the bond which links together sight and visibility, and great beyond other bonds by no small difference of nature; for light is their bond, and light is no ignoble thing.

Nay, he said, the reverse of ignoble.

And which, I said, of the gods in heaven would you say was the lord of this element? Whose is that light which makes the eye to see perfectly and the visible to appear?

You mean the sun, as you and all mankind say.

May not the relation of sight to this deity be described as follows?

How?

Neither sight nor the eye in which sight resides is the sun?

No.

Yet of all the organs of sense the eye is likest the sun?

Far the likest.

And the power which the eye possesses is a sort of effluence which is dispensed from the sun?

Exactly.

Then the sun is not sight, but the author of sight who is recognized by sight?

True, he said.

And this is he whom I call the child of the good, whom the good begat in his own likeness, to be in the visible world, in relation to sight and the things of sight, what the good is in the intellectual world in relation to mind and the things of mind?

Will you be a little more explicit? he said.

Why, you know, I said, that the eyes, when a person no longer directs them towards those objects on the colors of which the light of day is shining, but the moon and stars only, see dimly, and are nearly blind; they seem to have no clearness of vision in them?

Very true.

But when they are directed towards objects on which the sun shines, they see clearly and there is sight in them?

Certainly.

And the soul is like the eye: when resting upon that on which truth and being shines, the soul perceives and understands, and is radiant with intelligence; but when turning towards the twilight of generation and destruction, then she has opinion only, and goes blinking about, and is first of one opinion and then of another, and seems to have no intelligence?

Yes.

Now, that which imparts truth to the object and knowledge to the subject is what I would have you term the idea of good and that you will regard as the cause of science and of truth as known by us; beautiful too, as are both truth and knowledge, you will be right in esteeming this other nature as more beautiful than either; and, as in the previous instance, light and sight may be truly said to be like the sun, and yet not to be the sun, so in this other sphere, science and truth may be deemed like the good, but not the good: the good has a place of honor yet higher.

What a wonder of beauty that must be, he said, which is the author of science and truth, and yet surpasses them in beauty; for you surely cannot mean to say that the good is pleasure?

Speak not of that, I said, but please to consider the image in another point of view.

What is that?

Why, you would say that the sun is not only the author of visibility in all visible things, but of generation and nourishment and growth, though not himself a generation?

Certainly.

In like manner the good may be said to be not only the author of knowledge in all things known, but of their being and essence, and yet the good is not essence, but far exceeds essence in dignity and power.

Glaucon said, with ludicrous earnestness: By the light of heaven, how amazing!

Yes, I said, and that all comes of you, for you made me utter my fancies.

Aristotle
(384–322 B.C.)

Aristotle was born in Stagira, in Macedonia—the northern frontier of the Greek world. His father, Nicomachus, was physician to King Amyntas, grandfather to Alexander the Great. He went to Athens at eighteen, where he studied in Plato's Academy for some twenty years. Passed over to succeed Plato as head of the Academy, Aristotle traveled to the Greek colonies of Asia Minor. There he married the niece of King Hermias of Atarneus. In 343 B.C. he was summoned to the Macedonian court to tutor the young Alexander; but he left before Alexander embarked on his world conquests when his nephew, Callisthenes, was executed for refusing to worship Alexander as a god. (Other accounts have it that Callisthenes was implicated in an assassination plot against Alexander.) Aristotle returned to Athens with a hefty sum of seed money provided by his supporters in the Macedonian royal family and, in a gymnasium dedicated to Apollo Lyceus, opened a school devoted to comprehensive research in science and philosophy. Aristotle often lectured while strolling around the grounds of the Lyceum, and so he became known as the Peripatetic philosopher. Following Alexander's death in 323 B.C., Aristotle was charged with impiety. Unlike Socrates, however, Aristotle fled Athens, lest "The Athenians sin a second time against philosophy." He died in Chalcis a few months later.

Nicomachean Ethics*

Every art and every kind of inquiry, and likewise every act and purpose, seems to aim at some good: and so it has been well said that the good is that at which everything aims.

But a difference is observable among these aims or ends. What is aimed at is sometimes the exercise of a faculty, sometimes a certain result beyond that exercise. And where there is an end beyond the act, there the result is better than the exercise of the faculty.

Now since there are many kinds of actions and many arts and sciences, it

From Aristotle, *The Nichomachean Ethics of Aristotle*, translated by F. H. Peters (London: C. Kegan Paul and Co., 1881).

follows that there are many ends also; *e.g.* health is the end of medicine, ships of shipbuilding, victory of the art of war, and wealth of economy.

But when several of these are subordinated to some one art or science,—as the making of bridles and other trappings to the art of horsemanship, and this in turn, along with all else that the soldier does, to the art of war, and so on,—then the end of the master-art is always more desired than the ends of the subordinate arts, since these are pursued for its sake. And this is equally true whether the end in view be the mere exercise of a faculty or something beyond that, as in the above instances.

If then in what we do there be some end which we wish for on its own account, choosing all the others as means to this, but not every end without exception as a means to something else (for so we should go on *ad infinitum,* and desire would be left void and objectless),—this evidently will be the good or the best of all things.

And surely from a practical point of view it much concerns us to know this good; for then, like archers shooting at a definite mark, we shall be more likely to attain what we want.

If this be so, we must try to indicate roughly what it is, and first of all to which of the arts or sciences it belongs.

It would seem to belong to the supreme art or science, that one which most of all deserves the name of master-art or master-science.

Now Politics seems to answer to this description. For it prescribes which of the sciences a state needs, and which each man shall study, and up to what point; and to it we see subordinated even the highest arts, such as economy, rhetoric, and the art of war.

Since then it makes use of the other practical sciences, and since it further ordains what men are to do and from what to refrain, its ends must include the ends of the others, and must be the proper good of man.

For though this good is the same for the individual and the state, yet the good of the state seems a grander and more perfect thing both to attain and to secure; and glad as one would be to do this service for a single individual, to do it for a people and for a number of states is nobler and more divine.

This then is the aim of the present inquiry, which is a sort of political inquiry. . . .

Since—to resume—all knowledge and all purpose aims at some good, what is this which we say is the aim of Politics; or, in other words, what is the highest of all realizable goods?

As to its name, I suppose nearly all men are agreed; for the masses and the men of culture alike declare that it is happiness, and hold that to "live well" or to "do well" is the same as to be "happy."

But they differ as to what this happiness is, and the masses do not give the same account of it as the philosophers.

The former take it to be something palpable and plain, as pleasure or wealth or fame; one man holds it to be this, and another that, and often the same man is of different minds at different times,—after sickness it is health, and in poverty it is wealth; while when they are impressed with the consciousness of their ignorance, they admire most those who say grand things that are above their comprehension.

Some philosophers, on the other hand, have thought that, beside these several good things, there is an "absolute" good which is the cause of their goodness. . . .

Leaving these matters, then, let us return once more to the question, what this good can be of which we are in search.

It seems to be different in different kinds of action and in different arts,—one thing in medicine and another in war, and so on. What then is the good in each of these cases? Surely that for the sake of which all else is done. And that in medicine is health, in war is victory, in building is a house,—a different thing in each different case, but always, in whatever we do and in whatever we choose, the end. For it is always for the sake of the end that all else is done.

If then there be one end of all that man does, this end will be the realizable good,—or these ends, if there be more than one.

Our argument has thus come round by a different path to the same point as before. This point we must try to explain more clearly.

We see that there are many ends. But some of these are chosen only as means, as wealth, flutes, and the whole class of instruments. And so it is plain that not all ends are final.

But the best of all things must, we conceive, be something final.

If then there be only one final end, this will be what we are seeking,—or if there be more than one, then the most final of them.

Now that which is pursued as an end in itself is more final than that which is pursued as means to something else, and that which is never chosen as means than that which is chosen both as an end in itself and as means, and that is strictly final which is always chosen as an end in itself and never as means.

Happiness seems more than anything else to answer to this description: for we always choose it for itself, and never for the sake of something else; while honour and pleasure and reason, and all virtue or excellence, we choose partly indeed for themselves (for, apart from any result, we should choose each of them), but partly also for the sake of happiness, supposing that they will help to make us happy. But no one chooses happiness for the sake of these things, or as a means to anything else at all.

We seem to be led to the same conclusion when we start from the notion of self-sufficiency.

The final good is thought to be self-sufficing [or all-sufficing]. In applying this term we do not regard a man as an individual leading a solitary life, but we also take account of parents, children, wife, and, in short, friends and fellow-citizens generally, since man is naturally a social being. Some limit must indeed be set to this; for if you go on to parents and descendants and friends of friends, you will never come to a stop. But this we will consider further on: for the present we will take self-sufficing to mean what by itself makes life desirable and in want of nothing. Now happiness is believed to answer to this description.

And further, happiness is believed to be the most desirable thing in the world, and that not merely as one among other good things: if it were merely one among other good things [so that other things could be added to it], it is plain that the addition of the least of other goods must make it more desirable; for the addition becomes a surplus of good, and of two goods the greater is always more desirable.

Thus it seems that happiness is something final and self-sufficing, and is the end of all that man does.

But perhaps the reader thinks that though no one will dispute the statement that happiness is the best thing in the world, yet a still more precise definition of it is needed.

This will best be gained, I think, by asking, What is the function of man? For as the goodness and the excellence of a piper or a sculptor, or the practiser of any art, and generally of those who have any function or business to do, lies in that function, so man's good would seem to lie in his function, if he has one.

But can we suppose that, while a carpenter and a cobbler has a function and a business of his own, man has no business and no function assigned him by nature? Nay, surely as his several members, eye and hand and foot, plainly have each his own function, so we must suppose that man also has some function over and above all these.

What then is it?

Life evidently he has in common even with the plants, but we want that which is peculiar to him. We must exclude, therefore, the life of mere nutrition and growth.

Next to this comes the life of sense; but this too he plainly shares with horses and cattle and all kinds of animals.

There remains then the life whereby he acts—the life of his rational nature, with its two sides or divisions, one rational as obeying reason, the other rational as having and exercising reason.

But as this expression is ambiguous, we must be understood to mean thereby the life that consists in the exercise of the faculties; for this seems to be more properly entitled to the name.

The function of man, then, is exercise of his vital faculties [or soul] on one side in obedience to reason, and on the side with reason.

But what is called the function of a man of any profession and the function of a man who is good in that profession are generically the same, *e.g.,* of a harper and of a good harper; and this holds in all cases without exception, only that in the case of the latter his superior excellence at his work is added; for we say a harper's function is to harp, and a good harper's to harp well.

Man's function then being, as we say, a kind of life—that is to say, exercise of his faculties and action of various kinds with reason—the good man's function is to do this well and beautifully.

But the function of anything is done well when it is done in accordance with the proper excellence of that thing.

Putting all this together, then, we find that the good of man is exercise of his faculties in accordance with excellence or virtue, or, if there be more than one, in accordance with the best and most complete virtue.

But to this we must add that the external circumstances of his life must also be perfect and complete: if one swallow or one fine day does not make a spring, neither does one day or any small space of time make a blessed or happy man.

This, then, may be taken as a rough outline of the good; for this, I think, is the proper method,—first to sketch the outline, and then to fill in the details. But it would seem that, the outline once fairly drawn, any one can carry on the work and fit in the several items which time reveals to us or helps us to find. And this indeed is the way in which the arts and sciences have grown; for it requires no extraordinary genius to fill up the gaps. . . .

Since happiness is an exercise of the vital faculties in accordance with perfect virtue or excellence, we will now inquire about virtue or excellence; for this will probably help us in our inquiry about happiness.

And indeed the true statesman seems to be especially concerned with virtue, for he wishes to make the citizens good and obedient to the laws. Of this we have an example in the Cretan and the Lacedaemonian lawgivers, and any others who have resembled them. But if the inquiry belongs to Politics or the science of the state, it is plain that it will be in accordance with our original purpose to pursue it.

The virtue or excellence that we are to consider is, of course, the excellence of man; for it is the good of man and the happiness of man that we started to seek. And by the excellence of man I mean excellence not of body, but of soul; for happiness we take to be an activity of the soul.

If this be so, then it is evident that the statesman must have some knowledge of the soul, just as the man who is to heal the eye or the whole body must have some knowledge of them, and that the more in proportion as the science of the state is higher and better than medicine. But all educated physicians take much pains to know about the body.

As statesmen [or students of Politics], then, we must inquire into the nature of the soul, but in so doing we must keep our special purpose in view and go only so far as that requires; for to go into minuter detail would be too laborious for the present undertaking.

Now, there are certain points which are stated with sufficient precision even in the popular accounts of the soul, and these we will adopt.

For instance, they distinguish an irrational and a rational part.

Whether these are separated as are the parts of the body or any divisible thing, or whether they are only distinguishable in thought but in fact inseparable, like concave and convex in the circumference of a circle, makes no difference for our present purpose.

Of the irrational part, again, one division seems to be common to all things that live, and to be possessed by plants—I mean that which causes nutrition and growth; for we must assume that all things that take nourishment have a faculty of this kind, even when they are embryos, and have the same faculty when they are full grown; at least, this is more reasonable than to suppose that they then have a different one.

The excellence of this faculty, then, is plainly one that man shares with other beings, and not specifically human.

And this is confirmed by the fact that this part of the soul, or this faculty, is thought to be most active in sleep, while the distinction between the good and the bad man shows itself least in sleep—whence the saying that for half their lives there is no difference between the happy and the miserable. This indeed is what we should expect; for sleep is the cessation of the soul from those functions in respect of which it is called good or bad, except in so far as the motions of the body may sometimes make their way in, and give occasion to dreams which are better in the good man than in ordinary people.

However, we need not pursue this further, and may dismiss the nutritive principle, since it has no place in the excellence of man.

But there seems to be another vital principle that is irrational, and yet in some way partakes of reason. In the case of the continent and of the incontinent man alike, we praise the reason or the rational part, for it exhorts them rightly and urges them to do what is best; but there is plainly present in them another principle besides the rational one, which fights and struggles against the reason. For just as a paralyzed limb, when you will to move it to the right, moves on the contrary to the left, so it is with the soul; the incontinent man's impulses run counter to his reason. Only whereas we see the refractory member in the case of the body, we do not see it in the case of the soul. But we must nevertheless, I think, hold that in the soul, too, there is something beside the reason, which opposes and runs counter to it (though in what sense it is distinct from the reason does not matter here).

It seems, however, to partake of reason also, as we said: at least, in the continent man it submits to the reason; while in the temperate and courageous man we may say it is still more obedient; for in him it is altogether in harmony with the reason.

The irrational part, then, it appears, is twofold. There is the vegetative faculty, which has no share of reason; and the faculty of appetite or of desire in general, which partakes of reason in a manner—that is, in so far as it listens to reason and submits to its sway. But when we say "partakes of reason" or "listens to reason," we mean this in the sense in which we talk of "listening to reason" from parents or friends, not in the sense in which we talk of listening to reason from mathematicians.

Further, all advice and all rebuke and exhortation testifies that the irrational part is in some way amenable to reason.

If then we like to say that this part, too, has a share of reason, the rational part also will have two divisions: one rational in the strict sense as possessing reason in itself, the other rational as listening to reason as a man listens to his father.

Now, on this division of the faculties is based the division of excellence; for we speak of intellectual excellences and of moral excellences; wisdom and understanding and prudence we call intellectual, liberality and temperance we call moral virtues or excellences. When we are speaking of a man's moral character we do not say that he is wise or intelligent, but that he is gentle or temperate. But we praise the wise man, too, for his habit of mind or trained faculty; and a habit or trained faculty that is praiseworthy is what we call an excellence or virtue. . . .

Excellence, then, being of these two kinds, intellectual and moral, intellectual excellence owes its birth and growth mainly to instruction, and so requires time and experience, while moral excellence is the result of habit or custom (*ethos*), and has accordingly in our language received a name formed by a slight change from *ethos*.

From this it is plain that none of the moral excellences or virtues is implanted in us by nature; for that which is by nature cannot be altered by training. For instance, a stone naturally tends to fall downwards, and you could not train it to rise upwards, though you tried to do so by throwing it up ten thousand times, nor could you train fire to move downwards, nor accustom anything which naturally behaves in one way to behave in any other way.

The virtues, then, come neither by nature nor against nature, but nature gives the capacity for acquiring them, and this is developed by training.

Again, where we do things by nature we get the power first, and put this power forth in act afterwards: as we plainly see in the case of the senses; for it is not by constantly seeing and hearing that we acquire those faculties, but, on the contrary, we had the power first and then used it, instead of acquiring the power by the use. But the virtues we acquire by doing the acts, as is the case with the arts too. We learn an art by doing that which we wish to do when we have learned it; we become builders by building, and harpers by harping. And so by doing just acts we become just, and by doing acts of temperance and courage we become temperate and courageous.

This is attested, too, by what occurs in states; for the legislators make their citizens good by training; *i.e.* this is the wish of all legislators, and those who do not succeed in this miss their aim, and it is this that distinguishes a good from a bad constitution.

Again, both virtues and vices result from and are formed by the same acts in which they manifest themselves, as is the case with the arts also. It is by harping that good harpers and bad harpers alike are produced: and so with builders and the rest; by building well they will become good builders, and bad builders by building badly. Indeed, if it were not so, they would not want anybody to teach them, but would all be born either good or bad at their trades. And it is just the same with the virtues also. It is by our conduct in our intercourse with other men that we become just or unjust, and by acting in circumstances of danger, and training ourselves to feel fear or confidence, that we become courageous or cowardly. So, too, with our animal appetites and the passion of anger; for by behaving in this way or in that on the occasions with which these passions are concerned, some become temperate and gentle, and others profligate and ill-tempered. In a word, the several habits or characters are formed by the same kind of acts as those which they produce.

Hence we ought to make sure that our acts be of a certain kind; for the resulting character varies as they vary. It makes no small difference, therefore, whether a man be trained from his youth up in this way or in that, but a great difference, or rather all the difference.

But our present inquiry has not, like the rest, a merely speculative aim; we are not inquiring merely in order to know what excellence or virtue is, but in order to become good; for otherwise it would profit us nothing. We must ask therefore about these acts, and see of what kind they are to be; for, as we said, it is they that determine our habits of character.

First of all, then, that they must be in accordance with right reason is a common characteristic of them, which we shall here take for granted, reserving for future discussion the question what this right reason is, and how it is related to the other excellences.

But let it be understood, before we go on, that all reasoning on matters of practice must be in outline merely, and not scientifically exact: for, as we said at starting, the kind of reasoning to be demanded varies with the subject in hand; and in practical matters and questions of expediency there are no invariable laws, any more than in questions of health.

And if our general conclusions are thus inexact, still more inexact is all reasoning about particular cases; for these fall under no system of scientifically established rules or traditional maxims, but the agent must always consider for himself what the special occasion requires, just as in medicine or navigation.

But though this is the case we must try to render what help we can.

First of all, then, we must observe that, in matters of this sort, to fall short and to exceed are alike fatal. This is plain (to illustrate what we cannot see by what we can see) in the case of strength and health. Too much and too little exercise alike destroy strength, and to take too much meat and drink, or to take too little, is equally ruinous to health, but the fitting amount produces and increases and preserves them. Just so, then, is it with temperance also, and courage, and the other virtues. The man who shuns and fears everything and never makes a stand, becomes a coward; while the man who fears nothing at all, but will face anything, becomes foolhardy. So, too, the man who takes his fill of any kind of pleasure, and abstains from none, is a profligate, but the man who shuns all (like him whom we call a "boor") is devoid of sensibility.

For temperance and courage are destroyed both by excess and defect, but preserved by moderation.

But habits or types of character are not only produced and preserved and destroyed by the same occasions and the same means, but they also manifest themselves in the same circumstances. This is the case with palpable things like strength. Strength is produced by taking plenty of nourishment and doing plenty of hard work, and the strong man, in turn, has the greatest capacity for these. And the case is the same with the virtues: by abstaining from pleasure we become temperate, and when we have become temperate we are best able to abstain. And so with courage: by habituating ourselves to despise danger, and to face it, we become courageous; and when we have become courageous, we are best able to face danger. . . .

We have thus found the genus to which virtue belongs; but we want to know, not only that it is a trained faculty, but also what species of trained faculty it is.

We may safely assert that the virtue or excellence of a thing causes that thing both to be itself in good condition and to perform its function well. The excellence of the eye, for instance, makes both the eye and its work good; for it is by the excellence of the eye that we see well. So the proper excellence of the horse makes a horse what he should be, and makes him good at running, and carrying his rider, and standing a charge.

If, then, this holds good in all cases, the proper excellence or virtue of man will be a habit or trained faculty that makes a man good and makes him perform his function well.

How this is to be done we have already said, but we may exhibit the same conclusion in another way, by inquiring what the nature of this virtue is.

Now, if we have any quantity, whether continuous or discrete, it is possible to take either a larger (or too large), or a smaller (or too small), or an equal (or fair) amount, and that either absolutely or relatively to our own needs.

By an equal or fair amount I understand a mean amount, or one that lies between excess and deficiency.

By the absolute mean, or mean relatively to the thing itself, I understand that which is equidistant from both extremes, and this is one and the same for all.

By the mean relatively to us I understand that which is neither too much nor too little for us; and this is not one and the same for all.

For instance, if ten be larger (or too large) and two be smaller (or too small), if we take six we take the mean relatively to the thing itself (or the arithmetical mean); for it exceeds one extreme by the same amount by which it is exceeded by the other extreme: and this is the mean in arithmetical proportion.

But the mean relatively to us cannot be found in this way. If ten pounds of food is too much for a given man to eat, and two pounds too little, it does not follow that the trainer will order him six pounds: for that also may perhaps be too much for the man in question, or too little; too little for Milo, too much for the beginner. The same holds true in running and wrestling.

And so we may say generally that a master in any art avoids what is too much and what is too little, and seeks for the mean and chooses it—not the absolute but the relative mean.

Every art or science, then, perfects its work in this way, looking to the mean and bringing its work up to this standard; so that people are wont to say of a good work that nothing could be taken from it or added to it, implying that excellence is destroyed by excess or deficiency, but secured by observing the mean. And good artists, as we say, do in fact keep their eyes fixed on this in all that they do.

Virtue therefore, since like nature it is more exact and better than any art, must also aim at the mean—virtue of course meaning moral virtue or excellence; for it has to do with passions and actions, and it is these that admit of excess and deficiency and the mean. For instance, it is possible to feel fear, confidence, desire, anger, pity, and generally to be affected pleasantly and painfully, either too much or too little, in either case wrongly; but to be thus affected at the right times, and on the right occasions, and towards the right persons, and with the right object, and in the right fashion, is the mean course and the best course, and these are characteristics of virtue. And in the same way our outward acts also admit of excess and deficiency, and the mean or due amount.

Virtue, then, has to deal with feelings or passions and with outward acts, in which excess is wrong and deficiency also is blamed, but the mean amount is praised and is right—both of which are characteristics of virtue.

Virtue, then, is a kind of moderation (*mesotes tis*), inasmuch as it aims at the mean or moderate amount (*to meson*).

Again, there are many ways of going wrong (for evil is infinite in nature, to use a Pythagorean figure while good is finite), but only one way of going right; so that the one is easy and the other hard—easy to miss the mark and hard to hit. On this account also, then, excess and deficiency are characteristic of vice, hitting the mean is characteristic of virtue:

"Goodness is simple, ill takes any shape."

Virtue, then, is a habit or trained faculty of choice, the characteristic of which lies in observing the mean relatively to the persons concerned, and which is guided by reason, *i.e.* by the judgment of the prudent man.

And it is a moderation, firstly, inasmuch as it comes in the middle or mean between two vices, one on the side of excess, the other on the side of defect; and, secondly, inasmuch as, while these vices fall short of or exceed the due measure in feeling and in action, it finds and chooses the mean, middling, or moderate amount.

Regarded in its essence, therefore, or according to the definition of its nature, virtue is a moderation or middle state, but viewed in its relation to what is best and right it is the extreme of perfection. . . .

But it is not enough to make these general statements [about virtue and vice]: we must go on and apply them to particulars [*i.e.* to the several virtues and vices]. For in reasoning about matters of conduct general statements are too vague, and do not convey so much truth as particular propositions. It is with particulars that conduct is concerned: our statements; therefore, when applied to these particulars, should be found to hold good.

These particulars then [*i.e.* the several virtues and vices and the several acts and affections with which they deal], we will take from the following table.

Moderation in the feelings of fear and confidence is courage: of those that exceed, he that exceeds in fearlessness has no name (as often happens), but he that exceeds in confidence is foolhardly, while he that exceeds in fear, but is deficient in confidence, is cowardly.

Moderation in respect of certain pleasures and also (though to a less extent) certain pains is temperance, while excess is profligacy. But defectiveness in the matter of these pleasures is hardly ever found, and so this sort of people also have as yet received no name: let us put them down as "void of sensibility."

In the matter of giving and taking money, moderation is liberality, excess and deficiency are prodigality and illiberality. But these two vices exceed and fall short in contrary ways: the prodigal exceeds in spending, but falls short in taking; while the illiberal man exceeds in taking, but falls short in spending.

(For the present we are but giving an outline or summary, and aim at nothing more; we shall afterwards treat these points in greater detail.)

But, besides these, there are other dispositions in the matter of money: there is a moderation which is called magnificence (for the magnificent is not the same as the liberal man: the former deals with large sums, the latter with small), and an excess which is called bad taste or vulgarity, and a deficiency which is called meanness; and these vices differ from those which are opposed to liberality: how they differ will be explained later.

With respect to honour and disgrace, there is a moderation which is high-mindedness, an excess which may be called vanity, and a deficiency which is little-mindedness.

But just as we said that liberality is related to magnificence, differing only in that it deals with small sums, so here there is a virtue related to high-mindedness, and differing only in that it is concerned with small instead of great honours. A man may have a due desire for honour, and also more or less than a due desire: he that carries this desire to excess is called ambitious, he that has not enough of it is called unambitious, but he that has the due amount has no name. There are also no abstract names for the characters, except "ambition," corresponding to ambitious. And on this account those who occupy the extremes lay claim to the middle place. And in common parlance, too, the moderate man is sometimes called ambitious and sometimes unambitious, and sometimes the ambitious man is praised and sometimes the unambitious. Why this is we will explain afterwards; for the present we will follow out our plan and enumerate the other types of character.

In the matter of anger also we find excess and deficiency and moderation. The characters themselves hardly have recognized names, but as the moderate man is here called gentle, we will call his character gentleness; of those who go into extremes, we may take the term wrathful for him who exceeds, with wrathfulness for the vice, and wrathless for him who is deficient, with wrathlessness for his character.

Besides these, there are three kinds of moderation, bearing some resemblance to one another, and yet different. They all have to do with intercourse in speech and action, but they differ in that one has to do with the truthfulness of this intercourse, while the other two have to do with its pleasantness—one of the two with pleasantness in matters of amusement, the other with pleasantness in all the relations of life. We must therefore speak of these qualities also in order that we may the more plainly see how, in all cases, moderation is praiseworthy, while the extreme courses are neither right nor praiseworthy, but blamable.

In these cases also names are for the most part wanting, but we must try, here as elsewhere, to coin names ourselves, in order to make our argument clear and easy to follow.

In the matter of truth, then, let us call him who observes the mean a true [or truthful] person, and observance of the mean truth [or truthfulness]: pretence, when it exaggerates, may be called boasting, and the person a boaster; when it understates, let the names be irony and ironical.

With regard to pleasantness in amusement, he who observes the mean may be called witty, and his character wittiness; excess may be called buffoonery, and the man a buffoon; while boorish may stand for the person who is deficient, and boorishness for his character.

With regard to pleasantness in the other affairs of life, he who makes himself properly pleasant may be called friendly, and his moderation friendliness; he that exceeds may be called obsequious if he have no ulterior motive, but a flatterer if he has an eye to his own advantage; he that is deficient in this respect, and always makes himself disagreeable, may be called a quarrelsome or peevish fellow.

Moreover, in mere emotions and in our conduct with regard to them, there are ways of observing the mean; for instance, shame (*aidos*), is not a virtue, but yet the modest (*aidemon*) man is praised. For in these matters also we speak of this man as observing the mean, of that man as going beyond it (as the shame-faced man whom the least thing makes shy), while he who is deficient in the feeling, or lacks it altogether, is called shameless; but the term modest (*aidemon*) is applied to him who observes the mean.

Righteous indignation, again, hits the mean between envy and malevolence. These have to do with feelings of pleasure and pain at what happens to our neighbours. A man is called righteously indignant when he feels pain at the sight of undeserved prosperity, but your envious man goes beyond him and is pained by the sight of any one in prosperity, while the malevolent man is so far from being pained that he actually exults in the sight of prosperous iniquity.

But we shall have another opportunity of discussing these matters.

As for justice, the term is used in more senses than one; we will, therefore, after disposing of the above questions, distinguish these various senses, and show how each of these kinds of justice is a kind of moderation.

And then we will treat of the intellectual virtues in the same way.

There are, as we said, three classes of disposition, viz. two kinds of vice, one marked by excess, the other by deficiency, and one kind of virtue, the observance of the mean. . . .

Now that we have treated (sufficiently, though summarily) of these matters, and of the virtues, and also of friendship and pleasure, are we to suppose that we have attained the end we proposed? Nay, surely the saying holds good, that in practical matters, the end is not a mere speculative knowledge of what is to be done, but rather the doing of it. It is not enough to know about virtue, then, but we must endeavor to possess it and to use it, or to take any other steps that may make us good.

Now, if theories alone were sufficient to make people good, they would deservedly receive many and great rewards, to use the words of Theognis; but, in fact, it seems that though they are potent to guide and to stimulate liberal-minded young men, and though a generous disposition, with a sincere love of what is noble, may by them be opened to the influence of virtue, yet they are powerless to turn the mass of men to goodness. For the generality of men are naturally apt to be swayed by fear rather than by reverence, and to refrain from evil rather because of the punishment that it brings than because of its own foulness. For under the guidance of their passions they pursue the pleasures that suit their nature and the means by which those pleasures may be obtained, and avoid the opposite pains, while of that which is noble and truly pleasant they have not even a conception, as they have never tasted it.

What theories or arguments, then, can bring such men as these to order? Surely it is impossible, or at least very difficult, to remove by any argument what has long been ingrained in the character. For my part, I think we must be well content if we can get some modicum of virtue when all the circumstances are present that seem to make men good.

Now, what makes men good is held by some to be nature, by others habit [or training], by others instruction.

As for the goodness that comes by nature, it is plain that it is not within our control, but is bestowed by some divine agency on certain people who truly deserve to be called fortunate.

As for theory or instruction, I fear that it cannot avail in all cases, but that the hearer's soul must be prepared by training it to feel delight and aversion on the right occasions, just as the soil must be prepared if the seed is to thrive. For if he lives under the sway of his passions, he will not listen to the arguments by which you would dissuade him, nor even understand them. And when he is in this state, how can you change his mind by argument? To put it roundly, passion seems to yield to force only, and not to reason. The character, then, must be already formed, so as to be in some way akin to virtue, loving what is noble and hating what is base.

But to get right guidance from youth up in the road to virtue is hard, unless we are brought up under suitable laws; for to live temperately and regularly is not pleasant to the generality of men, especially to the young. Our nurture, then, should be prescribed by law, and our whole way of life; for it will cease to be painful as we get accustomed to it. And I venture to think that it is not enough to get proper nurture and training when we are young, but that as we ought to carry on the same way of life after we are grown up, and to confirm these habits, we need the intervention of the law in these matters also, and indeed, to put it roundly, in our whole life. For the generality of men are more readily swayed by compulsion than by reason, and by fear of punishment than by desire for what is noble.

For this reason, some hold that the legislator should, in the first instance, invite the people and exhort them to be virtuous because of the nobility of virtue, as those who have been well trained will listen to him; but that when they will not listen, or are of less noble nature, he should apply correction and punishment, and banish utterly those who are incorrigible. For the good man, who takes what is noble as his guide, will listen to reason, but he who is not good, whose desires are set on pleasure, must be corrected by pain like a beast of burden. And for this reason, also, they say the pains to be applied must be those that are most contrary to the pleasures which the culprit loves.

As we have said, then, he who is to be good must be well nurtured and trained, and thereafter must continue in a like excellent way of life, and must never, either voluntarily or involuntarily, do anything vile; and this can only be effected if men live subject to some kind of reason and proper regimen, backed by force.

Now, the paternal rule has not the requisite force or power of compulsion, nor has the rule of any individual, unless he be a king of something like one; but the law has a compulsory power, and at the same time is a rational ordinance proceeding from a kind of prudence or reason. And whereas we take offence at individuals who oppose our inclinations, even though their opposition is right, we do not feel aggrieved when the law bids us do what is right.

STUDY/DISCUSSION ELEMENTS I

1. Terms

a. Self-mastery
b. Good
c. End
d. Moderation
e. Guardian(s)
f. Happiness
g. (The) Function of a Thing
h. Final End
i. (A) State
j. Good Fortune
k. Vice
l. The Idea of the Good

m. Virtue (cf. Excellence)
n. (The) Irrational Part of Soul
o. Courage
p. Luxurious State
q. Art
r. Moral Virtue
s. Habit
t. Justice
u. Mean
v. Temperance
w. Self-sufficing

2. Theses

a. Good fortune follows wisdom (or knowledge).
b. Pleasure is not the good.
c. The final end of human action is happiness.
d. One who practices an art, insofar as he or she practices the art, can never err.
e. Whether a thing or possession is good or not good depends upon the guidance of wisdom.
f. One becomes virtuous by doing virtuous acts.
g. The good for humans is the excellent exercise of our vital functions with reason or in obedience to reason.
h. Each citizen in a state should do and practice one thing only.
i. A virtue is a habit which makes a person good and able to perform his or her function well.
j. The object of ruling is the good of a state's citizens.
k. Virtue always aims at the mean.

Chapter Three

Classical Developments

THEMES AND IDEAS

The final defeat of its Persian invaders in 449 B.C. ushered in classical Greece's so-called Golden Age. Centered in the city-state of Athens, Greece's Golden Age lasted less than half a century, ending when the Peloponnesian War between Athens and Sparta concluded with a Spartan victory in 404 B.C. As Greece's military power waned, that of its northern neighbor, Macedonia, grew stronger. In 337 B.C. the Greeks accepted King Philip of Macedonia's offer to form an alliance, the League of Corinth. Under Alexander the Great, Philip's son, the Macedonians and their Greek allies conquered Asia Minor and all of the eastern Mediterranean world. After his death in 322 B.C., Alexander's empire was divided among his three leading generals. In the next century, Greece and the lands conquered by Alexander were absorbed by the even greater empire of the Romans.

The Macedonians considered the Greeks their ethnic brethren, and they recognized the cultural superiority of Greek civilization. Alexander spread Greek culture throughout his empire. Indeed, his empire is known as the Hellenistic world, from the Greeks' own term for their people, *Hellenes*. The Romans, similarly impressed with Greek culture, established once and for all the dominant role of Greek culture—including, of course, Greek philosophy—in shaping Western civilization.

The readings in this section represent four major schools of thought during the Hellenistic and Roman periods of Western civilization: Epicureanism (Epicurus), Stoicism (Seneca and Epictetus), Skepticism (Sextus Empiricus), and Neoplatonism (Plotinus). Despite their differences, these schools shared Plato's and Aristotle's thesis that the ultimate end of human life is happiness. Indeed, the nature of happiness and how to achieve it constitute the main theme of this section. Plato's and Aristotle's identification of the well-lived (happy) life with the life of virtue and right action also remains largely in place, as does the link between moral conduct and civility.

Epicurus

Plato and Aristotle firmly established that living well is a rational undertaking, requiring an understanding of the nature of goodness and the capacity to act based on that understanding. Their emphasis on excellence or virtuosity also established the lofty—indeed, godlike, Plato says—character of the moral life. Epicurus' moral philosophy is the best-known expression of a view previously rejected by both Plato and Aristotle, that the main ingredient in or indicator of happiness is pleasure. The goal or end of all human behavior, Epicurus argued, is pleasure. A good meal, for example, is an enjoyable or pleasurable meal. When deciding what to eat, we primarily consider what foods are pleasurable to us. In saying this, however, we must keep in mind that the ultimate object of moral deliberation is the totality of our life, not just the present moment. Moral reasoning would not look at a meal as an isolated event, but as an integral part of our overall life. For, our ultimate goal in life is not just to be happy right now, but to live a happy life.

Epicurus insists that his philosophy, Epicureanism, must not be confused with hedonism. Hedonism, as Epicurus understood it, also takes pleasure to be the goal of all human action, but it states that at each moment we should act to maximize the amount of pleasure we may experience at that particular moment. Epicureanism, in contrast, pursues the maximum amount of pleasure attainable in life as a whole, not just at some particular moment of life; and it emphasizes the fact that what we do now may have future consequences as well as present effects. We must especially recognize the fact that pleasure exists only when pain is absent and that something which may give us pleasure now may cause us pain in the future. (Obvious examples would be the hangover that follows the morning after an intoxicating evening, or the indigestion that follows an all-you-can-eat buffet extravaganza.) To maximize the amount of pleasure in our lives, we must also minimize the amount of pain we experience; and Epicurus argues that we in fact achieve the most ideal balance between experiencing pleasure and avoiding pain when we pursue pleasure in moderation, or when we pursue "moderated pleasures." At times, he even suggests that the avoidance of (avoidable) pain or worry itself adds special pleasure to life, as do such nonsensual pursuits as intellectual activities and pleasant social discourse—thus distancing his own philosophy even further from hedonism.

Seneca and Epictetus

Epicureanism begins with the hedonistic-sounding doctrine that happiness is a function of pleasure. The sort of life that an Epicurean wise person supposedly attains, however, is not a continuous orgy of pleasure, pleasure, and more pleasure, but a life which is "even," "smooth," and "free from disturbance." It is a life of moderate pleasures and intellectual and social enjoyments, and it especially avoids unhealthy activities and intense pleasures which cause us pain in the long run. Of course, a certain amount of pain is inevitable in life; but at least the Epicurean life avoids self-inflicted calamities. Thus, the Epicurean wise person will also experience a continual sense of satisfaction or "moral pleasure" at knowing that he or she is living the healthiest, longest, and most pleasurable yet least painful life possible. Building on this last feature of Epicureanism, Stoicism argues that our internal, psychological condition alone is the ultimate goal of moral wisdom. Put differently, Stoicism views happiness as nothing but a state of mind, or a psychological condition, rather than as some special quality or effect of a well-lived life.

Stoic writings, including Seneca's and Epictetus', typically criticize Epicureanism. Pursuing pleasure, even moderate and "moral" pleasures, they argue, can never lead to happiness. Happiness is a state of mind that is "free and indefatigable." That is, it must never be influenced by outside forces, and it must persist through any and every situation we might encounter in life. Pleasure, however, is "servile and transitory." It exists only so long as some stimulus exists to produce it, and we can never expect it to last longer than for a moment. Insofar as our psychological condition is affected by any outside condition or force whatsoever—whether pleasure-producing stimuli or some other dependency, such as fame or material possessions—we are at its mercy. Our mental state will be "exalted and depressed" as conditions change, and especially as things change to better or to worse.

Stoicism emphasizes the classical thesis that wisdom is the key to happiness. Moral wisdom is not a matter of knowing some "goodness itself" (Plato) or of some normative principle (say, Aristotle's Golden Mean or Epicurus' moderate-pleasures principle), however, but a matter of understanding the necessary, lawlike nature of our world, and so of everything that happens in life. Since the universe is controlled by absolute, unbending laws, it is foolish to wish that things were different from the way they are, or that they would happen or turn out differently from the way they do in fact happen and turn out. Understanding this, a wise person accepts everything that exists and happens as just part of the way things are—indeed, must be. He or she is not surprised, "exalted or depressed" by anything. The wise person also considers things which others might consider bad or unfortunate to be simply opportunities to test and strengthen his or her mental resolve, his or her "stoic outlook" on life.

Stoic moral philosophy does have a normative as well as a psychological component, insofar as one's understanding of the lawlike order of nature is relevant to his or her moral deliberations. In particular, the Stoic wise person conforms his or her own wishes and desires to the natural order of things. Accordingly, this person will choose precisely those (physical) actions which his or her body would perform were it directly controlled by the laws of nature rather than by a human mind. The right action is thus always the "natural" action—i.e., the action which fits into or coheres with the natural order of events, as implied by the laws of nature.

Sextus Empiricus

How does moral philosophy relate to the rest of philosophy? Or, how does moral wisdom relate to wisdom generally? Plato's answer is a bit complicated, perhaps ambiguous. It can be summarized, however, in the thesis that knowledge of goodness itself is the highest form of all knowledge. Yet, his claim that "goodness itself" is the cause of rationality and truth seems to imply, insofar as a cause is always distinct from its effect, that "goodness itself" lies forever beyond (it transcends) all rationally obtainable truth. Accordingly, a philosopher cannot reason directly to knowledge of "goodness itself" but must ascend toward it step by step, by way of the various knowledges or arts that derive from it. Although moral wisdom is superior to all other areas of knowledge, it thus also depends on them, at least for its attainment. The relationship between moral wisdom and other areas of knowledge is even more complicated in Aristotle's philosophy; but, at least insofar as Aristotelian moral wisdom reduced to knowing and applying the principle of the golden mean, other areas of knowledge—natural philosophy (science), for example—do not appear to have any direct bearing on moral wisdom in his philosophy. In Stoicism, however, moral wisdom depends completely on, in particular, natural or scientific knowledge. The (morally) wise person understands the lawful order of nature and thereby becomes one with it in his or her attitudes and actions. Natural philosophy is not just a step on the path to moral wisdom; it defines the content and the viewpoint of moral wisdom.

Skepticism, as represented here by Sextus Empiricus, was largely a reaction to Stoicism. In one sense, it reverses and, in another sense, it rejects outright the relationship between moral wisdom and natural knowledge found in Stoicism. The ultimate end of all philosophical activity is the "moral" end of a serene, tranquil, unperturbed state of mind—in short, of Stoic happiness. At the same time, Sextus argues that no pursuit of wisdom, including the scientific pursuit of natural knowledge, can actually lead to happiness or quietude. The ultimate end of knowledge is truth. To know something is, most essentially, to discern the truth about it. The Stoic thesis, that pursuing knowledge will lead us to quietude, therefore assumes that we can discern truth. Sextus argues, however, that this assumption is wrong; human beings are utterly incapable of discerning truth. Truth lies forever beyond the grasp of human faculties. Now, one might conclude from this that happiness itself is likewise unattainable. Or, one might redefine happiness in terms of the pursuit of wisdom itself, as opposed to seeing it as an attainment or outcome of this pursuit. Sextus draws a different conclusion: that there must be another way for us to achieve quietude than through pursuing wisdom. In particular, he maintains that to achieve quietude we must tame, or even extinguish, our rational ("inquisitive") nature by recognizing the utter futility of searching for truth. Sextus introduces the method of equipoise as the way to achieve this recognition.

Quietude, Sextus maintains, is in fact the natural condition of the human mind. Disquiet or perplexity is a function of certain outside stimuli that tend to disturb this natural condition. The human mind is especially liable to having its natural balance or equilibrium disturbed by problematic and conflicting states of affairs—for example, by the fact that one and the same object may look large close up but tiny when seen from a distance, or by the fact that people do not always share the same beliefs about right and wrong. When such disturbances occur, our inquisitive nature mistakenly assumes that we can resolve our disquiet by discerning the truth—by figuring out what the true size of the object is, for example, or by discerning the truth about right and wrong. But the only effective way to return to our natural, undisturbed condition is to recognize that there is no single, "true" way that things are or, if there is, that we are incapable of discerning it. Every problem or conflict has a number of possible solutions capable of equally strong rational justification. Sextus' equipoise method is to counterbalance every possible solution ("proposition") with alternative possible solutions and every alleged proof of a solution with equally strong proofs for the alternative solutions. In so doing, the Skeptic comes to realize that puzzles, problematic states of affairs, and even outright inconsistencies are just part of life. There is nothing we can do about them but accept them. So far as moral wisdom is concerned, the Skeptic abandons all beliefs about what is "truly" good and "truly" bad, or about whether an action is "truly" right or "truly" wrong. Instead, moral deliberation becomes a matter of determining what action would be least disruptive, least likely to incite disquiet and adverse reactions, in one's society. In effect, the Skeptic accepts and conforms to the customs or prevailing opinions of his or her society.

Plotinus

The Stoics, we have seen, criticize Epicurus' conception of happiness as too servile and transitory to be the ultimate end of moral action. Sextus, in turn, accepted the Stoics' conception of happiness but rejected their method for attaining it. But Sextus' own method hardly seems a panacea. Indeed, Sextus himself claims just that his method is better than methods aimed at finding truth, not that it will relieve us of all disturbance or disquiet once and for all. Problematic states of affairs remain a part of life and are bound to affect our quietude from time to time. The Skeptic will not compound any unavoidable, "natural" disquiet, however, by embarking on an impossible quest for unattainable truth.

Plotinus began teaching in Rome soon after Sextus. His philosophy, known as Neoplatonism, was inspired largely by Plato's philosophy, but it incorporates features of other classical philosophies—most notably Aristotle's and the Stoics'—as well as original ideas of its own. At the heart of Plotinus' moral philosophy is his thesis that complete happiness (perfect tranquillity, serenity, or quietude) can exist only in a realm that is eternal, self-contained (immune to all outside forces), and absolutely unchanging. Human beings, of course, do not live in such a realm. Our universe is a temporal realm of continuous movement, change, and interaction. Such a realm does exist, however, and our soul is one of its progeny. Even now, the "better part" of our soul remains linked to that realm, making it possible for us to return intellectually and spiritually to it and to direct our lives in accordance with it. Plotinus' conception of an eternal realm of Being or intelligibles—the true objects of knowledge—also provided Neoplatonism with an answer to Sextus' Skepticism. Sextus' critique of "dogmatic philosophies"—philosophies which assume that we can discern truth—requires that every proposition and every proof of a proposition has alternatives. But, in eternity, things can never be in any way different from the way they in fact (eternally) are. There can be only one truth in that realm. Truth there is necessary; it is not just one among many possible truths.

Plotinus' doctrine of an eternal, self-contained, unchanging reality is the most salient Platonic feature of his Neoplatonism. Plato held that our universe is a "moving image of eternity"—a temporal manifestation of eternal principles called Forms, Archetypes, or Paradigms. This explains the regularity, indeed lawfulness, of natural processes. He also held that our soul, which includes our consciousness and initiates our actions, is composed of and contains certain features of that realm. This explains our inquisitive nature—our rational desire and capacity to discern truth. It also enables us to liberate ourselves from the circumstances and forces that impinge upon us in this world, to conform our lives and actions instead to the "divine" principles of that realm. Moreover, Plato held that this complex system of the eternal Forms, the temporal cosmos, and human thought and action is ordered and united by a single, absolutely first principle—goodness itself.

These Platonic ideas underlie Plotinus' Neoplatonism (and our reading). Plotinus insists, more clearly than Plato, however, that the absolutely first principle must transcend even the eternal Forms—the realm of "intelligence." He also insists that "goodness itself" is more properly called "the One." For, the first principle of all Form, truth, reality, and goodness must itself be utterly simple. It cannot contain or be composed of any parts, or of any other sort of multiplicity—unlike even the realm of the (many) eternal Forms (Intellect). Moreover, because of its own simplicity or "oneness," the One's creative activity always yields existents which are unified in some way—in themselves, and in their ordered relations with one another. Goodness in things is thus always a function of unity. Some thing (or group of things) is good just insofar as it in some way possesses unity or "oneness." Hence, right action produces or promotes unity.

Epicurus
(341–270 B.C.)

Born of Athenian parents on the isle of Samos, Epicurus wrote extensively, but only fragments and several of his "letters" remain. Neocles, his father, ran an elementary school—a lowly regarded profession at the time. This, plus the social contempt which mainland Athenians felt for "colonials," followed Epicurus throughout his life. Epicurus began studying philosophy at age fourteen, and at age eighteen he went to Athens for his two years of mandatory military service. He studied with a variety of Platonists, Peripatetics, and Democritean materialists, and he was very much aware of the teachings of Pyrrho of Elis on the importance of imperturbability to virtue and happiness. When he was thirty, Epicurus moved to Mytilene on the isle of Lesbos and began teaching his new philosophy. His teachings so incited the citizens and authorities in Mytilene, however, that he was forced to flee. After spending some time in Lampascus, where he was decidedly more successful, Epicurus returned to Athens and, in a house and surrounding gardens outside of Athens, established his school. Suffering from persistent ill health, Epicurus remained there until his death.

Letter to Menoeceus*

No one should postpone the study of philosophy when he is young, nor should he weary of it when he becomes mature, because the search for mental health is never untimely or out of season. To say that the time to study philosophy has not yet arrived or that it is past is like saying that the time for happiness is not yet at hand or is no longer present. Thus both the young and the mature should pursue philosophy, the latter in order to be rejuvenated as they age by the blessings that accrue from pleasurable past experience, and the youthful in order to become mature immediately through having no fear of the future. Hence we should make a practice of the things that make for happiness, for assuredly when we have this we have everything, and we do everything we can to get it when we don't have it.

From Epicurus, "Letter to Menoeceus," translated by George K. Strodach in *The Philosophy of Epicurus*, ed. George Strodach, pp. 178–185. Copyright © 1963 by Northwestern University Press, Evanston, Ill. Used with permission.

The Preconditions of Happiness

I. You should do and practice all the things I constantly recommended to you, with the knowledge that they are the fundamentals of the good life. (1) First of all, you should think of deity as imperishable and blessed being (as delineated in the universal conception of it common to all men), and you should not attribute to it anything foreign to its immortality or inconsistent with its blessedness. On the contrary, you should hold every doctrine that is capable of safeguarding its blessedness in common with its imperishability. The gods do indeed exist, since our knowledge of them is a matter of clear and distinct perception; but they are not like what the masses suppose them to be, because most people do not maintain the pure conception of the gods. The irreligious man is not the person who destroys the gods of the masses but the person who imposes the ideas of the masses on the gods. The opinions held by most people about the gods are not true conceptions of them but fallacious notions, according to which awful penalties are meted out to the evil and the greatest of blessings to the good. The masses, by assimilating the gods in every respect to their own moral qualities, accept deities similar to themselves and regard anything not of this sort as alien.

(2) Second, you should accustom yourself to believing that death means nothing to us, since every good and every evil lies in sensation; but death is the privation of sensation. Hence a correct comprehension of the fact that death means nothing to us makes the mortal aspect of life pleasurable, not by conferring on us a boundless period of time but by removing the yearning for deathlessness. There is nothing fearful in living for the person who has really laid hold of the fact that there is nothing fearful in not living. So it is silly for a person to say that he dreads death—not because it will be painful when it arrives but because it pains him now as a future certainty; for that which makes no trouble for us when it arrives is a meaningless pain when we await it. This, the most horrifying of evils, means nothing to us, then, because so long as we are existent death is not present and whenever it is present we are nonexistent. Thus it is of no concern either to the living or to those who have completed their lives. For the former it is nonexistent, and the latter are themselves nonexistent.

Most people, however, recoil from death as though it were the greatest of evils; at other times they welcome it as the end-all of life's ills. The sophisticated person, on the other hand, neither begs off from living nor dreads not living. Life is not a stumbling block to him, nor does he regard not being alive as any sort of evil. As in the case of food he prefers the most savory dish to merely the larger portion, so in the case of time he garners to himself the most agreeable moments rather than the longest span.

Anyone who urges the youth to lead a good life but counsels the older man to end his life in good style is silly, not merely because of the welcome character of life but because of the fact that living well and dying well are one and the same discipline. Much worse off, however, is the person who says it were well not to have been born "but once born to pass Hades' portals as swiftly as may be." Now if he says such a thing from inner persuasion why does he not withdraw from life? Everything is in readiness for him once he has firmly resolved on this course. But if he speaks facetiously he is a trifler standing in the midst of men who do not welcome him.

It should be borne in mind, then, that the time to come is neither ours nor altogether not ours. In this way we shall neither expect the future outright as something destined to be nor despair of it as something absolutely not destined to be.

The Good Life

II. It should be recognized that within the category of desire certain desires are natural, certain others unnecessary and trivial; that in the case of the natural desires certain ones are necessary, certain others merely natural; and that in the case of necessary desires certain ones are necessary for happiness, others to promote freedom from bodily discomfort, others for the maintenance of life itself. A steady view of these matters shows us how to refer all moral choice and aversion to bodily health and imperturbability of mind, these being the twin goals of happy living. It is on this account that we do everything we do—to achieve freedom from pain and freedom from fear. When once we come by this, the tumult in the soul is calmed and the human being does not have to go about looking for something that is lacking or to search for something additional with which to supplement the welfare of soul and body. Accordingly we have need of pleasure only when we feel pain because of the absence of pleasure, but whenever we do not feel pain we no longer stand in need of pleasure. And so we speak of pleasure as the starting point and the goal of the happy life because we realize that it is our primary native good, because every act of choice and aversion originates with it, and because we come back to it when we judge every good by using the pleasure feeling as our criterion.

Because of the very fact that pleasure is our primary and congenital good we do not select every pleasure; there are times when we forgo certain pleasures, particularly when they are followed by too much unpleasantness. Furthermore, we regard certain states of pain as preferable to pleasures, particularly when greater satisfaction results from our having submitted to discomforts for a long period of time. Thus every pleasure is a good by reason of its having a nature akin to our own, but not every pleasure is desirable. In like manner every state of pain is an evil, but not all pains are uniformly to be rejected. At any rate, it is our duty to judge all such cases by measuring pleasures against pains, with a view to their respective assets and liabilities, inasmuch as we do experience the good as being bad at times and, contrariwise, the bad as being good.

In addition, we consider limitation of the appetites a major good, and we recommend this practice not for the purpose of enjoying just a few things and no more but rather for the purpose of enjoying those few in case we do not have much. We are firmly convinced that those who need expensive fare least are the ones who relish it most keenly and that a natural way of life is easily procured, while trivialities are hard to come by. Plain foods afford pleasure equivalent to that of a sumptuous diet, provided that the pains of penury are wholly eliminated. Barley bread and water yield the peak of pleasure whenever a person who needs them sets them in front of himself. Hence becoming habituated to a simple rather than a lavish way of life provides us with the full complement of health; it makes a person ready for the necessary business of life; it puts us in a position of advantage when we happen upon sumptuous fare at intervals and prepares us to be fearless in facing fortune.

Thus when I say that pleasure is the goal of living I do not mean the pleasures of libertines or the pleasures inherent in positive enjoyment, as is supposed by certain persons who are ignorant of our doctrine or who are not in agreement with it or who interpret it perversely. I mean, on the contrary, the pleasure that consists in freedom from bodily pain and mental agitation. The pleasant life is not the product of one drinking party after another or of sexual intercourse with women and boys or of the sea food and other delicacies afforded by a luxurious table. On the contrary, it is the result of sober thinking—namely, investigation of the reasons for every act of choice and aversion and elimination of those false ideas about the gods and death which are the chief source of mental disturbances.

The starting point of this whole scheme and the most important of its values is good judgment, which consequently is more highly esteemed even than philosophy. All the other virtues stem from sound judgment, which shows us that it is impossible to live the pleasant Epicurean life without also living sensibly, nobly, and justly and, vice versa, that it is impossible to live sensibly, nobly, and justly without living pleasantly. The traditional virtues grow up together with the pleasant life; they are indivisible. Can you think of anyone more moral than the person who has devout beliefs about the gods, who is consistently without fears about death, and who has pondered man's natural end? Or who realizes that the goal of the good life is easily gained and achieved and that the term of evil is brief, both in extent of time and duration of pain? Or the man who laughs at the "decrees of Fate," a deity whom some people have set up as sovereign of all?

The good Epicurean believes that certain events occur deterministically, that others are chance events, and that still others are in our own hands. He sees also that necessity cannot be held morally responsible and that chance is an unpredictable thing, but that what is in our own hands, since it has no master, is naturally associated with blameworthiness and the opposite. (Actually it would be better to subscribe to the popular mythology than to become a slave by accepting the determinism of the natural philosophers, because popular religion underwrites the hope of supplicating the gods by offerings but determinism contains an element of necessity, which is inexorable.) As for chance, the Epicurean does not assume that it is a deity (as in popular belief) because a god does nothing irregular; nor does he regard it as an unpredictable cause of all events. It is his belief that good and evil are not the chance contributions of a deity, donated to mankind for the happy life, but rather that the initial circumstances for great good and evil are sometimes provided by chance. He thinks it preferable to have bad luck rationally than good luck irrationally. In other words, in human action it is better for a rational choice to be unsuccessful than for an irrational choice to succeed through the agency of chance.

Think about these and related matters day and night, by yourself and in company with someone like yourself. If you do, you will never experience anxiety, waking or sleeping, but you will live like a god among men. For a human being who lives in the midst of immortal blessings is in no way like mortal man!

Lucius Annaeus Seneca
(5 B.C.—65 A.D.)

Of the great classical philosophies, Stoicism came closest to achieving universal appeal and acceptance. Its founder, Zeno of Citium, was born in 350 B.C. He became a wealthy merchant, but lost much of his wealth in a shipwreck. Moving to Athens, Zeno was enamored with the life of Socrates and joined a Socratic sect known as the Cynics. He also studied Megarian philosophy with Xenocrates, who was head of Plato's Academy. In 310 B.C. he founded his school at the Painted Porch (*stoa*) outside of Athens. All of his writings are lost to modern scholars.

Seneca, one of Stoicism's most famous Roman adherents, was born in Cordoba, Spain, where his father was a Roman imperial procurator. At a young age, Seneca was sent to Egypt to live with his aunt, whose husband was a viceroy to the emperor Tiberius. In Egypt he studied administration, finance, and Pythagorean and Oriental philosophies before finally embracing Stoicism. Moving to Rome, he was elected quaestor and soon became a leading influence in the Roman senate. In 49 A.D. Seneca was appointed praetor and became tutor to the future emperor Nero. For the first five years of his reign, Nero placed all of his administrative powers in the hands of Seneca. Seneca's political enemies gained the ear of the emperor, however, and Seneca was forced to retire from public life. In 65 A.D. Seneca was implicated in a plot against Nero, who ordered him to commit suicide.

Of a Happy Life*

All men, brother Gallio, wish to live happily, but are dull at perceiving exactly what it is that makes life happy: and so far is it from being easy to attain to happiness that the more eagerly a man struggles to reach it the further he departs from it, if he takes the wrong road; for, since this leads in the opposite direction, his very swiftness carries him all the further away. We must therefore first define clearly what it is at which we aim: next we must consider by what path we may most speedily reach it, for on our journey itself, provided it be made in the right direction, we shall learn how

From Seneca, "Of a Happy Life," in *L. Annaeus Seneca: Minor Dialogues*, translated by Aubrey Stewart (London: George Bell and Sons, 1889).

much progress we have made each day, and how much nearer we are to the goal towards which our natural desires urge us. But as long as we wander at random, not following any guide except the shouts and discordant clamours of those who invite us to proceed in different directions, our short life will be wasted in useless roamings, even if we labour both day and night to get a good understanding. Let us not therefore decide whither we must tend, and by what path, without the advice of some experienced person who has explored the region which we are about to enter, because this journey is not subject to the same conditions as others; for in them some distinctly understood track and inquiries made of the natives make it impossible for us to go wrong, but here the most beaten and frequented tracks are those which lead us most astray. Nothing, therefore, is more important than that we should not, like sheep, follow the flock that has gone before us, and thus proceed not whither we ought, but whither the rest are going. . . .

I follow nature, which is a point upon which every one of the Stoic philosophers are agreed: true wisdom consists in not departing from nature and in moulding our conduct according to her laws and model. A happy life, therefore, is one which is in accordance with its own nature, and cannot be brought about unless in the first place the mind be sound and remain so without interruption, and next, be bold and vigorous, enduring all things with most admirable courage, suited to the times in which it lives, careful of the body and its appurtenances, yet not troublesomely careful. It must also set due value upon all the things which adorn our lives, without over-estimating any one of them, and must be able to enjoy the bounty of Fortune without becoming her slave. You understand without my mentioning it that an unbroken calm and freedom ensue, when we have driven away all those things which either excite us or alarm us: for in the place of sensual pleasures and those slight perishable matters which are connected with the basest crimes, we thus gain an immense, unchangeable, equable joy, together with peace, calmness and greatness of mind, and kindliness: for all savageness is a sign of weakness.

Our highest good may also be defined otherwise, that is to say, the same idea may be expressed in different language. Just as the same army may at one time be extended more widely, at another contracted into a smaller compass, and may either be curved towards the wings by a depression in the line of the centre, or drawn up in a straight line, while, in whatever figure it be arrayed, its strength and loyalty remain unchanged; so also our definition of the highest good may in some cases be expressed diffusely and at great length, while in others it is put into a short and concise form. Thus, it will come to the same thing, if I say "The highest good is a mind which despises the accidents of fortune, and takes pleasure in virtue": or, "It is an unconquerable strength of mind, knowing the world well, gentle in its dealings, showing great courtesy and consideration for those with whom it is brought into contact." Or we may choose to define it by calling that man happy who knows good and bad only in the form of good or bad minds: who worships honour, and is satisfied with his own virtue, who is neither puffed up by good fortune nor cast down by evil fortune, who knows no other good than that which he is able to bestow upon himself, whose real pleasure lies in despising pleasures. If you choose to pursue this digression further, you can put this same idea into many other forms, without impairing or weakening its meaning: for what prevents our saying that a happy life consists in a mind which is free, upright, undaunted, and steadfast, beyond the influence of fear or desire, which thinks nothing good except honour, and nothing bad except shame, and regards everything else as a mass of mean details which can neither add anything to nor take anything away from the happiness of life, but which come and go without either increasing or diminishing the highest good? A man of these principles, whether he will or no, must be accompanied by a continual cheerfulness, a high happiness, which comes indeed from on high because he delights in what he has, and desires no greater pleasures than those which his home affords. Is he not right in allowing these to turn the scale against petty, ridiculous, and shortlived movements of his wretched body? on the day on which he becomes proof against pleasure he also becomes proof against pain. See, on the other hand, how evil and guilty a slavery the man is forced to serve who is dominated in turn by pleasures and pains, those most untrustworthy and passionate of masters. We must, therefore, escape from them into freedom. This nothing will bestow upon us save contempt of Fortune: but if we attain to this, then there will dawn upon us those invaluable blessings, the repose of a mind that is at rest in a safe haven, its lofty imaginings, its great and steady delight at casting out errors and learning to know the truth, its courtesy, and its cheerfulness, in all of which we shall take delight, not regarding them as good things, but as proceeding from the proper good of man.

Since I have begun to make my definitions without a too strict adherence to the letter, a man may be called "happy" who, thanks to reason, has ceased either to hope or to fear: but rocks also feel neither fear nor sadness, nor do cattle, yet no one would call those things happy which cannot comprehend what happiness is. With them you may class men whose dull nature and want of self-knowledge reduces them to the level of cattle, mere animals: there is no difference between the one and the other, because the latter have no reason, while the former have only a corrupted form of it, crooked and cunning to their own hurt. For no one can be styled happy who is beyond the influence of truth: and consequently a happy life is unchangeable, and is founded upon a true and trustworthy discernment; for the mind is uncontaminated and freed from all evils only when it is able to escape not merely from wounds but also from scratches, when it will always be able to maintain the position which it has taken up, and defend it even against the angry assaults of Fortune: for with regard to sensual pleasures, though they were to surround one on every side, and use every means of assault, trying to win over the mind by caresses and making trial of every conceivable stratagem to attract either our entire selves or our separate parts, yet what mortal that retains any traces of human origin would wish to be tickled day and night, and, neglecting his mind, to devote himself to bodily enjoyments? . . .

The happy man, therefore, is he who can make a right judgment in all things: he is happy who in his present circumstances, whatever they may be, is satisfied and on friendly terms with the conditions of his life. That man is happy, whose reason recommends to him the whole posture of his affairs. . . .

[V]irtue is a lofty quality, sublime, royal, unconquerable, untiring: pleasure is low, slavish, weakly, perishable; its haunts and homes are the brothel and the tavern. You will meet virtue in the temple, the market-place, the senate house, manning the walls, covered with dust, sunburnt, horny-handed: you will find pleasure skulking out of sight, seeking for shady nooks at the public baths, hot chambers, and places which dread the visits of the aedile, soft, effeminate, reeking of wine and perfumes, pale or perhaps painted and made up with cosmetics. The highest good is immortal: it knows no ending, and does not admit of either satiety or regret: for a right-thinking mind never alters or becomes hateful to itself, nor do the best things ever undergo any change: but pleasure dies at the very moment when it charms us most: it has no great scope, and therefore it soon cloys and wearies us, and fades away as soon as its first impulse is over: indeed, we cannot depend upon anything whose nature is to change. Consequently it is not even possible that there should be any solid substance in that which comes and goes so swiftly, and which perishes by the very exercise of its own functions, for it arrives at a point at which it ceases to be, and even while it is beginning always keeps its end in view. . . .

[F]or it is Nature whom we ought to make our guide: let our reason watch her, and be advised by her. To live happily, then, is the same thing as to live according to Nature: what this may be, I will explain. If we guard the endowments of the body and the advantages of nature with care and fearlessness, as things soon to depart and given to us only for a day; if we do not fall under their dominion, nor allow ourselves to become the slaves of what is no part of our own being; if we assign to all bodily pleasures and external delights the same position which is held by auxiliaries and light-armed troops in a camp; if we make them our servants, not our masters—then and then only are they of value to our minds. A man should be unbiassed and not to be conquered by external things: he ought to admire himself alone, to feel confidence in his own spirit, and so to order his life as to be ready alike for good or for bad fortune. Let not his confidence be without knowledge; nor his knowledge without steadfastness: let him always abide by what he has once determined, and let there be no erasure in his doctrines. It will be understood, even though I append it not, that such a man will be tranquil and composed in his demeanour, high-minded and courteous in his actions. Let reason be encouraged by the senses to seek for the truth, and draw its first principles from thence: indeed it has no other base of operations or place from which to start in pursuit of truth: it must fall back upon itself. Even the all-embracing universe and God who is its guide extends himself forth into outward things, and yet altogether returns from all sides back to himself. Let our mind do the same thing: when, following its bodily senses it has by means of them sent itself forth into the things of the outward world, let it remain still their master and its own. By this means we shall obtain a strength and an ability which are united and allied together, and shall derive from it that reason which never halts between two opinions, nor is dull in forming its perceptions, beliefs, or convictions. Such a mind, when it has ranged itself in order, made its various parts agree together, and, if I may so express myself, harmonized them, has attained to the highest good: for it has nothing evil or hazardous remaining, nothing to shake it or make it stumble: it will do everything under the guidance of its own will, and nothing unexpected will befal it, but whatever may be done by it will turn out well, and that, too, readily and easily, without the doer having recourse to any underhand devices: for slow and hesitating action are the signs of discord and want of settled purpose. You may, then, boldly declare that the highest good is singleness of mind: for where agreement and unity are, there must the virtues be: it is the vices that are at war one with another. . . .

I do not call a man wise who is overcome by anything, let alone by pleasure: yet, if engrossed by pleasure, how will he resist toil, danger, want, and all the ills which surround and threaten the life of man? How will he bear the sight of death or of pain? How will he endure the tumult of the world, and make head against so many most active foes, if he be conquered by so effeminate an antagonist? He will do whatever pleasure advises him: well, do you not see how many things it will advise him to do? . . .

Let virtue lead the way and bear the standard: we shall have pleasure for all that, but we shall be her masters and controllers; she may win some concessions from us, but will not force us to do anything. On the contrary, those who have permitted pleasure to lead the van, have neither one nor the other: for they lose virtue altogether, and yet they do not possess pleasure, but are possessed by it, and are either tortured by its absence or choked by its excess, being wretched if deserted by it, and yet more wretched if overwhelmed by it, like those who are caught in the shoals of the Syrtes and at one time are left on dry ground and at another tossed on the flowing waves. . . .

Let the highest good, then, rise to that height from whence no force can dislodge it, whither neither pain can ascend, nor hope, nor fear, nor anything else that can impair the authority of the "highest good." Thither virtue alone can make her way: by her aid that hill must be climbed: she will bravely stand her ground and endure whatever may befal her not only resignedly, but even willingly: she will know that all hard times come in obedience to natural laws, and like a good soldier she will bear wounds, count scars, and when transfixed and dying will yet adore the general for whom she falls: she will bear in mind the old maxim "Follow God." On the other hand, he who grumbles and complains and bemoans himself is nevertheless forcibly obliged to obey orders, and is dragged away, however much against his will, to carry them out: yet what madness is it to be dragged rather than to follow? as great, by Hercules, as it is folly and ignorance of one's true position to grieve because one has not got something or because something has caused us rough treatment, or to be surprised or indignant at those ills which befal good men as well as bad ones, I mean diseases, deaths, illnesses, and the other cross accidents of human life. Let us bear with magnanimity whatever the system of the universe makes it needful for us to bear: we are all bound by this oath: "To bear the ills of mortal life, and to submit with a good grace to what we cannot avoid." We have been born into a monarchy: our liberty is to obey God.

True happiness, therefore, consists in virtue: and what will this virtue bid you do? Not to think anything bad or good which is connected neither with virtue nor with wickedness: and in the next place, both to endure unmoved the assaults of evil, and, as far as is right, to form a god out of what is good. What reward does she promise you for this campaign? an enormous one, and one that raises you to the level of the gods: you shall be subject to no restraint and to no want; you shall be free, safe, unhurt; you shall fail in nothing that you attempt; you shall be debarred from nothing; everything shall turn out according to your wish; no misfortune shall befal you; nothing shall happen to you except what you expect and hope for. "What! does virtue alone suffice to make you happy?" why, of course, consummate and god-like virtue such as this not only suffices, but more than suffices: for when a man is placed beyond the reach of any desire, what can he possibly lack? if all that he needs is concentred in himself, how can he require anything from without? . . .

If, therefore, any one of those dogs who yelp at philosophy were to say, as they are wont to do, "Why, then, do you talk so much more bravely than you live? why do you check your words in the presence of your superiors, and consider money to be a necessary implement? why are you disturbed when you sustain losses, and weep on hearing of the death of your wife or your friend? why do you pay regard to common rumour, and feel annoyed by calumnious gossip? why is your estate more elaborately kept than its natural use requires? why do you not dine according to your own maxims? . . .

"Philosophers do not carry into effect all that they teach." No; but they effect much good by their teaching, by the noble thoughts which they conceive in their minds: would, indeed, that they could act up to their talk: what could be happier than they would be? but in the meanwhile you have no right to despise good sayings and hearts full of good thoughts. Men deserve praise for engaging in profitable studies, even though they stop short of producing any results. Why need we wonder if those who begin to climb a steep path do not succeed in ascending it very high? yet, if you be a man, look with respect on those who attempt great things, even though they fall. It is the act of a generous spirit to proportion its efforts not to its own strength but to that of human nature, to entertain lofty aims, and to conceive plans which are too vast to be carried into execution. . . .

Epictetus
(55–135 A.D.)

The breadth of Stoicism's appeal among ancient Romans is evident in the sharp contrast between Seneca's and Epictetus' origins and social standings. Born of a slave woman in Hierapolis, in Asia Minor, Epictetus came to Rome as a member of Nero's bodyguard. Lamed by mistreatment as a slave, Epictetus became an administrator in the emperor's household. After Nero's death, Epictetus passed into the service of the emperor's administrative secretary, Epaphroditus, who gave him his freedom and sent him to study with the famous Stoic teacher Rufus. When the emperor Domitian banished all philosophers from Rome in 89 A.D., Epictetus fled to Nicopolis in Epirus and soon attracted a large following. One of his students, Flavius Arrianus, composed several books and a small "Handbook," a Stoic catechism, based on Epictetus' teachings.

The Manual*

Of things some are in our power, and others are not. In our power are opinion, movement towards a thing, desire, aversion (turning from a thing); and in a word, whatever are our own acts: not in our power are the body, property, reputation, offices (magisterial power), and in a word, whatever are not our own acts. And the things in our power are by nature free, not subject to restraint nor hindrance: but the things not in our power are weak, slavish, subject to restraint, in the power of others. Remember then that if you think the things which are by nature slavish to be free, and the things which are in the power of others to be your own, you will be hindered, you will lament, you will be disturbed, you will blame both gods and men: but if you think that only which is your own to be your own, and if you think that what is another's, as it really is, belongs to another, no man will ever compel you, no man will hinder you, you will never blame any man, you will accuse no man, you will do nothing involuntarily (against your will), no man will harm you, you will have no enemy, for you will not suffer any harm.

If then you desire (aim at) such great things, remember that you must not (attempt to) lay hold of them with small effort; but you must leave alone some things

From Epictetus, "The Manual" in *The Discourses of Epictetus*, translated by George Long (d. 1879) (New York: Hurst and Co.).

entirely, and postpone others for the present. But if you wish for these things also (such great things), and power (office) and wealth, perhaps you will not gain even these very things (power and wealth) because you aim also at those former things (such great things): certainly you will fail in those things through which alone happiness and freedom are secured. Straightway then practice saying to every harsh appearance, You are an appearance, and in no manner what you appear to be. Then examine it by the rules which you possess, and by this first and chiefly, whether it relates to the things which are in our power or to things which are not in our power: and if it relates to any thing which is not in our power, be ready to say, that it does not concern you.

Remember that desire contains in it the profession (hope) of obtaining that which you desire and the profession (hope) in aversion (turning from a thing) is that you will not fall into that which you attempt to avoid: and he who fails in his desire is unfortunate; and he who falls into that which he would avoid, is unhappy. If then you attempt to avoid only the things contrary to nature which are within your power, you will not be involved in any of the things which you would avoid. But if you attempt to avoid disease or death or poverty, you will be unhappy. Take away then aversion from all things which are not in our power, and transfer it to the things contrary to nature which are in our power. But destroy desire completely for the present. For if you desire anything which is not in our power, you must be unfortunate: but of the things in our power, and which it would be good to desire, nothing yet is before you. But employ only the power of moving towards an object and retiring from it; and these powers indeed only slightly and with exceptions and with remission. . . .

Men are disturbed not by the things which happen, but by the opinions about the things: for example, death is nothing terrible, for if it were, it would have seemed so to Socrates; for the opinion about death, that it is terrible, is the terrible thing. When then we are impeded or disturbed or grieved, let us never blame others, but ourselves, that is, our opinions. It is the act of an ill-instructed man to blame others for his own bad condition; it is the act of one who has begun to be instructed, to lay the blame on himself; and of one whose instruction is completed, neither to blame another, nor himself. . . .

Seek not that the things which happen should happen as you wish; but wish the things which happen to be as they are, and you will have a tranquil flow of life. . . .

Remember that thou art an actor in a play, of such a kind as the teacher (author) may choose; if short, of a short one; if long, of a long one: if he wishes you to act the part of a poor man, see that you act the part naturally: if the part of a lame man, of a magistrate, of a private person, (do the same). For this is your duty, to act well the part that is given to you; but to select the part, belongs to another.

We may learn the wish (will) of nature from the things in which we do not differ from one another: for instance, when your neighbour's slave has broken his cup, or any thing else, we are ready to say forthwith, that it is one of the things which happen. You must know then that when your cup is also broken, you ought to think as you did when your neighbour's cup was broken. Transfer this reflection to greater things also. Is another man's child or wife dead? There is no one who would not say, this is an event incident to man. But when a man's own child or wife is dead, forthwith he calls out, Wo to me, how wretched I am. But we ought to remember how we feel when we hear that it has happened to others. . . .

As to piety towards the Gods you must know that this is the chief thing, to have right opinions about them, to think that they exist, and that they administer the All well and justly; and you must fix yourself in this principle (duty), to obey them, and to yield to them in every thing which happens, and voluntarily to follow it as being accomplished by the wisest intelligence. For if you do so, you will never either blame the Gods, nor will you accuse them of neglecting you. And it is not possible for this to be done in any other way than by withdrawing from the things which are not in our power, and by placing the good and the evil only in those things which are in our power. For if you think that any of the things which are not in our power is good or bad, it is absolutely necessary that, when you do not obtain what you wish, and when you fall into those things which you do not wish, you will find fault and hate those who are the cause of them; . . .

Sextus Empiricus
(fl. c. 200 A.D.)

The brand of Skepticism, Pyrrhonism, made famous by the writings of Sextus Empiricus traces to Pyrrho of Elis (c. 360–275 B.C.) and his pupil, Timon of Phlius (c. 315–225 B.C.). After Timon's death, however, skeptical theory passed to a succession of Academic Skeptics who headed Plato's Academy during the second century B.C. Pyrrhonism was revived in the first century B.C. by Aenesidemus of Knossos in Crete, who devised many of the classic arguments against "dogmatism" and aetiology (scientific reasoning) found in Sextus' work. During the first and second centuries A.D. Pyrrhonism was linked first to "empiric" and then to "methodic" medical theory. Sextus, a Greek physician, succeeded Herodotus as the head of one of these medical schools. Little else is known about Sextus, except that he spent much of his time in Rome but maintained close ties to medical schools in Athens and Alexandria.

Outlines of Pyrrhonism and Against the Ethicists*

The natural result of any investigation is that the investigators either discover the object of search or deny that it is discoverable and confess it to be inapprehensible or persist in their search. So, too, with regard to the objects investigated by philosophy, this is probably why some have claimed to have discovered the truth, others have asserted that it cannot be apprehended, while others again go on inquiring. Those who believe they have discovered it are the "Dogmatists," specially so called—Aristotle, for example, and Epicurus and the Stoics and certain others; Cleitomachus and Carneades and other Academics treat it as inapprehensible: the Sceptics keep on searching. Hence it seems reasonable to hold that the main types of philosophy are three—the Dogmatic, the Academic, and the Sceptic. Of the other systems it will best become others to speak: our task at present is to describe in outline the Sceptic doctrine, first premising that of none of our future statements do

Reprinted by permission of the publishers and The Loeb Classical Library from "Outlines of Pyrrhonism" in *Sextus Empiricus I* and "Against the Ethicists" in *Sextus Empiricus III*, translated by Rev. R. G. Bury, Cambridge, Mass.: Harvard University Press, Copyright © 1976 and © 1968 by The President and Fellows of Harvard College.

we positively affirm that the fact is exactly as we state it, but we simply record each fact, like a chronicler, as it appears to us at the moment. . . .

The originating cause of Scepticism is, we say, the hope of attaining quietude. Men of talent, who were perturbed by the contradictions in things and in doubt as to which of the alternatives they ought to accept, were led on to inquire what is true in things and what false, hoping by the settlement of this question to attain quietude. The main basic principle of the Sceptic system is that of opposing to every proposition an equal proposition; for we believe that as a consequence of this we end by ceasing to dogmatize. . . .

We assert still that the Sceptic's End is quietude in respect of matters of opinion and moderate feeling in respect of things unavoidable. For the Sceptic, having set out to philosophize with the object of passing judgement on the sense-impressions and ascertaining which of them are true and which false, so as to attain quietude thereby, found himself involved in contradictions of equal weight, and being unable to decide between them suspended judgement; and as he was thus in suspense there followed, as it happened, the state of quietude in respect of matters of opinion. For the man who opines that anything is by nature good or bad is for ever being disquieted: when he is without the things which he deems good he believes himself to be tormented by things naturally bad and he pursues after the things which are, as he thinks, good; which when he has obtained he keeps falling into still more perturbations because of his irrational and immoderate elation, and in his dread of a change of fortune he uses every endeavour to avoid losing the things which he deems good. On the other hand, the man who determines nothing as to what is naturally good or bad neither shuns nor pursues anything eagerly; and, in consequence, he is unperturbed. . . .

* * *

He, then, is happy who lives to the end without perturbation and, as Timon said, existing in a state of quietness and calm—

For on all sides calm was prevailing,

and—

Him when thus I descried in a calm with no winds to disquiet.

And of the goods and evils which are said to exist some are introduced by belief, others by necessity. Thus by [rational] belief are introduced all those which men pursue or avoid of their own judgement,—as, for example, amongst things external, wealth and fame and noble birth and friendship, and everything of the kind, are called desirable and good; and, amongst qualities of the body, beauty and strength and sound condition; and, amongst qualities of the soul, courage and justice and wisdom and virtue in general; and the opposites of these are regarded as things to be avoided. But by necessity are brought about all such things as befall us because of an irrational affection of sense, and all that some natural necessity brings about, "but no one would willingly choose them," or avoid them,—such as pain and pleasure. Hence, since there exists such a difference as this in these things, the fact that it is only the man who suspends judgement about all things who lives to the end an unperturbed life in respect of the goods and evils due to belief we have already established, both in our previous discussion of the Sceptic "end," and also on the present occasion when we showed that it is not possible to be happy if one assumes the existence of anything good and evil by nature. For he who does this is tossed about with endless perturbations, through avoiding these things and pursuing those, and drawing upon himself many evils because of the goods, and being afflicted by many times more evils because of his belief about evils.—Thus the man who declares that wealth (shall we say?) is a good and poverty an evil is perturbed in two ways if he has not wealth,—both because he has not the good and because he is toiling for the acquisition of it,—and when he has acquired it he is punished in three ways,—because he is immoderately overjoyed, and because he toils to ensure that his wealth stays with him, and because he is painfully anxious and dreads the loss of it. But he who ranks wealth neither amongst the natural goods nor amongst the natural evils, but utters the formula "Not more," is neither perturbed at its absence nor overjoyed at its presence, but in either case remains unperturbed. So that in respect of the things held, as a matter of belief, to be good and bad, and in respect of the desires and avoidances thereof, he is perfectly happy, while in respect of the sensible and irrational affections he preserves a due mean. For the things which occur, not because of a distortion of the reason and foolish belief but, owing to an involuntary affection of the sense it is impossible to get rid of by means of the Sceptical argument; for in a man who is distressed because of hunger or thirst, it is not feasible to implant, by means of the Sceptical argument, the conviction that he is not in distress, and in the man who is overjoyed at getting relief from these sufferings it is not in its power to implant the belief that he is not overjoyed.—What help, then, towards happiness (ask the Dogmatists) do we get from suspension of judgement if one has to be perturbed in any case and unhappy because perturbed? Great help, we shall reply. For even though he who suspends judgement about all things is perturbed owing to the presence of what causes pain, yet as compared with the Dogmatist he bears the distress more lightly, because, firstly, to pursue goods and to shun evils'which are endless in number and thus to be harassed by the perturbations due to these pursuits and avoidances as by Furies is much worse than not to suffer thus but merely to be engaged in avoiding and guarding against only one isolated form of evil. And, secondly, even the thing which the Ephectics avoid as evil, is not excessively perturbing. For the suffering is either small, such as that which befalls us every day,—hunger or thirst or cold or heat or something similar;—or, on the contrary, it is very violent and intense, as in the case of those afflicted with incurable torments, during which the doctors often provide powerful anodynes to assist the patient in obtaining some relief; or else it is moderate and protracted, as in some diseases. And of these, that which faces us every day perturbs us least as the remedies for it (food and drink and shelter) are easy to provide; and that which is most intense and in the highest degree perturbing terrifies us, after all, but for a moment, like a lightning-flash, and then either destroys us or is destroyed. And the moderate and protracted kind neither remains all through life nor is continuous in its nature but has many intervals of rest and periods of relief; for were it unceasing it would not have been protracted.—The perturbation, then, which befalls the Sceptic is moderate and not so very alarming. Notwithstanding, even if it be very great, we ought not to blame those who suffer involuntarily and of necessity but Nature,

> Who recks not aught of custom,

and the man who through his beliefs and owing to his own judgement draws upon himself the evil. For just as the man with a fever is not to be blamed because he has a fever (for he has the fever involuntarily), but the man who does not abstain from things inexpedient is to be blamed (for it lay in his own power to abstain from things inexpedient),—so the man who is perturbed at the presence of painful things is not to be blamed; for the perturbation caused by the pain is not due to himself but is bound to occur of necessity whether he wishes it or not; but he who through his own imaginations invents for himself a host of things desirable and to be avoided is deserving of blame; for he stirs up for himself a flood of evils.—And one may see the same thing in the case of the so-called "evils" themselves. For he who has no additional belief about pain being an evil is merely affected by the necessitated motion of the pain; but he who imagines in addition that the pain is objectionable only, that it is evil only, doubles by this belief the distress which results from its presence. For do we not observe frequently how, in the case of those who are being cut, the patient who is being cut manfully endures the torture of the cutting—

> His fair hue paling not, nor from his cheeks
> Wiping the tears away,

because he is affected only by the motion due to the cutting; whereas the man who stands beside him, as soon as he sees a small flow of blood, at once grows pale, trembles, gets in a great sweat, feels faint, and finally falls down speechless, not because of the pain (for it is not present with him), but because of the belief he has about pain being an evil? Thus the perturbation due to the belief about an evil as evil is sometimes greater than that which results from the so-called evil itself.—He, then, who suspends judgement about all things which depend on belief wins happiness most fully, and during involuntary and irrational affections although he is perturbed—

> Yea, for he is not sprung from a rock or an oak primeval
> But of the race of men was he,

yet his state of feeling is moderate.

Plotinus
(205–269 A.D.)

Neoplatonism · View

True to his insistence on the supremacy of intellectual and spiritual pursuits over temporal or material concerns, Plotinus refused to discuss his own background and life with his disciples. Possibly related to Trajan or his wife Plotina, Plotinus apparently was raised in Egypt but spoke and read only Greek. At age twenty-eight Plotinus went to study philosophy in Alexandria under Ammonius Saccas, a Platonist. Moving to Rome when he was forty, Plotinus began teaching and, ten years later, began writing his series of sixty-four treatises known as the *Enneads*. Plotinus obviously had, or at least quickly made, wealthy friends in Rome, among them emperor Gallienus and his wife Salonino. He served as tutor and legal guardian to the children of several aristocratic families and attracted disciples of diverse social and philosophic backgrounds. Toward the end of his life Plotinus contracted a severe and debilitating illness—possibly tuberculosis or, according to other armchair diagnoses, leprosy—which led to the breakup of his school. He also had exceptionally weak eyesight, which prevented him from rereading and editing his treatises. His treatises were compiled and edited after his death by Porphyry, who also alleges that Plotinus was capable of ecstatic religious experiences and, in fact, that he experienced union with God four times during the six years that Porphyry was with him.

Enneads I.7 & V.1*

Could one say that the good for a thing was anything else than the full natural activity of its life? If the thing was made up of many parts, would not its good be the proper, natural, and never-failing activity of the better part of it? So the soul's activity will be its natural good. Now if it is of the best sort itself and its activity is directed towards the best, this best will not only be the good for it but it will be the good absolutely. Then if something does not direct its activity towards another thing, since it is the

Reprinted by permission of the publishers and The Loeb Classical Library from "On the Primal Good and the Other Goods" in *Plotinus I* and "On the Primary Hypostases" in *Plotinus V*, translated by A. H. Armstrong, Cambridge, Mass.: Harvard University Press, Copyright © 1966 and © 1984 by The President amd Fellows of Harvard College best of beings and transcends all beings, and all other things direct their activities towards it, it is obvious that this will be the Good, through which other things are enabled to participate in good. All the other things which have the good like this will have it in two ways, by being made like it and by directing their activity towards it. So if the aspiration and activity towards the best is good, the Good must not look or aspire to something else, but stay quiet and be the "spring and origin" of natural activities, and give other things the form of good, not by its activity directed to them— for they are directed to it, their source. It must not be the Good by activity or thought, but by reason of its very abiding. For because it is "beyond being," it transcends activity and transcends mind and thought. For, to put it another way, one must assume the Good to be that on which everything else depends and which itself depends on nothing; for so the statement is true that it is that "to which everything aspires." So it must stay still, and all things turn back to it, as a circle does to the centre from which all the radii come. The sun, too, is an example, since it is like a centre in relation to the light which comes from it and depends on it; for the light is everywhere with it and is not cut off from it; even if you want to cut it off on one side, the light remains with the sun.

And how is everything else directed towards it? Soulless things are directed towards soul, and soul to the Good through intellect. But soulless things too have something of it, because each particular thing is one somehow and is existent somehow. Soulless things, too, share in form; and as they share in unity, existence and form so they share in the Good. In an image of the Good, that is to say; for what they share in are images of existence and the One, and their form is an image too. But the life of soul, of the first soul which comes next after intellect, is nearer to truth, and this first soul has through intellect the form of good. It can have the Good if it looks to it (Intellect comes after the Good). Life, then, is the good to that which lives, and intellect to that which has a share in intellect; so that if something has life and intellect, it has a twofold approach to the Good. . . .

* * *

What is it, then, which has made the souls forget their father, God, and be ignorant of themselves and him, even though they are parts which come from his higher world and altogether belong to it? The beginning of evil for them was audacity and coming to birth and the first otherness and the wishing to belong to themselves. Since they were clearly delighted with their own independence, and made great use of self-movement, running the opposite course and getting as far away as possible, they were ignorant even that they themselves came from that world. . . .

Let every soul, then, first consider this, that it made all living things itself, breathing life into them, those that the earth feeds and those that are nourished by the sea, and the divine stars in the sky; it made the sun itself, and this great heaven, and adorned it itself, and drives it round itself, in orderly movement; it is a nature other than the things which it adorns and moves and makes live; and it must necessarily be more honourable than they, for they come into being or pass away when the soul leaves them or grants life to them, but soul itself exists for ever because "it does not depart from itself." This is how soul should reason about the manner in which it grants life in the whole universe and in individual things. Let it look at the great soul, being itself another soul which is no small one, which has become worthy to look by being freed from deceit and the things that have bewitched the other souls, and is established in quietude. Let not only its encompassing body and the body's raging sea be quiet, but all its environment: the earth quiet, and the sea and air quiet, and the heaven itself at peace. Into this heaven at rest let it imagine soul as if flowing in from outside, pouring in and entering it everywhere and illuminating it: as the rays of the sun light up a dark cloud, and make it shine and give it a golden look, so soul entering into the body of heaven gives it life and gives it immortality and wakes what lies inert. And heaven, moved with an everlasting motion by the wise guidance of soul, becomes a "fortunate living being" and gains its value by the indwelling of soul; before soul it was a dead body, earth and water, or rather the darkness of matter and non-existence, and "what the gods hate," as a poet says. . . . For soul has given itself to the whole magnitude of heaven, as far as it extends, and every stretch of space, both great and small, is ensouled . . . And by its power the heaven is one, though it is multiple with one part in one place and one in another, and our universe is a god by the agency of this soul. And the sun also is a god because it is ensouled, and the other heavenly bodies, and we, if we are in any way divine, are so for this reason: for "corpses are more throwable away than dung". But that which is for the gods the cause of their being gods must necessarily be a divinity senior to them. But our soul is of the same kind, and when you look at it without its accretions and take it in its purified state you will find that very same honourable thing which [we said] was soul, more honourable than everything which is body. For all bodily things are earth. . .

Since the soul is so honourable and divine a thing, be sure already that you can attain God by reason of its being of this kind, and with this as your motive ascend to him: in all certainty you will not look far; and the stages between are not many. Grasp then the soul's upper neighbour, more divine than this divine thing, after which and from which the soul comes. For, although it is a thing of the kind which our discussion has shown it to be, it is an image of Intellect; just as a thought in its utterance is an image of the thought in soul, so soul itself is the expressed thought of Intellect. . . .

But one might see this also from what follows: if someone admires this perceptible universe, observing its size and beauty and the order of its everlasting course, and the gods in it, some of whom are seen and some are invisible, and the spirits, and all animals and plants, let him ascend to its archetypal and truer reality and there see them all intelligible and eternal in it, in its own understanding and life; and let him see pure Intellect presiding over them, and immense wisdom, and the true life of Kronos, a god who is fulness and intellect. For he encompasses in himself all things immortal, every intellect, every god, every soul, all for ever unmoving. For why should it seek to change when all is well with it? Where should it seek to go away to when it has everything in itself? But it does not even seek to increase, since it is most perfect. Therefore all things in it are perfect, that it may be altogether perfect, having nothing which is not so, having nothing in itself which does not think; but it thinks not by seeking but by having. Its blessedness is not something acquired, but all things are in eternity, and the true eternity, which time copies, running round the soul, letting some things go and attending to others. For around Soul things come one after another: now Socrates, now a horse, always some one particular reality; but Intellect is all things. It has therefore everything at rest in the same place, and it only is, and its "is" is for ever, and there is no place for the future for then too it is—or for the past—for nothing there has passed away—but all things remain stationary for ever, since they are the same, as if they were satisfied with themselves for being so. . . .

This god, then, which is over the soul, is multiple; and soul exists among the intelligible realities in close unity with them, unless it wills to desert them. When it has come near then to him and, in a way, become one with him, it lives for ever. Who is it, then, who begat this god? The simple god, the one who is prior to this kind of multiplicity, the cause of this one's existence and multiplicity, the maker of number. For number is not primary: the One is prior to the dyad, but the dyad is secondary and, originating from the One, has it as definer. . . .

Since, then, there exists soul which reasons about what is right and good, and discursive reasoning which enquires about the rightness and goodness of this or that particular thing, there must be some further permanent rightness from which arises the discursive reasoning in the realm of soul. Or how else would it manage to reason? And if soul sometimes reasons about the right and good and sometimes does not, there must be in us Intellect which does not reason discursively but always possesses the right, and there must be also the principle and cause and God of Intellect. . . .

STUDY/DISCUSSION ELEMENTS II

1. Terms

a. Good
b. Natural Desire (cf. Appetites)
c. Things in Our Power
d. Determinism
e. Virtue
f. Archetypal Reality
g. Happiness
h. Suspension of Judgment
i. The Highest Good

j. Piety
k. Mental Disturbance(s)
l. Dogmatist
m. Freedom
n. The One
o. Right Judgment
p. Irrational Affection(s)
q. Soul
r. Tranquillity (cf. Quietude)

2. Theses

a. Whoever believes that anything is good or evil by nature cannot be happy.
b. Death should mean nothing to us.
c. No misfortune can befall a virtuous person.
d. Physical things are good or divine only through the agency of soul.
e. Pleasure is our primary native good and the goal of the happy life.
f. We live happily by living according to nature.
g. We should desire only what is in our power.
h. True happiness is found only through Intellect, in the One.
i. Happiness depends upon right judgment and reason.
j. Whoever suspends judgment is happy and bears necessary perturbations moderately.
k. A life mastered by pleasure and pain cannot be happy.
l. Absolute good depends upon nothing, whereas all else depends upon it.
m. An unhappy person should blame nothing or no one but himself.

Chapter Four

Medieval Developments

THEMES AND IDEAS

The early fifth century A.D. saw the final breakup of the Roman Empire, the hub of Western civilization for almost six hundred years. The political, social, and economic structure of the West was devastated by Rome's fall. Its effects on Western philosophy were equally dramatic. Since educated Romans read Greek, very little Greek philosophy had been translated into Latin, the language of the Romans. For the next seven centuries, Greek philosophical writings were largely inaccessible to Latin thinkers. During this time, philosophy in the Latin West was dominated by the Christian Neoplatonism of St. Augustine, who lived and wrote during the final days of the Roman Empire.

Greek philosophical writings began finding their way into Latin universities during the eleventh century, by way of Islamic scholars in Moorish Spain and through eastern Italy. During the twelfth century, more and more Greek philosophy was translated into Latin, including almost all of Aristotle's writings. Latin philosophers were particularly overwhelmed by the breadth, depth, and careful logic of Aristotle's philosophy, which also challenged centuries-old doctrines and ideas. In the thirteenth century, St. Thomas Aquinas sought to harmonize Aristotelian concepts and principles with basic theological tenets of Christian Neoplatonism. He encountered stiff opposition, but, after his death, Greek (and especially Aristotle's) philosophy increasingly influenced the direction of Western thought once more. Indeed, the pace of Western philosophical development was so quickened by the rediscovery of Greek learning that it was hardly affected by the events in the fourteenth century which marked the end of the so-called Middle Ages. These included the growing strength of the European monarchies and a corresponding decline in the temporal power of the Roman Catholic Church; the devastating Hundred Years' War between France and England; the Black Death (bubonic plague), which swept across Europe killing over one-half of the population in some areas; the schism between the Italian papacy and its hitherto faithful ally, France; and an economic depression which paralyzed Europe and hastened the end of feudalism.

In the Latin Middle Ages, all philosophy revolved around theology. Christian Neoplatonists identified Plotinus' absolutely first principle (the One) with God, and so they viewed theology—the study of God—as the consummation of philosophy's search for knowledge, as the highest form of rational investigation. Moreover, since God is the source of all truth, knowledge, reality, and goodness, every intellectual endeavor must sooner or later rely upon theology to complete its understanding of its particular subject matter. Moral philosophy continued to focus on the nature of happiness and how to achieve it, and Medieval thinkers all accepted some version of Plotinus' doctrine that perfect happiness can only be found in God (the One). Despite this "other-worldly" dimension to their moral philosophies, the Neoplatonic thesis that our world is an image of the divine realm and our soul a progeny of that realm led Medieval thinkers increasingly to reemphasize the importance of individual responsibility and conduct in the moral life. Thus, already in St. Augustine, we see a renewed emphasis on Plato's concept of the well-ordered soul and on the social nature of morality; and by the time of St. Thomas Aquinas, right action, moral responsibility, and moral deliberation—increasingly peripheral concerns during the Later Classical (Hellenistic and Roman) period—are once again central to moral philosophy.

St. Augustine and Boethius

Much of St. Augustine's influence and genius lay in his skill at adapting Neoplatonic principles to Christian theological concerns and at rendering them more accessible to a wider audience than they were in Plotinus' *Enneads*. He derives the Neoplatonic conception of happiness, for example, from the rather mundane principles that we achieve happiness by satisfying our wants or desires; that, conversely, we seek to satisfy our wants or desires in order to achieve happiness; and that to be assured of happiness, the object(s) of our wants or desires must be something we can possess whenever we desire it, for however long we desire it, and without having to worry that it might be taken from us against our will. This last principle implies, however, that the object(s) of our desire must not be subject to the uncertainties and ever-changing reality of our world. It (or they) must be eternal and unchanging, attributes which belong to God—or to the divine realm—alone. To satisfy a desire, however, we must possess its object. How could we possibly "possess" God? We possess God, Augustine argues, insofar as our soul, and so also the choices we make, are governed by reason or wisdom—the proper "measure" of the human soul.

Augustine builds on this in other writings by introducing the idea of "eternal law": God is eternally the ultimate source and absolutely first principle, or highest law, of all creation. Hence, our soul is governed by wisdom just insofar as it conforms its choices to the highest possible conception of law, this being the idea of perfect order. Moreover, the temporal or "human" laws of a society or state also conform to this conception just insofar as they promote social order. Just as the ultimate object of God's eternal law is the good or welfare of all creation, so too should a state aim at the common good or public welfare of its citizens.

Boethius' *Consolation of Philosophy,* which he wrote in prison while awaiting execution, more obviously reflects Stoicism's influence on classical Neoplatonism and explores the moral implications of Neoplatonism's doctrine that our world is an image of the divine realm. Boethius, a wealthy and influential man, was convicted—unjustly, he maintains—of treason. He is distraught and angry with God for permitting such an injustice. His *Consolation of Philosophy* is an inner dialogue between Boethius and the goddess Philosophy, who diagnoses the source of his misery and anger, and who reminds him of the true nature and source of happiness.

Philosophy links "human happiness"—happiness as we humans commonly conceive of it—to Fortune, the personification of a person's experiences and circumstances in life. We typically consider ourselves to be happy just so long as we have good fortune, or just so long as Fortune is treating us well. Insofar as Fortune is treating us badly, we consider our lives, and so ourselves, to be unhappy. To see the true nature and source of happiness, however, we must first recognize the utterly false, illusory character of "human happiness." This conception of happiness is false, first, because it ignores the fact that change is part of the very nature of Fortune and, second, because it is a mistake to link happiness to Fortune in the first place. Everyone desires to be happy and, indeed, to remain happy always. But change is a universal, necessary feature of our universe and of everything in it, including our experiences and situation in life (Fortune). Changes in our Fortune are as inevitable as changes in the weather or as the process of life itself. To desire always to be happy while also linking happiness to Fortune is either irrational or, more likely, is simply to ignore this basic fact about Fortune's nature. Moreover, linking happiness to Fortune is, by itself, a mistake. Whether an experience or circumstance in life is good or bad depends on whether or not it conforms to our desires; we consider ourselves fortunate just in case Fortune is treating us the way we want her to treat us. But then, Fortune alone cannot be the source even just of "human" happiness (or unhappiness). Our own desires and expectations are as much sources of our happiness (or unhappiness) as Fortune is. Moreover, this fact indicates the only sure way for us to satisfy our desire always to be happy: Instead of sitting around and hoping that Fortune will conform to our desires, we should align our desires with Fortune. Moreover, this Stoic-sounding approach to life is proper and rational because everything that transpires in the natural world, and so everything that happens to us, is in fact good.

In nature, Philosophy argues, goodness is a function of unity. A natural thing is good just insofar as its form and its efficient power are one. Every natural thing possesses a form, which defines the kind of thing it is, and certain efficient powers—capacities which determine and control its natural processes and activities. A thing's form and efficient powers are "one" just in case it possesses precisely those efficient powers which things of its kind are supposed to possess. But this is true for every natural thing. Indeed, everything that transpires in the natural world happens precisely the way it is supposed to happen, based on the natural laws defining and governing our world. Hence, every natural event or thing is good. In nature, form and efficient power are always one. Indeed, once we recognize that Fortune is just the changing face of Providence—God's natural laws—we also see that there is no such thing as "bad fortune," but only opportunities to test our understanding of Providence and to align our desires with the wholly good natural order created by God.

Aquinas

Efforts by St. Thomas' predecessors—St. Anselm, for example—to focus on goodness as the (normative) standard as well as the ultimate end of human action reach fruition in Aquinas' moral philosophy. Aquinas views every human action as the overt, physical expression of (i) an apprehension of some goal or end; (ii) a disposition or inclination to attain it; (iii) deliberation concerning how to attain it; and (iv) a willful act of choosing that action identified by deliberation as the means to attaining it. Human actions are thus inherently goal-directed. Every (human) action aims at some goal and is chosen for the sake of attaining that goal. Aristotle's identification of goodness with the ultimate aim of all action leads Aquinas to conclude that ultimately everyone seeks goodness. Goodness is thus the universal, ultimate, and natural object of the human will. Moreover, happiness results from the ultimate satisfaction of our inclinations. Hence, we can achieve happiness only by attaining goodness. But goodness, as the universal object of the human will, cannot be identified with any particular instance or kind of goodness since we would then always be inclined just toward that particular goodness or thing—say, toward money, chocolate brownies, or our house pet. Instead, we are inclined toward different particular objects, and even toward different kinds of objects, at different times. Goodness, as the omnipresent or universal motivator of our will, must therefore be some wholly universal—nonparticular, nonspecific— "kind" of goodness. It must also be absolutely permanent or unchanging, if it is to satisfy our will completely and forevermore, and so to make us completely and forever happy. It must, in other words, be identical to God.

Like Augustine, Aquinas maintains that "possessing" God is a matter of apprehension rather than a physical act of some sort. Once again, however, Aquinas uses Aristotelian concepts in analyzing the nature of this apprehension. He distinguishes two basic apprehensive faculties: sense experience, which apprehends particular things by means of the five senses; and reason or intellect, which apprehends universals—objects not localized in particular places or times. Intellect, in turn, apprehends universals in two different ways: "Practical intellect" apprehends universals as instantiated by particular things in space and time while "speculative intellect" apprehends universals as such, apart from any instantiations of them. Thus, by sense experience I apprehend a particular tree—say, the tree outside my office window right now; by practical intellect I apprehend treeness as instantiated by this, that, and other particular trees; and by speculative intellect I apprehend treeness itself, apart from any instantiations of it. Now, Aquinas' thesis that God (goodness itself) is neither a particular thing nor even a specific kind of (good) thing implies that we cannot apprehend God by sense experience or practical intellect. But nor can we apprehend God by the "natural" functioning of our speculative intellect. Our speculative intellect "naturally" apprehends universals-as-such by defining them—by identifying their essential features or "parts." But God is absolutely universal and permanent, according to Christian Neoplatonists, because He has no "features" or "parts." He is absolutely simple and "one." We can apprehend God as such only by an immediate, absolutely simple act of our speculative intellect, one in which its "natural" mode of operation has been circumvented. We cannot attain such an apprehension on our own, however, but only through God's miraculous help.

Aquinas' Aristotelianized Neoplatonism links happiness with human conduct by virtue of the fact that goodness includes justice. God is perfect goodness, and so He must also be perfectly just; and justice implies rewarding right action and punishing wrong action. God does this by bestowing perfect happiness—i.e., the intellectual vision of His divine essence—on those who act rightly, or live virtuously, and by withholding it from those who act wrongly, or live unvirtuously. But, when is an action right? How do we live virtuously? Aquinas gives two answers, one "speculative" in defining the nature of right action and the other "practical" in stating a normative principle to guide our deliberations and choices of action. His speculative answer defines right action as action willed in conformity with God's will. An action is right, in other words, just in case it is willfully chosen and is an action which God Himself would choose if He were choosing instead of us. Aquinas' practical answer derives from the fact that the ultimate object of God's will is the entire created universe, or the common good of all creation. It states that, in willfully choosing an action, we should always refer it "to the common good as its end."

St. Aurelius Augustine
(354–430)

Augustine was born in the Roman province of Numidia, in North Africa. His father, Patricius, was a pagan while his mother, Monica, was a Christian. After completing his elementary education, Augustine studied classical literature for four years in Madaura. Aided by a wealthy benefactor, Romanianus, Augustine went to Carthage for advanced studies in rhetoric, in preparation for a career in law or government. In Carthage, however, Augustine was drawn toward theological studies by Manicheism and its doctrine of two coeternal divinities, Good and Evil. He failed to be fully convinced by the arguments of the Manichees and their bishop, Faustus; and in 383 he moved to Rome, where he studied Academic Skepticism. After a year, Augustine moved on to Milan, where he taught rhetoric and met St. Ambrose. He also studied Neoplatonism, which answered, he thought, the theological and philosophical questions that had troubled him at least since Carthage. Augustine was baptized in 387 and returned to North Africa, where he established a school for lay Christians. In 391, he was ordained to minister in the Church at Hippo. Consecrated Bishop of Hippo in 395, Augustine spent the next thirty years developing his theological views and responding to numerous theological controversies and "heresies."

The Happy Life*

Then I spoke again: "We wish to be happy, do we not?"
No sooner had I said this, than they agreed, with one voice.
I asked: "In your opinion, is a person happy who does not possess what he wants?"
They said: "By no means."
"What? Everyone who possesses what he wants is happy?"

From St. Augustine, "The Happy Life," translated by Ludwig Schopp in *Writings of Saint Augustine*, ed. Ludwig Schopp, The Fathers of the Church (Washington, D.C.: Catholic University of America Press, 1948). Used with permission.

At this point our mother said: "If he wishes and possesses good things, he is happy; if he desires evil things—no matter if he possesses them—he is wretched."

I smiled at her and said cheerfully: "Mother, you have really gained the mastery of the very stronghold of philosophy. For, undoubtedly you were wanting the words to express yourself like Tullius, who also has dealt with this matter. In his *Hortensius,* a book written in the praise and defense of philosophy, he said: 'Behold, not the philosophers, but only people who like to argue, state that all are happy who live according to their own will. This, of course, is not true, for, to wish what is not fitting is the worst of wretchedness. But it is not so deplorable to fail of attaining what we desire as it is to wish to attain what is not proper. For, greater evil is brought about through one's wicked will than happiness through fortune.' "

At these words our mother exclaimed in such a way that we, entirely forgetting her sex, thought we had some great man in our midst, while in the meantime I became fully aware whence and from what divine source this flowed.

Then Licentius spoke up: "You must tell us what a person has to wish in order to be happy, and what kind of things he must desire."

"Invite me," I said, "to your birthday party, and I will accept gladly what you serve. In this manner, please, be my guest today and do not ask for something that perhaps is not prepared."

When he felt sorry because of his request, though it was modest and not out of place, I asked: "Do we all now agree that nobody can be happy without possessing what he desires, and that not everyone who has what he wants is happy?"

They all expressed their approval.

"But what about this?" I asked. "Do you grant that everyone who is not happy is wretched?"

They had no doubt about this.

"Everyone, then," I continued, "who does not possess what he wants, is miserable."

All assented.

"But what preparation should a man make to gain happiness?" I asked. "For this, perhaps, is also a question to serve up at our banquet, so that the eagerness of Licentius may not be disregarded. In my opinion, what a man possesses ought to be obtained by him when he wants it."

"That is evident," they said.

"It must be something," I remarked, "that ever remains, and is neither dependent upon fate nor subject to any mishap. For, whatever is mortal and transitory we cannot possess whenever we wish it, and as long as we wish to have it."

All agreed.

But Trygetius said: "Many favorites of fortune possess abundantly and plentifully those things which, though frail and subject to mishaps, are pleasant for this earthly life. And they lack nothing that they desire."

To him I replied: "In your opinion, is a person happy who has fear?"

"It does not seem so," he answered.

"If, then, someone is likely to lose what he loves, can he be without fear?"

"No," he said.

"All those fortuitous things can be lost. No one, then, who possesses and loves them can ever be happy."

He did not refute this.

At this point, however, our mother said: "Even if somebody were certain that he would not lose all those things, he still could not be satisfied with such possessions. Hence, he is miserable because he is ever needy."

"But, in your opinion would not somebody be happy," I asked, "who has all these things in abundance and superfluity, if he is moderate in his desires, and enjoys them with contentment properly and pleasantly?"

"In this case," she replied, "he is not happy through the possession of these things, but through the moderation of his mind."

"Very well expressed," I said. "No better answer to my question could be expected, and no other one from you. Therefore, we do not have the slightest doubt that anyone setting out to be happy must obtain for himself that which always endures and cannot be snatched away through any severe misfortune."

Trygetius said: "We have already agreed to this."

"Is God, in your opinion, eternal and ever remaining?" I asked.

"This, of course, is so certain," replied Licentius, "that the question is unnecessary." All the others agreed with pious devotion.

"Therefore," I concluded, "whoever possesses God is happy."

As they readily and joyfully agreed to this, I continued: "It seems to me, therefore, that we have only to inquire what man really possesses God, for he, certainly, will be happy. It is your opinion about this that I now ask." . . .

"Now we have to inquire who it is that is not in want, for it is he who will be wise and happy. Now, foolishness is want and a term of want, while this word 'want' usually signifies a sort of sterility and lack. Kindly pay close attention to the great case with which the ancients have created either all or, as is evident, some words, especially designating those things the knowledge of which was very necessary.

"You now agree that every fool is in want, and that every person in want is a fool. And I think you also concede that a foolish soul is faulty, and that all faults of the mind can be included in that one term foolishness.

"On the first day of our discussion we said that the term *nequitia* [worthlessness] is so called because it comes from 'not anything,' while its opposite, *frugalitas* [frugality] comes from *frux* [fruit]. Therefore, in those two opposites, frugality and worthlessness, two things seem to be evident, namely, *esse* [to be] and *non esse* [not to be]. Of what, then, do we conceive as the opposite of 'want,' about which we are speaking?"

While the others hesitated, Trygetius said: "If I speak of wealth, I see that poverty is its opposite."

"This is almost right," I answered. "For poverty and want are usually understood in the same sense. But, another word has to be found so that the commendable side may not lack a term. Otherwise, the one side would have two terms [poverty and want], confronted on the other side by the one term [wealth] . . . For, nothing could be more absurd than to lack a word where one is needed in opposition to 'want.' "

Licentius said: "If we may say so, the word 'fullness' [*plenitudo*] seems to be the proper opposite of 'want.' "

"Perhaps," I said, "we will inquire later about this word a little more carefully. For this is not important for the quest of truth. Although Sallust, (that most excellent weigher of words), has chosen 'opulence' as the opposite of 'want,' I accept your 'fullness.' Here we will not labor in dread of the grammarians, nor will we fear that, for a careless use of words, we will be chastised by those who have permitted us to use their property."

When they smilingly had given their approval, I said: "While your thoughts are directed toward God, since I did not intend to disregard your minds, as oracles, so to speak, let us examine the meaning of this term, for I think no term is more adapted to the truth. 'Fullness' and 'want,' then, are opposites. As in the case of 'worthlessness' and 'frugality,' here, too, appear the concepts 'to be' and 'not to be.'

"If 'want' is identical with 'foolishness,' 'fullness' will be 'wisdom.' And, quite correctly, many have called frugality the mother of all virtues. Tullius also agrees with them, when, in one of his popular orations, he says: 'Whatever may be others' opinion, I think that frugality, that is, moderation and restraint, is the greatest virtue.' This is very learnedly and becomingly said, for he considered the fruit, that is, what we call 'to be,' whose contrary is 'not to be.' But, because of the common manner of speech, according to which 'frugality' means the same as 'thriftiness,' he illustrates what he has in mind by adding 'moderation' and 'restraint.' Let us now consider these two words more closely."

"The word *modestia* [moderation] is derived from *modus* [measure], and the word *temperantia* [restraint] from *temperies* [proper mixture]. Wherever measure and proper mixture are, there is nothing either too much or too little. Here, then, we have the precise sense of 'fullness' [*plenitudo*] which is the word we chose as the opposite of 'want' [*egestas*], and more suitably than if we were to use 'abundance' [*abundantia*]. For, by 'abundance' is understood a profusion and a sort of pouring forth of something excessively plentiful.

"If this happens in excess, there, also, measure is lacking, and the thing that is in excess stands in want of measure. Want, then, is not alien even to excess, but both 'the more' and 'the less' are alien to measure. If you discuss opulence, you will find that it also contains measure, for the word *opulentia* has no other derivation than from *ops* [wealth]. But, how does that enrich which is too much, since this is often more inconvenient than too little? Therefore, whatever is either too little or too much is subject to want, since it is in want of measure.

"But the measure of the soul is wisdom. Wisdom, however, is undeniably the opposite of foolishness, and foolishness is want, but fullness is the opposite of want. Therefore, wisdom is fullness. Yet, in fullness is measure. Hence, the measure of the soul is in wisdom. Hence, the very famous proverb rightly known as the most useful principle in life: 'Not anything too much.' "

"At the beginning of our discussion today we intended to call that man happy who is not in want, in case we should find misery identical with want. This is now found to be so. Therefore, 'to be happy' means nothing else than 'not to be in want,' that is, 'to be wise.'

"If now you ask what wisdom is—our reason has also explained and developed this as far as was at present possible—the answer is that wisdom is nothing but the measure of the soul, that is, that through which the soul keeps its equilibrium so that it neither runs over into too much nor remains short of its fullness. It runs over into luxuries, despotism, pride, and other things of this kind, through which the souls of immoderate and miserable men believe they get joy and might. But it is narrowed down by meanness, fear, grief, passion, and many other things through which miserable men make acknowledgement of their misery.

"However, when it [the soul] beholds the wisdom found and, to use the word of the boy here, devotes itself to it, and, without being moved by mere empty vanity, is not seduced to the treachery of images, weighed down in whose embrace it generally deserts God and finds a pernicious end, it then fears no immoderateness, and therefore no want and hence no misery. Thus, whoever is happy possesses his measure, that is, wisdom."

"But what wisdom should be so called, if not the wisdom of God? We have also heard through divine authority that the Son of God is nothing but the wisdom of God, and the Son of God is truly God. Thus, everyone having God is happy—a statement already acclaimed by everyone at the beginning of our symposium. But, do you believe that wisdom is different from truth? For it has also been said: 'I am the Truth.' The truth, however, receives its being through a supreme measure, from which it emanates and into which it is converted when perfected. However, no other measure is imposed upon the supreme measure. For, if the supreme measure exists through the supreme measure, it is measure through itself.

"Of course, the supreme measure also must be a true measure. But, just as the truth is engendered through measure, so measure is recognized in truth. Thus, neither has truth ever been without measure, nor measure without truth.

"Who is the Son of God? It has been said: The Truth. Who is it that has no father? Who other than the supreme measure? Whoever attains the supreme measure, through the truth, is happy. This means, to have God within the soul, that is, to enjoy God. Other things do not have God, although they are possessed by God."

"A certain admonition, flowing from the very fountain of truth, urges us to remember God, to seek Him, and thirst after Him tirelessly. This hidden sun pours into our innermost eyes that beaming light. His is all the truth that we speak, even though, in our anxiety, we hesitate to turn with courage toward this light and to behold it in its entirety, because our eyes, recently opened, are not yet strong enough. This light appears to be nothing other than God, who is perfect without any fault. Because there is entirety and perfection, at the same time He is the most omnipotent God.

"But, as long as we are still seeking, and not yet satiated by the fountain itself—to use our word—by fullness [*plenitudo*]—we must confess that we have not yet reached our measure; therefore, notwithstanding the help of God, we are not yet wise and happy.

"This, then, is the full satisfaction of souls, this the happy life: to recognize piously and completely the One through whom you are led into the truth, the nature of the truth you enjoy, and the bond that connects you with the supreme measure."

Ancius Boethius
(480–524)

Boethius was born into a wealthy and powerful Roman Christian family. His ancestors and relatives included two emperors, a pope, and several Roman consuls. After his father died, Boethius was raised by Quintus Symmachus, who became Prefect of Rome and Head of the State. Boethius was thoroughly educated in literature and philosophy at an early age and, under King Theodoric, the first "barbarian" ruler of Rome, became sole (and last) consul of Rome at age thirty. Boethius set, as his ultimate goal in life, to translate the complete works of Aristotle into Latin. He fell well short of this goal, but it was through his efforts alone that at least some of Aristotle's philosophy survived for the Latin Middle Ages. A staunch proponent of unification between the eastern and western Roman empires, Boethius fell out of favor with Theodoric. Perceiving him a threat to his rule, Theodoric had Boethius arrested, convicted, tortured, and bludgeoned to death.

The Consolation of Philosophy*

. . . [S]he thus began to speak: "If I have thoroughly learned the causes and the manner of your sickness, your former good fortune has so affected you that you are being consumed by longing for it. The change of this alone has overturned your peace of mind through your own imagination. I understand the varied disguises of that unnatural state. I know how Fortune is ever most friendly and alluring to those whom she strives to deceive, until she overwhelms them with grief beyond bearing, by deserting them when least expected. If you recall her nature, her ways, or her deserts, you will see that you never had in her, nor have lost with her, aught that was lovely. Yes, I think I shall not need great labour to recall this to your memory. For then too, when she was at your side with all her flattery, you were wont to reproach her in strong and manly terms; and to revile her with the opinions that you had gathered in worship of me with favoured ones. But no sudden change of outward affairs can ever come without some upheaval in the mind. Thus has it followed that you, like others, have fallen somewhat away from your calm peace of mind. But it is time now for you to make trial of some gentle and pleasant draught, which by reaching your inmost parts shall prepare the way for yet stronger healing draughts. Try therefore the assuring influence of gentle argument which keeps its straight path only when it holds fast to my instructions. And with this art of orators let my handmaid, the art of song, lend her aid in chanting light or weighty harmonies as we desire.

"What is it, mortal man, that has cast you down into grief and mourning? You have seen something unwonted, it would seem, something strange to you. But if you think that Fortune has changed towards you, you are wrong. These are ever her ways: this is her very nature. She has with you preserved her own constancy by her very change. She was ever changeable at the time when she smiled upon you, when she was mocking you with the allurements of false good fortune. You have discovered both the different faces of the blind goddess. To the eyes of others she is veiled in part: to you she has made herself wholly known. If you find her welcome, make use of her ways, and so make no complaining. If she fills you with horror by her treachery, treat her with despite; thrust her away from you, for she tempts you to your ruin. For though she is the cause of this great trouble for you, she ought to have been the subject of calmness and peace. For no man can ever make himself sure that she will never desert him, and thus has she deserted you. Do you reckon such happiness to be prized, which is sure to pass away? Is good fortune dear to you, which is with you for a time and is not sure to stay, and which is sure to bring you unhappiness when it is gone? But seeing that it cannot be stayed at will, and that when it flees away it leaves misery behind, what is such a fleeting thing but a sign of coming misery? Nor should it ever satisfy any man to look only at that which is placed before his eyes. Prudence takes measure of the results to come from all things. The very changeableness of good and bad makes Fortune's threats no more fearful, nor her smiles to be desired. And lastly, when you have once put your neck beneath the yoke of Fortune, you must with steadfast heart bear whatever comes to pass within her realm. But if you would dictate the law by which she whom you have freely chosen to be your mistress must stay or go, surely you will be acting without justification; and your very impatience will make more bitter a lot which you cannot change. If you set your sails before the wind, will you not move forward whither the wind drives you, not whither your will may choose to go? If you intrust your seed to the furrow, will you not weigh the rich years and the barren against each other? You have given yourself over to Fortune's rule, and you must bow yourself to your mistress's ways. Are you trying to stay the force of her turning wheel? Ah! dull-witted mortal, if Fortune begin to stay still, she is no longer Fortune." . . .

"Thus there is nothing wretched unless you think it to be so: and in like manner he who bears all with a calm mind finds his lot wholly blessed. Who is so happy but would wish to change his estate, if he yields to impatience of his lot? With how much bitterness is the sweetness of man's life mingled! For even though its enjoyment seem pleasant, yet it may not be surely kept from departing when it will. It is plain then how wretched is the happiness of mortal life which neither endures for ever with men of calm mind, nor ever wholly delights the care-ridden. Wherefore, then, O mortal men, seek ye that happiness without, which lies within yourselves? Ye are confounded by error and ignorance. I will shew you as shortly as I may, the pole on which turns the highest happiness. Is there aught that you value more highly than your own self? You will answer that there is nothing. If then you are master of yourself, you will be in possession of that which you will never wish to lose, and which Fortune will never be able to take from you. Yet consider this further, that you may be assured that happiness cannot be fixed in matters of chance: if happiness is the highest good of a man who lives his life by reason, and if that which can by any means be snatched away, is not the highest good (since that which is best cannot be snatched away), it is plain that Fortune by its own uncertainty can never come near to reaching happiness. Further, the man who is borne along by a happiness which may stumble, either knows that it may change, or knows it not: if he knows it not, what happiness can there be in the blindness of ignorance? If he knows it, he must needs live in fear of losing that which he cannot doubt that he may lose; wherefore an ever-present fear allows not such an one to be happy. Or at any rate, if he lose it without unhappiness, does he not think it worthless? For that, whose loss can be calmly borne, is indeed a small good." . . .

"There is then no doubt that these roads to happiness are no roads, and they cannot lead any man to any end whither they profess to take him. I would shew you shortly with what great evils they are bound up. Would you heap up money? You will need to tear it from its owner. Would you seem brilliant by the glory of great honours? You must kneel before their dispenser, and in your desire to surpass other men in honour, you must debase yourself by setting aside all pride. Do you long for power? You will be subject to the wiles of all over whom you have power, you will be at the mercy of many dangers. You seek fame? You will be drawn to and fro among rough paths, and lose all freedom from care. Would you spend a life of pleasure? Who would not despise and cast off such servitude to so vile and brittle a thing as your body? How petty are all the aims of those who put before themselves the pleasures of the body, how uncertain is the possession of such? In bodily size will you ever surpass the elephant? In strength will you ever lead the bull, or in speed the tiger? Look upon the expanse of heaven, the strength with which it stands, the rapidity with which it moves, and cease for a while to wonder at base things. This heaven is not more wonderful for those things than for the design which guides it. How sweeping is the brightness of outward form, how swift its movement, yet more fleeting than the passing of the flowers of spring." . . .

"Then you have before you the form of false happiness, and its causes; now turn your attention in the opposite direction, and you will quickly see the true happiness which I have promised to shew you."

"But surely this is clear even to the blindest, and you shewed it before when you were trying to make clear the causes of false happiness. For if I mistake not, true and perfect happiness is that which makes a man truly satisfied, powerful, venerated, renowned, and happy. And (for I would have you see that I have looked deeply into the matter) I realize without doubt that that which can truly yield any one of these, since they are all one, is perfect happiness."

"Ah! my son," said she, "I do see that you are blessed in this opinion, but I would have you add one thing."

"What is that?" I asked.

"Do you think that there is anything among mortals, and in our perishable lives, which could yield such a state?"

"I do not think that there is, and I think that you have shewn this beyond the need of further proof."

"These then seem to yield to mortals certain appearances of the true good, or some such imperfections; but they cannot give true and perfect good."

"No."

"Since, then, you have seen what is true happiness, and what are the false imitations thereof, it now remains that you should learn whence this true happiness may be sought." . . .

"Now consider," she continued, "where it lies. The universally accepted notion of men proves that God, the fountainhead of all things, is good. For nothing can be thought of better than God, and surely He, than whom there is nothing better, must without doubt be good. Now reason shews us that God is so good, that we are convinced that in Him lies also the perfect good. For if it is not so, He cannot be the fountainhead; for there must then be something more excellent, possessing that perfect good, which appears to be of older origin than God: for it has been proved that all perfections are of earlier origin than the imperfect specimens of the same: wherefore, unless we are to prolong the series to infinity, we must allow that the highest Deity must be full of the highest, the perfect good. But as we have laid down that true happiness is perfect good, it must be that true happiness is situated in His Divinity."

"Yes, I accept that; it cannot be in any way contradicted." . . .

Then she said, "At what would you value this, namely if you could find out what is the absolute good?"

"I would reckon it," I said, "at an infinite value, if I could find out God too, who is the good."

"And that too I will make plain by most true reasoning, if you will allow to stand the conclusions we have just now arrived at."

"They shall stand good."

"Have I not shewn," she asked, "that those things which most men seek are for this reason not perfect goods, because they differ between themselves; they are lacking to one another, and so cannot afford full, absolute good? But when they are gathered together, as it were, into one form and one operation, so that complete satisfaction, power, veneration, renown, and pleasure are all the same, then they become the true good. Unless they are all one and the same, they have no claim to be reckoned among the true objects of men's desires."

"That has been proved beyond all doubt."

"Then such things as differ among themselves are not goods, but they become so when they begin to be a single unity. Is it not then the case these become goods by the attainment of unity?"

"Yes," I said, "it seems so."

"But I think you allow that every good is good by participation in good?"

"Yes, I do."

"Then by reason of this likeness both unity and good must be allowed to be the same thing; for such things as have by nature the same operation, have the same essence."

"Undeniably."

"Do you realise that everything remains existent so long as it keeps its unity, but perishes in dissolution as soon as it loses its unity?"

"How so?" I asked.

"In the case of animals," she said, "so long as mind and body remain united, you have what you call an animal. But as soon as this unity is dissolved by the separation of the two, the animal perishes and can plainly be no longer called an animal. In the case of the body, too, so long as it remains in a single form by the union of its members, the human figure is presented. But if the division or separation of the body's parts drags that union asunder, it at once ceases to be what it was. In this way one may go through every subject, and it will be quite evident that each thing exists individually, so long as it is one, but perishes so soon as it ceases to be one."

"Yes, I see the same when I think of other cases."

"Is there anything," she then asked, "which, in so far as it acts by nature, ever loses its desire for self-preservation, and would voluntarily seek to come to death and corruption?"

"No," I said; "while I think of animals which have volition in their nature, I can find in them no desire to throw away their determination to remain as they are, or to hasten to perish of their own accord, so long as there are no external forces compelling them thereto. Every animal labours for its preservation, shunning death and extinction. But about trees and plants, I have great doubts as to what I should agree to in their case, and in all inanimate objects."

"But in this case too," she said, "you have no reason to be in doubt, when you see how trees and plants grow in places which suit them, and where, so far as nature is able to prevent it, they cannot quickly wither and perish. For some grow in plains, others on mountains; some are nourished by marshes, others cling to rocks; some are fertilised by otherwise barren sands, and would wither away if one tried to transplant them to better soil. Nature grants to each what suits it, and works against their perishing while they can possibly remain alive. I need hardly remind you that all plants seem to have their mouths buried in the earth, and so they suck up nourishment by their roots and diffuse their strength through their pith and bark: the pith being the softest part is always hidden away at the heart and covered, protected, as it were, by the strength of the wood; while outside, the bark, as being the defender who endures the best, is opposed to the unkindness of the weather. Again, how great is nature's care, that they should all propagate themselves by the reproduction of their seed; they all, as is so well known, are like regular machines not merely for lasting a time, but for reproducing themselves for ever, and that by their own kinds. Things too which are supposed to be inanimate, surely do all seek after their own by a like process. For why is flame carried upward by its lightness, while solid things are carried down by their weight, unless it be that these positions and movements are suitable to each? Further, each thing preserves what is suitable to itself, and what is harmful, it destroys. Hard things, such as stones, cohere with the utmost tenacity of their parts, and resist easy dissolution; while liquids, water, and air, yield easily to division, but quickly slip back to mingle their parts which have been cut asunder. And fire cannot be cut at all.

"We are not now discussing the voluntary movements of a reasoning mind, but the natural instinct. For instance, we unwittingly digest the food we have eaten, and unconsciously breathe in sleep. Not even in animals does this love of self-preservation come from mental wishes, but from elementary nature. For often the will, under stress of external causes, embraces the idea of death, from which nature revolts in horror. And, on the other hand, the will sometimes restrains what nature always desires, namely the operation of begetting, by which alone the continuance of mortal things becomes enduring. Thus far, then, this love of self-preservation arises not from the reasoning animal's intention, but from natural instinct. Providence has given to its creatures this the greatest cause of permanent existence, the instinctive desire to remain existent so far as possible. Wherefore you have no reason to doubt that all things, which exist, seek a permanent existence by nature, and similarly avoid extinction."

"Yes," I said, "I confess that I see now beyond all doubt what appeared to me just now uncertain."

"But," she continued, "that which seeks to continue its existence, aims at unity; for take this [a]way, and none will have any chance of continued existence."

"That is true."

"Then all things desire unity," she said, and I agreed.

"But we have shewn unity to be identical with the good?".

"Yes," said I.

"Then all things desire the good; and that you may define as being the absolute good which is desired by all."

"Nothing could be more truthfully reasoned. For either everything is brought back to nothing, and all will flow on at random with no guiding head; or if there is any universal aim, it will be the sum of all good."

"Great is my rejoicing, my son," said she, "for you have set firmly in your mind the mark of the central truth. And hereby is made plain to you that which you a short time ago said that you knew not."

"What was that?"

"What was the final aim of all things," she said, "for that is plainly what is desired by all: since we have agreed that that is the good, we must confess that the good is the end of all things." . . .

"This universe would never have been suitably put together into one form from such various and opposite parts, unless there were some One who joined such different parts together; and when joined, the very variety of their natures, so discordant among themselves, would break their harmony and tear them asunder unless the One held together what it wove into one whole. Such a fixed order of nature could not continue its course, could not develop motions taking such various directions in place, time, operation, space, and attributes, unless there were One who, being immutable, had the disposal of these various changes. And this cause of their remaining fixed and their moving, I call God, according to the name familiar to all."

Then said she, "Since these are your feelings, I think there is but little trouble left me before you may revisit your home with happiness in your grasp. But let us look into the matter we have set before ourselves. Have we not shewn that complete satisfaction exists in true happiness, and we have agreed that God is happiness itself, have we not?"

"We have."

"Wherefore He needs no external aid in governing the universe, or, if He had any such need, He would not have this complete sufficiency."

"That of necessity follows," I said.

"Then He arranges all things by Himself."

"Without doubt He does."

"And God has been shewn to be the absolute good."

"Yes, I remember."

"Then He arranges all things by good, if He arranges them by Himself, whom we have agreed to be the absolute good. And so this is the tiller and rudder by which the ship of the universe is kept sure and unbreakable." . . .

"The engendering of all things, the whole advance of all changing natures, and every motion and progress in the world, draw their causes, their order, and their forms from the allotment of the unchanging mind of God, which lays manifold restrictions on all action from the calm fortress of its own directness. Such restrictions are called Providence when they can be seen to lie in the very simplicity of divine understanding; but they were called Fate in old times when they were viewed with reference to the objects which they moved or arranged. It will easily be understood that these two are very different if the mind examines the force of each. For Providence is the very divine reason which arranges all things, and rests with the supreme disposer of all; while Fate is that ordering which is a part of all changeable things, and by means of which Providence binds all things together in their own order. Providence embraces all things equally, however different they may be, even however infinite: when they are assigned to their own places, forms, and times, Fate sets them in an orderly motion; so that this development of the temporal order, unified in the intelligence of the mind of God, is Providence. The working of this unified development in time is called Fate. These are different, but the one hangs upon the other. For this order, which is ruled by Fate, emanates from the directness of Providence. Just as when a craftsman perceived in his mind the form of the object he would make, he sets his working power in motion, and brings through the order of time that which he had seen directly and ready present to his mind. So by Providence does God dispose all that is to be done, each thing by itself and unchangeably; while these same things which Providence has arranged are worked out by Fate in many ways and in time." . . .

"For a definite order embraces all things, so that even when some subject leaves the true place assigned to it in the order, it returns to an order, though another, it may be, lest aught in the realm of Providence be left to random chance. But 'hard is it for me to set forth all these matters as a god,' nor is it right for a man to try to comprehend with his mind all the means of divine working, or to explain them in words. Let it be enough that we have seen that God, the Creator of all nature, directs and disposes all things for good. And while He urges all, that He has made manifest, to keep His own likeness, He drives out by the course of Fate all evil from the bounds of His state. Wherefore if you look to the disposition of Providence, you will reckon naught as bad of all the evils which are held to abound upon earth." . . .

"For this reason a wise man should never complain, whenever he is brought into strife with fortune; just as a brave man cannot properly be disgusted whenever the noise of battle is heard, since for both of them their very difficulty is their opportunity, for the brave man of increasing his glory, for the wise man of confirming and strengthening his wisdom. From this is virtue itself so named, because it is so supported by its strength that it is not overcome by adversity." . . .

St. Thomas Aquinas
(1225–1274)

Son to a count of Aquino, Thomas was also related to the imperial family
and several royal houses of Italy. Born in the castle of Rocca Secca near
Aquino, in southern Italy, he became an oblate in the nearby Benedictine
abbey of Monte Cassino at the age of six. When he was ten, Thomas was
sent to study liberal arts at the University of Naples. There he joined the
Dominican Order despite opposition from his father, who at one point
imprisoned him in the castle of San Giovanni for two years, to no avail. In
1248, Thomas went to Cologne, where he studied with St. Albert the Great.
After additional studies at the convent of St. James in Paris, he became a
Doctor of Theology in 1257. Thomas returned to Italy, where he taught in
the Papal Curia and met William of Moerbeke, a fellow Dominican whom
he encouraged to produce a complete set of Latin translations from Greek
manuscripts of Aristotle's writings. It was at this time that Thomas began
writing his commentaries on Aristotle's philosophy and transforming Latin
theology and philosophy. Returning to Paris in 1268, Thomas' teachings
encountered bitter opposition from Augustinians and Latin Averroists. In
1272 Thomas was relieved of his teaching duties at Paris and went to
Naples, where he established a Dominican university. He lectured and
traveled widely on behalf of his order and died on his way to the Council of
Lyons. In 1277 his doctrines were condemned at Oxford and at Paris but,
in 1323, he was canonized by Pope John XXII. In 1567 Pope Pius V
proclaimed him the Angelic Doctor and, in 1880, he was named the Patron
of Catholic Schools by Pope Leo XIII.

Treatise on Happiness[*]

QI, art. 1: DOES MAN ACT FOR AN END?

Only those actions of man are properly called human which are characteristic of man
as man. Now the difference between man and irrational creatures is that he is the
master of his actions. Hence the actions of which man is the master are the only ones

that can properly be called human. But man is master of his actions through his reason and will; hence free judgment of choice is said to be "a power of will and reason." Therefore actions that are deliberately willed are properly called human. If there are other actions that belong to man, they can be called *actions of man* but not *human actions* strictly speaking, since they are not actions of man as man. Now it is clear that all actions which proceed from a power are caused by that power in conformity with the nature of its object. But the object of the will is an end and a good. Therefore all human actions are for the sake of an end.

QVIII, art. 1: DOES THE WILL WILL ONLY THE GOOD?

The will is a rational appetite. Now appetite is only for the good. The reason for this is that appetite is simply an inclination for something on the part of the one who desires it. Now nothing is favorably disposed to something unless it is like or suitable to it. Hence, since everything, insofar as it is a being and a substance, is a good, every inclination is to a good. Therefore the Philosopher says that the good is "that which all desire."

But it must be noted that since every inclination arises from some form, natural appetite arises from the form that is present in the natural thing, whereas sense appetite as well as rational appetite—the will—arises from a form as known. Hence just as natural appetite tends to a good that is in fact good, so sense appetite as well as the will tend to the good as known. Consequently, for the will to tend to something, it is not required that it be in truth good, but that it be apprehended as good. This is why the Philosopher says that "the end is the good or the apparent good."

QVIII, art. 2: DO WE WILL THE END ONLY OR ALSO THE MEANS?

Sometimes by "will" we mean the power itself by which we will and sometimes we mean the will's act. If in speaking of the will we mean the power, then it extends both to the end and to the means. For any power extends to those things in which its kind of object can be found in any way; for example, sight extends to all things what-soever which in any way share color. But the aspect of good, which is the object of the power of the will, is found not only in the end but also in the means.

However, if we are speaking of the will as it means particularly the act, then it relates to the end only. For every act denominated from a power designates the simple act of that power; for example, "understanding" designates the simple act of the intellect. Now the simple act of a power is referred to that which is in itself the object of that power. But that which is good and willed for itself is the end. Hence,

From St. Thomas Aquinas, *Treatise on Happiness*, translated by John A. Oesterle (Notre Dame, University of Notre Dame Press, 1983). Used with permission.

strictly speaking, the simple act of willing is of the end itself. The means, on the other hand, are good or willed, not in themselves, but only as referred to the end. Hence the will is directed to the means only as it is directed to an end, so that what is willed in the means is the end. . . .

QI, art. 6: DOES MAN WILL ALL THAT HE WILLS FOR AN ULTIMATE END?

All things which man desires he necessarily desires for an ultimate end. This is made clear by two arguments. First, because whatever man desires, he desires under the aspect of a good. If it is not desired as his complete good, which is the ultimate end, he must desire it as tending toward his complete good because a beginning of something is always ordered to its completion, as is evident both in what is brought about by nature and what is made by art. Thus every beginning of fulfillment is ordered to complete fulfillment, which is achieved through the ultimate end.

Second, because the ultimate end as moving the appetite is like the first mover in other motions. But clearly, secondary moving causes move only insofar as they are moved by a first mover. Hence secondary desirable things move the appetite only as ordered to a primary desirable thing, which is the ultimate end.

QI, art. 7: IS THERE ONE ULTIMATE END FOR ALL MEN?

We can speak of the ultimate end in two ways, having in mind in one case the notion of the ultimate end, and in the other that in which the notion of the ultimate end is realized. With respect to the notion of the ultimate end, all agree in desiring the ultimate end, since all desire their good to be complete, which is what the ultimate end is, as we have said. But with respect to that in which this kind of thing is realized, all men are not agreed as to their ultimate end, for some desire riches as their complete good, some sense pleasure, and others something else. . . .

QII, art. 8: DOES MAN'S HAPPINESS CONSIST IN ANY CREATED GOOD?

It is impossible for man's happiness to consist in a created good, for happiness is the perfect good which wholly brings desire to rest, for it would not be an ultimate end if something should still remain to be desired. Now the object of the will, or human appetite, is the universal good, just as the object of the intellect is universal truth. Hence it is evident that nothing can bring the will of man to rest except the universal good. This is not found in any created thing but only in God, for all creatures have goodness by participation. Hence only God can satisfy the will of man, as is said (*Psalms 102:5*), "Who satisfieth thy desire with good things." Therefore man's happiness consists in God alone.

QXIX, art. 3: DOES THE GOODNESS OF THE WILL DEPEND UPON REASON?

As we have said, the goodness of the will depends properly upon the object. Now the object of the will is presented to it by reason, for the good known by the intellect is the object proportioned to the will. A sensible or imaginary good is not proportioned to the will but to sense desire, for the will can tend to the universal good, which reason apprehends, whereas sense desire tends only to the particular good, which is grasped by a sense knowing power. Hence the goodness of the will depends upon reason in the same way as it depends on its object.

QIII, art. 4: GIVEN THAT HAPPINESS IS AN ACTIVITY OF THE INTELLECTUAL PART, IS IT AN ACT OF THE INTELLECT OR OF THE WILL?

Two things are required for happiness, as we have stated. One refers to the very being of happiness and the other is a sort of per se accident of it, namely, the delight connected with it. Now with respect to what happiness is essentially, I maintain that it is impossible for it to consist in an act of the will. For it is evident from what has been said, that happiness is the attainment of the ultimate end. But the attainment of the end does not consist in an act itself of the will, for the will is directed to the end both as absent and present—absent, when it desires it; and present, when it delights in resting in it. Now it is clear that desire for the end is not attainment of it, but a movement toward the end. Now delight is in the will as a result of the end being present; but the converse is not true, that a thing becomes present because the will delights in it. Therefore it must be something other than an act of the will by which the end becomes present to the one willing it.

This is clearly the case in regard to ends which are sensed, for if the acquiring of money were a result of an act of the will, an avaricious man would have it from the very moment he willed to have it. But at the outset he does not have it; he attains it when he gets it in his hands or in some such way, and then he takes delight in the money possessed. It is the same with an intelligible end. At the outset, we wish to attain it; we attain it when it becomes present to us by an act of the intellect, and then the delighted will rests in the end now attained.

Consequently the essence of happiness consists in an act of the intellect, but the delight resulting from happiness belongs to the will. As Augustine says, happiness is "joy in the truth," because joy itself is the fulfillment of happiness.

QIII, art. 8: DOES THE HAPPINESS OF MAN CONSIST IN THE VISION OF THE DIVINE ESSENCE?

Ultimate and perfect happiness can only be in the vision of the divine essence. To make this evident, two points must be noted. First, man is not perfectly happy as long as something remains for him to desire and seek; second, the perfection of a power is judged in terms of its object. Now the object of the intellect is *what a thing is,* that is, the essence of a thing. Hence the intellect is perfected in the measure that it knows the essence of a thing. If, then, an intellect knows the essence of some effect but through it is not able to know the essence of the cause, that is, to know the *what it is* of the cause, that intellect is not said to know the cause absolutely, although it may be able to gather from the effect the knowledge that the cause exists. Consequently, when man knows an effect and knows that it has a cause, he still has a natural desire to know the cause as to *what it is.* And that desire is one of wonder, and is a cause of inquiry, as is said in the *Metaphysics.* For example, if a man, knowing that the sun is eclipsed, takes into account that it comes from some cause which he does not know as to what it is, he wonders about it, and from wondering begins to inquire about it, and he goes on inquiring until he comes to know the essence of the cause.

If therefore the human intellect knows the essence of some created effect and knows no more about God than that He exists, the perfection of that intellect has not reached the point of knowing the first cause absolutely, and there still remains in it a natural desire to seek out the cause. Hence it is not yet completely happy. Consequently, for perfect happiness, the intellect must reach the very essence of the first cause. Thus its perfection will be had by its union with God as an object, and only in this does man's happiness consist, as has been pointed out.

QV, art. 3: CAN ONE BE HAPPY IN THIS LIFE?

Some participation in happiness can be had in this life, but true and perfect happiness cannot be had in this life. This can be shown in two ways. The first way is taken from the common notion of happiness, for happiness, since it is "the complete and sufficient good," excludes all evil and fulfills all desire. Now in this life all evil cannot be excluded. The present life is subject to many evils which cannot be avoided: the evil of ignorance on the part of the intellect, the evil of inordinate affection on the part of desire, and the evil of much suffering on the part of the body, as Augustine carefully sets forth. Likewise, the desire for good cannot be fully satisfied in this life, for man naturally desires the good he has to be permanent. Now what is good in the present life is transitory; for life itself, which we naturally desire, passes away, and we would like to hold on to it for ever, since man naturally shrinks from death. Hence it is impossible for true happiness to be had in this life.

The second way is taken from what happiness specifically consists in, the vision of the divine essence, which man cannot attain in this life, as has been shown. It is thus clearly evident that no one can attain true and perfect happiness in this life.

QV, art. 5: CAN MAN ATTAIN HAPPINESS BY HIS NATURAL POWERS?

The imperfect happiness which man can have in this life can be acquired by his natural powers, as can virtue, which is the activity happiness consists in, as we shall see later on. But, as we have already said, man's perfect happiness consists in the vision of the divine essence. Now to see the essence of God is beyond the nature not only of man but of every creature, as we have shown. For the natural knowledge of any creature is in accordance with the type of substance it is; thus it is said of a purely intellectual being that "it knows what is above it and what is below it in a way corresponding to its substance." But all knowledge which is according to the mode of created substance falls short of the vision of the divine essence, which infinitely exceeds all created substance. Hence neither man, nor any other creature, can attain ultimate happiness by his own natural powers.

QV, art. 6: CAN MAN ATTAIN HAPPINESS THROUGH THE ACTION OF SOME HIGHER CREATURE?

Every creature is subject to the laws of nature, since each has limited power and action; therefore, whatever exceeds created nature cannot be brought about by the power of a creature. Hence if anything needs to be accomplished that is beyond nature, it is done directly by God, such as raising the dead, restoring sight to the blind, and things of this kind. Now we have shown that happiness is a good which exceeds created nature. Consequently it cannot be bestowed through the action of any creature; on the contrary, man is made happy by God alone, if we are speaking of perfect happiness. But if it is a question of imperfect happiness, the same thing will be said of it as is said of virtue, in whose act it consists.

QXIX, art. 9: DOES THE GOODNESS OF THE WILL DEPEND UPON ITS CONFORMITY TO THE DIVINE WILL?

As we have said, the goodness of the will depends upon the intention of the end. Now the ultimate end of the human will is the supreme good, which is God, as we have also said. Therefore in order that the human will be good it must be ordered to the supreme good, which is God.

Now this supreme good is primarily and per se related to the divine will as its proper object, and that which is first in any genus is the measure and explanation of everything which belongs to that genus. But everything is right and good insofar as it reaches a proper measure. Therefore, in order that the human will be good, it must be conformed to the divine will.

QXIX, art. 4: DOES THE GOODNESS OF THE WILL DEPEND ON ETERNAL LAW?

In all causes ordered to one another, the effect depends more upon the first cause than upon a second cause, since a second cause acts only in virtue of a first cause. Now human reason's capacity to be the rule of the human will, by which its goodness is measured, is derived from eternal law, which is divine reason. Hence, "Many say: Who shows us good things? The light of Thy countenance, O Lord, is signed upon us" (*Psalms 4:7*). In other words: "The light of reason which is in us, to the extent it can show us what is good and regulates our will, to that extent is the light of Thy countenance, i.e., is derived from Thy countenance." Hence it is clear that the goodness of the human will depends much more upon the eternal law than upon human reason, and when human reason fails, we must have recourse to the eternal reason.

QXIX, art. 10: IS IT NECESSARY FOR THE HUMAN WILL, IN ORDER TO BE GOOD, TO BE CONFORMED TO THE DIVINE WILL WITH REGARD TO THE THING WILLED?

As we have said, the will tends to its object insofar as it is proposed by reason. Now a thing may be considered in various ways by reason; hence a thing may be good from one point of view and not good from another point of view. Consequently, if one man wills that a thing take place, inasmuch as it is accounted as good, his will is good; and the will of another man when he wills that the same thing not take place, inasmuch as it is accounted as evil, is also good. For example, the judge's will is good when he wills the death of a criminal, because this realizes justice; whereas the will of someone else—the criminal's wife or son who does not wish him killed because it is an evil for the family—is also good.

Now since the will follows the apprehension of reason or the intellect, the more universal the nature of the good which is apprehended the more universal is the good which the will tends to. This is evident in the example we have just given. The judge has to guard the common good, with which justice is concerned, and as a consequence he wills the death of the criminal, which is counted as good in relation to the common welfare, whereas the wife of the criminal has to concern herself with the private domestic good, and from this point of view she wills that her husband, the criminal, not be put to death. Now God, who is the maker and ruler of the universe, apprehends the good of the entire universe, and hence whatever He wills, He wills with a view to the common good; and this is His own goodness and the good of the whole universe. A creature, on the other hand, in accord with its nature, apprehends a particular good proportionate to such a nature. Now it is possible for something to be good in view of a particular consideration which is not good in view of a universal one, or conversely. Hence it happens that one's will is good in willing something from a particular point of view which nevertheless God does not will from a universal point of view, and vice versa. Hence various wills of various men can be good in respect to opposite things, inasmuch as they will a particular thing to be or not to be for different reasons.

Now one's will is not right in willing some particular good unless he refers it to the common good as to an end, since the natural appetite of any part is ordered to the common good of the whole. Now it is the end that provides the formal reason for willing whatever is directed to the end. Hence, in order that a man will a particular good with a right will, he must will that particular good materially while willing the common and divine good formally. Therefore the human will must be conformed to the divine will, with regard to that which is willed formally, for it is bound to will the divine and common good; but not materially, for the reason just given. But in any event the human will is in a certain way conformed to the divine will in both respects. For, inasmuch as it is conformed to the divine will with regard to the common nature of what is willed, it is conformed to the divine will with regard to the ultimate end. And in the event that it is not conformed to the divine will in what is willed materially, it is still conformed to the divine will considered as an efficient cause, for the proper inclination following upon nature, or upon the particular grasp of this or that thing, comes to it from God as from its efficient cause. Hence, in this regard it is customary to say that the human will is conformed to the divine will in that it wills what God wills it to will.

There is also another kind of conformity, from the point of view of the formal cause, such that man wills something from charity, as God wills it. This conformity is also reduced to a conformity of form, which is taken from the order to the ultimate end, which is the proper object of charity.

STUDY/DISCUSSION ELEMENTS III

1. Terms

a. Fullness
b. False Happiness
c. Fortune
d. Means
e. Ultimate End
f. Appetite(s)
g. Measure
h. Good
i. Will
j. Perfect Happiness

k. Moderation
l. Virtue
m. Good Will
n. Essence
o. Absolute Goodness
p. Wisdom
q. Imperfect Happiness
r. True Happiness
s. Eternal Law
t. Providence

2. Theses

a. Every human action is deliberately willed.
b. Whoever desires earthly and fortuitous things cannot be happy.
c. A person is happy by possessing wisdom.
d. Every human action is willed for the sake of complete (perfect) happiness.
e. The essence of happiness is an act of intellect.
f. Fortune cannot make us happy.
g. The good is the end of all things. (cf. All things desire the good.)
h. Whoever possesses God is happy. (cf. Happiness is found only in God.)
i. A human will is good insofar as it is conformed to the divine will.
j. Perfect happiness is impossible in this life.
k. In willing some particular good, one should refer it to the common good as its ultimate end.
l. Everything from God is good.

Chapter Five

Modern Developments

THEMES AND IDEAS

This section includes major figures in moral philosophy from the late sixteenth to the late nineteenth centuries. Dubbed the Modern era, many of the ideas and concerns which developed during these three centuries are likely to strike twentieth-century readers as, indeed, decidedly "modern." Significant developments, for example, in science, technology, and global politics in the late nineteenth and early twentieth centuries provide some justification for demarcating our own century from its immediate precursors. For purposes of intellectual and cultural history, however, this demarcation is largely a matter of convenience, allowing us to give special treatment to most recent and current intellectual activity. It also reflects the fact that it becomes increasingly difficult to identify what or who will prove to be truly significant in the larger context of Western history as we approach our own day and time, as well as the importance of paying special attention to most recent and current developments to orderly, continued progress in philosophy.

In this section, we shall observe a growing emphasis on the individuality and independence, or autonomy (from the Greek, for "self-rule," or "rule of and by the self"), of moral agents and on the social nature of morality. These themes are by no means new. Autonomy has been a central concept in moral philosophy from the very beginning, and Plato, for example, placed special emphasis on the relationship between morality and civility. Still, these themes became increasingly more implicit than explicit after Plato's time, and in Medieval philosophy, both the self and society were always viewed in the wider context of universal creation and in terms of their relationships to God as the supreme lawgiver and source of all goodness. Modern thinkers, in contrast, tend to view moral agents not only as responsible for their own beliefs and actions but as individual, independent (autonomous) sources of moral value and conduct—as deriving moral ends and standards from their own particular humanity. At the same time, Modern thinkers repeatedly emphasize the social nature of morality. Some even held that moral concepts—rightness, goodness, etc.—presuppose a social context. On this extreme view, moral concepts lose all purpose or meaning when isolated or abstracted from any social context; human actions have moral significance only in the context of some social or political structure. This tension between, on the one hand, the individuality and autonomy of moral agents and, on the other hand, the social nature of morality may even be the central problem of moral philosophy during the Modern era.

Actually, this tension is already latent in the so-called Renaissance. The Renaissance is often viewed less as a distinct historical period than as a spirit which infused European civilization beginning in the late fourteenth century. The Renaissance was itself inspired by the recovery of classical learning, art, and outlooks which began in the later Middle Ages. The late Medieval spirit of recovery and "rebirth" was intensified, however, by a number of developments in the fifteenth and sixteenth centuries. The temporal, political power of the Roman Catholic papacy was finally supplanted by the emerging sovereign nations of Europe. Europeans saw themselves less and less as members of a single, universal order centering on the Church of Rome and more and more as citizens of diverse nations, each with its own political institutions, laws, and mores. Expanding economies and national interests increased European contacts with the rest of the world, inspiring a sense of adventure, curiosity, and of the value of individual achievement. Discoveries of new oceans and worlds, economic prosperity underscored by acquisitions of personal wealth through manufacturing and trade, and a dramatic rise in secular learning deeply affected European attitudes and interests.

The "rebirth" of Europe—which literally is what *renaissance* means—has always been most closely associated, however, with the recovery of Greek and Roman culture. The late Medieval recovery of Greek philosophy continued to spread and was augmented by a growing interest in classical literature, art, and science. Earlier Latin translations of Greek philosophy were translated into the various national vernaculars of Europe. This, and the invention of printing in the mid-fifteenth century, greatly increased the availability of classical learning to secular scholars. An appetite for all manner of intellectual and artistic achievement and the erosion among secular thinkers of the Medieval focus on theology gave the Renaissance its distinctive, humanistic character. The Renaissance humanists, who first characterized the preceding centuries as the "Middle Ages" (in Latin, the "Medieval" period), discovered a wealth of new ideas and viewpoints in classical writings which they applied in their own, more "self-" or "human-centered" approach to nature and human conduct.

Erasmus

Erasmus, a late Renaissance Christian humanist, provides an excellent bridge between Medieval philosophy and the more secular outlook of the Modern era. Erasmus, like the Medieval Neoplatonists, sees God's goodness reflected in the order and harmony of the natural world. The laws of nature bind all things and natural processes together to form a single, unified, smoothly functioning universe. The order and harmony of nature, in particular, has normative significance for Erasmus, providing us with a standard or model to emulate in our dealings with one another. Peace is the natural condition of our universe, an expression of God's goodness, and it is the source of all goodness—including human goodness. Human peace—"the concord of all men"—is thus the ultimate, natural end of human conduct, a fact which Erasmus sees confirmed in the New Testament gospels on the life and teachings of Jesus Christ.

Thomas Hobbes

With Hobbes, a number of themes and problems in Modern—and twentieth-century—moral philosophy become explicit. The tendency, already present in Erasmus, to focus on human conduct and relationships becomes central to Hobbes' moral philosophy. Moral concepts—good and evil, for example—are meaningful only in relation to human actions; and they have moral (normative) meaning only in relation to social institutions, relationships, and laws. No "common rule of good and evil" can be discovered in the nature of the universe or its laws, Hobbes insists, nor in God as the first principle and creator of our universe. Instead, Hobbes looks to human nature and the inner psychological causes of human conduct and society. In so doing, however, he articulates an ongoing problem for subsequent moral philosophies: In the absence of a universal basis for, author of, or authority behind moral truth, how can moral wisdom have any genuine normative force? How can we justify, or even explain, the sense of responsibility, even obligation, commonly associated with the idea of *moral* conduct? This problem is especially acute for Hobbes because his conception of human nature—called psychological egoism—implies that the natural condition of human relationships is decidedly nonsocial and uncivil. Human nature, for Hobbes, is no surrogate for the moral status of God in Medieval thought.

Every human action, Hobbes maintains, is an attempt to pursue something or to avoid something, based on an inclination toward that object or away from it. Inclinations to pursue objects are called desires, and inclinations to avoid objects are called aversions. In this context, where human conduct is analyzed in terms of its most basic psychological causes, an object is good just in case it is an object of desire and evil (or bad) just in case it is an object of aversion. Moreover, since human goodness is the same as happiness, a person's happiness ("felicity") is measured by the degree to which he or she satisfies his or her desires. Every individual's desires thus determine the nature of goodness and happiness for that individual; and since satisfying one's own desires is the fundamental natural motive for our actions, their effects on others or on our relationships with others—what Hobbes calls questions of justice and injustice—are irrelevant. Indeed, our only natural interest in others is as potential threats to our own capacity to satisfy our desires and achieve happiness, insofar as it is always possible for two people to desire the same object(s) even though only one of them can actually possess it (them). This fact naturally inclines us to want to dominate one another. Indeed, it makes us want to destroy one another, since only then are we assured that others will not impede our own pursuit of happiness. The natural state of human relationships is thus unceasing warfare, "every man against every man."

Erasmus viewed warfare and purely self-interested behavior as perversions of the natural order established by God. Hobbes, in contrast, derives his understanding of the natural state of human conduct and relationships from human nature, and his conception of human nature implies that we are anything but naturally peaceful, civil beings. Hobbes also recognizes, however, that people in fact do live (more or less) at peace with one another—that we in fact do consider one another's needs and interests and manage to cooperate with one another, enough at least to have social order. Clearly, we are able somehow to restrain and reform our natural inclinations, and so avoid the solitary, poor, nasty, brutish, and short natural state of human life. Indeed, the fact that we must restrain and reform our selfish natures if we are to avoid a life of utter misery and unhappiness is what gives unselfish, civilized behavior its moral meaning. Social relationships and civility are not natural, however, but "invented." We invent them by entering into "social contracts"—by establishing institutions and laws which impose and maintain order. These, in turn, define the proper order of human relationships in a society and, more important, the proper (or "just") way to act in that society. These contracts, along with the demands placed upon us by nature that require us to restrain our selfishness, thereby also gives objectivity to civil morality (or justice) despite its "invented" character. Hobbes explains our ability to invent society (and justice) in terms of a capacity for "enlightened self-interest." But while this capacity enables us to educate our natural inclinations, it cannot extinguish them. Morality, as defined by a society's institutions and laws, depends on the establishment of a civil power stronger than the collection of selfish individuals within society. Only then is moral conduct not only just but truly binding, and so obligatory.

John Locke

John Locke, like Hobbes, also bases morality on his conception of our natural state. But, whereas Hobbes bases his conception on his egoistic psychology, Locke focuses on individual liberty—the lack of constraining institutions, law, and civil powers—as the distinguishing feature of humanity in a natural state. In the state of nature, no one person (or group of persons) has authority or moral power over others; and, this being the right state of human relationships from the viewpoint of nature, everyone has a natural right to his or her own "liberty, life, and property." Or, since social institutions and authorities do not exist in nature, nature clearly permits self-determination; hence, self-determination is naturally right, and so a natural right of ours. The fact that self-determination is naturally right also implies that it is naturally wrong for one person to infringe on another's liberty, life, or possessions. In this way, "nature wills the peace and preservation of all mankind"; and social institutions and laws which promote, protect, and sustain our natural rights are expressions of what is naturally right.

David Hume

Hobbes and Locke illustrate the growing debate in Modern thought over the relationship between nature and morality. This is by no means a new debate. Indeed, our very first reading saw Socrates reacting to Thrasymachus' claim that right and wrong are matters of convention, not knowledge. For centuries, however, Latin philosophers had adhered to the Neoplatonic doctrine that morality flows from the same divine will which established the natural order, effectively silencing the debate. As Modern secular philosophy separated, or at least distinguished, itself from the Christian Neoplatonists' approach to morality, the issue became more acute than ever. In the twentieth century, the issue most commonly takes the form of debating the relationship between factual judgments and moral (or, more generally, value) judgments. This formulation of the issue is rooted in David Hume, who recognized an important difference between Hobbes' attempt to base morality on human inclination, appetites, or "sentiments" and Locke's attempt to base morality on a rational understanding of nature, or at least of the natural state of human relationships.

A *judgment,* let us say, is a belief about the nature or character of some object. Let us define a *factual* judgment, in turn, as a judgment about an object as it exists in nature, and a *value* judgment as a judgment about an object insofar as it relates to a certain set of "value" characteristics—for example, goodness or badness, rightness or wrongness. Notice that these definitions do not, by themselves, imply that factual judgments and value judgments constitute distinct classes of judgments. They allow for the possibility that value judgments may in fact also be factual judgments—in particular, if value characteristics are natural features of objects. The perennial debate over the relationship between morality and nature thus becomes a matter of determining whether value judgments are also factual judgments, rather than a distinct kind of (nonfactual) judgments.

Hume, in his classic investigation of this issue, identifies (human) reason—which he sharply distinguishes from sentiment—as the source of factual judgments. Accordingly, if reason is not also the source of value judgments—in particular, if sentiment is instead—then value judgments cannot be a kind of factual judgment, and our beliefs about the goodness or badness, or the rightness or wrongness, of objects could not refer to any sort of natural features of objects. It might seem also to follow that our moral (or value) beliefs are based solely on convention or human artifice, so that there is nothing objective about morality at all. Hume's genius, however, lies in his declining to take this final, Hobbesian step. Pure conventionality, or subjectivism, is not the only alternative to maintaining that value judgments are also factual. The normative force of morality does not depend on its being natural but on its being universal and social—on certain actions being right (and others wrong) for anyone and everyone, and on right action being civil, socially valuable, and unselfish. Though morality is grounded in sentiment, Hume argues, human sentiment is neither capricious nor wholly selfish. In particular, Hume maintains, human sentiment universally approves what is useful and abhors what is harmful; and it especially approves what is useful in promoting social order and human well-being while abhorring social chaos and human suffering. Hume thus refocuses the debate over the nature of morality, from a question of whether it is "natural" or "conventional," to a question of whether there exist universal standards of moral judgment or whether moral standards are universally binding on all human beings. He also enunciates what comes to be known as the Principle of Utility: A universal standard does exist, and this standard is usefulness or utility.

Immanuel Kant

Both Hobbes and Hume link morality to human sentiment, on the one hand, and to social institutions and rules, on the other. This way of viewing morality may seem refreshingly down-to-earth and realistic, especially to a twentieth-century reader. Yet, it also conflicts with some widely held views about morality. We think, for example, that if something is morally wrong (say, murder), then it is wrong regardless of how an individual might feel about it and regardless of what the laws of a particular society might say about it. We distinguish good laws from bad laws, even good social structures from bad ones, and believe that good laws and good societies reflect or conform to moral goodness instead of somehow inventing it. Similarly, we distinguish good people from bad people and believe that good people embody moral goodness rather than just somehow inventing and approving it. Morality is not determined by how an individual (or a group of individuals) happens to feel or what he or she happens to like and dislike. Rather, morality tells us how we should feel about things, or what things we should desire, like, or approve. Indeed, if an action is morally right, we should do it even if we do not feel like doing it or do not want to do it, or even if our society and its laws do not sanction it. At the very least, the moral value of our conduct is most evident in situations where doing the right thing requires that we act contrary to our own desires, inclinations, or society's laws. Precisely these sorts of reservations about Hobbes' and Hume's view of morality motivated Immanuel Kant.

Kant's primary objective is to identify the "moral motive"—the essence and source of moral conduct. He insists that it must transcend societal custom and laws, and even our own desires, feelings, or inclinations. But he also wants to render moral philosophy scientific; that is, he wants to determine if moral philosophy, like natural science, can discern a universal law—a moral law which binds everyone's conduct, regardless of any individual, distinctive facts about them or their particular circumstance in life. Kant believes that he can achieve both of these objectives by analyzing the concept of a good will.

Traditionally, moral philosophers have identified the essence of morality with its highest, final, or ultimate end; and, Kant argues, this can be nothing other than the good will: Only the good will can be good absolutely, unconditionally, or in and of itself. Likewise, a universal moral law could be found only in the good will, since this is the essence of (all) morality and because human deliberation and action is free (autonomous). In nature, things cannot choose whether or not to obey the laws of nature. Natural laws govern natural processes and activities, not just universally, but with necessity. Similarly, a universal moral law must also, if it is to be a genuine law, compel our obedience to it. At the same time, however, the "universe" that it must govern is a universe of free (human) wills. Moral laws, unlike natural laws, must be accepted *as law* before they can wield any authority or "compelling force" over us. They must, in other words, be necessarily binding on our conduct while somehow also respecting our will's freedom. To do this, they must be laws which every will would freely impose upon itself just insofar as it strives to act morally, or laws which every good will would impose upon itself just because it is a good will.

Kant's derivation of a universal moral law from the concept of a good will relies on the fact that our will is not only free but also rational. Indeed, Kant identifies our will with practical reason: A willful act is a deliberate act; and we act deliberately when we evaluate a situation and determine how we ought to act in that situation. Every willful act thus implies a belief about what we ought to do. Kant calls these beliefs "maxims" or "particular conceptions of moral law." Now, a willful act is (morally) good just in case its maxim is also a moral law. Thus, a good will formulates, or self-legislates, maxims which are also moral laws. This analysis of how a good will functions leads Kant to discover at least one universal moral law, or categorical imperative: Act only according to that maxim whereby you can at the same time will that it become a universal law.

Kantian scholars disagree over the precise meaning of Kant's concept of the good will. His reasoning becomes somewhat clearer, however, if we understand goodness—or at least highest or ultimate goodness—to mean excellent functioning. A good car, for example, is a car that functions (or runs) excellently; and a good worker is one who does excellent work. A good will, similarly, is an excellently functioning will. Moreover, Kant attributes two main characteristics to our will: It is free, and it is rational. The preceding derivation of a categorical imperative focuses on the second characteristic: Rational excellence is knowing universal laws. So, a rationally excellent will is one whose "particular conceptions" of moral law are in fact (universal) moral laws. Alternatively, a will exercises freedom most excellently when it legislates not just for itself but is a universal legislator—when it functions as a will which legislates what should and should not be done throughout an entire universe. Thus, again, a good will would be a will whose self-legislations (maxims) can in fact obtain universally, or for an entire universe—in particular, for what Kant calls a kingdom of ends.

The precise meaning and application of Kant's categorical imperative is an unending matter of debate among historians of moral philosophy. Some reduce it to a question of whether you would be willing to see everyone else also acting on whatever maxim you are contemplating for yourself. Others take Kant's insistence that a maxim be capable of functioning as a law of the universe more literally—as demanding, for example, that you adopt a more objective, impersonal attitude toward your maxims and examine whether they really could order and preserve an entire ("moral") universe, these being the essential functions of every law-of-a-universe. Moreover, some historians argue that Kant intends his categorical imperative to establish the rightness (or wrongness) of any and every possible action whatsoever. Others hold that, while his categorical imperative may establish the rightness (or wrongness) of certain types of actions— for example, the so-called perfect and imperfect duties in his examples—it is primarily meant to establish certain boundaries within which moral beings are free to establish, perhaps negotiate, more specific rules of conduct among themselves.

John Stuart Mill

Kant is the first philosopher in this text to explicitly deny the classical doctrine that the ultimate end of moral action is (human) happiness. Kant believes that happiness is far too vague and ambiguous a concept to provide us with a universal end or standard for our actions. He may also be reacting to Modern thinkers' tendency to portray happiness as an inherently selfish goal that conflicts with civilized, social behavior—Hobbes, of course, being the most extreme example of this. John Stuart Mill also wants morality to focus on a universal moral law, but he believes that such a law need not—indeed, must not—forgo linking (human) goodness with happiness. Mill's moral law is usually called the Principle of Utility, or the Utilitarian Principle, and it states: That action is right which promotes the greatest amount of happiness for the greatest number of persons.

Mill rejects Kant's attempt to insulate the "moral motive" from human desire, inclinations, or sentiment. He would agree that the essence of morality lies in free will, but he disagrees with Kant's conception of free will. Kant believes that our will is truly free only when its choices are determined by nothing outside of its own rational, self-legislating nature—including our own desires and wants as much as social institutions, political authorities, and the like. For Mill, in contrast, the elements of human psychology are inseparably linked to one another. Our desires and wants are integral parts of our autonomous being. Indeed, Mill holds that we act freely just insofar as we are able to do what we *desire* or *want* to do. Hence, the ultimate end (good) of human conduct must be the ultimate end of human desire; and this is happiness. Everything we desire, Mill argues, must either be integral to our happiness or be a means to attaining happiness. Hume's classic statement of the Principle of Utility—that an action is right if it is useful or beneficial to humanity—is thus modified by Mill's identification of what benefits humanity with what promotes happiness.

But, what is happiness? Mill's teacher, Jeremy Bentham, defined happiness in terms of pleasure. In our reading, Mill defends the Epicurean conception of happiness (as he calls it), and he insists that there are various kinds and levels of pleasure, some being "higher" and so intrinsically more valuable than others. Perhaps the most significant feature of Mill's discussion, however, is the connection he establishes between individual happiness and the aggregate happiness of a moral community—hence, with "the greatest happiness for the greatest number of persons." In *Utilitarianism*, Mill argues that just as one's own happiness is the ultimate object of each person's desires, so too must the general happiness be the ultimate object of the aggregate desires of all persons constituting a moral community. The basis for Mill's communal outlook can be seen more fully, however, in his essay "Civilization," in which he demonstrates the sheer perversity, as Mill sees it, of Hobbes' view that the individual pursuit of happiness somehow conflicts with the communal ends and accomplishments of unselfish, civil beings.

Hobbes (and also Locke) investigated the nature and source of morality by distinguishing civilized society from a presocial state of nature. Mill considers this approach too simplistic, arguing that we must distinguish two degrees or levels of civilization. The establishment of social institutions and relationships distinguishes human communities from mere, unorganized collections of distinct ("state of nature") individuals; but this is just the first step on the road to true civilization. Even groups of humans who we would otherwise describe as savages or barbarians exhibit this level of civility. "True," or second-level, civility involves more than just some sort of "social contract." Second-level civility requires that citizens be inculcated with a social conscience—that they sacrifice "some portion of individual will, for a common purpose," and subdue their self "to act as interdependent parts of a complex whole." Indeed, only such (second-level) civilizations know true prosperity and human improvement and are truly "advanced on the road to perfection; happier, nobler, wise." Paradoxical though it may seem, only people who view themselves dispassionately as integral parts of the aggregate of persons constituting their society, and so who subsume their own happiness under the general happiness, are capable of attaining the fullest measure of happiness possible for human beings.

Desiderius Erasmus
(1466–1536)

Erasmus was born in Rotterdam. His father, a parish priest, entered him in the monastery of Steyr against his wishes. In 1493 Erasmus became secretary to the bishop of Cambrai, left the monastery, and studied at the University of Paris. Erasmus traveled to England in 1499, where he befriended Colet and More. Already a superb Latin scholar, Erasmus was inspired by Colet's biblical lectures to study classical Greek. Erasmus became an avid proponent of classicism and was instrumental in developing humanistic studies in classical languages and literature, and in the early Christian fathers. After the Reformation, Erasmus lived in Louvain and Basel. At first refusing to take sides, Erasmus finally came out against Lutheranism in 1524. His final years were uneventful, however, as he remained largely aloof from the bitter disputes between Catholics and Protestants.

The Complaint of Peace*

Peace Speaks:
Though I certainly deserve no ill treatment from mortals, yet, if the insults and repulses I receive were attended with any advantage to them, I would content myself with lamenting in silence my own unmerited indignities and man's injustice. But since, in driving me away from them, they remove the source of all human blessings, and let in a deluge of calamities on themselves, I am more inclined to bewail their misfortune, than complain of ill usage to myself; and I am reduced to the necessity of weeping over and commiserating those whom I wished to view, rather as objects of indignation than of pity.

For, though rudely to reject one who loves them as I do, may appear to be savage cruelty; to feel an aversion for one who has deserved so well of them, base ingratitude; to trample on one who has nursed and fostered them with all a parent's care, an unnatural want of filial affection; yet voluntarily to renounce so many and so great advantages as I always bring in my train, to go in quest of evils, infinite in

From Erasmus, *The Complaint of Peace* (Boston, Mass. and Burlington, N.J.: Charles Williams and O. Allison, 1813).

number and shocking in nature, how can I account for such perverse conduct, but by attributing it to downright madness? We may be angry with the wicked, but we can only pity the insane. What can I do but weep over them? And I weep over them the more bitterly, because they weep not for themselves. No part of their misfortune is more deplorable than their insensibility to it. It is one great step to convalescence, to know the extent and inveteracy of a disease.

Now, if I, whose name is Peace, am a personage glorified by the united praise of God and man, as the fountain, the parent, the nurse, the patroness, the guardian of every blessing which either heaven or earth can bestow; if, without me nothing is flourishing, nothing safe, nothing pure or holy, nothing pleasant to mortals, or grateful to the Supreme Being: if, on the contrary, War is one vast ocean, rushing on mankind, of all the united plagues and pestilences in nature; if, at its deadly approach, every blossom of happiness is instantly blasted, every thing that was improving gradually degenerates and dwindles away to nothing, every thing that was firmly supported totters on its foundation, every thing that was formed for long duration comes to a speedy end, and every thing that was sweet, by nature, is turned into bitterness; if war is so unhallowed, that it becomes the deadliest bane of piety and religion; if there is nothing more calamitous to mortals, and more detestable to heaven, I ask, how in the name of God, can I believe those beings to be rational creatures; how can I believe them to be otherwise than stark mad; who, with such a waste of treasure, with so ardent a zeal, with so great an effort, with so many arts, so much anxiety, and so much danger, endeavour to drive me away from them, and purchase endless misery and mischief at a price so high?

If they were wild beasts who thus despised and rejected me, I could bear it more patiently; because I should impute the affront to nature, who had implanted in them so savage a disposition. If I were an object of hatred to dumb creatures, I could overlook their ignorance, because the powers of mind necessary to perceive my excellence have been denied to them. But it is a circumstance equally shameful and marvellous, that, though nature has formed one animal, and one alone, with powers of reason, and a mind participating of divinity; one animal, and one alone, capable of sentimental affection and social union; I can find admission among the wildest of wild beasts, and the most brutal of brutes, sooner than with this one animal; the rational, immortal animal, called man.

Among the celestial bodies that are revolving over our heads, though the motions are not the same, and though the force is not equal, yet they move, and ever have moved, without clashing, and in perfect harmony. The very elements themselves, though repugnant in their nature, yet, by a happy equilibrium, preserve eternal peace; and amid the discordancy of their constituent principles, cherish, by a friendly intercourse and coalition, an uninterrupted concord.

In living bodies, how all the various limbs harmonize, and mutually combine, for common defence against injury! What can be more heterogeneous, and unlike, than the body and the soul? And yet with what strong bonds nature has united them, is evident from the pang of separation. As life itself is nothing else but the concordant union of body and soul, so is health the harmonious co-operation of all the parts and functions of the body.

Animals destitute of reason, live with their own kind in a state of social amity. Elephants herd together; sheep and swine feed in flocks; cranes and craws take their flight in troops; storks have their public meetings to consult previously to their emigration, and feed their parents when unable to feed themselves; dolphins defend each other by mutual assistance; and every body knows, that both ants and bees have respectively established, by general agreement, a little friendly community.

But I need dwell no longer on animals, which, though they want reason, are evidently furnished with sense. In trees and plants, one may trace the vestiges of amity and love. Many of them are barren, unless the male plant is placed on their vicinity. The vine embraces the elm, and other plants cling to the vine. So that things which have no powers of sense to perceive any thing else, seem strongly to feel the advantages of union.

But plants, though they have not powers of perception, yet, as they have life, certainly approach very nearly to those things which are endowed with sentient faculties. What then is so completely insensible as stony substance? Yet even in this, there appears to be a desire of union. Thus, the loadstone attracts iron to it, and holds it fast in its embrace, when so attracted. Indeed, the attraction of cohesion, as a law of love, takes place throughout all inanimate nature.

I need not repeat, that the most savage of the savage tribe, in the forest, live among each other in amity. Lions shew no fierceness to the lion race. The boar does not brandish his deadly tooth against his brother boar. The lynx lives in peace with the lynx. The serpent shews no venom in his intercourse with his fellow serpent; and the loving kindness of wolf to wolf is proverbial.

But I will add a circumstance still more marvellous. The accursed Spirits, by whom the concord between heavenly and human beings was originally interrupted, and to this day continues interrupted, hold union with one another, and preserve their usurped power, such as it is, by humanity!

Yet man to man, whom, of all created beings, concord would most become, and who stands most in need of it, neither nature, so powerful and irresistible in every thing else can reconcile; neither human compacts unite; neither the great advantages, which would evidently arise from unanimity combine, nor the actual feeling and experience of the dreadful evils of discord cordially endear. To all men the human form is the same, the sound made by the organs of utterance similar; and while other species of animals differ from each other chiefly in the shape of their bodies, to men alone is given a reasoning power, which is, indeed, common to all men, yet in a manner so exclusive, that it is not at the same time common to any other living creature. To this distinguished being is also given the power of speech, the most conciliating instrument of social connexion and cordial love. Throughout the whole race of men are sown by nature the seeds of virtue, and of every excellent quality. From nature man receives a mild and gentle disposition, so prone to reciprocal benevolence, that he delights to be loved for the pleasure of being loved, without any view to interest; and feels a satisfaction in doing good, without a wish or prospect of remuneration. This disposition to do disinterested good, is natural to man, unless in a few instances, where, corrupted by depraved desires, which operate like the drugs of Circe's cup, the human being has degenerated to the brute. Hence, even the common people, in the ordinary language of daily conversation, denominate whatever is connected with mutual good will, humane; so that the word humanity no longer describes man's nature, merely in a physical sense; but signifies humane manners, or a behaviour, worthy the nature of man, acting his proper part in civil society.

Tears also are a distinctive mark fixed by nature, and appropriated to her favourite, man. They are a proof of placability, a forgiving temper; so that if any trifling offence be given or taken, if a little cloud of ill humour darken the sunshine, there soon falls a gentle shower of tears, and the cloud melts into a sweet serenity.

Thus, it appears in what various ways, nature has taught man her first great lesson of love and union. . . .

But such and so many plain indications of her meaning, has nature taught mankind to seek peace, and ensure it. She invites them to it by various allurements, she draws them to it by gentle violence, she compels them to it by the strong arm of necessity. After all, then, what infernal being, all-powerful in mischief, bursting every bond of nature asunder, fills the human bosom with an insatiable rage for war! If familiarity with the sight had not first destroyed all surprise at it, and custom, soon afterwards, blunted the sense of its evil, who could be prevailed upon to believe, that those wretched beings are possessed of rational souls, the intellects and feelings of human creatures, who contend, with all the rage of furies, in everlasting feuds and litigations, ending in murder! Robbery, blood, butchery, desolation, confound, without distinction, every thing sacred and profane. The most hallowed treaties, mutually confirmed by the strongest sanctions, cannot stop the enraged parties from rushing on to mutual destruction, whenever passion or mistaken interest, urges them to the irrational decision of the battle.

Though there were no other motive to preserve peace, one would imagine that the common name of man might be sufficient to secure concord between all who claim it. But, be it granted, that nature has no effect on men as men, though we have seen that nature rules, as she ought to do, in the brute creation, yet must not Christ, therefore, avail with christians? Be it granted, that the suggestions of nature have no effect with a rational being, though we see them have great weight even on inanimate things without sense, yet, as the suggestions of the christian religion are far more excellent than those of nature, why does not the christian religion persuade those who profess it, of a truth which it recommends above all others, that is, the expediency and necessity of peace on earth, and good will towards men; or, at least, why does it fail of effectually dissuading from the unnatural, and more than brutal madness of waging war? . . .

Such then and so fierce, ought not men to blush at the appellation of christians, differing, as they do essentially, from the peculiar and distinguishing excellence of Christ? Consider the whole of his life; what is it, but one lesson of concord and mutual love? What do his precepts, what do his parables inculcate, but peace and charity? Did that excellent prophet Isaiah, when he foretold the coming of Christ as an universal reconciler, represent him as an earthly lord, a satrap, a grandee, or courtier? Did he announce him as a mighty conqueror, a burner of villages, a destroyer of towns, as one who was to triumph over the slaughter and misery of wretched mortals? No. How then did he announce him? As the Prince of Peace. The prophet intending to describe him as the most excellent of all the princes that ever came into the world, drew the title of that superior excellence, from what is itself the most excellent of all things, peace. Nor is it to be wondered, that Isaiah, an inspired prophet, viewed Peace in this light, when Silius Italicus, a heathen poet, has written my character in these words:

"No boon that Nature ever gave to man,
May be compared with Peace."

The mystic minstrel, the sweet Psalmist, has also sung:

"In Salem (a place of peace) is his tabernacle."

Not in tents, not in camps, did this Prince, mighty to save, fix his residence; but in Salem, the city of peace. He is, indeed, the prince of peace; Peace is his dear delight, and War his abomination.

Thomas Hobbes
(1588–1697)

Hobbes was a clergyman's son, born in Malmesbury, England. Educated in classical languages and literature at an early age, Hobbes was translating Euripides from Greek into Latin by age fourteen. At fifteen he went to Oxford, where he studied logic and Aristotelian philosophy. At twenty Hobbes became tutor to Lord Hardwicke, Earl of Devonshire, and his son, William Lord Cavendish. During his residence at Devonshire, Hobbes nurtured his interest in the classics while also studying science and mathematics, including Galileo, Kepler, and Euclid. He became close friends with Ben Jonson and Bacon and, after Cavendish's death, studied in Europe, where he met Gassendi, Descartes, and even Galileo. Hobbes' travels were instigated by political events as much as by intellectual curiosity. A staunch royalist during the Puritan Revolution, Hobbes became Prince Charles' tutor in 1647 while the future King Charles II was in exile in France. In 1651 he published *Leviathan*, which managed to upset both the prince (because it did not uphold the divine right of kings) and Hobbes' French hosts (because it was seen as anti-Catholic). As a result, Hobbes returned to England, where Oliver Cromwell allowed him to live in peace provided he refrain from politics. After the Restoration of the English monarchy, Hobbes was a favorite in Charles II's court. Suspicions over his alleged atheism, however, required Hobbes to publish his remaining works abroad.

Leviathan*

There be in animals, two sorts of "motions" peculiar to them: one called "vital;" begun in generation, and continued without interruption through their whole life; such as are the "course" of the "blood," the "pulse," the "breathing," the "concoction, nutrition, excretion," &c., to which motions there needs no help of imagination: the other is "animal motion," otherwise called "voluntary motion;" as to "go," to "speak," to "move" any of our limbs, in such manner as is first fancied in our minds. That sense is motion in the organs and interior parts of man's body, caused by the action of the things we see, hear, &c.; and that fancy is but the relics of the same motion,

From Thomas Hobbes, *Leviathan* (London: George Routledge and Sons, 1887).

remaining after sense, has been already said in the first and second chapters. And because "going," "speaking," and the like voluntary motions, depend always upon a precedent thought of "whither," "which way," and "what;" it is evident, that the imagination is the first internal beginning of all voluntary motion. And although unstudied men do not conceive any motion at all to be there, where the thing moved is invisible; or the space it is moved in is, for the shortness of it, insensible; yet that doth not hinder, but that such motions are. For let a space be never so little, that which is moved over a greater space, whereof that little one is part, must first be moved over that. These small beginnings of motion, within the body of man, before they appear in walking, speaking, striking, and other visible actions, are commonly called "endeavour."

This endeavour, when it is toward something which causes it, is called "appetite," or "desire;" the latter being the general name; and the other oftentimes restrained to signify the desire of food, namely "hunger" and "thirst." And when the endeavour is fromward something, it is generally called "aversion." These words, "appetite" and "aversion," we have from the Latins; and they both of them signify the motions, one of approaching, the other of retiring. . . .

That which men desire, they are also said to "love" and to "hate" those things for which they have aversion. So that desire and love are the same thing; save that by desire, we always signify the absence of the object; by love, most commonly the presence of the same. So also by aversion, we signify the absence; and by hate, the presence of the object.

Of appetites and aversions, some are born with men; as appetite of food, appetite of excretion, and exoneration, which may also and more properly be called aversions, from somewhat they feel in their bodies; and some other appetites, not many. The rest, which are appetites of particular things, proceed from experience, and trial of their effects upon themselves or other men. For of things we know not at all, or believe not to be, we can have no further desire, than to taste and try. But aversion we have for things, not only which we know have hurt us, but also that we do not know whether they will hurt us, or not. . . .

But whatsoever is the object of any man's appetite or desire, that is it which he for his part calleth "good:" and the object of his hate and aversion, "evil;" and of his contempt, "vile" and "inconsiderable." For these words of good, evil, and contemptible, are ever used with relation to the person that useth them: there being nothing simply and absolutely so; nor any common rule of good and evil, to be taken from the nature of the objects themselves; but from the person of the man, where there is no commonwealth; or, in a commonwealth, from the person that representeth it; or from an arbitrator or judge, whom men disagreeing shall by consent set up, and make his sentence the rule thereof. . . .

When in the mind of man, appetites, and aversions, hopes, and fears, concerning one and the same thing, arise alternately; and divers good and evil consequences of the doing, or omitting the thing propounded, come successively into our thoughts; so that sometimes we have an appetite to it; sometimes an aversion from it; sometimes hope to be able to do it; sometimes despair, or fear to attempt it; the whole sum of desires, aversions, hopes and fears continued till the thing be either done, or thought impossible, is that we call "deliberation." . . .

In "deliberation," the last appetite, or aversion, immediately adhering to the action, or to the omission thereof, is that we call the "will;" the act, not the faculty of "willing." And beasts that have "deliberation," must necessarily also have "will." The definition of the "will," given commonly by the Schools, that it is a "rational appetite," is not good. For if it were, then could there be no voluntary act against reason. For a "voluntary act" is that, which proceedeth from the "will," and no other. But if instead of a rational appetite, we shall say an appetite resulting from a precedent deliberation, then the definition is the same that I have given here. Will, therefore, is the last appetite in deliberating. And though we say in common discourse, a man had a will once to do a thing, that nevertheless he forbore to do; yet that is properly but an inclination, which makes no action voluntary; because the action depends not of it, but of the last inclination, or appetite. For if the intervenient appetites, make any action voluntary; then by the same reason all intervenient aversions, should make the same action involuntary; and so one and the same action, should be both voluntary and involuntary.

By this it is manifest, that not only actions that have their beginning from covetousness, ambition, lust, or other appetites to the thing propounded; but also those that have their beginning from aversion, or fear of those consequences that follow the omission, are "voluntary actions." . . .

"Continual success" in obtaining those things which a man from time to time desireth, that is to say, continual prospering, is that men call "felicity;" I mean the felicity of this life. For there is no such thing as perpetual tranquillity of mind, while we live here; because life itself is but motion, and can never be without desire, nor without fear, no more than without sense. What kind of felicity God hath ordained to them that devoutly honour Him, a man shall no sooner know, than enjoy; being joys, that now are as incomprehensible, as the word of school-men "beatifical vision" is unintelligible. . . .

"Nature" hath made men so equal, in the faculties of the body, and mind; as that though there be found one man sometimes manifestly stronger in body or of quicker mind than another; yet when all is reckoned together, the difference between man, and man, is not so considerable, as that one man can thereupon claim to himself any benefit, to which another may not pretend, as well as he. For as to the strength of body, the weakest has strength enough to kill the strongest, either by secret machination, or by confederacy with others, that are in the same danger with himself.

And as to the faculties of the mind, setting aside the arts grounded upon words, and especially that skill of proceeding upon general, and infallible rules, called science; which very few have, and but in few things; as being not a native faculty, born with us; nor attained, as prudence, while we look after somewhat else, I find yet a greater equality amongst men, than that of strength. For prudence, is but experience; which equal time, equally bestows on all men, in those things they equally apply themselves unto. . . .

From this equality of ability, ariseth equality of hope in the attaining of our ends. And therefore if any two men desire the same thing, which nevertheless they cannot both enjoy, they become enemies; and in the way to their end, which is principally their own conservation, and sometimes their delectation only, endeavour to destroy, or subdue one another. And from hence it comes to pass, that where an invader hath no more to fear, than another man's single power; if one plant, sow, build, or possess a convenient seat, others may probably be expected to come prepared with forces united, to dispossess, and deprive him, not only of the fruit of his labour, but also of his life, or liberty. And the invader again is in the like danger of another.

And from this diffidence of one another, there is no way for any man to secure himself, so reasonable, as anticipation; that is, by force, or wiles, to master the persons of all men he can, so long, till he see no other power great enough to endanger him: and this is no more than his own conservation requireth, and is generally allowed. . . .

Hereby it is manifest, that during the time men live without a common power to keep them all in awe, they are in that condition which is called war; and such a war, as is of every man, against every man. For "war" consisteth not in battle only, or the act of fighting; but in a tract of time, wherein the will to contend by battle is sufficiently known: and therefore the notion of "time" is to be considered in the nature of war; as it is in the nature of weather. For as the nature of foul weather, lieth not in a shower or two of rain; but in an inclination thereto of many days together: so the nature of war, consisteth not in actual fighting, but in the known disposition thereto, during all the time there is no assurance to the contrary. All other time is "peace."

Whatsoever therefore is consequent to a time of war, where every man is enemy to every man, the same is consequent to the time, wherein men live without other security than what their own strength and their own invention shall furnish them withal. In such condition there is no place for industry, because the fruit thereof is uncertain, and consequently no culture of the earth; no navigation, nor use of the commodities that may be imported by sea; no commodious building; no instruments of moving and removing, such things as require much force; no knowledge of the face of the earth; no account of time; no arts; no letters; no society; and which is worst of all, continual fear, and danger of violent death; and the life of man, solitary, poor, nasty, brutish, and short. . . .

To this war of every man, against every man, this also is consequent; that nothing can be unjust. The notions of right and wrong, justice and injustice, have there no place. Where there is no common power, there is no law: where no law, no injustice. Force and fraud, are in war the two cardinal virtues. Justice and injustice are none of the faculties neither of the body nor mind. If they were, they might be in a man that were alone in the world, as well as his senses, and passions. They are qualities that relate to men in society, not in solitude. It is consequent also to the same condition, that there be no propriety, no dominion, no "mine" and "thine" distinct; but only that to be every man's, that he can get; and for so long, as he can keep it. And thus much for the ill condition, which man by mere nature is actually placed in; though with a possibility to come out of it, consisting partly in the passions, partly in his reason.

The passions that incline men to peace, are fear of death; desire of such things as are necessary to commodious living; and a hope by their industry to obtain them. And reason suggesteth convenient articles of peace, upon which men may be drawn to agreement. . . .

But because covenants of mutual trust, where there is a fear of not performance on either part, . . . are invalid; though the original of justice be the making of covenants; yet injustice actually there can be none, till the cause of such fear be taken away; which while men are in the natural condition of war, cannot be done. Therefore before the names of just and unjust can have place, there must be some coercive power, to compel men equally to the performance of their covenants, by the terror of some punishment, greater than the benefit they expect by the breach of their covenant; and to make good that propriety, which by mutual contract men acquire, in recompense of the universal right they abandon: and such power there is none before the erection of a commonwealth. And this is also to be gathered out of the ordinary definition of justice in the Schools: for they say, that "justice is the constant will of giving to every man his own." And therefore where there is no "own," that is no propriety, there is no injustice; and where there is no coercive power erected, that is, where there is no commonwealth, there is no propriety; all men having right to all things: therefore where there is no commonwealth, there nothing is unjust. So that the nature of justice, consisteth in keeping of valid covenants: but the validity of covenants begins not but with the constitution of a civil power, sufficient to compel men to keep them; and then it is also that propriety begins.

John Locke
(1632–1704)

A Puritan, Locke sided with Parliament in the political upheavals which transformed seventeenth-century England. Locke's father, a member of the landed gentry, was a captain in the parliamentary army and legal clerk to the Justices of Somerset. At twenty, Locke went to Oxford, where he studied botany and earned a bachelor's degree in medicine. At Oxford he met the Earl of Shaftesbury, future Lord Chancellor of England. Locke became an instant celebrity after performing a delicate operation on Shaftesbury, who repaid him with generous financial support and several offers of government appointments. A lifelong academic, Locke declined most of these offers. Banished from Oxford in 1684 on the king's orders, Locke became the central intellectual force behind the bloodless Glorious Revolution of 1688. He spent the remainder of his life in Essex. Through his writing and correspondence, Locke continued to influence English politics, most especially a group of Lockean parliamentarians known simply as "the College."

Essay Concerning Civil Government[*]

To understand political power aright, and derive it from its original, we must consider what estate all men are naturally in, and that is, a state of perfect freedom to order their actions, and dispose of their possessions, and persons as they think fit, within the bounds of the law of Nature, without asking leave, or depending upon the will of any other man.

A state also of equality, wherein all the power and jurisdiction is reciprocal, no one having more than another, there being nothing more evident, than the creatures of the same species and rank promiscuously born to all the same advantages of Nature, and the use of the same faculties, should also be equal one amongst another without subordination or subjection, unless the lord and master of them all, should by any manifest declaration of his will set one above another, and confer on him by an evident and clear appointment an undoubted right to dominion and sovereignty. . . .

But though this be a state of liberty, yet it is not a state of license, though man in

From John Locke, "Essay Concerning Civil Government" in *Two Treatises of Government* (London: Awnsham and J. Churchill, 1698).

that state have an uncontrollable liberty, to dispose of his person or possessions, yet he has not liberty to destroy himself, or so much as any creature in his possession, but where some nobler use, than its bare preservation calls for it. The state of Nature has a law of Nature to govern it which obliges every one, and reason, which is that law, teaches all mankind, who will but consult it; that being all equal and independent, no one ought to harm another in his life, health, liberty or possessions; for men being all the workmanship of one omnipotent, and infinitely wise Maker; all the servants of one sovereign Master, sent into the world by his order and about his business, they are his property, whose workmanship they are, made to last during his, not one another's pleasure. And being furnished with like faculties, sharing all in one community of Nature, there cannot be supposed any such subordination among us, that may authorize us to destroy one another, as if we were made for one anothers uses, as the inferior ranks of creatures are for ours, every one as he is bound to preserve himself, and not to quit his station willfully, so by the like reason when his own preservation comes not in competition, ought he as much as he can to preserve the rest of mankind, and not unless it be to do justice on an offender, take away, or impair the life or what tends to the preservation of life, the liberty, health, limb or goods of another.

And that all men may be restrained from invading others rights, and from doing hurt to one another, and the law of Nature be observed, which willeth the peace and preservation of all mankind, the execution of the law of Nature is in that state, put into every mans hands, whereby every one has a right to punish the transgressors of that law to such a degree, as may hinder its violation. For the law of Nature would as all other laws that concern men in this world be in vain, if there were no body that in the state of Nature, had a power to execute that law, and thereby preserve the innocent and restrain offenders, and if any one in the state of Nature may punish another, for any evil he has done, every one may do so. For in that state of perfect equality, where naturally there is no superiority or jurisdiction of one, over another, what any may do in prosecution of that law, every one must needs have a right to do.

And thus, in the state of Nature, one man comes by a power over another; but yet no absolute or arbitrary power, to use a criminal when he has got him in his hands, according to the passionate heats or boundless extravagancy of his own will, but only to retribute to him, so far as calm reason and conscience dictates, what is proportionate to his transgression, which is so much as may serve for reparation and restraint. For these two are the only reasons why one man may lawfully do harm to another, which is that we call punishment. In transgressing the law of Nature, the offender declares himself to live by another rule, than that of reason and common equity, which is that measure God has set to the actions of men, for their mutual security, and so he becomes dangerous to mankind, the tie, which is to secure them from injury and violence, being slighted and broken by him, which being a trespass against the whole species, and the peace and safety of it, provided for by the law of Nature, every man upon this score, by the right he hath to preserve mankind in general, may restrain, or where it is necessary, destroy things noxious to them, and so may bring such evil on any one, who hath transgressed that law, as may make him repent the doing of it, and thereby deter him, and by his example others, from doing the like mischief. And in this case, and upon this ground, every man hath a right to punish the offender, and be executioner of the law of Nature. . . .

Besides the crime which consists in violating the law, and varying from the right rule of reason, whereby a man so far becomes degenerate, and declares himself to quit the principles of human nature, and to be a noxious creature, there is commonly injury done, and some person or other, some other man, receives damage by his transgression, in which case he who hath received any damage, has besides the right of punishment common to him with other men, a particular right to seek reparation from him that hath done it. And any other person who finds it just, may also join with him that is injured, and assist him in recovering from the offender, so much as may make satisfaction for the harm he hath suffered. . . .

To this strange doctrine, *viz.* That in the state of Nature every one has the executive power of the law of Nature, I doubt not but it will be objected, that it is unreasonable for men to be judges in their own cases, that self-love will make men partial to themselves and their friends. And on the other side, ill nature, passion and revenge will carry them too far in punishing others. And hence nothing but confusion and disorder will follow, and that therefore God hath certainly appointed government to restrain the partiality and violence of men. I easily grant, that civil government is the proper remedy for the inconveniences of the state of Nature, which must certainly be great, where men may be judges in their own case, since 'tis easy to be imagined, that he who was so unjust as to do his brother an injury, will scarce be so just as to condemn himself for it: But I shall desire those who make this objection, to remember that absolute monarchs are but men, and if government is to be the remedy of those evils, which necessarily follow from men being judges in their own cases, and the state of Nature is therefore not to be endured, I desire to know what kind of government that is, and how much better it is than the state of Nature, where one man commanding a multitude, has the liberty to be judge in his own case, and may do to all his subjects whatever he pleases, without the least question or controle of those who execute his pleasure? And in whatsoever he doth, whether led by reason, mistake or passion, must be submitted to? Which men in the state of Nature are not bound to do one to another. And if he that judges, judges amiss in his own, or any other case, he is answerable for it to the rest of mankind. . . .

To those that say, there were never any men in the state of Nature; I will not only oppose the authority of the judicious *Hooker*, (*Eccl. Pol. Lib.I.Sect.10*) where he says, *the laws which have been hitherto mentioned*, i.e. the laws of Nature, *to bind men absolutely, even as they are men, although they have never any settled fellowship, never any solemn agreement amongst themselves what to do or not to do, but for as much as we are not by our selves sufficient to furnish our selves with competent store of things, needful for such a life, as our Nature doth desire, a life, fit for the dignity of man; therefore to supply those defects and imperfections which are in us, as living single and solely by our selves, we are naturally induced to seek communion and fellowship with others, this was the cause of mens uniting themselves, at first in politick societies.* But I moreover affirm, that all men are naturally in that state, and remain so till by their own consents they make themselves members of some politick society. . . .

David Hume
(1711–1776)

Hume was born in Edinburgh, Scotland. His father was related to the Earl of Hume and his mother was the daughter of Sir David Falconer, president of the College of Justice. His family wanted him to pursue a legal career, but Hume's own interests lay in literature, philosophy, and history. His first major work, *A Treatise on Human Nature*, appeared in 1739. Contrary to Hume's own expectations, however, the book—and his "new" philosophical method and ideas—was hardly noticed. Bitterly disappointed, Hume spent the next several years traveling and finding employment as a tutor and as secretary to several government missions. Appointed librarian to the Faculty of Advocates at Edinburgh in 1752, Hume began composing his histories of England. He also held a number of government appointments, including chargé d'affaires to the French embassy and undersecretary of state in the Foreign Office.

Enquiry Concerning the Principles of Morals*

DISPUTES with men, pertinaciously obstinate in their principles, are, of all others, the most irksome; except, perhaps, those with persons, entirely disingenuous, who really do not believe the opinions they defend, but engage in the controversy, from affectation, from a spirit of opposition, or from a desire of showing wit and ingenuity, superior to the rest of mankind. The same blind adherence to their own arguments is to be expected in both; the same contempt of their antagonists; and the same passionate vehemence, in inforcing sophistry and falsehood. And as reasoning is not the source, whence either disputant derives his tenets; it is in vain to expect, that any logic, which speaks not to the affections, will ever engage him to embrace sounder principles.

Those who have denied the reality of moral distinctions, may be ranked among the disingenuous disputants; nor is it conceivable, that any human creature could ever seriously believe, that all characters and actions were alike entitled to the affection and regard of every one. The difference, which nature has placed between one man and another, is so wide, and this difference is still so much farther widened,

From David Hume, "Enquiry Concerning the Principles of Morals" in *Essays and Treatises on Several Subjects*, vol. II (London: T. Cadell, A. Donaldson and W. Creech, 1777).

by education, example, and habit, that, where the opposite extremes come at once under our apprehension, there is no scepticism so scrupulous, and scarce any assurance so determined, as absolutely to deny all distinction between them. Let a man's insensibility be ever so great, he must often be touched with the images of Right and Wrong; and let his prejudices be ever so obstinate, he must observe, that others are susceptible of like impressions. The only way, therefore, of converting an antagonist of this kind, is to leave him to himself. For, finding that nobody keeps up the controversy with him, it is probable he will, at last, of himself, from mere weariness, come over to the side of common sense and reason.

There has been a controversy started of late, much better worth examination, concerning the general foundation of MORALS; whether they be derived from REASON, or from SENTIMENT; whether we attain the knowledge of them by a chain of argument and induction, or by an immediate feeling and finer internal sense; whether, like all sound judgement of truth and falsehood, they should be the same to every rational intelligent being; or whether, like the perception of beauty and deformity, they be founded entirely on the particular fabric and constitution of the human species. . . .

It must be acknowledged, that both sides of the question are susceptible of specious arguments. Moral distinctions, it may be said, are discernible by pure *reason*: Else, whence the many disputes that reign in common life, as well as in philosophy, with regard to this subject: The long chain of proofs often produced on both sides; the examples cited, the authorities appealed to, the analogies employed, the fallacies detected, the inferences drawn, and the several conclusions adjusted to their proper principles. Truth is disputable; not taste: What exists in the nature of things is the standard of our judgement; what each man feels within himself is the standard of sentiment. Propositions in geometry may be proved, systems in physics may be controverted; but the harmony of verse, the tenderness of passion, the brilliancy of wit, must give immediate pleasure. No man reasons concerning another's beauty; but frequently concerning the justice or injustice of his actions. In every criminal trial the first object of the prisoner is to disprove the facts alleged, and deny the actions imputed to him: The second to prove, that, even if these actions were real, they might be justified, as innocent and lawful. It is confessedly by deduction of the understanding, that the first point is ascertained: How can we suppose that a different faculty of the mind is employed in fixing the other?

On the other hand, those who would resolve all moral determinations into *sentiment*, may endeavour to show, that it is impossible for reason ever to draw conclusions of this nature. To virtue, say they, it belongs to be *amiable*, and vice *odious*. This forms their very nature or essence. But can reason or argumentation distribute these different epithets to any subjects, and pronounce before-hand, that this must produce love, and that hatred? Or what other reason can we ever assign for these affections, but the original fabric and formation of the human mind, which is naturally adapted to receive them?

The end of all moral speculations is to teach us our duty; and, by proper representations of the deformity of vice and beauty of virtue, beget correspondent habits, and engage us to avoid the one, and embrace the other. But is this ever to be expected from inferences and conclusions of the understanding, which of themselves have no hold of the affections, or set in motion the active powers of men? They discover truths: But where the truths which they discover are indifferent, and beget no desire or aversion, they can have no influence on conduct and behaviour. What is honourable, what is fair, what is becoming, what is noble, what is generous, takes possession of the heart, and animates us to embrace and maintain it. What is intelligible, what is evident, what is probable, what is true, procures only the cool assent of the understanding; and gratifying a speculative curiosity, puts an end to our researches.

Extinguish all the warm feelings and prepossessions in favour of virtue, and all disgust or aversion to vice: Render men totally indifferent towards these distinctions; and morality is no longer a practical study, nor has any tendency to regulate our lives and actions.

These arguments on each side (and many more might be produced) are so plausible, that I am apt to suspect, they may, the one as well as the other, be solid and satisfactory, and that *reason* and *sentiment* concur in almost all moral determinations and conclusions. . . .

If the foregoing hypothesis be received, it will now be easy for us to determine the question first started, concerning the general principles of morals; and though we postponed the decision of that question, lest it should then involve us in intricate speculations, which are unfit for moral discourses, we may resume it at present, and examine how far either *reason* or *sentiment* enters into all decisions of praise or censure.

One principal foundation of moral praise being supposed to lie in the usefulness of any quality or action, it is evident, that *reason* must enter for a considerable share in all decisions of this kind; since nothing but that faculty can instruct us in the tendency of qualities and actions, and point out their beneficial consequences to society and to their possessor. In many cases, this is an affair liable to great controversy: Doubts may arise; opposite interests may occur; and a preference must be given to one side, from very nice views, and a small overbalance of utility. This is particularly remarkable in questions with regard to justice; as is, indeed, natural to suppose, from that species of utility, which attends this virtue. Were every single instance of justice, like that of benevolence, useful to society; this would be a more simple state of the case, and seldom liable to great controversy. But as single instances of justice are often pernicious in their first and immediate tendency, and as the advantage to society results only from the observance of the general rule, and from the concurrence and combination of several persons in the same equitable conduct; the case here becomes more intricate and involved. The various circumstances of society; the various consequences of any practice; the various interests which may be proposed; These, on many occasions, are doubtful, and subject to great discussion and enquiry. The object of municipal laws is to fix all the questions with regard to justice: The debates of civilians; the reflections of politicians; the precedents of history and public records, are all directed to the same purpose. And a very accurate *reason* or *judgement* is often requisite, to give the true determination, amidst such intricate doubts arising from obscure or opposite utilities.

But though reason, when fully assisted and improved, be sufficient to instruct us in the pernicious or useful tendency of qualities and action; it is not alone sufficient to produce any moral blame or approbation. Utility is only a tendency to a certain end; and were the end totally indifferent to us, we should feel the same indifference towards the means. It is requisite a *sentiment* should here display itself, in order to give a preference to the useful above the pernicious tendencies. This sentiment can be no other than a feeling for the happiness of mankind, and a resentment of their misery; since these are the different ends which virtue and vice have a tendency to promote. Here, therefore, *reason* instructs us in the several tendencies of actions, and *humanity* makes a distinction in favour of those which are useful and beneficial. . . .

Examine the crime of *ingratitude*, for instance; which has place, wherever we observe good-will, expressed and known, together with good-offices performed, on the one side, and a return of ill-will or indifference, with ill-offices or neglect on the other: Anatomize all these circumstances, and examine, by your reason alone, in what consists the demerit or blame. You never will come to any issue or conclusion. Reason judges either of *matter of fact* or of *relations*. Enquire then, *first*, where is that matter of fact, which we here call *crime*; point it out; determine the time of its existence; describe its essence or nature; explain the sense or faculty, to which it discovers itself. It resides in the mind of the person, who is ungrateful. He must, therefore, feel it, and be conscious of it. But nothing is there, except the passion of ill-will or absolute indifference. You cannot say, that these, of themselves, always, and in all circumstances, are crimes. No: they are only crimes, when directed towards persons, who have before expressed and displayed good-will towards us. Consequently, we may infer, that the crime of ingratitude is not any particular individual *fact*; but arises from a complication of circumstances, which, being presented to the spectator, excites the *sentiment* of blame, by the particular structure and fabric of his mind. . . .

The hypothesis which we embrace is plain. It maintains, that morality is determined by sentiment. It defines virtue to be *whatever mental action or quality gives to a spectator the pleasing sentiment of approbation;* and vice the contrary. We then proceed to examine a plain matter of fact, to wit, what actions have this influence. We consider all the circumstances, in which these actions agree: And thence endeavour to extract some general observations with regard to these sentiments. If you call this metaphysics, and find any thing abstruse here, you need only conclude, that your turn of mind is not suited to the moral sciences.

When a man, at any time, deliberates concerning his own conduct (as, whether he had better, in a particular emergence, assist a brother or a benefactor), he must consider these separate relations, with all the circumstances and situations of the persons, in order to determine the superior duty and obligation: And in order to determine the proportion of lines in any triangle, it is necessary to examine the nature of that figure, and the relations which its several parts bear to each other. But notwithstanding this appearing similarity in the two cases, there is, at bottom, an extreme difference between them. A speculative reasoner concerning triangles or circles considers the several known and given relations of the parts of these figures; and thence infers some unknown relation, which is dependent on the former. But in moral deliberations, we must be acquainted, before-hand, with all the objects, and all their relations to each other; and from a comparison of the whole, fix our choice or approbation. No new fact to be ascertained: No new relation to be discovered. All the circumstances of the case are supposed to be laid before us, ere we can fix any sentence of blame or approbation. If any material circumstance be yet unknown or doubtful, we must first employ our enquiry or intellectual faculties to assure us of it; and must suspend for a time all moral decision or sentiment. While we are ignorant, whether a man were aggressor or not, how can we determine whether the person who killed him, be criminal or innocent? But after every circumstance, every relation is known, the understanding has no farther room to operate, nor any object on which it could employ itself. The approbation or blame, which then ensues, cannot be the work of the judgement, but of the heart; and is not a speculative proposition or affirmation, but an active feeling or sentiment. In the disquisitions of the understanding, from known circumstances and relations, we infer some new and unknown. In moral decisions, all the circumstances and relations must be previously known; and the mind, from the contemplation of the whole, feels some new impression of affection or disgust, esteem or contempt, approbation or blame. . . .

It appears evident, that the ultimate ends of human actions can never, in any case, be accounted for by *reason*, but recommend themselves entirely to the sentiments and affection of mankind, without any dependence on the intellectual faculties. Ask a man, *why he uses exercise*; he will answer, *because he desires to keep his health*. If you then enquire, *why he desires health*, he will readily reply, *because sickness is painful*. If you push your enquiries farther, and desire a reason, *why he hates pain*, it is impossible he can ever give any. This is an ultimate end, and is never referred to any other object.

Perhaps, to your second question, *why he desires health*, he may also reply, that *it is necessary for the exercise of his calling*. If you ask, *why he is anxious on that head*, he will answer, *because he desires to get money*. If you demand *Why? It is the instrument of pleasure*, says he. And beyond this it is an absurdity to ask for a reason. It is impossible there can be a progress *in infinitum*; and that one thing can always be a reason, why another is desired. Something must be desirable on its own account, and because of its immediate accord or agreement with human sentiment and affection.

Now as virtue is an end, and is desirable on its own account, without fee and reward, merely, for the immediate satisfaction which it conveys; it is requisite that there should be some sentiment, which it touches; some internal taste or feeling, or whatever you may please to call it, which distinguishes moral good and evil, and which embraces the one and rejects the other.

Thus the distinct boundaries and offices of *reason* and of *taste* are easily ascertained. The former conveys the knowledge of truth and falsehood: The latter gives the sentiment of beauty and deformity, vice and virtue. The one discovers objects, as they really stand in nature, without addition or diminution: The other has a productive faculty, and gilding or staining all natural objects with the colours, borrowed from internal sentiment, raises, in a manner, a new creation. Reason, being cool and disengaged, is not motive to action, and directs only the impulse received from appetite or inclination, by showing us the means of attaining happiness or avoiding misery: Taste, as it gives pleasure or pain, and thereby constitutes happiness or misery, becomes a motive to action, and is the first spring or impulse to desire and volition. From circumstances and relations, known or supposed, the former leads us to the discovery of the concealed and unknown: After all circumstances and relations are laid before us, the latter makes us feel from the whole a new sentiment of blame or approbation. The standard of the one, being founded on the nature of things, is eternal and inflexible, even by the will of the Supreme Being: The standard of the other, arising from the internal frame and constitution of animals, is ultimately derived from that Supreme Will, which bestowed on each being its peculiar nature, and arranged the several classes and orders of existence. . . .

IT may be esteemed, perhaps, a superfluous task to prove, that the benevolent or softer affections are ESTIMABLE; and wherever they appear, engage the approbation, and good-will of mankind. The epithets *sociable, good-natured, humane, merciful, grateful, friendly, generous, beneficent,* or their equivalents, are known in all languages, and universally express the highest merit, which *human nature* is capable of attaining. Where these amiable qualities are attended with birth and power and eminent abilities, and display themselves in the good government or useful instruction of mankind, they seem even to raise the possessors of them above the rank of *human nature*, and make them approach in some measure to the divine. Exalted capacity, undaunted courage, prosperous success; these may only expose a hero or politician to the envy and ill-will of the public: But as soon as the praises are added of humane and beneficent; when instances are displayed of lenity, tenderness, or friendship; envy itself is silent, or joins the general voice of approbation and applause. . . .

But I forget, that it is not my present business to recommend generosity and benevolence, or to paint, in their true colours, all the genuine charms of the social virtues. These, indeed, sufficiently engage every heart, on the first apprehension of them; and it is difficult to abstain from some sally of panegyric, as often as they occur in discourse or reasoning. But our object here being more the speculative, than the practical part of morals, it will suffice to remark, (what will readily, I believe, be allowed) that no qualities are more intitled to the general good-will and approbation of mankind than beneficence and humanity, friendship and gratitude, natural affection and public spirit, or whatever proceeds from a tender sympathy with others, and a generous concern for our kind and species. These, wherever they appear, seem to transfuse themselves, in a manner, into each beholder, and to call forth, in their own behalf, the same favourable and affectionate sentiments, which they exert on all around.

We may observe, that, in displaying the praises of any humane, beneficent man, there is one circumstance which never fails to be amply insisted on, namely, the happiness and satisfaction, derived to society from his intercourse and good offices. To his parents, we are apt to say, he endears himself by his pious attachment and duteous care, still more than by the connexions of nature. His children never feel his authority, but when employed for their advantage. With him, the ties of love are consolidated by beneficence and friendship. The ties of friendship approach, in a fond observance of each obliging office, to those of love and inclination. His domestics and dependants have in him a secure resource; and no longer dread the power of fortune, but so far as she exercises it over him. From him the hungry receive food, the naked cloathing, the ignorant and slothful skill and industry. Like the sun, an inferior minister of providence, he cheers, invigorates, and sustains the surrounding world.

If confined to private life, the sphere of his activity is narrower; but his influence is all benign and gentle. If exalted into a higher station, mankind and prosterity reap the fruit of his labours.

As these topics of praise never fail to be employed, and with success, where we would inspire esteem for any one; may it not thence be concluded, that the UTILITY, resulting from the social virtues, forms, at least, a *part* of their merit, and is one source of that approbation and regard so universally paid to them?

When we recommend even an animal or a plant as *useful* and *beneficial,* we give it an applause and recommendation suited to its nature. As, on the other hand, reflection on the baneful influence of any of these inferior beings always inspires us with the sentiment of aversion. The eye is pleased with the prospect of corn-fields and loaded vineyards; horses grazing, and flocks pasturing: But flies the view of briars and brambles, affording shelter to wolves and serpents.

A machine, a piece of furniture, a vestment, a house well contrived for use and convenience, is so far beautiful, and is contemplated with pleasure and approbation. An experienced eye is here sensible to many excellencies, which escape persons ignorant and uninstructed.

Can any thing stronger be said in praise of a profession, such as merchandize or manufacture, than to observe the advantages which it procures to society? And is not a monk and inquisitor enraged when we treat his order as useless or pernicious to mankind?

The historian exults in displaying the benefit arising from his labours. The writer of romance alleviates or denies the bad consequences ascribed to his manner of composition.

In general, what praise is implied in the simple epithet *useful*! What reproach in the contrary! . . .

In all determinations of morality, this circumstance of public utility is ever principally in view; and wherever disputes arise, either in philosophy or common life, concerning the bounds of duty, the question cannot, by any means, be decided with greater certainty, than by ascertaining, on any side, the true interests of mankind. If any false opinion, embraced from appearances, has been found to prevail; as soon as farther experience and sounder reasoning have given us juster notions of human affairs; we retract our first sentiment, and adjust anew the boundaries of moral good and evil.

Giving alms to common beggars is naturally praised; because it seems to carry relief to the distressed and indigent: But when we observe the encouragement thence arising to idleness and debauchery, we regard that species of charity rather as a weakness than a virtue. . . .

Upon the whole, then, it seems undeniable, *that* nothing can bestow more merit on any human creature than the sentiment of benevolence in an eminent degree; and *that* a *part*, at least, of its merit arises from its tendency to promote the interests of our species, and bestow happiness on human society. We carry our view into the salutary consequences of such a character and disposition; and whatever has so benign an influence, and forwards so desirable an end, is beheld with complacency and pleasure. The social virtues are never regarded without their beneficial tendencies, nor viewed as barren and unfruitful. The happiness of mankind, the order of society, the harmony of families, the mutual support of friends, are always considered as the result of their gentle dominion over the breasts of men. . . .

The social virtues must, therefore, be allowed to have a natural beauty and amiableness, which, at first, antecedent to all precept or education, recommends them to the esteem of uninstructed mankind, and engages their affections. And as the public utility of these virtues is the chief circumstance, whence they derive their merit, it follows, that the end, which they have a tendency to promote, must be some way agreeable to us, and take hold of some natural affection. It must please, either from considerations of self-interest, or from more generous motives and regards.

It has often been asserted, that, as every man has a strong connexion with society, and perceives the impossibility of his solitary subsistence, he becomes, on that account, favourable to all those habits or principles, which promote order in society, and insure to him the quiet possession of so inestimable a blessing. As much as we value our own happiness and welfare, as much must we applaud the practice of justice and humanity, by which alone the social confederacy can be maintained, and every man reap the fruits of mutual protection and assistance. . . .

Usefulness is agreeable, and engages our approbation. This is a matter of fact, confirmed by daily observation. But, *useful?* For what? For some body's interest, surely. Whose interest then? Not our own only: For our approbation frequently extends farther. It must, therefore, be the interest of those, who are served by the character or action approved of; and these we may conclude, however remote, are not totally indifferent to us. . . .

[W]e must renounce the theory, which accounts for every moral sentiment by the principle of self-love. We must adopt a more public affection, and allow, that the interests of society are not, even on their own account, entirely indifferent to us. Usefulness is only a tendency to a certain end; and it is a contradiction in terms, that any thing pleases as means to an end, where the end itself no wise affects us. If usefulness, therefore, be a source of moral sentiment, and if this usefulness be not always considered with a reference to self; it follows, that every thing, which contributes to the happiness of society, recommends itself directly to our approbation and good-will. Here is a principle, which accounts, in great part, for the origin of morality: And what need we seek for abstruse and remote systems, when there occurs one so obvious and natural?

Have we any difficulty to comprehend the force of humanity and benevolence? Or to conceive, that the very aspect of happiness, joy, prosperity, gives pleasure; that of pain, suffering, sorrow, communicates uneasiness? The human countenance, says HORACE, borrows smiles or tears from the human countenance. Reduce a person to solitude, and he loses all enjoyment, except either of the sensual or speculative kind; and that because the movements of his heart are not forwarded by correspondent movements in his fellow-creatures. The signs of sorrow and mourning, though arbitrary, affect us with melancholy; but the natural symptoms, tears and cries and groans, never fail to infuse compassion and uneasiness. And if the effects of misery touch us in so lively a manner; can we be supposed altogether insensible or indifferent towards its causes; when a malicious or treacherous character and behaviour are presented to us? . . .

THAT JUSTICE is useful to society, and consequently that *part* of its merit, at least, must arise from that consideration, it would be a superfluous undertaking to prove. That public utility is the *sole* origin of justice, and that reflections on the beneficial consequences of this virtue are the *sole* foundation of its merit; this proposition, being more curious and important, will better deserve our examination and enquiry.

Let us suppose, that nature has bestowed on the human race such profuse *abundance* of all *external* conveniences, that, without any uncertainty in the event, without any care or industry on our part, every individual finds himself fully provided with whatever his most voracious appetites can want, or luxurious imagination wish or desire. His natural beauty, we shall suppose, surpasses all acquired ornaments: The perpetual clemency of the seasons renders useless all cloaths or covering: The raw herbage affords him the most delicious fare; the clear fountain, the richest beverage. No laborious occupation required: No tillage: No navigation. Music, poetry, and contemplation form his sole business: Conversation, mirth, and friendship his sole amusement.

It seems evident, that, in such a happy state, every other social virtue would flourish, and receive tenfold encrease; but the cautious, jealous virtue of justice would never once have been dreamed of. For what purpose make a partition of goods, where every one has already more than enough? Why give rise to property, where there cannot possibly by any injury? Why call this object *mine*, when, upon the seizing of it by another, I need but stretch out my hand to possess myself of what is equally valuable? Justice, in that case, being totally USELESS, would be an idle ceremonial, and could never possibly have place in the catalogue of virtues.

We see, even in the present necessitous condition of mankind, that, wherever any benefit is bestowed by nature in an unlimited abundance, we leave it always in common among the whole human race, and make no subdivisions of right and property. Water and air, though the most necessary of all objects, are not challenged as the property of individuals; nor can any man commit injustice by the most lavish use and enjoyment of these blessings. In fertile extensive countries, with few inhabitants, land is regarded on the same footing. And no topic is so much insisted on by those, who defend the liberty of the seas, as the unexhausted use of them in navigation. Were the advantages, procured by navigation, as inexhaustible, these reasoners had never had any adversaries to refute; nor had any claims ever been advanced of a separate, exclusive dominion over the ocean. . . .

To make this truth more evident, let us reverse the foregoing suppositions; and carrying every thing to the opposite extreme, consider what would be the effect of these new situations. Suppose a society to fall into such want of all common necessaries, that the utmost frugality and industry cannot preserve the greater number from perishing, and the whole from extreme misery: It will readily, I believe, be admitted, that the strict laws of justice are suspended, in such a pressing emergence, and give place to the stronger motives of necessity and self-preservation. Is it any crime, after a shipwreck, to seize whatever means or instrument of safety one can lay hold of, without regard to former limitations of property? Or if a city besieged were perishing with hunger; can we imagine, that men will see any means of preservation before them, and lose their lives, from a scrupulous regard to what, in other situations, would be the rules of equity and justice? The USE and TENDENCY of that virtue is to procure happiness and security, by preserving order in society: But where the society is ready to perish from extreme necessity, no greater evil can be dreaded from violence and injustice; and every man may now provide for himself by all the means, which prudence can dictate, or humanity permit. The public, even in less urgent necessities, opens granaries, without the consent of proprietors; as justly supposing, that the authority of magistracy may, consistent with equity, extend so far: But were any number of men to assemble, without the type of laws or civil jurisdiction; would an equal partition of bread in a famine, though effected by power and even violence, be regarded as criminal or injurious? . . .

When any man, even in political society, renders himself, by his crimes, obnoxious to the public, he is punished by the laws in his goods and person; that is, the ordinary rules of justice are, with regard to him suspended for a moment, and it becomes equitable to inflict on him, for the *benefit* of society, what, otherwise, he could not suffer without wrong or injury.

The rage and violence of public war; what is it but a suspension of justice among the warring parties, who perceive, that this virtue is now no longer of any *use* or advantage to them? The laws of war, which then succeed to those of equity and justice, are rules calculated for the *advantage* and *utility* of that particular state, in which men are now placed. And were a civilized nation engaged with barbarians, who observed no rules even of war; the former must also suspend their observance of them, where they no longer serve to any purpose; and must render every action or recounter as bloody and pernicious as possible to the first aggressors.

Thus, the rules of equity or justice depend entirely on the particular state and condition, in which men are placed, and owe their origin and existence to that UTILITY, which results to the public from their strict and regular observance. Reserve, in any considerable circumstance, the condition of men: Produce extreme abundance or extreme necessity: Implant in the human breast perfect moderation and humanity, or perfect rapaciousness and malice: By rendering justice totally *useless*, you thereby totally destroy its essence, and suspend its obligation upon mankind.

The common situation of society is a medium amidst all these extremes. We are naturally partial to ourselves, and to our friends; but are capable of learning the advantage resulting from a more equitable conduct. Few enjoyments are given us from the open and liberal hand of nature; but by art, labour, and industry, we can extract them in great abundance. Hence the ideas of property become necessary in all civil society: Hence justice derives its usefulness to the public: And hence alone arises its merit and moral obligation.

Immanuel Kant
(1724–1804)

Kant was born in Konigsberg, East Prussia, where he remained his entire life. His family, Scotch by descent, were Pietists—a Protestant sect which emphasized the importance of virtuous conduct over theological orthodoxy. Kant enrolled in the University of Konigsberg at sixteen and, after completing his studies, tutored for several aristocratic families in the area. In 1755 he became an unsalaried instructor at the university. In 1770 Kant was appointed Professor of Logic and Metaphysics at Konigsberg, a position he held until his death in 1804. Despite not fitting the mold of the well-traveled European academic, Kant was exceptionally well-read and kept up with the latest developments in science, historiography, and philosophy. His work habits and "time management" were legendary. It was said that the citizens of Konigsberg could set their watches as Kant passed by on his daily constitutionals through the town. Yet he was anything but rigid or authoritarian with his students, who found him cheerful, compassionate, witty, and nondogmatic.

Metaphysical Foundations of Morals*

NOTHING CAN POSSIBLY BE CONCEIVED IN THE WORLD, OR even out of it, which can be called good without qualification, except a GOOD WILL. Intelligence, wit, judgment, and the other *talents* of the mind, however they may be named, or courage, resolution, perseverance, as qualities of temperament, are undoubtedly good and desirable in many respects. But these gifts of nature may also become extremely bad and mischievous if the will which is to make use of these gifts, and which therefore constitutes what is called *character*, is not good. It is the same with the *gifts of fortune.* Power, riches, honor, even health, and the general well-being and contentment with one's condition which is called *happiness*, all inspire pride and often presumption if there is not a good will to correct the influence of these on the mind, and with this to rectify also the whole principle of acting and adapt it to its end. The sight of a being, not adorned with a single feature of a pure and good will, enjoying unbroken prosperity can never give pleasure to an impartial rational spectator. Thus a good will appears to constitute the indispensable condition for being even worthy of happiness.

Indeed, quite a few qualities are of service to this good will itself and may facilitate its action, yet have no intrinsic, unconditional value, but are always presupposing a good will; this qualifies the esteem that we justly have for these qualities and does not permit us to regard them as absolutely good. Moderation in the affections and passions, self-control and calm deliberation are not only good in many respects, but even seem to constitute part of the intrinsic worth of a person; but they are far from deserving to be called good without qualification, although they have been so unconditionally praised by the ancients. For without the principles of a good will, these qualities may become extremely bad. The coolness of a villain not only makes him far more dangerous, but also immediately makes him more abominable in our eyes than he would have been without it.

A good will is good not because of what it performs or effects, nor by its aptness for attaining some proposed end, but simply by virtue of the volition; that is, it is good in itself and when considered by itself is to be esteemed much higher than all that it can bring about in pursuing any inclination, nay even in pursuing the sum total of all inclinations. It might happen that, owing to special misfortune, or to the niggardly provision of a step-motherly nature, this will should wholly lack power to accomplish its purpose. If with its greatest efforts this will should yet achieve nothing and there should remain only good will (to be sure, not a mere wish but the summoning of all means in our power), then, like a jewel, good will would still shine by its own light as a thing having its whole value in itself. Its usefulness or fruitlessness can neither add to nor detract anything from this value. It would be, as it were, only the setting to enable us to handle it the more conveniently in common commerce and to attract to it the attention of those who are not yet experts, but not to recommend it to true experts or to determine its value. . . .

Everything in nature works according to laws. Rational beings alone have the faculty for acting according *to the concept* of laws; that is, according to principles. [In other words, rational beings alone] have a will. Since deriving actions from principles requires *reason*, the will is nothing more than practical reason. If reason infallibly determines the will, then the actions of such a being that are recognized as objectively necessary are also subjectively necessary. The will is a faculty for choosing *only that* which reason, independently of inclination, recognizes as practically necessary; that is, as good. But if reason does not sufficiently determine the will by itself, if the latter is also subject to the subjective conditioning of particular impulses which do not always coincide with the objective conditions; in a word, if the will *in itself* does not completely accord with reason, as is actually the case with men, then the actions which are objectively recognized as necessary are subjectively contingent. Determining such a will according to objective laws is compulsory (*Notigung*). This means that the relation of objective laws to a will not thoroughly good is conceived as the determination of the will of a rational being by principles of reason which the will, because of its nature, does not necessarily follow.

The concept of an objective principle, in so far as it is compulsory for a will, is called a command of reason and the formulation of such a command is called an IMPERATIVE.

All imperatives are expressed by the word *ought* (or *shall*) and are indicating thereby the relation of an objective law of reason to a will, which, because of its subjective constitution, is not necessarily determined by this [compulsion]. Such imperatives may state that something would be good to do or to forbear from doing, but they are addressing themselves to a will which does not always do a thing merely because that thing is represented as good to do. The practically *good* determines the will by means of the concepts of reason, and consequently from objective, not subjective causes; that is, [it determines them] on principles which are valid for every rational being as such. The practically good is distinguishable from the *pleasant* which influences the will only by means of sensations from subjective causes and which is valid only for the particular sense of this or that man and is not a principle of reason holding true for everyone.

Therefore a perfectly good will would be equally subject to objective laws of good [action], but could not be conceived thereby as *compelled* to act lawfully by itself. Because of its subjective constitution it can only be determined by the concept of the good. Consequently no imperatives hold true for the Divine will, or in general for a *holy* will. *Ought* is out of place here because the act of willing is already necessarily in unison with the law. Therefore imperatives are only formulations for expressing the relation of the objective laws of all volition to the subjective imperfections of the will of this or that rational being; that is, the human will.

All *imperatives* command either *hypothetically* or *categorically*. . . . Since every practical law represents a possible action as good, and on this account as necessary for a subject who can determine practically by reason, all imperatives are formulations determining an action which is necessary according to the principle of a will in some respects good. If the action is good only as a means *to something else*, then the imperative is *hypothetical*. If the action is conceived as good *in itself* and consequently as necessarily being the principle of a will which of itself conforms to reason then it is *categorical*. . . .

When I conceive of a hypothetical imperative at all, I do not know previously what it will contain until I am given the condition. But when I conceive of a categorical imperative I know at once what it contains. In addition to the law, the imperative contains only the necessity that the maxim conform to this law. As the maxim contains no condition restricting the maxim, nothing remains but the general statement of the law to which the maxim of the action should conform, and it is only this conformity that the imperative properly represents as necessary.

Therefore there is only one categorical imperative, namely this: *Act only on a maxim by which you can will that it, at the same time, should become a general law.*

Now, if all imperatives of duty can be deduced from this one imperative as easily as from their principle, then we shall be able at least to show what we understand by it and what this concept means, although it would remain undecided whether what is called duty is not just a vain notion.

Since the universality of the law constitutes what is properly called *nature* in the most general sense [as to form]; that is, the existence of things as far as determined by general laws, the general imperative duty may be expressed thus: *Act as if the maxim of your action were to become by your will a general law of nature.*

We will now enumerate a few duties, adopting the usual division of duties to ourselves and to others, and of perfect and imperfect duties.

1. A man, while reduced to despair by a series of misfortunes and feeling wearied of life, is still so far in possession of his reason that he can ask himself whether it would not be contrary to his duty to himself to take his own life. Now he

inquires whether the maxim of his action could become a general law of nature. His maxim is: Out of self-love I consider it a principle to shorten my life when continuing it is likely to bring more misfortune than satisfaction. The question then simply is whether this principle of self-love could become a general law of nature. Now we see at once that a system of nature, whose law would be to destroy life by the very feeling designed to compel the maintenance of life, would contradict itself, and therefore could not exist as a system of nature; hence that maxim cannot possibly be a general law of nature and consequently it would be wholly inconsistent with the supreme principle of all duty.

2. Another man finds himself forced by dire need to borrow money. He knows that he will not be able to repay it, but he also sees that nothing will be lent him unless he promises firmly to repay it within a definite time. He would like to make this promise but he still has enough conscience to ask himself: Is it not unlawful and contrary to my duty to get out of a difficulty in this way? However, suppose that he does decide to do so, the maxim of his action would then be expressed thus: When I consider myself in want of money, I shall borrow money and promise to repay it although I know that I never can. Now this principle of self-love or of one's own advantage may perhaps be agreeable to my whole future well-being; but the question is now: Is it right? Here I change the suggestion of self-love into a general law and state the question thus: How would it be if my maxim were a general law? I then realize at once that it could never hold as a general law of nature but would necessarily contradict itself. For if it were a general law that anyone considering himself to be in difficulties would be able to promise whatever he pleases intending not to keep his promise, the promise itself and its object would become impossible since no one would believe that anything was promised him, but would ridicule all such statements as vain pretenses.

3. A third man finds in himself a talent which with the help of some education might make him a useful man in many respects. But he finds himself in comfortable circumstances, and prefers to indulge in pleasure rather than to take pains in developing and improving his fortunate natural capacities. He asks, however, whether his maxim of neglecting his natural gifts, besides agreeing with his inclination toward indulgence, agrees also with what is called duty. He sees then that nature could indeed subsist according to such a general law, though men (like the South Sea Islanders) let their talents rust and devote their lives merely to idleness, amusement, and the propagation of their species, in a word, to enjoyment. But he cannot possibly *will* that this should be a general law of nature or be implanted in us as such by an instinct of nature. For, as a rational being, he necessarily wills that his faculties be developed, since they have been given to serve him for all sorts of possible purposes.

4. A fourth, prosperous man, while seeing others whom he could help having to struggle with great hardship thinks: What concern is it of mine? Let everyone be as happy as heaven pleases or as he can make himself. I will take nothing from him nor even envy him, but I do not wish either to contribute anything to his welfare or assist him in his distress. There is no doubt that if such a way of thinking were a general law, society might get along very well and doubtless even better than if everyone were to talk of sympathy and good will or even endeavor occasionally to put it into practice, but then [were to] cheat when one could and so betray the rights of man or otherwise violate them. But although it is possible that a general law of nature might exist in

terms of that maxim, it is impossible to *will* that such a principle should have the general validity of a law of nature. For a will which resolved this would contradict itself, inasmuch as many a time one would need the love and sympathy of others and by such a law of nature, sprung from one's own will, one would deprive himself of all hope of the aid he desires.

These are a few of the many actual duties, or at least what we regard as such, which derive clearly from the one principle that we have established. We must be *able to will* that a maxim of our action should be a general law. This is the canon of any moral assessment at all of such action. Some actions are such that their maxims cannot even be *conceived* as a general law of nature without contradiction, let alone that one could *will* that these maxims *should* become such laws. Other actions reveal no such intrinsic impossibility, but still it is impossible to *will* that their maxim should be elevated to the universality of a law of nature, since such a will would contradict itself. It can be easily seen that the former would conflict with strict or more specific, inexorable duty, the latter merely with a broader (meritorious) duty. Therefore, all duties, in regard to their compulsory nature (not the object of their action), depend on the same principle as the above illustrations conclusively show. . . .

The will is conceived as a faculty impelling a man to action *in accordance with the concept of certain laws.* Such a faculty can be found only in rational beings. Now, that which serves the will as the objective ground for its self-determination is the *end*, and if the end if given by reason alone, it must be so given for all rational beings. On the other hand, that which merely contains the ground of a possibility of action is called the *means*. The subjective ground of desire is the *main-spring*, the objective ground of volition is the *motive*; hence the distinction [arises] between subjective ends resting on main-springs, and objective ends depending on motives that hold for every rational being. Practical principles are *formal* when they abstract from all subjective ends, they are *material* when they assume these and, therefore, particular main-springs of action. The ends which a rational being chooses to set himself as *effects* of his action (material ends) are altogether merely relative as only their relation to the specific capacity for desire of the subject gives them their value. Such value therefore cannot furnish general principles, i.e., practical laws valid and necessary for all rational beings and for every volition. Hence all these relative ends can only give rise to hypothetical imperatives. However, supposing that there were something *whose existence* was *in itself* of absolute value, something which, as an *end in itself*, could be a ground for definite laws, then this end and it alone, would be the ground for a possible categorical imperative, i.e., a practical law. Now I say that man, and generally every rational being, *exists* as an end in himself, *not merely as a means* for the arbitrary use of this or that will; he must always be regarded as an end in all his actions whether aimed at himself or at other rational beings. All objects of the inclinations have only a conditional value since, but for the inclinations and their respective wants, their object would be without value. But the inclinations them-selves, being sources of want, are so far from having an absolute value that instead of relishing them it must rather be the general wish of every rational being to be wholly free from them. Hence the value of any object which *can be acquired* by our action is always conditional. Beings whose existence depends not on our will but on nature have, nevertheless, if they are irrational beings, only a relative value as means and are therefore called *things*; rational beings, on the other hand, are called *persons*. Their very nature constitutes them as ends in themselves; that is, as something which must not be used merely as means. To that extent, a person is limiting freedom of action and is an object of respect. Therefore persons are not merely subjective ends whose existence is an end for us as the result of our action, but they are objective ends; that is, things whose existence in itself is an end. No other end can be substituted (as a justification) for such an end, making it *merely* serve as a means, because otherwise nothing whatever could be found that would possess *absolute value*. If all value were conditional and therefore contingent, reason would have no supreme practical principle whatever.

Now, if a supreme practical principle ought to exist, or a categorical imperative with respect to the human will, it must be one which turns the concept of what is necessarily an end for everybody because it is *an end in itself* into an *objective* principle of the will which can serve as a general practical law. The basis of this principle is that *rational nature exists as an end in itself*. Man necessarily conceives his own existence as being this rational nature, to the extent that it is a *subjective* principle of human actions. But every other rational being regards its existence similarly for the same rational reason that holds true for me, so at the same time it is an objective principle from which, as a supreme practical ground, all laws of the will must needs be deductible. Accordingly, the practical imperative will be as follows: *Act so as to treat man, in your own person as well as in that of anyone else, always as an end, never merely as a means.* We shall now inquire whether this principle can be realized.

To use the previous examples:

First: In regard to the concept of necessary duty to oneself, whoever contemplates suicide will ask himself whether his action is consistent with the idea of man as an end in itself. If he destroys himself to escape onerous conditions, he uses a person merely as a *means* to maintain a tolerable condition until life ends. But man is not a thing, that is to say, something which can be used *merely* as means, but in all his actions must always be considered as an end in itself. Therefore I cannot dispose in any way of man in my own person so as to mutilate, damage or kill him. (It is a matter of morals proper to define this principle more precisely to avoid all misunderstanding. Therefore I bypass such questions as that of the amputation of the limbs in order to preserve one's life, and of exposing one's life to danger with a view to preserving it, etc.)

Second: As regards necessary or obligatory duties toward others, whoever is thinking of making a lying promise to others will see at once that he would be using another man *merely as a means*, without the latter being the end in itself at the same time. The person whom I propose to use by such a promise or my own purposes cannot possibly assent to my way of acting toward him. . . . This conflict with the principle of duty toward others becomes more obvious if we consider examples of attacks on the liberty and property of others. Here it is clear that whoever transgresses the rights of men intends to use the person of others merely as means without considering that as rational beings they shall always be regarded as ends also; that is, as beings who could possibly be the end of the very same action.

Third: As regards contingent (meritorious) duties to oneself, it is not enough that the action does not violate humanity in our own person as an end in itself; [such action] must also *be congruous to it*. Now, there are in mankind capacities for greater perfection which belong to the end of nature regarding humanity. . . . To neglect these capacities might at best be consistent with the *survival* of humanity as an end in itself, but [it is not consistent] with the *promotion* of nature's end regarding humanity.

Fourth: As regards meritorious duties toward others, the natural end which all men have is their own happiness. Now, humanity might indeed subsist if no one contributed anything to the happiness of others as long as he did not deliberately diminish it; but this would be only negatively congruous to *humanity as an end in itself* if everyone does not also endeavor to promote the ends of others as far as he is able. For the ends of any subject which is an end in himself must be my ends too as far as possible, if that idea is to be *fully* effective in me.

This principle of man, and any rational creature, being *an end in itself*, which is the main limiting condition of every man's freedom of action, is not taken from experience for two reasons. First, its universal character, applying as it does to all rational beings whatever, is a fact which no experience can determine; second, because this principle does not present humanity as a subjective end of men; that is, as an object which actually we set ourselves as an end, but it [presents humanity as] an objective end which, whatever [subjective] ends we may have, is to constitute as a law the supreme limiting condition of all subjective ends. It must, therefore, derive from pure reason. In fact, according to the first principle, *the rule* and its universal character which enables [such legislation] to be some kind of law, for example, a law of nature, the *subjective* ground is the *end*. Since, according to the second principle the subject of all ends is some rational being, each being an end in itself, the third practical principle of the will follows as the ultimate prerequisite for the congruity [of will] with general practical reason; viz, the idea that *the will of every rational being is a will giving general laws*.

By virtue of this principle all maxims are rejected which cannot co-exist with the will as the general legislator. Thus the will is not being subjected simply to law, but is so subjected that it must be regarded *as giving itself the law*, and for this very reason is subject to the law of which it may consider itself the author. . . . Although a will *which is subject to laws* may be attached to such a law through interest, yet a will which is itself a supreme law-giver cannot possibly depend on any interest, since such a dependent will would still need another law which would restrict the interest of its self-love by the condition that it should be valid as a general law.

Thus the principle that every human will *gives general laws through all its maxims* i, otherwise correct, could very well be *suited as* the categorical imperative because it is *not grounded in any interest* but rather in the idea of universal lawgiving. Therefore, it alone among all possible imperatives can be *unconditional*. Or better still, to reverse the proposition: If there is a categorical imperative, i.e., a law for every [act of] willing by a rational being, it can only command that everything be done on account of maxims of a will which could at the same time consider itself the object of its general laws, because only then both the practical principle and the imperative which it obeys are unconditional, the latter not being based on any interest.

John Stuart Mill
(1806–1873)

John Mill was the eldest of James Mill's nine children. His early education was directed exclusively by his father. An exceptionally precocious child, he was studying Greek at age three and had read Herodotus, Plato, Gibbons, and Hume before he was eight. Logic, economics, and political theory came next. At fourteen, Mill was sent to France for a year to learn French and to study mathematics, science, and more economics. At seventeen, Mill went to work in the India House, where he later succeeded his father as chief examiner. A disciple of Wordsworth and Carlyle, Mill wrote extensively on literary as well as political and philosophical topics. He was pensioned in 1858 when the government overhauled the British colonial system and dissolved the East India Company. Elected to Parliament in 1865, Mill lobbied vigorously for "radical" political causes, including the reformation of Irish land laws and women's suffrage. He failed to be reelected, however, and, after several years of declining health, died in 1873.

Utilitarianism*

. . . On the present occasion, I shall, without further discussion of the other theories, attempt to contribute something toward the understanding and appreciation of the Utilitarian or Happiness theory, and toward such proof as it is susceptible of. . . .

The creed which accepts as the foundation of morals, Utility, or the Greatest Happiness Principle, holds that actions are right in proportion as they tend to promote happiness, wrong as they tend to produce the reverse of happiness. By happiness is intended pleasure, and the absence of pain; by unhappiness, pain, and the privation of pleasure. To give a clear view of the moral standard set up by the theory, much more requires to be said; in particular, what things it includes in the ideas of pain and pleasure; and to what extent this is left an open question. But these supplementary explanations do not affect the theory of life on which this theory of morality is grounded—namely, that pleasure and freedom from pain, are the only things desirable as ends; and that all desirable things (which are as numerous in the

From John Stuart Mill, "Utilitarianism" in *Utilitarianism, Liberty & Representative Government*, Everyman's Library (London: J.M. Dent & Sons). Used with permission.

utilitarian as in any other scheme) are desirable either for pleasure inherent in themselves, or as means to the promotion of pleasure and the prevention of pain.

Now, such a theory of life excites in many minds, and among them in some of the most estimable in feeling and purpose, inveterate dislike. To suppose that life has (as they express it) no higher end than pleasure—no better and nobler object of desire and pursuit—they designate as utterly mean and groveling; as a doctrine worthy only of swine, to whom the followers of Epicurus were, at a very early period, contemptuously likened; and modern holders of the doctrine are occasionally made the subject of equally polite comparisons by its German, French, and English assailants.

When thus attacked, the Epicureans have always answered, that it is not they, but their accusers, who represent human nature in a degrading light; since the accusation supposes human beings to be capable of no pleasure except those of which swine are capable. If this supposition were true, the charge could not be gainsaid, but would then be no longer an imputation; for if the sources of pleasure were precisely the same to human beings and to swine, the rule of life which is good enough for the one would be good enough for the other. The comparison of the Epicurean life to that of beasts is felt as degrading, precisely because a beast's pleasures do not satisfy a human being's conceptions of happiness. Human beings have faculties more elevated than the animal appetites, and when once made conscious of them, do not regard anything as happiness which does not include their gratification. . . . It is quite compatible with the principle of utility to recognize the fact, that some *kinds* of pleasure are more desirable and more valuable than others. It would be absurd that, while, in estimating all other things, quality is considered as well as quantity, the estimation of pleasure should be supposed to depend on quantity alone.

If I am asked, what I mean by difference of quality in pleasures, or what makes one pleasure more valuable than another, merely as a pleasure, except its being greater in amount, there is but one possible answer. Of two pleasures, if there be one to which all or almost all who have experience of both give a decided preference, irrespective of any feeling of moral obligation to prefer it, that is the more desirable pleasure. If one of the two is, by those who are competently acquainted with both, placed so far above the other that they prefer it, even though knowing it to be attended with a greater amount of discontent, and would not resign it for any quantity of the other pleasure which their nature is capable of, we are justified in ascribing to the preferred enjoyment a superiority in quality, so far outweighing quantity as to render it, in comparison, of small account.

Now it is an unquestionable fact that those who are equally acquainted with, and equally capable of appreciating and enjoying, both do give a most marked preference to the manner of existence which employs their higher faculties. Few human creatures would consent to be changed into any of the lower animals, for a promise of the fullest allowance of a beast's pleasures; no intelligent human being would consent to be a fool, no instructed person would be an ignoramus, no person of feeling and conscience would be selfish and base, even though they should be persuaded that the fool, the dunce, or the rascal is better satisfied with his lot than they are with theirs. They would not resign what they possess more than he for the most complete satisfaction of all the desires which they have in common with him. . . . Whoever supposes that this preference takes place at a sacrifice of happiness—

that the superior being, in anything like equal circumstances, is not happier than the inferior—confounds the two very different ideas of happiness and content. It is indisputable that the being whose capacities of enjoyment are low, has the greatest chance of having them fully satisfied; and a highly endowed being will always feel that any happiness which he can look for, as the world is constituted, is imperfect. But he can learn to bear its imperfections, if they are at all bearable; and they will not make him envy the being who is indeed unconscious of the imperfections, but only because he feels not at all the good which those imperfections qualify. It is better to be a human being dissatisfied than a pig satisfied; better to be Socrates dissatisfied than a fool satisfied. And if the fool, or the pig, are of a different opinion, it is because they only know their own side of the question. The other party of the comparison knows both sides. . . .

I have dwelt on this point, as being part of a perfectly just conception of Utility or Happiness, considered as the directive rule of human conduct. But it is by no means an indispensable condition to the acceptance of the utilitarian standard; for that standard is not the agent's own greatest happiness, but the greatest amount of happiness altogether; and if it may possibly be doubted whether a noble character is always the happier for its nobleness, there can be no doubt that it makes other people happier, and that the world in general is immensely a gainer by it. Utilitarianism, therefore, could only attain its end by the general cultivation of nobleness of character, even if each individual were only benefited by the nobleness of others, and his own, so far as happiness is concerned, were a sheer deduction from the benefit. But the bare enunciation of such an absurdity as this last, renders refutation superfluous.

According to the Greatest Happiness Principle, as above explained, the ultimate end, with reference to and for the sake of which all other things are desirable (whether we are considering our own good or that of other people), is an existence exempt as far as possible from pain, and as rich as possible in enjoyments, both in point of quantity and quality; the test of quality, and the rule for measuring it against quantity, being the preference felt by those who in their opportunities of experience, to which must be added their habits of self-consciousness and self-observation, are best furnished with the means of comparison. This, being, according to the utilitarian opinion, the end of human action, is necessarily also the standard of morality; which may accordingly be defined, the rules and precepts for human conduct, by the observance of which an existence such as has been described might be, to the greatest extent possible, secured to all mankind; and not to them only, but, so far as the nature of things admits, to the whole sentient creation. . . .

The main constituents of a satisfied life appear to be two, either of which by itself is often found sufficient for the purpose: tranquillity, and excitement. With much tranquillity, many find that they can be content with very little pleasure: with much excitement, many can reconcile themselves to a considerable quantity of pain. There is assuredly no inherent impossibility in enabling even the mass of mankind to unite both; since the two are so far from being incompatible that they are in natural alliance, the prolongation of either being a preparation for, and exciting a wish for, the other. It is only those in whom indolence amounts to a vice, that do not desire excitement after an interval of repose: it is only those in whom the need of excitement is a disease, that feel the tranquillity which follows excitement dull and insipid, instead of pleasurable in direct proportion to the excitement which preceded it.

When people who are tolerably fortunate in their outward lot do not find in life sufficient enjoyment to make it valuable to them, the cause generally is, caring for nobody but themselves. To those who have neither public nor private affections, the excitements of life are much curtailed, and in any case dwindle in value as the time approaches when all selfish interests must be terminated by death: while those who leave after them objects of personal affection, and especially those who have also cultivated a fellow-feeling with the collective interests of mankind, retain as lively an interest in life on the eve of death as in the vigor of youth and health. Next to selfishness, the principal cause which makes life unsatisfactory is want of mental cultivation. A cultivated mind—I do not mean that of a philosopher, but any mind to which the fountains of knowledge have been opened, and which has been taught, in any tolerable degree, to exercise its faculties—finds sources of inexhaustible interests in all that surrounds it; in the objects of nature, the achievements of art, the imaginations of poetry, the incidents of history, the ways of mankind, past and present, and their prospects in the future. It is possible, indeed, to become indifferent to all this, and that too without having exhausted a thousandth part of it; but only when one has had from the beginning no moral or human interest in these things, and has sought in them only the gratification of curiosity. . . .

As for vicissitudes of fortune, and other disappointments connected with worldly circumstances, these are principally the effect either of gross imprudence, of ill-regulated desires, or of bad or imperfect social institutions. All the grand sources, in short, of human suffering are in a great degree, many of them almost entirely, conquerable by human care and effort; and though their removal is grievously slow—though a long succession of generations will perish in the breach before the conquest is completed, and this world becomes all that, if will and knowledge were not wanting, it might easily be made—yet every mind sufficiently intelligent and generous to bear a part, however small and inconspicuous, in the endeavor, will draw a noble enjoyment from the contest itself, which he would not for any bribe in the form of selfish indulgence consent to be without. . . .

I must again repeat, what the assailants of utilitarianism seldom have the justice to acknowledge, that the happiness which forms the utilitarian standards of what is right in conduct, is not the agent's own happiness, but that of all concerned. As between his own happiness and that of others, utilitarianism requires him to be as strictly impartial as a disinterested and benevolent spectator. In the golden rule of Jesus of Nazareth, we read the complete spirit of the ethics of utility. To do as you would be done by, and to love your neighbor as yourself, constitute the ideal perfection of utilitarian morality. As the means of making the nearest approach to this ideal, utility would enjoin, first, that laws and social arrangements should place the happiness, or (as speaking practically it may be called) the interest, of every individual, as nearly as possible in harmony with the interest of the whole; and secondly, that education and opinion, which have so vast a power over human character, should so use that power as to establish in the mind of every individual an indissoluble association between his own happiness and the good of the whole; especially between his own happiness and the practice of such modes of conduct, negative and positive, as regard for the universal happiness prescribes; so that not only he may be unable to conceive the possibility of happiness to himself, consistently with conduct opposed to the general good but also that a direct impulse to promote the general good may be in every individual one of the habitual motives of action, and the sentiments connected therewith may fill a large and prominent place in every human being's sentient existence. If the impugners of the utilitarian morality represented it to their own minds in this its true character, I know not what recommendation possessed by any other morality they could possibly affirm to be wanting to it; what more beautiful or more exalted developments of human nature any other ethical system can be supposed to foster, or what springs of action, not accessible to the utilitarian, such systems rely on for giving effect to their mandates.

The objectors to utilitarianism cannot always be charged with representing it in a discreditable light. On the contrary, those among them who entertain anything like a just idea of its disinterested character, sometimes find fault with its standard as being too high for humanity. They say it is exacting too much to require that people shall always act from the inducement of promoting the general interest of society. But . . . it is a misapprehension of the utilitarian mode of thought, to conceive it as implying that people should fix their minds upon so wide a generality as the world, or society at large. The great majority of good actions are intended not for the benefit of the world, but for that of individuals, of which the good of the world is made up; and the thoughts of the most virtuous man need not on these occasions travel beyond the particular persons concerned, except so far as is necessary to assure himself that in benefiting them he is not violating the rights, that is, the legitimate and authorized expectations, of any one else. The multiplication of happiness is, according to the utilitarian ethics, the object of virtue: the occasions on which any person (except one in a thousand) has it in his power to do this on an extended scale, in other words to be a public benefactor, are but exceptional; and on these occasions alone is he called on to consider public utility; in every other case, private utility, the interest or happiness of some few persons, is all he has to attend to. Those alone the influence of whose actions extends to society in general need concern themselves habitually about so large an object. . . .

Again, defenders of utility often find themselves called upon to reply to such objections as this—that there is not time, previous to action, for calculating and weighing the effects of any line of conduct on the general happiness. This is exactly as if anyone were to say that it is impossible to guide our conduct by Christianity, because there is not time, on every occasion on which anything has to be done, to read through the Old and New Testaments. The answer to the objection is that there has been ample time, namely, the whole past duration of the human species. During all that time, mankind have been learning by experience the tendencies of actions; on which experience all the prudence, as well as all the morality of life, are dependent. People talk as if the commencement of this course of experience had hitherto been put off, and as if, at the moment when some man feels tempted to meddle with the property or life of another, he had to begin considering for the first time whether murder and theft are injurious to human happiness. Even then I do not think that he would find the question very puzzling; but, at all events, the matter is now done to his hand. It is truly a whimsical supposition that, if mankind were agreed in considering utility to be the test of morality, they would remain without any agreement as to what *is* useful, and would take no measures for having their notions on the subject taught to the young, and enforced by law and opinion. There is no difficulty in proving any ethical standard whatever to work ill, if we suppose universal idiocy to be conjoined with it; but on any hypothesis short of that, mankind must by this time have acquired positive beliefs as to the effects of some actions on their happiness; and the beliefs which have thus come down are the rules of morality for the multitude, and for the philosopher until he has succeeded in finding better. . . .

It has already been remarked, that questions of ultimate ends do not admit of proof, in the ordinary acceptation of the term. To be incapable of proof by reasoning is common to all first principles; to the first premises of our knowledge, as well as to those of our conduct. But the former, being matters of fact, may be the subject of a direct appeal to the faculties which judge of fact—namely, our senses and our internal consciousness. Can an appeal be made to the same faculties on questions of practical ends? Or by what other faculty is cognisance taken of them?

Questions about ends are, in other words, questions what things are desirable. The utilitarian doctrine is, that happiness is desirable, and the only thing desirable, as an end; all other things being only desirable as means to that end. What ought to be required of this doctrine—what conditions is it requisite that the doctrine should fulfill—to make good its claim to be believed?

The only proof capable of being given that an object is visible, is that people actually see it. The only proof that a sound is audible, is that people hear it: and so of the other sources of our experience. In like manner, I apprehend, the sole evidence it is possible to produce that anything is desirable, is that people do actually desire it. If the end which the utilitarian doctrine proposes to itself were not, in theory and in practice, acknowledged to be an end, nothing could ever convince any person that it was so. No reason can be given why the general happiness is desirable, except that each person, so far as he believes it to be attainable, desires his own happiness. This, however, being a fact, we have not only all the proof which the case admits of, but all which it is possible to require, that happiness is a good: that each person's happiness is a good to that person, and the general happiness, therefore, a good to the aggregate of all persons. Happiness has made out its title as *one* of the ends of conduct, and consequently one of the criteria of morality.

But it has not, by this alone, proved itself to be the sole criterion. To do that, it would seem, by the same rule, necessary to show, not only that people desire happiness, but that they never desire anything else. Now it is palpable that they do desire things which, in common language, are decidedly distinguished from happiness. They desire, for example, virtue, and the absence of vice, no less really than pleasure and the absence of pain. The desire of virtue is not as universal, but it is as authentic a fact, as the desire of happiness. And hence the opponents of the utilitarian standard deem that they have a right to infer that there are other ends of human action besides happiness, and that happiness is not the standard of approbation and disapprobation.

But does the utilitarian doctrine deny that people desire virtue, or maintain that virtue is not a thing to be desired? The very reverse. It maintains not only that virtue is to be desired, but that it is to be desired disinterestedly, for itself. Whatever may be the opinion of utilitarian moralists as to the original conditions by which virtue is made virtue; however they may believe (as they do) that actions and dispositions are only virtuous because they promote another end than virtue; yet this being granted, and it having been decided, from considerations of this description, what *is* virtuous, they not only place virtue at the very head of the things which are good as means to the ultimate end, but they also recognize as a psychological fact the possibility of its being, to the individual, a good in itself, without looking to any end beyond it; and hold, that the mind is not in a right state, not in a state conformable to Utility, not in the state most conducive to the general happiness, unless it does love virtue in this manner—as a thing desirable in itself, even although, in the individual instance, it should not produce those other desirable consequences which it tends to produce, and on account of which it is held to be virtue. This opinion is not, in the smallest degree, a departure from the Happiness principle. The ingredients of happiness are very various, and each of them is desirable in itself, and not merely when considered as swelling an aggregate. The principle of utility does not mean that any given pleasure, as music, for instance, or any given exemption from pain, as for example health, is to be looked upon as means to a collective something termed happiness, and to be desired on that account. They are desired and desirable in and for themselves; besides being means, they are a part of the end. Virtue, according to the utilitarian doctrine, is not naturally and originally part of the end, but it is capable of becoming so; and in those who love it disinterestedly it has become so, and is desired and cherished, not as a means to happiness, but as a part of their happiness.

To illustrate this farther, we may remember that virtue is not the only thing, originally a means, and which if it were not a means to anything else, would be and remain indifferent, but which by association with what it is a means to, comes to be desired for itself, and that too with the utmost intensity. What, for example, shall we say of the love of money? There is nothing originally more desirable about money than about any heap of glittering pebbles. Its worth is solely that of the things which it will buy; the desires for other things than itself, which it is a means of gratifying. Yet the love of money is not only one of the strongest moving forces of human life, but money is, in many cases, desired in and for itself; the desire to possess it is often stronger than the desire to use it, and goes on increasing when all the desires which point to ends beyond it, to be compassed by it, are falling off. It may, then, be said truly, that money is desired not for the sake of an end, but as part of the end. From being a means to happiness, it has come to be itself a principal ingredient of the individual's conception of happiness. The same may be said of the majority of the great objects of human life—power, for example, or fame, except that to each of these there is a certain amount of immediate pleasure annexed, which has at least the semblance of being naturally inherent in them—a thing which cannot be said of money. Still, however, the strongest natural attraction, both of power and of fame, is the immense aid they give to the attainment of our other wishes; and it is the strong association thus generated between them and all our objects of desire which gives to the direct desire of them the intensity it often assumes, so as in some characters to surpass in strength all other desires. In these cases the means have become a part of the end, and a more important part of it than any of the things which they are means to. What was once desired as an instrument for the attainment of happiness, has come to be desired for its own sake. In being desired for its own sake it is, however, desired as *part* of happiness. The person is made, or thinks he would be made, happy by its mere possession; and is made unhappy by failure to obtain it. The desire of it is not a different thing from the desire of happiness, any more than the love of music, or the desire of health. They are included in happiness. They are some of the elements of which the desire of happiness is made up. Happiness is not an abstract idea, but a concrete whole; and these are some of its parts. And the utilitarian standard sanctions and approves their being so. Life would be a poor thing, very ill provided with sources of happiness, if there were not this provision of nature, by which things originally indifferent, but conducive to, or otherwise associated with, the satisfaction of our primitive desires, become in themselves sources of pleasure more valuable than the primitive pleasures, both in permanency, in the space of human existence that they are capable of covering, and even in intensity.

Civilization*

The word civilization, like many other terms of the philosophy of human nature, is a word of double meaning. It sometimes stands for *human improvement* in general, and sometimes for *certain kinds* of improvement in particular.

We are accustomed to call a country more civilized if we think it more improved; more eminent in the best characteristics of Man and Society; further advanced in the road to perfection; happier, nobler, wiser. This is one sense of the word civilization. But in another sense it stands for that kind of improvement only which distinguishes a wealthy and populous nation from savages or barbarians. . . .

We shall in the present article invariably use the word civilization in the narrow sense: not that in which it is synonymous with improvement, but that in which it is the direct converse or contrary of rudeness or barbarism. Whatever be the characteristics of what we call savage life, the contrary of these, or rather the qualities which society puts on as it throws off these, constitute civilization. Thus, a savage tribe consists of a handful of individuals, wandering or thinly scattered over a vast tract of country: a dense population, therefore, dwelling in fixed habitations, and largely collected together in towns and villages, we term civilized. In savage life there is no commerce, no manufactures, no agriculture, or next to none: a country rich in the fruits of agriculture, commerce, and manufactures, we call civilized. In savage communities each person shifts for himself; except in war (and even then very imperfectly) we seldom see any joint operations carried on by the union of many; nor do savages find much pleasure in each other's society. Wherever, therefore, we find human beings acting together for common purposes in large bodies, and enjoying the pleasures of social intercourse, we term them civilized. In savage life there is little or no law, or administration of justice; no systematic employment of the collective strength of society, to protect individuals against injury from one another; every one trusts to his own strength or cunning, and where that fails, he is without resource. We accordingly call a people civilized, where the arrangements of society, for protecting the persons and property of its members, are sufficiently perfect to maintain peace among them; *i.e.* to induce the bulk of the community to rely for their security mainly upon the social arrangements, and renounce for the most part, and in ordinary circumstances, the vindication of their interests (whether in the way of aggression or of defence) by their individual strength or courage.

These ingredients of civilization are various, but consideration will satisfy us that they are not improperly classed together. History, and their own nature, alike show, that they begin together, always coexist, and accompany each other in their growth. Wherever there has introduced itself sufficient knowledge of the arts of life, and sufficient security of property and person, to render the progressive increase of

From John Stuart Mill, "Civilization" in *The London and Westminister Review* (April 1836), 1–16.

wealth and population possible, the community becomes and continues progressive in all the elements which we have just enumerated. . . .

Look at the savage: he has bodily strength, he has courage, enterprise, and is often not without intelligence; what makes all savage communities poor and feeble? The same cause which prevented the lions and tigers from long ago extirpating the race of men—incapacity of co-operation. It is only civilized beings who càn combine. All combination is compromise: it is the sacrifice of some portion of individual will, for a common purpose. The savage cannot bear to sacrifice, for any purpose, the satisfaction of his individual will. His impulses cannot bend to his calculations. Look again at the savage: he is used indeed to make his will give way; but to the commands of a master, not to a superior purpose of his own. He is wanting in intelligence to form such a purpose; above all, he cannot frame to himself the conception of a fixed rule; nor if he could, has he the capacity to adhere to it; he is habituated to control, but not to self-control; when a driver is not standing over him with a cart-whip, he is found more incapable of withstanding any temptation, or constraining any inclination, than the savage himself.

We have taken extreme cases, that the fact we seek to illustrate might stand out more conspicuously. But the remark itself applies universally. As any people approach to the condition of savages or of slaves, so are they incapable of acting in concert. Look even at war, the most serious business of a barbarous people; see what a figure rude nations, or semicivilized and enslaved nations, have made against civilized ones, from Marathon downwards. Why? Because discipline is more powerful than numbers, and discipline, that is, perfect co-operation, is an attribute of civilization. . . .

STUDY/DISCUSSION ELEMENTS IV

1. Terms

a. Unconditional Value
   (cf. Intrinsic Worth)
b. (The) Will
c. Peace
d. Imperative(s)
e. Facts (cf. Matters of Fact)
f. Good Will
g. Vital Motion
h. Law(s) of Nature
i. Moral Distinctions
j. Liberty
k. Good
l. Subjectively Necessary
m. Civilization
n. Sentiment(s)
o. Deliberation
p. Ultimate End(s)
q. Utility
r. Right(s)
s. (The) Greatest
   Happiness Principle

t. Maxim(s)
u. Evil
v. Contingent
w. Hypothetical Imperative(s)
x. Duty(ies)
y. (The) Satisfied Life
z. Social Virtue(s)
aa. Impartial
bb. State of Nature
cc. Human Nature (cf. Humanity)
dd. Retribution
ee. Happiness (cf. Felicity)
ff. Equality
gg. Self-love
hh. War
ii. Quality of (in) Pleasure(s)
jj. (An) End in Itself
kk. Justice
ll. Covenants of Mutual Trust
mm. Coercive Power
nn. Universal Legislator

2. Theses

a. Whoever transgresses the law of nature quits human nature and becomes a noxious beast.
b. Objects of inclination have only conditional worth and are incapable of furnishing general principles.
c. Reason and sentiment concur in almost all moral determinations and conclusions.
d. Peace is the source and guardian of all good things.
e. Equity and justice depend completely on public utility.
f. Only the good will is good in itself, without qualification.
g. Harmony and peace are natural to our universe.
h. Good and evil do not exist in the natures of objects themselves.
i. Whatever we desire we desire as a means to our own happiness or as a part of our happiness.
j. The compulsory nature of duty derives from the categorical principle(s) of the good will.
k. One should always act for the preservation of humankind—oneself and also the rest of humankind—except where another impairs one's life, health, liberty, or possessions.
l. The ultimate source of all moral distinctions is sentiment.

m. A categorical imperative consists in nothing but the conception of law, a general statement of the law to which a maxim should conform, and the necessity of this conformity.

n. Happiness as perpetual tranquillity of mind is impossible in this life.

o. Pleasures which depend upon employing our higher faculties are more valuable than those of our lower faculties. (cf. Better Socrates dissatisfied than a pig or a fool satisfied.)

p. Fear is the source of all peace and society.

q. Public utility recommends itself to human affection directly, naturally, and universally.

r. Just and unjust exist only in relation to society.

s. Without a common power to keep them in awe, human beings will live in a state of war—everyone against everyone.

t. Civilized people alone are capable of progressive increases in wealth and happiness.

u. Rational natures alone are not merely conditional, subjective ends but are grounds for an unconditional, practical imperative.

Chapter Six

Contemporary Perspectives

THEMES AND IDEAS

Modern universities are organized around academic departments: physics, chemistry, mathematics, history, psychology, philosophy, and so forth. This departmentalizing of humanity's intellectual labors is a relatively recent phenomenon, rooted in Medieval distinctions among the liberal arts but inspired more by the rapid development of diverse and highly specialized areas of scientific inquiry during the eighteenth and nineteenth centuries. Natural science, especially physics, led the way in the explosion of knowledge that has occurred just in the last few centuries. In the ever-expanding yet specialized and fragmented world of Modern thought, science soon supplanted philosophy and theology as the paradigm of rational investigation and knowledge. The idea that moral wisdom could somehow be on a par with scientific knowledge, already challenged by David Hume in the eighteenth century, appeared increasingly doubtful in the nineteenth century. Immanuel Kant's attempt to ground morality in a uniquely moral yet wholly rational and lawful motive only accelerated the tendency to view morality as a unique—a *sui generis*, or "of its own kind"— sphere of human activity, distinct from strictly intellectual and scientific endeavors. At the same time, the need to address the deep social changes and upheavals wrought by the industrial revolution solidified the secular and "practical" tendencies of Modern moral thought, especially among British utilitarians. The precise nature of moral wisdom, especially in relation to other intellectual endeavors, in an increasingly secular, pluralistic, scientific, and mechanized world, became a central concern of moral philosophers by the beginning of our century.

Analyzing the intellectual character and movements of an age becomes increasingly difficult the less we are afforded the luxury of historical distance and hindsight. Nonetheless, this final section distinguishes three main phases in contemporary (twentieth-century) moral philosophy: (1) an initial phase of critique, of reconsidering the nature and proper subject matter of moral philosophy, as begun by G. E. Moore and extended by A. J. Ayer; (2) an intermediate phase, motivated in part by Ayer's work, when moral philosophers focused on "meta" rather than "normative" ethics; and (3) a third phase, beginning roughly in the late 1960s, which has witnessed a rebirth of interest in normative ethics while remaining acutely aware of the special concerns of the preceding phases.

George Edward Moore

G. E. Moore's moral philosophy combines elements from two competing traditions in nineteenth-century British thought: utilitarianism and intuitionism. These traditions argued markedly different accounts of how we discern whether something is good or bad, right or wrong. Utilitarians maintained that reason is the source of moral judgment. We discern the moral significance of our actions by examining their consequences, especially for human happiness. Intuitionists, in contrast, believed that we possess a special mental faculty, distinct from reason, which directly apprehends the goodness or badness, rightness or wrongness, of things and actions. Moore's teacher, Henry Sidgwick (1838–1900), combined elements from both traditions in his own moral philosophy. Moore does likewise, though in a way that makes utilitarianism the more basic of the two for moral philosophy as such.

Moore insists that we distinguish rightness, as a property of actions, from goodness, as a property of ends and objects. Strictly speaking, ends and objects are not right or wrong, but good or bad; and actions are not good or bad, but right or wrong. Moreover, the proper subject matter of moral philosophy is human conduct—more precisely, right action. Goodness, of course, is the end or object of right action, but not only of right action. Goodness is also the end or object of art, for example. Hence, it is not the proper subject matter of moral philosophy as such. In addition, goodness by itself is a unique and utterly simple property. Goodness is distinct from any and every other property, and so we cannot define it or identify its essence with anything other than itself. When a philosopher says that goodness is pleasure, happiness, or anything other than just goodness, this can mean only that things which possess goodness are also things which give us pleasure, make us happy, or whatever. Since goodness cannot, in particular, be identified with, or defined in terms of, any of the properties we apprehend by reason or by our five senses, Moore adopts an intuitionist account of goodness as an object of moral discernment.

The proper subject matter of moral philosophy, Moore has argued, is not its "ultimate end," goodness, but right action; and Moore adopts a utilitarian account of right action: Right action produces or promotes goodness. (Of course, since Moore denies that goodness is identical to pleasure or to happiness, he rejects Mill's version of utilitarianism.) Even here, however, Moore sharply limits what moral philosophy can accomplish. Not only are moral philosophers unable to define the nature or essence of goodness, they also cannot determine whether an action is an absolute duty, or is universally, categorically obligatory. The Principle of Utility implies that an action is not merely right but obligatory just in case it produces or promotes the greatest possible amount of goodness; but we can never determine absolutely whether an action satisfies this demand, much less precisely which action this might be. For, to do so, we would have to know every single action which could possibly be chosen in a particular situation and, for each and every one of them, exactly how much goodness it would add to the universe; but we can never know all of these things, or at least not with absolute certainty. The best we can do is imagine a certain limited number of possible actions and make a reasonable, educated guess as to whether one of these actions would probably add more goodness to the universe than the others, or as to which of these actions would probably add the greatest amount of goodness to the universe.

Sometimes the rules, customs, and traditions of one's society may recommend a certain course of action; and Moore argues that it is always reasonable to listen to these. Other times, we may be completely on our own. In such cases, our moral intuition must discern what would be good in the particular situation, and we would then act to produce or attain that good. Insofar as we discern a number of goods which would require us to choose among different possible actions, Moore recommends several guidelines for us to keep in mind. These guidelines are all based on the idea that it is more reasonable to pursue a good which we are more likely actually to obtain than to pursue one which we are less likely actually to obtain. In particular, Moore observes the following: (1) We are more likely to attain a good for which we have a strong preference or desire. (2) We are more likely to attain a good which affects ourselves and people in whom we have a strong interest. And (3) we are more likely to attain a good which can be attained in the very near future. Indeed, except for the general utilitarian principle that right action produces or promotes goodness, all (normative) moral principles are nothing more than guidelines or rules of thumb, derived from our sense of reasonableness or human rationality.

Alfred Jules Ayer

A. J. Ayer was a key figure in a twentieth-century philosophical movement known as logical positivism. The term *positivism* is traced to a nineteenth-century philosopher, Auguste Comte (1798–1857), who advocated the use of scientific principles, first, to understand all aspects of human life—the psychological, the social, and the spiritual, as well as the obviously physical or natural—and, then, to establish rational goals and effective techniques for individual, social, and political improvement. The "hard-headed," or logical, positivists of the twentieth century shared Comte's belief in the primacy of scientific knowledge and principles, though they generally avoided politicizing their positivist outlook and rejected Comte's attempt, not merely to critique theology and other metaphysical disciplines, but in fact to replace them with his "religion" of positivism. In this regard, they were more directly influenced by such late nineteenth-century positivists as Ernst Mach (1838–1916) and by Ludwig Wittgenstein (1889–1951), who studied at Cambridge University soon after G. E. Moore and Bertrand Russel's ground-breaking work in the foundations of mathematics and logic. Twentieth-century, or logical, positivism was thus motivated mainly by an empiricist conception of scientific knowledge and by a general disdain for issues, concepts, methodologies, and outlooks which do not rigorously adhere to empirical, scientific, or (formal) logical principles.

The term *empiricism* comes from the Greek word *empeiria*, meaning direct experience in or acquaintance with something—as opposed, especially, to secondhand, abstract, or indirectly acquired knowledge or proficiencies. In Modern philosophy, the idea of empiricism was especially associated with certain views on the relationship between knowledge and *sense* experience, meaning our awareness of things around us through our five bodily senses: sight, hearing, taste, touch, and smell. Empiricism insists, in particular, that all (human) knowledge comes from, or must be based on, sense experience. The logical positivists expressed their empiricism in a verification principle of truth: The truth (or falsity) of a statement—a linguistic expression of some factual judgment—can be determined only by sense experience. The logical positivists also articulated a verification principle of meaning: The very meaning of a statement is determined by the sense experiences which would verify it if it were true.

Before we can determine whether a statement is true, we must know what it means. Suppose someone states that there are mountains on the far side of the moon. The verification principle of meaning directs us to find out what (sorts of) sense experiences would demonstrate that there in fact are mountains on the far side of the moon; and it implies that when we find this out, we thereby know what this statement means. (The verification principle of truth, in turn, adds that this statement is true just in case we would in fact have those sense experiences were we to travel to the far side of the moon.) But what if no sense experience whatsoever could demonstrate that this statement is true? What if, no matter what we saw, heard, tasted, touched, or smelled were we to travel to the far side of the moon, we would still not know whether or not there are mountains on the far side of the moon? In that case, the verification principle of meaning implies that this statement has no meaning—it is a meaningless statement. Alternatively, if we presume that every statement must have some empirical meaning or other, the principle would tell us that this string of written marks or verbal utterances is not really a statement to begin with. It may be an instance of some other kind of linguistic activity, but it is not a "statement-making" activity.

Our reading from A. J. Ayer is a classic example of logical positivist critiques of moral philosophy. Ayer applies the verification principle of meaning to the various kinds of things that a moral philosopher might write or say. Like Moore, Ayer is interested as well in identifying moral philosophy's distinctive subject matter. Ayer distinguishes three kinds of linguistic activity in the writings or utterances of moral philosophers: (1) Descriptions of "moral phenomena"—for example, how people act; what people believe or say about goodness, rightness, and the like; or what makes people act, believe, or say the things they do. (2) Instructions or recommendations about how people ought to act. And (3) definitions of moral terms—for example, *good* and *right*; or, analyses of how these terms function in moral discourse, deliberation, and conduct. Only the first kind of linguistic activity, Ayer argues, are empirically verifiable—hence, meaningful—statements. (Or, alternatively, only the first kind are really statements at all.) However, these sorts of statements are not distinctive of moral philosophy. Indeed, ascertaining such phenomena are more properly the job of the human sciences—psychology, sociology, and so on. The second kind of linguistic activity is also inappropriate to philosophy. Moral instruction or advice is for sermonizers and moralizers, not philosophers. Philosophers should be interested in understanding and truth, not in preaching. This leaves only the third sort of linguistic activity as a possible subject matter for moral philosophy. Definition or functional analysis is empirical—and, so, meaningful—insofar as it is based on observing how moral terms function in our language and in connection with what people do and say. Unlike the human sciences, however, this activity abstracts from observable facts about "moral" language and reflects upon precisely what makes certain terms "moral" terms. Ayer concludes that the distinctive subject matter of moral philosophy is thus discerning the function or "meanings" of moral terms. Moral philosophers should, in particular, give up searching for standards of moral conduct since this yields only preachments, not (empirical) truths.

Ayer's own analysis of moral discourse leads to the view called emotivism. Moral discourse is distinguished by its use of certain "moral" terms— *good, bad, right, wrong,* and the like. Ayer accepts Moore's position that at least the most basic of these terms, *good,* is indefinable. However, he denies that goodness is therefore a (simple) property of ends and objects, directly apprehended by moral intuition. A strict empiricist, Ayer maintains that our five bodily senses are our only means of directly apprehending objects or their properties; and sense experience apprehends only such properties as colors, shapes, sounds, odors, textures, and flavors. We do not somehow see, hear, feel, taste, or smell goodness as a distinct, simple, sensory property of things. As for moral terms, Ayer thus concludes that they do not add any empirically verifiable (hence, meaningful or statement-making) content to moral discourse. Their function is purely emotive. They express our emotional reactions—especially, feelings of approval and disapproval— toward things or actions.

John Rawls and J. J. C. Smart (Utilitarianism)

The foregoing introduction to Ayer's moral philosophy may seem out of proportion to the length of the reading selection. This is warranted, however, by logical positivism's immense influence, especially on Anglo-American moral philosophy, during the middle decades of this century. After Ayer, many Anglo-American thinkers considered metaethics to be the only legitimate activity for moral philosophers. By the late 1960s, however, philosophers returned increasingly to normative ethics, finding much in traditional moral philosophy that is carefully reasoned and genuinely normative, not merely either emotive or moralistic. During the interim, the most influential moral philosophy among normative ethicists was utilitarianism.

John Rawls and J. J. C. Smart debate two ways of interpreting utilitarianism's claim that the Principle of Utility is the universal law or ultimate standard of right action. Smart calls these interpretations extreme utilitarianism and restricted utilitarianism. They are also known as act utilitarianism and rule utilitarianism. The debate centers on the fact that societies have many rules, or customary ways of acting, which dictate how people ought to behave in certain situations. Moreover, in many cases, these rules and customs are not, at least in any obvious way, just special cases of the Principle of Utility. The rule that people ought to keep their promises is a good example. The customary belief that criminals should be punished is another. Indeed, we can easily imagine situations where following such rules and customs would not promote the greatest amount of happiness or goodness (for the greatest number of persons). Would punishing the president of the United States for any and every crime he or she might commit always be in the best interest of the United States or its citizens? Would it be wrong to break a promise made to a foreign government if doing so would further the interests of our country or its citizens? Notice, however, that these examples presuppose that we can distinguish determining whether an action would be right according to a specific moral rule from determining whether it would be right according to the Principle of Utility (and vice versa). Rawls argues, however, that this is not always the case. When an action is an instance of what he calls a "practice," the very nature of the action is determined by the practice of which it is an instance; and a practice is partly defined by certain (normative) rules. In such cases, we cannot directly apply the Principle of Utility to the action itself at all since the action derives its nature from some practice and, for that practice, right and wrong are determined by the rules of the practice. It makes no sense, in other words, to use the Principle of Utility as if it were an alternative way to evaluate the action independent of the rules of the practice.

Generalizing Rawls' discussion leads to rule utilitarianism: Every (deliberate) human action is an instance of some practice, and so its rightness (or wrongness) is determined by the specific normative rules of the practice rather than by the Principle of Utility itself. The Principle of Utility remains the ultimate standard of morality, however, because it determines what practices should be adopted: We ought to adopt those practices which would promote the greater amount of happiness or goodness overall. Smart, however, argues that rule utilitarianism offers a "monstrous" account of moral rationality. Supposing that every human action must be an instance of some practice, or conform to some specific normative rule, reduces moral deliberation to a kind of rule worshiping. Surely, if the Principle of Utility is the ultimate moral standard, it must be the first principle of all moral reasoning, not just when we consider what practices or rules to adopt. If morality is indeed a rational activity, we should strive always to act in the (morally) most rational way; and act utilitarianism insists that this means always choosing that action which promotes the greatest amount of happiness or goodness. Act utilitarianism thus insists that the rightness (or wrongness) of each and every action is determined directly by the Principle of Utility.

John Rawls' *Theory of Justice*

Utilitarianism remains an important and influential theory in contemporary moral philosophy. Like every true renaissance, the recent "rebirth" of normative ethics has led to a diversity of approaches, many of which modify and adapt earlier philosophies in light of current issues and concerns. While recognizing the important role of the utilitarian tradition and of certain metaethical discussions—for example, concerning universalizability, and the nature of moral reasoning or rationality—probably no single work stimulated this "rebirth" more than John Rawls' *Theory of Justice* (first published in 1971). Like Plato's *Republic* and Hobbes *Leviathan*, Rawls' work focuses on the relationship between individual action and social conduct, between morality as it applies to individuals and morality as encompassing certain concepts and practices pertaining to civilized society. The most basic of these "social" concepts is the concept of justice. The most basic concept of individual or "agent-centered" morality is goodness. These two sides to morality are tied together in Rawls' work by the dual role of rationality in establishing principles of justice, on the one hand, and in defining the moral ends, the "life plans" of individuals, on the other.

Rawls' theory of justice retains certain features of utilitarianism but is closer to social contract theory in approach. Justice—rightness, in the classical Greek sense—exists only when there is an explicit or implicit social contract establishing what is just (or unjust) in a society. This does not mean establishing specific rules to govern every single action or social behavior. Rather, social contracts establish certain fundamental principles which, in particular, assign basic rights and duties to citizens and place limits on individual action by circumscribing the ways in which citizens can legitimately pursue their own interests and goals while sharing the benefits of society. Moreover, genuine "principles of justice" do not merely establish what is just (or unjust) in a society. They must also establish a just society. They must, in other words, themselves be just principles; and principles of justice will themselves be just when they are rationally derived (or derivable) from an "original position" which is fair and impartial.

Rawls argues for two (genuine) principles of justice, arguing that rational persons placed in a fair and impartial original position—one characterized by his "veil of ignorance"—would always agree to these two principles. The first principle states that each member of society should enjoy the maximum amount of basic liberties possible, with the proviso that everyone must posses the same amount of basic liberties. The second states that as the members of society pursue their own interests and goals and reap society's benefits, any inequalities that arise must still leave everyone in society better off than they would have been had they not lived in that society; and these inequalities must be due to certain structural features of the society—"positions and offices"—which are fully and equally open to every citizen.

Rawls' thesis that justice demands a fair and impartial outlook is in the spirit of nineteenth-century utilitarianism. At the same time, however, he believes that the Principle of Utility could not itself be a fundamental principle of justice, because rational beings would never consent to a principle that could make some of them worse off than they might have been had they not consented to it; and the Principle of Utility has this potential since it permits sacrificing the rights, liberties, and interests of individuals—indeed, of whole minorities—for the greater good of the majority. A just principle of justice must, in other words, preserve the fairness and impartiality of the original position; and the Principle of Utility does not do this. It is, in effect, inherently partial to majorities and unfair to individuals or minorities. The Principle of Utility might, however, prove useful for debating specific rules and policies, so long as these respect the limits imposed on civil conduct by the principles of justice.

As principles of justice are to civil conduct, standards of goodness are to individual action; and, to have moral force, each must be rational in the appropriate way. Thus, just principles of justice are ones which rational beings would adopt in a fair and impartial original position. Analogously, good standards of goodness establish ends or goals which rational individuals would pursue when the "veil of ignorance" is lifted and they become aware of their own desires, interests, circumstances, and abilities. A rational being acts rationally, and we act rationally when we establish a set of ends or goals (a "plan of life") and choose our actions for the sake of achieving those goals. Moreover, a rational being does not establish just any plan of life or, say, just the first one that comes to mind but seeks to establish a rational plan of life. Finally, a plan of life is itself rational—hence, good, or morally binding on rational beings—when one selects it from among the various plans available to him or her on the basis of three "principles of rational choice": the principle of effective means, the principle of inclusiveness, and the principle of greater likelihood.

Interlude: Moral Relativism

From the very beginning, moral philosophers have been acutely aware of a conception of morality which, more than any other, questions the very idea (or ideal) of moral wisdom. This conception, known as relativism, may also be behind a number of remarks that people sometimes make about morality—for example, that what's right for me might not be right for you; that right and wrong is just a matter of opinion; or, going even further, that there really is no right or wrong, but only people's opinions. The importance of relativism in contemporary discussions of morality, both in philosophy and in everyday life, makes this an especially appropriate place to discuss it.

The basic idea of relativism is that there is no one, single moral truth (or set of moral truths) which applies to any and every moral being, regardless of his or her own moral ideas, or intentions—his or her moral psychology, as it were. "Moral truth," insofar as there is such a thing at all, is a relational concept which, in particular, must refer to the moral psychologies of individual agents as its primary source. Of course, even nonrelativists can recognize that the rightness (or wrongness) of actions may depend in part on individual persons' moral psychologies. If, for example, I truly believe that an action is morally right, could I be morally blamed for doing it? And, if not, could my action be judged morally wrong? Some philosophers would respond in the affirmative to both, or at least to the second, of these questions. But, many philosophers, including a number of nonrelativists, would answer no to both questions, on the grounds that an individual's intentions and beliefs do affect the moral value of his or her actions. Relativism, however, goes further. It claims that anything other than the agent's moral psychology can, at best, be incidental to the moral value of his or her actions. In the end, an agent's moral psychology alone makes his or her actions right (or wrong). A person's intentions, beliefs, and ideas ultimately determine not only his or her own moral outlook, or what that person thinks is right and wrong, but what in fact is right and wrong—at least regarding his or her own actions. Put another way, if "moral truth" refers to whatever it is that determines whether actions are right or wrong, then relativism holds that moral truth is identical with the moral psychologies of individual agents. Moral truth is, as it were, just whatever each individual believes it to be.

Relativism can take various forms, depending on precisely how one develops or interprets the foregoing general relativist ideas. For one thing, one can focus on different aspects of our moral psychologies. Some elements in our moral psychologies may be more important than others, perhaps even to the exclusion of all other elements. Thus, insofar as right and wrong are made to depend upon our preferences, desires, or wants, the result is an egoistic relativism. Or, insofar as right and wrong are made to depend upon the members of some group accepting or agreeing to certain normative standards, the result is a contractarian relativism. There is also a more general view, social relativism, which claims that right and wrong depend upon certain elements in our moral psychologies which, for whatever reason or cause, are shared by all or most members of a given society. Finally, insofar as right and wrong are made to depend just on whatever an individual agent happens to judge or believe to be right (or wrong), we have the most extreme form of relativism: subjectivism.

The basic relativist claim—that there is no one, single moral truth (or set of moral truths) which applies to any and every moral being—can also be interpreted in various ways, some of which are not utterly opposed to nonrelativism. One might hold, for example, a nonglobal form of relativism by making this claim only about certain aspects of morality, forms of "moral truth," spheres of human conduct, or whatever, rather than about all of morality. Or, one might combine a nonrelativist view about fundamental normative principles with a restricted relativism, which claims that subsidiary or specific rules are needed which cannot be derived from the fundamental principles but which, instead, are relativistic in nature—with the proviso only that they must respect any boundaries established by the fundamental principles. Kant's moral philosophy, on one interpretation, permits such a restricted form of relativism; and John Rawls' theory of justice may also. Finally, a moderated relativism would hold that there might exist a single moral truth that applies to everyone, but not because of the nature of morality or of moral truth itself. Rather, if there is such a moral truth, this is contingent upon some fact about human nature or psychology which just happens to be universally true. Hume, for example, argued that the source of morality is sentiment, but that everyone in fact approves of what is useful and disdains what is harmful. Hence, the Principle of Utility applies to everyone, but is contingent upon this universal fact about human sentiment.

Alan Gewirth

Contemporary debates over relativism often focus on questions of universality. Indeed, disproving the existence of any universal moral truths or principles is sometimes taken as sufficient to establish relativism; and conversely, establishing their existence is sometimes taken as sufficient to refute relativism. This depends, however, on the precise form of relativism being debated. For, in the case of moderated relativism, for example, a nonrelativist must demonstrate not only that universal moral truth (or truths) exists but that its universality is necessary—that is, that it applies not only to any existing moral agent but to every possible moral agent whatsoever. Alan Gewirth's moral philosophy, with roots in both the Kantian and the Lockean natural rights traditions, tries to do just this.

Gewirth argues that there does indeed exist a moral principle which is necessarily binding on every actual and possible moral agent whatsoever. This principle, the Principle of Generic Consistency, is not based merely on the moral psychologies of (existing) agents but on the very nature of moral agency itself. The very concept of moral agency, of acting to achieve some end or goal, entails the existence of certain "generic goods"—things which are good for moral agents solely because of the kind of thing they are (viz., moral agents). Since these goods follow from the very nature of moral agency, they are necessary goods for every moral agent. Hence, no moral agent, insofar as he or she is rational, could ever deny that they are good. Gewirth argues that there are two basic generic goods: the voluntariness, autonomy, or liberty of moral agents to determine their own actions, and the purposive or goal-directed character of their moral agency. The second of these basic generic goods, in turn, implies three other sorts of generic goods: basic goods, nonsubtractive goods, and additive goods. Moreover, since these several generic goods all follow from the very nature of moral agency, every moral agent has a right to them just by virtue of being a moral agent. Insofar as a moral agent is rational, he or she must recognize the (necessary) universality of this right for all agents and be opposed to anything which would interfere with this right or its exercise by any moral agent.

Dorothy Emmet

Relativism should not be confused with Skepticism. (Moral) relativism is a view about the nature of moral truth. (Moral) Skepticism, on the other hand, concerns our ability to attain moral truth. In particular, the Skeptic doubts that we can ever attain moral truth. Indeed, Skeptics often presuppose a nonrelativist concept of moral truth, though their Skepticism regarding (nonrelative) moral truth sometimes leads them to adopt a relativistic conception of moral truth instead—thereby resolving their Skepticism. (Moral) Skepticism can also lead to (moral) nihilism, the view that there is no such thing as moral truth at all—neither nonrelative nor relative.

(Moral) Skepticism itself is sometimes motivated by descriptive pluralism—by the fact that many different moral ideas and beliefs exist in the world—and sometimes by the additional fact that even moral philosophers seem unable to agree on a single moral philosophy or "truth." Indeed, these were the primary motivations behind Sextus Empiricus' classical Skepticism. Observation, history, and the tradition of moral philosophy itself suggested to Sextus that human beings are incapable of determining which, if any, moral beliefs or philosophies are in fact true. Notice, however, that this assumes that whenever two beliefs or philosophies conflict, only one of them can be true. Perhaps, however, this assumption is mistaken, or at least is too hasty. At least certain kinds of moral beliefs—perhaps, the normative proposals of moral philosophers, for example—may seem to conflict, not because at most one of them can in fact be true, but because each is only a partial expression of moral truth and each captures a different "part" or aspect of the truth. Thus, Dorothy Emmet argues that a number of ideas developed and debated over the years by moral philosophers capture or illuminate various aspects of morality. She also argues, however, that the idea of "goodness itself"—that is, of a single, ultimate goal or (nonrelativistic) standard for moral conduct—deserves a special place among the ideas of moral philosophers. Continued moral growth and improvement is essential to moral maturity and responsibility. A mature moral outlook demands, above all else, remaining open to the possibility that one's own moral judgments might in fact be incorrect, that one could always become wiser and better as a moral agent, or, in short, that moral judgments are "problematic"; and this outlook requires, or at least is best fostered by, the belief that goodness has a "transcendental reference"—i.e., (1) that things are in fact good or bad, or that there is indeed such a thing as moral truth, and (2) that goodness depends upon a source or standard which lies outside of individual agent's own moral psychologies and experiences.

Gilbert Harman

Gilbert Harman argues in favor of relativism. Morality is indeed a rational activity, he maintains, since a person can be morally obligated to do something only if he or she has a reason to be obligated to do it. But, moral reasons (and reasoning) cannot be isolated from the interests and the assumptions, or prior beliefs, of individual agents. A person's moral obligations—those things which he or she has reason(s) to be obligated to do—are, therefore, contingent on his or her own interests and moral beliefs. Harman goes on to argue that the "moral" beliefs typically assumed by individual agents in their moral reasoning are best viewed as resulting from tacit agreements, conventions, or contracts that bind peoples together to form societies. Hence, the reasons people have for doing things, and so any normative standards one might abstract from these reasons, are partly functions of their particular interests and partly a function of their society. Of course, it is certainly possible that certain interests are common to all people or that certain conventions exist in every society—hence, that universal moral reasons, and so obligations and standards, do exist; but Harman sees no reason to believe that this is in fact the case. Indeed, he believes that this probably is not the case; and so that there are no universal normative truths at all—not even contingently universal ones.

Alasdair MacIntyre

No previous moral philosopher has influenced contemporary moral philosophers' conception of their subject matter more than Immanuel Kant. In particular, Kant's categorical imperative was supposed to establish the rightness or wrongness of an action (or at least of certain kinds of actions) once and for all, and wholly apart from an agent's particular circumstances, sentiments, or prior beliefs about it. Ever since Kant, moral philosophers, meta- as well as normative ethicists, have tended to take individual actions or moral judgments about individual actions to be the primary datum of morality—whether or not they agreed with Kant's moral philosophy as such. Alasdair MacIntyre challenges this preoccupation with the rightness (or wrongness) of individual actions, and with moral judgments about individual actions. MacIntyre's work has, in particular, renewed interest in a central concept of moral philosophers from Plato and Aristotle well into the nineteenth century: the concept of virtue. Contemporary moral philosphers—including relativists, oddly enough, despite their emphasis on individual moral psychologies—often insist that questions about an agent's moral qualities and capabilities should be sharply separated from questions about the rightness or wrongness of his or her actions. Partly, this reflects the fact that it may sometimes be helpful for us to ask whether or not a certain action, considered just in or by itself, is (or would be) right—say, as we seek to develop or refine our own moral sensibilities or reasoning. But, if proceeding to act on our moral sensibilities—that is, if proceeding actually to perform or to refrain from performing that sort of action—requires that we also possess certain moral qualities or capabilities, then focusing just on actions by themselves, in abstraction from their agents, or insisting that we separate moral conduct from moral character, would seem not to be all that helpful after all. Indeed, some virtue theorists—Aristotle, for example—maintain that moral sensibility, reasoning, or judgment is itself contingent upon moral character.

MacIntyre develops his concept of virtue in three stages: First, in relation to "practices"; second, in relation to the "good life" for human beings; and, finally, in relation to the social, historical, and "narrative" nature of the moral identity of the self. A practice is a socially established, cooperative activity that promotes goods which are obtainable only by means of that activity and in proportion to the level of excellence attained by its practitioners. In this context, virtues are character traits, or capacities, which maintain the social relationships required by (or for) the practice, and which promote excellence in pursuing its good(s). The virtues of justice, courage, and honesty are prime examples of such capacities or character traits. Indeed, MacIntyre suggests that virtue, here and again in the two subsequent stages of its conceptual development, may in fact constitute moral philosophy's most basic subject matter. Civil conduct always encompasses a plurality of different practices. Insofar as normative standards are always internal to particular practices, this pluralism suggests relativism. The "primary virtues," however, promote and sustain any and every practice. Hence, they may be the nonrelative ties which bind the patchwork of human practices together into a single, universal "metapractice" called morality.

Turning to the good life for human beings, MacIntyre argues that a human life is not a series of discrete actions which can be isolated and separated from its agent or environment for the purpose of moral analysis and evaluation. To understand any given action—indeed, even just to define or describe it—we must take into account a number of things, including its time and setting, the intentions of its agent, both its and its agent's relation to other people, and the historical antecedents to all of these things. We must see it as an integral part of some "narrative history"—a "story," if you will, encompassing all of these past and present realities. In this context, virtues are capacities and propensities which, amid the complex narrative nature of human conduct, enable us to order our lives, and especially to order them toward some end or "good."

Finally, the self, the bearer of virtue(s) and the author of one's actions, also cannot be isolated and separated from its narrative context. MacIntyre argues that a person's identity or self is especially rooted in his or her society, its culture, and in the interpersonal groupings to which that person belongs—his or her family, career, place of employment, school, religious congregation, and so forth; and all of these, though most especially culture, are defined as much by their historical antecedents as by their present reality. Indeed, MacIntyre here emphasizes the special importance of historical sensitivity and perspective as itself a virtue—as a character trait or propensity which sustains and promotes (human) goodness.

George Edward Moore

Moore, born in London in 1873, received his early education at Dulwich College—a boys' "prep" school—where he matriculated the classical side of the curriculum for ten years. At eighteen, he entered Trinity College, Cambridge, where he was encouraged to study philosophy by Bertrand Russell. In 1898 Moore was awarded a Prize Fellowship for his dissertation on Kant's philosophy. The fellowship provided him an annual stipend and living quarters at Cambridge for six years, during which time he published several articles, lectured occasionally, and wrote *Principia Ethica*. From 1904 to 1911, Moore lived in Edinburgh and London, studying and writing on various philosophical topics and remaining active in the Aristotelian Society of London. In 1911 he assumed a lectureship in moral science at Cambridge; in 1916 he was elected a Fellow of the British Academy; and in 1925 Moore was appointed Professor of Mental Philosophy and Logic. After he retired from Cambridge in 1939, Moore lectured briefly at Oxford and then traveled extensively in the United States, where he lectured at a number of colleges and universities. He died in 1958.

Principles of Ethics (1903)*

It is very easy to point out some among our every-day judgments, with the truth of which Ethics is undoubtedly concerned. Whenever we say, "So and so is a good man," or "That fellow is a villain"; whenever we ask, "What ought I to do?" or "Is it wrong for me to do like this?"; whenever we hazard such remarks as "Temperance is a virtue and drunkenness a vice"—it is undoubtedly the business of Ethics to discuss such questions and such statements; to argue what is the true answer when we ask what it is right to do, and to give reasons for thinking that our statements about the character of persons or the morality of actions are true or false. In the vast majority of cases, where we make statements involving any of the terms "virtue," "vice," "duty," "right," "ought," "good," "bad," we are making ethical judgments; and if we wish to discuss their truth, we shall be discussing a point of Ethics.

From George Edward Moore, *Principia Ethica* (New York: Cambridge University Press, 1903), Published by the Syndics of the Cambridge University Press. Reprinted with the permission of Cambridge University Press.

So much of this is not disputed; but it falls very far short of defining the province of Ethics. That province may indeed be defined as the whole truth about that which is at the same time common to all such judgments and peculiar to them. But we have still to ask the question: What is it that is thus common and peculiar? And this is a question to which very different answers have been given by ethical philosophers of acknowledged reputation, and none of them perhaps, completely satisfactory.

If we take such examples as those given above, we shall not be far wrong in saying that they are all of them concerned with the questions of "conduct"—with the question, what, in the conduct of us, human beings, is good, and what is bad, what is right, and what is wrong. For when we say that a man is good, we commonly mean that he acts rightly; when we say that drunkenness is a vice, we commonly mean that to get drunk is a wrong or wicked action. And this discussion of human conduct is, in fact, that with which the name "Ethics" is most intimately associated. It is so associated by derivation; and conduct is undoubtedly by far the commonest and most generally interesting object of ethical judgments. . . .

Ethics is undoubtedly concerned with the question what good conduct is; but, being concerned with this, it obviously does not start at the beginning, unless it is prepared to tell us what is good as well as what is conduct. For "good conduct" is a complex notion: all conduct is not good; for some is certainly bad and some may be indifferent. And on the other hand, other things, beside conduct, may be good; and if they are so, then, "good" denotes some property, that is common to them and conduct; and if we examine good conduct alone of all good things, then we shall be in danger of mistaking for this property, some property which is not shared by those other things: and thus we shall have made a mistake about Ethics even in this limited sense; for we shall not know what good conduct really is. This is a mistake which many writers have actually made, from limiting their enquiry to conduct. And hence I shall try to avoid it by considering first what is good in general; hoping, that if we can arrive at any certainty about this, it will be much easier to settle the question of good conduct: for we all know pretty well what "conduct" is. This, then, is our first question: What is good? and What is bad? and to the discussion of this question (or these questions) I give the name of Ethics, since that science must, at all events, include it. . . .

If am asked "What is good?" my answer is that good is good, and that is the end of the matter. Or if I am asked "How is good to be defined?" my answer is that it cannot be defined, and that is all I have to say about it. But disappointing as these answers may appear, they are of the very last importance. To readers who are familiar with philosophic terminology, I can express their importance by saying that they amount to this: That propositions about the good are all of them synthetic and never analytic; and that is plainly no trivial matter. And the same thing may be expressed more popularly, by saying that, if I am right, then nobody can foist upon us such an axiom as that "Pleasure is the only good" or that "The good is the desired" on the pretence that this is "the very meaning of the word."

Let us, then consider this position. My point is that "good" is a simple notion, just as "yellow" is a simple notion; that, just as you cannot, by any manner of means, explain to any one who does not already know it, what yellow is, so you cannot explain what good is. Definitions of the kind that I was asking for, definitions which describe the real nature of the object or notion denoted by a word, and which do not merely tell us what the word is used to mean, are only possible when the object or notion in question is something complex. You can give a definition of a horse, because a horse has many different properties and qualities, all of which you can enumerate. But when you have enumerated them all, when you have reduced a horse to his simplest terms, then you can no longer define those terms. They are simply something which you think of or perceive, and to any one who cannot think of or perceive them, you can never, by any definition, make their nature known. It may perhaps be objected to this that we are able to describe to others, objects which they have never seen or thought of. We can, for instance, make a man understand what a chimaera is, although he has never heard of one or seen one. You can tell him it is an animal with a lioness's head and body, with a goat's head growing from the middle of its back, and with a snake in place of a tail. But here the object which you are describing is a complex object; it is entirely composed of parts, with which we are all perfectly familiar—a snake, a goat, a lioness; and we know, too, the manner in which those parts are to be put together, because we know what is meant by the middle of a lioness's back, and where her tail is wont to grow. And so it is with all objects, not previously known, which we are able to define: they are all complex; all composed of parts, which may themselves, in the first instance, be capable of similar definition, but which must in the end be reducible to simplest parts, which can no longer be defined. But yellow and good, we say, are not complex: they are notions of that simple kind, out of which definitions are composed and with which the power of further defining ceases. . . .

"Good," then, if we mean by it that quality which we assert to belong to a thing, when we say that the thing is good, is incapable of any definition, in the most important sense of that word. The most important sense of "definition" is that in which a definition states what are the parts which invariably compose a certain whole; and in this sense "good" has no definition because it is simple and has no parts. It is one of those innumerable objects of thought which are themselves incapable of defini- tion, because they are the ultimate terms by reference to which whatever *is* capable of definition must be defined. That there must be an indefinite number of such terms is obvious, on reflection; since we cannot define anything except by an analysis, which, when carried as far as it will go, refers us to something, which is simply different from anything else, and which by that ultimate difference explains the peculiarity of the whole which we are defining: for every whole contains some parts which are common to other wholes also. There is, therefore, no intrinsic difficulty in the contention that "good" denotes a simple and indefinable quality. There are many other instances of such qualities.

Consider yellow, for example. We may try to define it, by describing its physical equivalent; we may state what kind of light-vibrations must simulate the normal eye, in order that we may perceive it. But a moment's reflection is sufficient to shew that those light-vibrations are not themselves what we mean by yellow. *They* are not what we perceive. Indeed we should never have been able to discover their existence, unless we had first been struck by the patent difference of quality between the different colours. The most we can be entitled to say of those vibrations is that they are what corresponds in space to the yellow which we actually perceive.

Yet a mistake of this simple kind has commonly been made about "good." It may be true that all things which are good are *also* something else, just as it is true that all things which are yellow produce a certain kind of vibration in the light. And it is a fact, that Ethics aims at discovering what are those other properties belonging to all things which are good. But far too many philosophers have thought that when they named those other properties they were actually defining good; that these properties, in fact, were simply not "other," but absolutely and entirely the same with goodness. This view I propose to call the "naturalistic fallacy". . . .

To ask what kind of actions we ought to perform, or what kind of conduct is right, is to ask what kind of effects such action and conduct will produce. Not a single question in practical Ethics can be answered except by a causal generalisation. All such questions do, indeed, *also* involve an ethical judgment proper—the judgment that certain effects are better, in themselves, than others. But they *do* assert that these better things are effects—are causally connected with the actions in question. Every judgment in practical Ethics may be reduced to the form: This is a cause of that good thing. . . .

All moral laws, I wish to shew, are merely statements that certain kinds of actions will have good effects. The very opposite of this view has been generally prevalent in Ethics. "The right" and "the useful" have been supposed to be at least *capable* of conflicting with one another, and, at all events, to be essentially distinct. It has been characteristic of a certain school of moralists, as of moral common sense, to declare that the end will never justify the means. What I wish first to point out is that "right" does and can mean nothing but "cause of a good result," and is thus identical with "useful"; whence it follows that the end always will justify the means, and that no action which is not justified by its results can be right. That there may be a true proposition, meant to be conveyed by the assertion "The end will not justify the means," I fully admit; but that, in another sense, and a sense far more fundamental for ethical theory, it is utterly false, must first be shewn.

That the assertion "I am morally bound to perform this action" is identical with the assertion "This action will produce the greatest possible amount of good in the Universe" has already been briefly shewn . . .; but it is important to insist that this fundamental point is demonstrably certain. This may, perhaps, be best made evident in the following way. It is plain that when we assert that a certain action is our absolute duty, we are asserting that the performance of that action at that time is unique in respect of value. But no dutiful action can possibly have unique value in the sense that it is the sole thing of value in the world; since, in that case, *every* such action would be the *sole* good thing, which is a manifest contradiction. And for the same reason its value cannot be unique in the sense that it has more intrinsic value than anything else in the world; since *every* act of duty would then be the *best* thing in the world, which is also a contradiction. It can, therefore, be unique only in the sense that the whole world will be better, if it be performed, than if any possible alternative were taken. . . .

Our "duty," therefore, can only be defined as that action, which will cause more good to exist in the Universe than any possible alternative. And what is "right" or "morally permissible" only differs from this, as what will *not* cause *less* good than any possible alternative. When, therefore, Ethics presumes to assert that certain ways of acting are "duties" it presumes to assert that to act in those ways will always produce the greatest possible sum of good. If we are told that to "do no murder" is a duty, we are told that the action, whatever it may be, which is called murder, will under no circumstances cause so much good to exist in the Universe as its avoidance. . . .

In order to shew that any action is a duty, it is necessary to know both what are the other conditions, which will, conjointly with it, determine its effects; to know exactly what will be the effects of these conditions; and to know all the events which will be in any way affected by our action throughout an infinite future. We must have all this causal knowledge, and further we must know accurately the degree of value both of the action itself and of all these effects; and must be able to determine how, in conjunction with the other things in the Universe, they will affect its value as an organic whole. And not only this: we must also possess all this knowledge with regard to the effects of every possible alternative; and must then be able to see by comparison that the total value due to the existence of the action in question will be greater than that which would be produced by any of these alternatives. But it is obvious that our causal knowledge alone is far too incomplete for us ever to assure ourselves of this result. Accordingly it follows that we never have any reason to suppose that an action is our duty: we can never be sure that any action will produce the greatest value possible.

Ethics, therefore, is quite unable to give us a list of duties: but there still remains a humbler task which may be possible for Practical Ethics. Although we cannot hope to discover which, in a given situation, is the best of all possible alternative actions, there may be some possibility of shewing which among the alternatives, *likely to occur to any one,* will produce the greatest sum of good. This second task is certainly all that Ethics can ever have accomplished: and it is certainly all that it has ever collected materials for proving; since no one has ever attempted to exhaust the possible alternative actions in any particular case. . . .

If, now, we confine ourselves to a search for actions which are *generally* better as means than any probable alternative, it seems possible to establish as much as this in defence of most of the rules most universally recognized by Common Sense. I do not propose to enter upon this defence in detail, but merely to point out what seem to be the chief distinct principles by the use of which it can be made.

In the first place, then, we can only shew that one action is generally better than another as a means, provided that certain other circumstances are given. We do, as a matter of fact, only observe its good effects under certain circumstances; and it may be easily seen that a sufficient change in these would render doubtful what seem the most universally certain of general rules. Thus, the general disutility of murder can only be proved, provided the majority of the human race will certainly persist in existing. In order to prove that murder, if it were so universally adopted as to cause the speedy extermination of the race, would not be good as a means, we should have to disprove the main contention of pessimism—namely that the existence of human life is on the whole an evil. And the view of pessimism, however strongly we may be convinced of its truth or falsehood, is one which never has been either proved or refuted conclusively. That universal murder would not be a good thing at this moment can therefore not be proved. But, as a matter of fact, we can and do assume with certainty that, even if a few people are willing to murder, most people will not be willing. When, therefore, we say that murder is in general to be avoided, we only mean that it is so, so long as the majority of mankind will certainly not agree to it, but will persist in living. And that, under these circumstances, it is generally wrong for any single person to commit murder seems capable of proof. For, since there is in any case no hope of exterminating the race, the only effects which we have to consider are those which the action will have upon the increase of the goods and the diminution of the evils of human life. Where the best is not attainable (assuming extermination to be the best) one alternative may still be better than another. And, apart from the immediate evils which murder generally produces, the fact that, if it were a common practice, the feeling of insecurity, thus caused, would absorb much time, which might be spent to better purpose, is perhaps conclusive against it. So long as men desire to live as strongly as they do, and so long as it is certain that they will continue to do so, anything which hinders them from devoting their energy to the attainment of positive goods, seems plainly bad as a means. And the general practice of murder, falling so far short of universality as it certainly must in all known conditions of society, seems certainly to be a hindrance of this kind.

A similar defence seems possible for most of the rules, most universally enforced by legal sanctions, such as respect of property; and for some of those most commonly recognised by Common Sense, such as industry, temperance and the keeping of promises. In any state of society in which men have that intense desire for property of some sort, which seems to be universal, the common legal rules for the protection of property must serve greatly to facilitate the best possible expenditure of energy. And similarly: Industry is a means to the attainment of those necessaries, without which the further attainment of any great positive goods is impossible; temperance merely enjoins the avoidance of those excesses, which, by injuring health, would prevent a man from contributing as much as possible to the acquirement of these necessaries; and the keeping of promises greatly facilitates cooperation in such acquirement.

Now all these rules seem to have two characteristics to which it is desirable to call attention. (1) They seem all to be such that, in any known state of society, a *general* observance of them *would* be good as a means. The conditions upon which their utility depends, namely the tendency to preserve and propagate life and the desire of property, seem to be so universal and so strong, that it would be impossible to remove them; and, this being so, we can say that, under any conditions which could actually be given, the general observance of these rules would be good as a means. For, while there seems no reason to think that their observance ever makes a society worse than one in which they are not observed, it is certainly necessary as a means for any state of things in which the greatest possible goods can be attained. And (2) these rules, since they can be recommended as a means to that which is itself only a necessary condition for the existence of any great good, can be defended independently of correct views upon the primary ethical question of what is good in itself. On any view commonly taken, it seems certain that the preservation of civilized society, which these rules are necessary to effect, is necessary for the existence, in any great degree, of anything which may be held to be good in itself. . . .

So much, then, for moral rules or laws, in the ordinary sense—rules which assert that it is generally useful, under more or less common circumstances, for *everybody* to perform or omit some definite kind of action. It remains to say something with regard to the principles by which *the individual* should decide what he ought to do, *(a)* with regard to those actions as to which some general rule is certainly true, and *(b)* with regard to those where such a certain rule is wanting.

(a) Since, as I have tried to shew, it is impossible to establish that any kind of action will produce a better total result than its alternative *in all cases,* it follows that in some cases the neglect of an established rule will probably be the best course of action possible. The question then arises: Can the individual ever be justified in

assuming that his is one of these exceptional cases? And it seems that this question may be definitely answered in the negative. For, if it is certain that in a large majority of cases the observance of a certain rule is useful, it follows that there is a large probability that it would be wrong to break the rule in any particular case; and the uncertainty of our knowledge both of effects and of their value, in particular cases, is so great, that it seems doubtful whether the individual's judgment that the effects will probably be good in his case can ever be set against the general probability that that kind of action is wrong. Added to this general ignorance is the fact that, if the question arises at all, our judgment will generally be biassed by the fact that we strongly desire one of the results which we hope to obtain by breaking the rule. It seems, then, that with regard to any rule which is *generally* useful, we may assert that it ought *always* to be observed, not on the ground that in *every* particular case it will be useful, but on the ground that in *any* particular case the probability of its being so is greater than that of our being likely to decide rightly that we have before us an instance of its disutility. In short, though we may be sure that there are cases where the rule should be broken, we can never know which those cases are, and ought, therefore, never to break it. It is this fact which seems to justify the stringency with which moral rules are usually enforced and sanctioned, and to give a sense in which we may accept as true the maxims that "The end never justifies the means" and "That we should never do evil that good may come." The "means" and the "evil," intended by these maxims, are, in fact, the breaking of moral rules generally recognised and practised, and which, therefore, we may assume to be generally useful. Thus understood, these maxims merely point out that, in any particular case, although we cannot clearly perceive any balance of good produced by keeping the rule and do seem to see one that would follow from breaking it, nevertheless the rule should be observed. It is hardly necessary to point out that this is so only because it is certain that, in general, the end does justify the means in question, and that therefore there is a *probability* that in this case it will do so also, although we cannot see that it will.

But moreover the universal observance of a rule which is generally useful has, in many cases, a special utility, which seems deserving of notice. This arises from the fact that, even if we can clearly discern that our case is one where to break the rule is advantageous, yet, so far as our example has any effect at all in encouraging similar action, it will certainly tend to encourage breaches of the rule which are not advantageous. . . .

(b) This next division consists in the discussion of the method by which an individual should decide what to do with regard to possible actions of which the general utility cannot be proved. And it should be observed, that, according to our previous conclusions, this discussion will cover almost all actions, except those which, in our present state of society, are generally practised. For it has been urged that a proof of general utility is so difficult, that it can hardly be conclusive except in a very few cases. It is certainly not possible with regard to all actions which *are* generally practised; though here, if the sanctions are sufficiently strong, they are sufficient by themselves to prove the general utility of the individual's conformity to custom. And if it is possible to prove a general utility in the case of some actions, *not* generally practised, it is certainly not possible to do so by the ordinary method, which tries to shew in them a tendency to that preservation of society, which is itself a mere means, but only by the method, by which in any case, as will be urged, the

individual ought to guide his judgment—namely, by shewing their direct tendency to produce what is good in itself or to prevent what is bad. . . .

It seems, therefore, that, in cases of doubt, instead of following rules, of which he is unable to see the good effects in his particular case,that the individual should rather guide his choice by a direct consideration of the intrinsic value or vileness of the effects which his action may produce. Judgments of intrinsic value have this superiority over judgments of means that, if once true, they are always true; whereas what is a means to a good effect in one case, will not be so in another. For this reason the department of Ethics, which it should be most useful to elaborate for practical guidance, is that which discusses what things have intrinsic value and in what degrees; and this is precisely that department which has been most uniformly neglected, in favour of attempts to formulate rules of conduct.

We have, however, not only to consider the relative goodness of different effects, but also the relative probability of their being attained. A less good, that is more likely to be attained, is to be preferred to a greater, that is less probable, if the difference in probability is great enough to outweigh the difference in goodness. And this fact seems to entitle us to assert the general truth of three principles, which ordinarily moral rules are apt to neglect. (1) That a lesser good, for which any individual has a strong preference (if only it be a good, and not an evil), is more likely to be a proper object for him to aim at, than a greater one, which he is unable to appreciate. For natural inclination renders it immensely more easy to attain that for which such inclination is felt. (2) Since almost every one has a much stronger preference for things which closely concern himself, it will in general be right for a man to aim rather at goods affecting himself and those in whom he has a strong personal interest, than to attempt a more extended beneficence. Egoism is undoubtedly superior to Altruism as a doctrine of means: in the immense majority of cases the best thing we can do is to aim at securing some good in which we are concerned, since for that very reason we are far more likely to secure it. (3) Goods, which can be secured in a future so near as to be called "the present," are in general to be preferred to whose which, being in a further future, are, for that reason, far less certain of attainment.

Alfred Jules Ayer

Born in London, England, in 1910, Ayer was educated at Eton College and at Christ Church, Oxford. His academic career includes appointments as dean of Wadham College, Oxford, in 1945–1946, Grote Professor of the Philosophy of Mind and Logic at Oxford from 1946 to 1959, and Wykeham Professor of Logic at Oxford from 1959 to 1978. After serving in the Welsh Guards and British Intelligence during World War II, Ayer was attaché in the British Embassy in Paris for a short time after the war. Knighted in 1970, Ayer is a Chevalier of the Legion d'Honneur, an honorary member of the American Academy of Arts and Sciences, and a foreign member of the Royal Danish Academy of Sciences and Letters. Among his may philosophical works are *Thinking and Meaning, Metaphysics and Common Sense, The Central Questions of Philosophy,* and *Freedom and Morality.*

Language, Truth, and Logic (1936)*

. . . [T]he function of philosophy is wholly critical. In what exactly does its critical activity consist?

One way of answering this question is to say that it is the philosopher's business to test the validity of our scientific hypotheses and everyday assumptions. But this view, though very widely held, is mistaken. If a man chooses to doubt the truth of all the propositions he ordinarily believes, it is not in the power of philosophy to reassure him. The most that philosophy can do, apart from seeing whether his beliefs are self-consistent, is to show what are the criteria which are used to determine the truth or falsehood of any given proposition: and then, when the sceptic realises that certain observations would verify his propositions, he may also realize that he could make those observations, and so consider his original beliefs to be justified. But in such a case one cannot say that it is philosophy which justifies his beliefs. Philosophy merely shows him that experience can justify them. We may look to the philosopher to show us what we accept as constituting sufficient evidence for the truth of any given empirical proposition. But whether the evidence is forthcoming or not is in every case a purely empirical question. . . .

From Alfred Jules Ayer, *Language, Truth and Logic* (London: Victor Gollancz Ltd., 1936, 1967). Used with permission.

We shall set ourselves to show that in so far as statements of value are significant, they are ordinarily "scientific" statements; and that in so far as they are not scientific, they are not in the literal sense significant, but are simply expressions of emotion which can be neither true nor false. In maintaining this view, we may confine ourselves for the present to the case of ethical statements. What is said about them will be found to apply, *mutatis mutandis,* to the case of aesthetic statements also.

The ordinary system of ethics, as elaborated in the works of ethical philosophers, is very far from being a homogeneous whole. Not only is it apt to contain pieces of metaphysics, and analyses of non-ethical concepts: its actual ethical contents are themselves of very different kinds. We may divide them, indeed, into four main classes. There are, first of all, propositions which express definitions of ethical terms, or judgments about the legitimacy or possibility of certain definitions. Secondly, there are propositions describing the phenomena of moral experience, and their causes. Thirdly, there are exhortations to moral virtue. And, lastly, there are actual ethical judgments. It is unfortunately the case that the distinction between these four classes, plain as it is, is commonly ignored by ethical philosophers; with the result that it is often very difficult to tell from their works what it is that they are seeking to discover or prove.

In fact, it is easy to see that only the first of our four classes, namely that which comprises the propositions relating to the definitions of ethical terms, can be said to constitute ethical philosophy. The propositions which describe the phenomena of moral experience, and their causes, must be assigned to the science of psychology, or sociology. The exhortations to moral virtue are not propositions at all, but ejaculations or commands which are designed to provoke the reader to action of a certain sort. Accordingly, they do not belong to any branch of philosophy or science. As for the expressions of ethical judgments, we have not yet determined how they should be classified. But inasmuch as they are certainly neither definitions nor comments upon definitions, nor quotations, we may say decisively that they do not belong to ethical philosophy. A strictly philosophical treatise on ethics should therefore make no ethical pronouncements. But it should, by giving an analysis of ethical terms, show what is the category to which all such pronouncements belong. And this is what we are now about to do.

A question which is often discussed by ethical philosophers is whether it is possible to find definitions which would reduce all ethical terms to one or two fundamental terms. But this question, though it undeniably belongs to ethical philosophy, is not relevant to our present enquiry. We are not now concerned to discover which term, within the sphere of ethical terms, is to be taken as fundamental; whether, for example, "good" can be defined in terms of "right" or "right" in terms of "good," or both in terms of "value." What we are interested in is the possibility of reducing the whole sphere of ethical terms to non-ethical terms. We are enquiring whether the statements of ethical value can be translated into statements of empirical fact.

That they can be so translated is the contention of those ethical philosophers who are commonly called subjectivists, and of those who are known as utilitarians. For the utilitarian defines the rightness of actions, and the goodness of ends, in terms of the pleasure, or happiness, or satisfaction, to which they give rise; the subjectivist, in terms of the feelings of approval which a certain person, or group of people, has towards them. Each of these types of definition makes moral judgments into a sub-class of psychological or sociological judgments; and for this reason they are very attractive to us. For, if either was correct, it would follow that ethical assertions were not generically different from the factual assertions which are ordinarily contrasted with them; and the account which we have already given of empirical hypotheses would apply to them also.

Nevertheless we shall not adopt either a subjectivist or a utilitarian analysis of ethical terms. We reject the subjectivist view that to call an action right, or a thing good, is to say that it is generally approved of, because it is not self-contradictory to assert that some actions which are generally approved of are not right, or that some things which are generally approved of are not good. And we reject the alternative subjectivist view that a man who asserts that a certain action is right, or that a certain thing is good, is saying that he himself approves of it, on the ground that a man who confessed that he sometimes approved of what was bad or wrong would not be contradicting himself. And a similar argument is fatal to utilitarianism. We cannot agree that to call an action right is to say that of all of the actions possible in the circumstances it would cause, or be likely to cause, the greatest happiness, or the greatest balance of pleasure over pain, or the greatest balance of satisfied over unsatisfied desire, because we find that it is not self-contradictory to say that it is sometimes wrong to perform the action which would actually or probably cause the greatest happiness, or the greatest balance of pleasure over pain, or of satisfied over unsatisfied desire. And since it is not self-contradictory to say that some pleasant things are not good, or that some bad things are desired, it cannot be the case that the sentence "*x* is good" is equivalent to "*x* is pleasant," or to "*x* is desired." And to every other variant of utilitarianism with which I am acquainted the same objection can be made. And therefore we should, I think, conclude that the validity of ethical judgments is not determined by the felicific tendencies of actions, any more than by the nature of people's feelings; but that it must be regarded as "absolute" or "intrinsic," and not empirically calculable.

If we say this, we are not, of course, denying that it is possible to invent a language in which all ethical symbols are definable in non-ethical terms, or even that it is desirable to invent such a language and adopt it in place of our own; what we are denying is that the suggested reduction of ethical to non-ethical statements is consistent with the conventions of our actual language. That is, we reject utilitarianism and subjectivism, not as proposals to replace our existing ethical notions by new ones, but as analyses of our existing ethical notions. Our contention is simply that, in our language, sentences which contain normative ethical symbols are not equivalent to sentences which express psychological propositions, or indeed empirical proposition of any kind.

It is advisable here to make it plain that it is only normative ethical symbols, and not descriptive ethical symbols, that are held by us to be indefinable in factual terms. There is a danger of confusing these two types of symbols, because they are commonly constituted by signs of the same sensible form. Thus a complex sign of the form "*x* is wrong" may constitute a sentence which expresses a moral judgement concerning a certain type of conduct, or it may constitute a sentence which states that a certain type of conduct is repugnant to the moral sense of a particular society. In the latter case, the symbol "wrong" is a descriptive ethical symbol, and the sentence in which it occurs expresses an ordinary sociological proposition; in the former case, the symbol "wrong" is a normative ethical symbol, and the sentence in which it occurs does not, we maintain, express an empirical proposition at all. It is only with normative ethics that we are at present concerned; so that whenever ethical symbols are used in the course of this argument without qualification, they are always to be interpreted as symbols of the normative type.

In admitting that normative ethical concepts are irreducible to empirical concepts, we seem to be leaving the way clear for the "absolutist" view of ethics—that is, the view that statements of value are not controlled by observation, as ordinary empirical propositions are, but only by a mysterious "intellectual intuition." A feature of this theory, which is seldom recognized by its advocates, is that it makes statements of value unverifiable. For it is notorious that what seems intuitively certain to one person may seem doubtful, or even false, to another. So that unless it is possible to provide some criterion by which one may decide between conflicting intuitions, a mere appeal to intuition is worthless as a test of a proposition's validity. But in the case of moral judgements, no such criterion can be given. Some moralists claim to settle the matter by saying that they "know" that their own moral judgements are correct. But such an assertion is of purely psychological interest, and has not the slightest tendency to prove the validity of any moral judgment. For dissentient moralists may equally well "know" that their ethical views are correct. And, as far as subjective certainty goes, there will be nothing to choose between them. When such differences of opinion arise in connection with an ordinary empirical proposition, one may attempt to resolve them by referring to, or actually carrying out, some relevant empirical test. But with regard to ethical statements, there is, on the "absolutist" or "intuitionist" theory, no relevant empirical test. We are therefore justified in saying that on this theory ethical statements are held to be unverifiable. They are, of course, also held to be genuine synthetic propositions.

Considering the use which we have made of the principle that a synthetic proposition is significant only if it is empirically verifiable, it is clear that the acceptance of an "absolutist" theory of ethics would undermine the whole of our main argument. And as we have already rejected the "naturalistic" theories which are commonly supposed to provide the only alternative to "absolutism" in ethics, we seem to have reached a difficult position. We shall meet the difficulty by showing that the correct treatment of ethical statements is afforded by a third theory, which is wholly compatible with our radical empiricism.

We begin by admitting that the fundamental ethical concepts are unanalysable, inasmuch as there is no criterion by which one can test the validity of the judgements in which they occur. So far we are in agreement with the absolutists. But, unlike the absolutists, we are able to give an explanation of this fact about ethical concepts. We say that the reason why they are unanalysable is that they are mere pseudo-concepts. The presence of an ethical symbol in a proposition adds nothing to its factual content. Thus if I say to someone, "You acted wrongly in stealing that money," I am not stating anything more than if I had simply said, "You stole that money." In adding that this action is wrong I am not making any further statement about it. I am simply evincing my moral disapproval of it. It is as if I had said, "You stole that money," in a peculiar tone of horror, or written it with the addition of some special exclamation marks. The tone, or the exclamation marks, adds nothing to the literal meaning of the sentence. It merely serves to show that the expression of it is attended by certain feelings in the speaker.

If now I generalise my previous statement and say, "Stealing money is wrong," I produce a sentence which has no factual meaning—that is, expresses no proposition which can be either true or false. It is as if I had written "Stealing money!!"— where the shape and thickness of the exclamation marks show, by a suitable convention, that a special sort of moral disapproval is the feeling which is being expressed. It is clear that there is nothing said here which can be true or false. Another man may disagree with me about the wrongness of stealing, in the sense that he may not have the same feelings about stealing as I have, and he may quarrel with me on account of my moral sentiments. But he cannot, strictly speaking, contradict me. For in saying that a certain type of action is right or wrong, I am not making any factual statement, not even a statement about my own state of mind. I am merely expressing certain moral sentiments. And the man who is ostensibly contradicting me is merely expressing his moral sentiments. So that there is plainly no sense in asking which of us is in the right. For neither of us is asserting a genuine proposition.

What we have just been saying about the symbol "wrong" applies to all normative ethical symbols. Sometimes they occur in sentences which record ordinary empirical facts besides expressing ethical feeling about those facts: sometimes they occur in sentences which simply express ethical feeling about a certain type of action, or situation, without making any statement of fact. But in every case in which one would commonly be said to be making an ethical judgement, the function of the relevant ethical word is purely "emotive." It is used to express feeling about certain objects, but not to make any assertion about them.

It is worth mentioning that ethical terms do not serve only to express feeling. They are calculated also to arouse feeling, and so to stimulate action. Indeed some of them are used in such a way as to give the sentences in which they occur the effect of commands. Thus the sentence "It is your duty to tell the truth" may be regarded both as the expression of a certain sort of ethical feeling about truthfulness and as the expression of the command "Tell the truth." The sentence "You ought to tell the truth" also involves the command "Tell the truth," but here the tone of the command is less emphatic. In the sentence "It is good to tell the truth" the command has become little more than a suggestion. And thus the "meaning" of the word "good," in its ethical usage, is differentiated from that of the word "duty" or the word "ought." In fact we may define the meaning of the various ethical words in terms both of the different feelings they are ordinarily taken to express, and also the different responses which they are calculated to provoke.

We can now see why it is impossible to find a criterion for determining the validity of ethical judgements. It is not because they have an "absolute" validity which is mysteriously independent of ordinary sense-experience, but because they have no objective validity whatsoever. If a sentence makes no statement at all, there is obviously no sense in asking whether what it says is true or false. And we have seen that sentences which simply express moral judgements do not say anything. They are pure expressions of feeling and as such do not come under the category of truth and falsehood. They are unverifiable for the same reason as a cry of pain or a word of command is unverifiable—because they do not express genuine propositions. . . .

[A]rgument is possible on moral questions only if some system of values is presupposed. If our opponent concurs with us in expressing moral disapproval of all actions of a given type *t*, then we may get him to condemn a particular action *A*, by bringing forward arguments to show that *A* is of type *t*. For the question whether *A* does or does not belong to that type is a plain question of fact. Given that a man has certain moral principles, we argue that he must, in order to be consistent, react morally to certain things in a certain way. What we do not and cannot argue about is the validity of these moral principles. We merely praise or condemn them in the light of our own feelings. . . .

[E]thical philosophy consists simply in saying that ethical concepts are pseudo-concepts and therefore unanalysable. The further task of describing the different feelings that the different ethical terms are used to express, and the different reactions that they customarily provoke, is a task for the psychologist. There cannot be such a thing as ethical science, if by ethical science one means the elaboration of a "true" system of morals. For we have seen that, as ethical judgements are mere expressions of feelings, there can be no way of determining the validity of any ethical system, and, indeed, no sense in asking whether any such system is true. All that one may legitimately enquire in this connection is, What are the moral habits of a given person or group of people, and what causes them to have precisely those habits and feelings? And this enquiry falls wholly within the scope of the existing social sciences.

John Rawls
(Rule Utilitarianism)

Rawls was born in Baltimore, Maryland, in 1921, and was educated at Kent School and at Princeton and Cornell. After serving in the U.S. Army during World War II, Rawls taught at Princeton, Cornell, Harvard, and M.I.T. before being appointed Professor of Philosophy at Harvard University in 1962. Rawls has been James Bryant Conant University Professor at Harvard since 1979. A member of the American Academy of Arts and Sciences, Rawls is also a past president of the American Philosophical Association and of the American Association of Political and Legal Philosophy. He has authored numerous articles in scholarly journals.

Two Concepts of Rules (1955)*

IN THIS paper I want to show the importance of the distinction between justifying a practice and justifying a particular action falling under it, and I want to explain the logical basis of this distinction and how it is possible to miss its significance. While the distinction has frequently been made, and is now becoming commonplace, there remains the task of explaining the tendency either to overlook it altogether, or to fail to appreciate its importance.

To show the importance of the distinction I am going to defend utilitarianism against those objections which have traditionally been made against it in connection with punishment and the obligation to keep promises. I hope to show that if one uses the distinction in question then one can state utilitarianism in a way which makes it a much better explication of our considered moral judgments than these traditional objections would seem to admit. Thus the importance of the distinction is shown by the way it strengthens the utilitarian view regardless of whether that view is completely defensible or not.

To explain how the significance of the distinction may be overlooked, I am going to discuss two conceptions of rules. One of these conceptions conceals the importance of distinguishing between the justification of a rule or practice and the justification of a particular action falling under it. The other conception makes it clear why this distinction must be made and what is its logical basis.

From John Rawls, "Two Concepts of Rules," *The Philosophical Review*, 64 (1955), 3–32. Used with permission.

The subject of punishment, in the sense of attaching legal penalties to the violation of legal rules, has always been a troubling moral question. The trouble about it has not been that people disagree as to whether or not punishment is justifiable. Most people have held that, freed from certain abuses, it is an acceptable institution. Only a few have rejected punishment entirely, which is rather surprising when one considers all that can be said against it. The difficulty is with the justification of punishment: various arguments for it have been given by moral philosophers, but so far none of them has won any sort of general acceptance; no justification is without those who detest it. I hope to show that the use of the aforementioned distinction enables one to state the utilitarian view in a way which allows for the sound points of its critics.

For our purposes we may say that there are two justifications of punishment. What we may call the retributive view is that punishment is justified on the grounds that wrongdoing merits punishment. It is morally fitting that a person who does wrong should suffer in proportion to his wrongdoing. That a criminal should be punished follows from his guilt, and the severity of the appropriate punishment depends on the depravity of his act. The state of affairs where a wrongdoer suffers punishment is morally better than the state of affairs where he does not; and it is better irrespective of any of the consequences of punishing him.

What we may call the utilitarian view holds that on the principle that bygones are bygones and that only future consequences are material to present decisions, punishment is justifiable only by reference to the probable consequences of maintaining it as one of the devices of the social order. Wrongs committed in the past are, as such, not relevant considerations for deciding what to do. If punishment can be shown to promote effectively the interest of society it is justifiable, otherwise it is not.

I have stated these two competing views very roughly to make one feel the conflict between them: one feels the force of *both* arguments and one wonders how they can be reconciled. From my introductory remarks it is obvious that the resolution which I am going to propose is that in this case one must distinguish between justifying a practice as a system of rules to be applied and enforced, and justifying a particular action which falls under these rules; utilitarian arguments are appropriate with regard to questions about practices, while retributive arguments fit the application of particular rules to particular cases.

We might try to get clear about this distinction by imagining how a father might answer the question of his son. Suppose the son asks, "Why was *J* put in jail yesterday?" The father answers, "Because he robbed the bank at *B*. He was duly tried and found guilty. That's why he was put in jail yesterday." But suppose the son had asked a different question, namely, "Why do people put other people in jail?" Then the father might answer, "To protect good people from bad people" or "To stop people from doing things that would make it uneasy for all of us; for otherwise we wouldn't be able to go to bed at night and sleep in peace." There are two very different questions here. One question emphasizes the proper name: it asks why *J* was punished rather than someone else, or it asks what he was punished for. The other question asks why we have the institution of punishment: why do people punish one another rather than, say, always forgiving one another?

Thus the father says in effect that a particular man is punished, rather than some other man, because he is guilty, and he is guilty because he broke the law (past tense). In his case the law looks back, the judge looks back, the jury looks back, and a penalty is visited upon him for something he did. That a man is to be punished, and what his punishment is to be, is settled by its being shown that he broke the law and that the law assigns that penalty for the violation of it.

On the other hand we have the institution of punishment itself, and recommend and accept various changes in it, because it is thought by the (ideal) legislator and by those to whom the law applies that, as a part of a system of law impartially applied from case to case arising under it, it will have the consequence, in the long run, of furthering the interests of society.

One can say, then, that the judge and the legislator stand in different positions and look in different directions: one to the past, the other to the future. The justification of what the judge does, *qua* judge, sounds like the retributive view; the justification of what the (ideal) legislator does, *qua* legislator, sound like the utilitarian view. Thus both views have a point (this is as it should be since intelligent and sensitive persons have been on both sides of the argument); and one's initial confusion disappears once one sees that these views apply to persons holding different offices with different duties, and situated differently with respect to the system of rules that make up the criminal law.

One might say, however, that the utilitarian view is more fundamental since it applies to a more fundamental office, for the judge carries out the legislator's will so far as he can determine it. Once the legislator decides to have laws and to assign penalties for their violation (as things are there must be both the law and the penalty) an institution is set up which involves a retributve conception of particular cases. It is part of the concept of the criminal law as a system of rules that the application and enforcement of these rules in particular cases should be justifiable by arguments of a retributive character. The decision whether or not to use law rather than some other mechanism of social control, and the decision as to what laws to have and what penalties to assign, may be settled by utilitarian arguments; but if one decides to have laws then one has decided on something whose working in particular cases is retributive in form. . . .

I shall now consider the question of promises. The objection to utilitarianism in connection with promises seems to be this: it is believed that on the utilitarian view when a person makes a promise the only ground upon which he should keep it, if he should keep it, is that by keeping it he will realize the most good on the whole. So that if one asks the question "Why should I keep *my* promise?" the utilitarian answer is understood to be that doing so in *this* case will have the best consequences. And this answer is said, quite rightly, to conflict with the way in which the obligation to keep promises is regarded.

Now of course critics of utilitarianism are not unaware that one defense sometimes attributed to utilitarians is the consideration involving the practice of promise-keeping. In this connection they are supposed to argue something like this: it must be admitted that we feel strictly about keeping promises, more strictly than it might seem our view can account for. But when we consider the matter carefully it is always necessary to take into account the effect which our action will have on the practice of making promises. The promisor must weigh, not only the effects of breaking his promise on the particular case, but also the effect which his breaking his promise will have on the practice itself. Since the practice is of great utilitarian value, and since breaking one's promise always seriously damages it, one will seldom be justified in breaking one's promise. If we view our individual promises in the wider context of the practice of promising itself we can account for the strictness of the obligation to keep promises. There is always one very strong utilitarian consideration in favor of keeping them, and this will insure that when the question arises as to whether or not to keep a promise it will usually turn out that one should, even where the facts of the particular case taken by itself would seem to justify one's breaking it. In this way the strictness with which we view the obligation to keep promises is accounted for.

Ross has criticized this defense as follows: however great the value of the practice of promising, on utilitarian grounds, there must be some value which is greater, and one can imagine it to be obtainable by breaking a promise. Therefore there might be a case where the promisor could argue that breaking his promise was justified as leading to a better state of affairs on the whole. And the promisor could argue in this way no matter how slight the advantage won by breaking the promise. If one were to challenge the promisor his defense would be that what he did was best on the whole in view of all the utilitarian considerations, which in this case *include* the importance of the practice. Ross feels that such a defense would be unacceptable. I think he is right insofar as he is protesting against the appeal to consequences in general and without further explanation. Yet it is extremely difficult to weigh the force of Ross's argument. The kind of case imagined seems unrealistic and one feels that it needs to be described. One is inclined to think that it would either turn out that such a case came under an exception defined by the practice itself, in which case there would not be an appeal to consequences in general on the particular case, or it would happen that the circumstances were so peculiar that the conditions which the practice presupposes no longer obtained. But certainly Ross is right in thinking that it strikes us as wrong for a person to defend breaking a promise by a general appeal to consequences. For a general utilitarian defense is not open to the promisor: it is not one of the defenses allowed by the practice of making promises.

Ross gives two further counterarguments: First, he holds that it overestimates the damage done to the practice of promising by a failure to keep a promise. One who breaks a promise harms his own name certainly, but it isn't clear that a broken promise always damages the practice itself sufficiently to account for the strictness of the obligation. Second, and more important, I think, he raises the question of what one is to say of a promise which isn't known to have been made except to the promisor and the promisee, as in the case of a promise a son makes to his dying father concerning the handling of the estate. In this sort of case the consideration relating to the practice doesn't weigh on the promisor at all, and yet one feels that this sort of promise is as binding as other promises. The question of the effect which breaking it has on the practice seems irrelevant. The only consequence seems to be that one can break the promise without running any risk of being censured; but the obligation itself seems not the least weakened. Hence it is doubtful whether the effect on the practice ever weighs in the particular case; certainly it cannot account for the strictness of the obligation where it fails to obtain. It seems to follow that a utilitarian account of the obligation to keep promises cannot be successfully carried out.

From what I have said in connection with punishment, one can foresee what I am going to say about these arguments and counterarguments. They fail to make the distinction between the justification of a practice and the justification of a particular action falling under it, and therefore they fall into the mistake of taking it for granted that the promisor, like Carritt's official, is entitled without restriction to bring utilitarian considerations to bear in deciding whether to keep *his* promise. But if one considers what the practice of promising is one will see, I think, that it is such as not to allow this sort of general discretion to the promisor. Indeed, the point of the practice is to abdicate one's title to act in accordance with utilitarian and prudential considerations in order that the future may be tied down and plans coordinated in advance. There are obvious utilitarian advantages in having a practice which denies to the promisor, as a defense, any general appeal to the utilitarian principle in accordance with which the practice itself may be justified. There is nothing contradictory, or surprising, in this: utilitarian (or aesthetic) reasons might properly be given in arguing that the game of chess, or baseball, is satisfactory just as it is, or in arguing that it should be changed in various respects, but a player in a game cannot properly appeal to such considerations as reasons for his making one move rather than another. It is a mistake to think that if the practice is justified on utilitarian grounds then the promisor must have complete liberty to use utilitarian arguments to decide whether or not to keep his promise. The practice forbids this general defense; and it is a purpose of the practice to do this. Therefore what the above arguments presuppose—the idea that if the utilitarian view is accepted then the promisor is bound if, and only if, the application of the utilitarian principle to his own case shows that keeping it is best on the whole—is false. The promisor is bound because he promised: weighing the case on its merits is not open to him.

Is this to say that in particular cases one cannot deliberate whether or not to keep one's promise? Of course not. But to do so is to deliberate whether the various excuses, exceptions and defenses, which are understood by, and which constitute an important part of, the practice, apply to one's own case. Various defenses for not keeping one's promise are allowed, but among them there isn't the one that, on general utilitarian grounds, the promisor (truly) thought his action best on the whole, even though there may be the defense that the consequences of keeping one's promise would have been *extremely* severe. While there are too many complexities here to consider all the necessary details, one can see that the general defense isn't allowed if one asks the following question: what would one say of someone who, when asked why he broke his promise, replied simply that breaking it was best on the whole? Assuming that his reply is sincere, and that his belief was reasonable (i.e., one need not consider the possibility that he was mistaken), I think that one would question whether or not he knows what it means to say "I promise" (in the appropriate circumstances). It would be said of someone who used this excuse without further explanation that he didn't understand what defenses the practice, which defines a promise, allows to him. If a child were to use this excuse one would correct him; for it is part of the way one is taught the concept of a promise to be corrected if one uses this excuse. The point of having the practice would be lost if the practice did allow this excuse.

It is no, doubt part of the utilitarian view that every practice should admit the defense that the consequences of abiding by it would have been extremely severe; and utilitarians would be inclined to hold that some reliance on people's good sense and some concession to hard cases is necessary. They would hold that a practice is justified by serving the interests of those who take part in it; and as with any set of rules there is understood a background of circumstances under which it is expected to be applied and which need not—indeed which cannot—be fully stated. Should these circumstances change, then even if there is no rule which provides for the case, it may still be in accordance with the practice that one be released from one's obligation. But this sort of defense allowed by a practice must not be confused with the general option to weigh each particular case on utilitarian grounds which critics of utilitarianism have thought it necessarily to involve.

The concern which utilitarianism raises by its justification of punishment is that it may justify too much. The question in connection with promises is different: it is how utilitarianism can account for the obligation to keep promises at all. One feels that the recognized obligation to keep one's promise and utilitarianism are incompatible. And to be sure, they are incompatible if one interprets the utilitarian view as necessarily holding that each person has complete liberty to weigh every particular action on general utilitarian grounds. But must one interpret utilitarianism in this way? I hope to show that, in the sorts of cases I have discussed, one cannot interpret it in this way.

So far I have tried to show the importance of the distinction between the justification of a practice and the justification of a particular action falling under it by indicating how this distinction might be used to defend utilitarianism against two longstanding objections. One might be tempted to close the discussion at this point by saying that utilitarian considerations should be understood as applying to practices in the first instance and not to particular actions falling under them except insofar as the practices admit of it. One might say that in this modified form it is a better account of our considered moral opinions and let it go at that. But to stop here would be to neglect the interesting question as to how one can fail to appreciate the significance of this rather obvious distinction and can take it for granted that utilitarianism has the consequence that particular cases may always be decided on general utilitarian grounds. I want to argue that this mistake may be connected with misconceiving the logical status of the rules of practices; and to show this I am going to examine two conceptions of rules, two ways of placing them within the utilitarian theory.

The conception which conceals from us the significance of the distinction I am going to call the summary view. It regards rules in the following way: one supposes that each person decides what he shall do in particular cases by applying the utilitarian principle; one supposes further that different people will decide the same particular case in the same way and that there will be recurrences of cases similar to those previously decided. Thus it will happen that in cases of certain kinds the same decision will be made either by the same person at different times or by different persons at the same time. If a case occurs frequently enough one supposes that a rule is formulated to cover that sort of case. I have called this conception the summary view because rules are pictured as summaries of past decisions arrived at by the *direct* application of the utilitarian principle to particular cases. Rules are regarded as reports that cases of a certain sort have been found on *other* grounds to be properly decided in a certain way (although, of course, they do not *say* this).

There are several things to notice about this way of placing rules within the utilitarian theory.

1. The point of having rules derives from the fact that similar cases tend to recur and that one can decide cases more quickly if one records past decisions in the form of rules. If similar cases didn't recur, one would be required to apply the utilitarian principle directly, case by case, and rules reporting past decisions would be of no use.

2. The decisions made on particular cases are logically prior to rules. Since

rules gain their point from the need to apply the utilitarian principle to many similar cases, it follows that a particular case (or several cases similar to it) may exist whether or not there is a rule covering that case. We are pictured as recognizing particular cases prior to there being a rule which covers them, for it is only if we meet with a number of cases of a certain sort that we formulate a rule. Thus we are able to describe a particular case as a particular case of the requisite sort whether there is a rule regarding *that* sort of case or not. Put another way: what the *A*'s and the *B*'s refer to in rules of the form "Whenever *A* do *B*" may be described as *A*'s and *B*'s whether or not there is the rule. "Whenever *A* do *B*", or whether or not there is any body of rules which make up a practice of which that rule is a part.

To illustrate this consider a rule, or maxim, which could arise in this way: suppose that a person is trying to decide whether to tell someone who is fatally ill what his illness is when he has been asked to do so. Suppose the person to reflect and then decide, on utilitarian grounds, that he should not answer truthfully; and suppose that on the basis of this and other like occasions he formulates a rule to the effect that when asked by someone fatally ill what his illness is, one should not tell him. The point to notice is that someone's being fatally ill and asking what his illness is, and someone's telling him, are things that can be described as such whether or not there is this rule. The performance of the action to which the rule refers doesn't require the stage-setting of a practice of which this rule is a part. This is what is meant by saying that on the summary view particular cases are logically prior to rules.

3. Each person is in principle always entitled to reconsider the correctness of a rule and to question whether or not it is proper to follow it in a particular case. As rules are guides and aids, one may ask whether in past decisions there might not have been a mistake in applying the utilitarian principle to get the rule in question, and wonder whether or not it is best in this case. The reason for rules is that people are not able to apply the utilitarian principle effortlessly and flawlessly; there is need to save time and to post a guide. On this view a society of rational utilitarians would be a society without rules in which each person applied the utilitarian principle directly and smoothly, and without error, case by case. On the other hand, ours is a society in which rules are formulated to serve as aids in reaching these ideally rational decisions on particular cases, guides which have been built up and tested by the experience of generations. If one applies this view to rules, one is interpreting them as maxims, as "rules of thumb"; and it is doubtful that anything to which the summary conception did apply would be called a *rule*. Arguing as if one regarded rules in this way is a mistake one makes while doing philosophy.

4. The concept of a *general* rule takes the following form. One is pictured as estimating on what percentage of the cases likely to arise a given rule may be relied upon to express the correct decision, that is, the decision that would be arrived at if one were to correctly apply the utilitarian principle case by case. If one estimates that by and large the rule will give the correct decision, or if one estimates that the likelihood of making a mistake by applying the utilitarian principle directly on one's own is greater than the likelihood of making a mistake by following the rule, and if these considerations held of persons generally, then one would be justified in urging its adoption as a general rule. In this way *general* rules might be accounted for on the summary view. It will still make sense, however, to speak of applying the utilitarian principle case by case, for it was by trying to foresee the results of doing this that one

got the initial estimates upon which acceptance of the rule depends. That one is taking a rule in accordance with the summary conception will show itself in the naturalness with which one speaks of the rules as a guide, or as a maxim, or as a generalization from experience, and as something to be laid aside in extraordinary cases where there is no assurance that the generalization will hold and the case must therefore be treated on its merits. Thus there goes with this conception the notion of a particular exception which renders a rule suspect on a particular occasion.

The other conception of rules I will call the practice conception. On this view rules are pictured as defining a practice. Practices are set up for various reasons, but one of them is that in many areas of conduct each person's deciding what to do on utilitarian grounds case by case leads to confusion, and that the attempt to coordinate behavior by trying to foresee how others will act is bound to fail. As an alternative one realizes that what is required is the establishment of a practice, the specification of a new form of activity; and from this one sees that a practice necessarily involves the abdication of full liberty to act on utilitarian and prudential grounds. It is the mark of a practice that being taught how to engage in it involves being instructed in the rules which define it, and that appeal is made to those rules to correct the behavior of those engaged in it. Those engaged in a practice recognize the rules as defining it. The rules cannot be taken as simply describing how those engaged in the practice in fact behave: it is not simply that they act as if they were obeying the rules. Thus it is essential to the notion of a practice that the rules are publicly known and understood as definitive; and it is essential also that the rules of a practice can be taught and can be acted upon to yield a coherent practice. On this conception, then, rules are not generalizations from the decisions of individuals applying the utilitarian principle directly and independently to recurrent particular cases. On the contrary, rules define a practice and are themselves the subject of the utilitarian principle.

To show the important differences between this way of fitting rules into the utilitarian theory and the previous way, I shall consider the differences between the two conceptions on the points previously discussed.

1. In contrast with the summary view, the rules of practices are logically prior to particular cases. This is so because there cannot be a particular case of an action falling under a rule of a practice unless there is the practice. This can be made clearer as follows: in a practice there are rules setting up offices, specifying certain forms of action appropriate to various offices, establishing penalties for the breach of rules and so on. We may think of the rules of a practice as defining offices, moves and offenses. Now what is meant by saying that the practice is logically prior to particular cases is this: given any rule which specifies a form of action (a move), a particular action which would be taken as falling under this rule given that there is the practice would not be *described as* that sort of action unless there was the practice. In the case of actions specified by practices it is logically impossible to perform them outside the stage-setting provided by those practices, for unless there is the practice, and unless the requisite proprieties are fulfilled, whatever one does, whatever movements one makes, will fail to count as a form of action which the practice specifies. What one does will be described in some *other* way.

One may illustrate this point from the game of baseball. Many of the actions one performs in a game of baseball one can do by oneself or with others whether there is the game or not. For example, one can throw a ball, run, or swing a peculiarly shaped piece of wood. But one cannot steal base, or strike out, or draw a walk, or make an error, or balk; although one can do certain things which appear to resemble these actions such as sliding into a bag, missing a grounder and so on. Striking out, stealing a base, balking, etc., are all actions which can only happen in a game. No matter what a person did, what he did would not be described as stealing a base or striking out or drawing a walk unless he could also be described as playing baseball, and for him to be doing this presupposes the rule-like practice which constitutes the game. The practice is logically prior to particular cases: unless there is the practice the terms referring to actions specified by it lack a sense.

2. The practice view leads to an entirely different conception of the authority which each person has to decide on the propriety of following a rule in particular cases. To engage in a practice, to perform those actions specified by a practice, means to follow the appropriate rules. If one wants to do an action which a certain practice specifies then there is no way to do it except to follow the rules which define it. Therefore, it doesn't make sense for a person to raise the question whether or not a rule of a practice correctly applies to *his* case where the action he contemplates is a form of action defined by a practice. If someone were to raise such a question, he would simply show that he didn't understand the situation in which he was acting. If one wants to perform an action specified by a practice, the only legitimate question concerns the nature of the practice itself ("How do I go about making a will?").

This point is illustrated by the behavior expected by a player in games. If one wants to play a game, one doesn't treat the rules of the game as guides as to what is best in particular cases. In a game of baseball if a batter were to ask "Can I have four strikes?" it would be assumed that he was asking what the rule was; and if, when told what the rule was, he were to say that he meant that on this occasion he thought it would be best on the whole for him to have four strikes rather than three, this would be most kindly taken as a joke. One might contend that baseball would be a better game if four strikes were allowed instead of three; but one cannot picture the rules as guides to what is best on the whole in particular cases, and question their applicability to particular cases as particular cases.

3 and 4. To complete the four points of comparison with the summary conception, it is clear from what has been said that rules of practices are not guides to help one decide particular cases correctly as judged by some higher ethical principle. And neither the quasi-statistical notion of generality, nor the notion of a particular exception, can apply to the rules of practices. A more or less general rule of a practice must be a rule which according to the structure of the practice applies to more or fewer of the kinds of cases arising under it; or it must be a rule which is more or less basic to the understanding of the practice. Again, a particular case cannot be an exception to a rule of a practice. An exception is rather a qualification or a further specification of the rule.

It follows from what we have said about the practice conception of rules that if a person is engaged in a practice, and if he is asked why *he* does what *he* does, or if he is asked to defend what he does, then his explanation, or defense, lies in referring the questioner to the practice. He cannot say of *his* action, if it is an action specified by a practice, that he does it rather than some other because he thinks it is best on the whole. When a man engaged in a practice is queried about his action he must assume that the questioner either doesn't know that he is engaged in it ("Why are you in a hurry to pay him?" "I promised to pay him today") or doesn't know what the practice is. One doesn't so much justify one's particular action as explain, or show, that it is in accordance with the practice. The reason for this is that it is only against the stage-setting of the practice that one's particular action is described as it is. Only by reference to the practice one *say* what one is doing. To explain or to defend one's own action, as a particular action, one fits it into the practice which defines it. If this is not accepted it's a sign that a different question is being raised as to whether one is justified in accepting the practice, or in tolerating it. When the challenge is to the practice, citing the rules (saying what the practice is) is naturally to no avail. But when the challenge is to the particular action defined by the practice, there is nothing one can do but refer to the rules. Concerning particular actions there is only a question for one who isn't clear as to what the practice is, or who doesn't know that it is being engaged in. This is to be contrasted with the case of a maxim which may be taken as pointing to the correct decision on the case as decided on *other* grounds, and so giving a challenge on the case a sense by having it question whether these other grounds really support the decision on this case.

If one compares the two conceptions of rules I have discussed, one can see how the summary conception misses the significance of the distinction between justifying a practice and justifying actions falling under it. On this view rules are regarded as guides whose purpose it is to indicate the ideally rational decision on the given particular case which the flawless application of the utilitarian principle would yield. One has, in principle, full option to use the guides or to discard them as the situation warrants without one's moral office being altered in any way: whether one discards the rules or not, one always holds the office of a rational person seeking case by case to realize the best on the whole. But on the practice conception, if one holds an office defined by a practice then questions regarding one's actions in this office are settled by reference to the rules which define the practice. If one seeks to question these rules, then one's office undergoes a fundamental change: one then assumes the office of one empowered to change and criticize the rules, or the office of a reformer, and so on. The summary conception does away with the distinction of offices and the various forms of argument appropriate to each. On that conception there is one office and so no offices at all. It therefore obscures the fact that the utilitarian principle must, in the case of actions and offices defined by a practice, apply to the practice, so that general utilitarian arguments are not available to those who act in offices so defined. . . .

What I have tried to show by distinguishing between two conceptions of rules is that there is a way of regarding rules which allows the option to consider particular cases on general utilitarian grounds; whereas there is another conception which does not admit of such discretion except insofar as the rules themselves authorize it. I want to suggest that the tendency while doing philosophy to picture rules in accordance with the summary conception is what may have blinded moral philosophers to the significance of the distance between justifying a practice and justifying a particular action falling under it; and it does so by misrepresenting the logical force of the reference to the rules in the case of a challenge to a particular action falling under a practice, and by obscuring the fact that where there is a practice, it is the practice itself that must be the subject of the utilitarian principle.

J. J. C. Smart
(Act Utilitarianism)

John Jamieson Carswell Smart was born in Cambridge, England, in 1920. After serving as lieutenant· in the British Army during World War II, Smart completed his Master of Arts degree at Glasgow University in 1946, graduating with honors in philosophy, mathematics, and natural philosophy. He was also named Ferguson Scholar of the Scottish Universities. After completing his graduate studies at Queen's College, Oxford, in 1948, Smart taught as Hughes Professor of Philosophy at the University of Adelaide, Reader in Philosophy at La Trobe University, and Professor of Philosophy at the Australian National University. He has also lectured at Princeton, Harvard, Yale and Stanford and is presently Emeritus Professor of Philosophy at Adelaide and the Australian University and Gavin David Young Lecturer at Adelaide. A Fellow of the Australian Academy of the Humanities and a member of the Institut International de Philosophie, Smart has also served on the Council of the Australian Academy of the Humanities and on the Governing Board of the Philosophy of Science Association. He is past president of the Australian Association of Philosophy and has served on the editorial boards of several prestigious journals. Smart also received an honorary D. Litt. from the University of St. Andrews in 1983. His major writings include *An Outline of a System of Utilitarian Ethics, Philosophy and Scientific Realism, Ethics, Persuasion and Truth,* and *Essays Metaphysical and Moral.*

Extreme and Restricted Utilitarianism (1956)*

Utilitarianism is the doctrine that the rightness of actions is to be judged by their consequences. What do we mean by "actions" here? Do we mean particular actions or do we mean classes of actions? According to which way we interpret the word "actions" we get two different theories, both of which merit the appellation "utilitarian".

(1) If by "actions" we mean particular individual actions we get the sort of

From J.J.C. Smart, "Extreme and Restricted Utilitarianism," *The Philosophical Quarterly*, 6 (1956), 344–354. Used with permission: amended as requested by Professor Smart.

doctrine held by Bentham, Sidgwick, and Moore. According to this doctrine we test individual actions by their consequences, and general rules, like "keep promises", are more rules of thumb which we use only to avoid the necessity of estimating the probable consequences of our actions at every step. The rightness or wrongness of keeping a promise on a particular occasion depends only on the goodness or badness of the consequences of keeping or breaking the promise on that particular occasion. Of course part of the consequences of breaking the promise, and a part to which we will normally ascribe decisive importance, will be the weakening of faith in the institution of promising. However, if the goodness of the consequences of breaking the rule is *in toto* greater than the goodness of the consequences of keeping it, then we must break the rule, irrespective of whether the goodness of the consequences of *everybody's* obeying the rule is or is not greater than the consequences of *everybody's* breaking it. To put it shortly, rules do not matter, save *per accidens* as rules of thumb and as *de facto* social institutions with which the utilitarian has to reckon when estimating consequences. I shall call this doctrine "extreme utilitarianism".

(2) A more modest form of utilitarianism has recently become fashionable. The doctrine is to be found in Toulmin's book *The Place of Reason in Ethics,* in Nowell-Smith's *Ethics* (though I think Nowell-Smith has qualms), in John Austin's *Lectures on Jurisprudence* (Lecture II), and even in J. S. Mill, if Urmson's interpretation of him is correct(*Philosophical Quarterly,* Vol. 3, pp. 33–39, 1953). Part of its charm is that it appears to resolve the dispute in moral philosophy between intuitionists and utilitarians in a way which is very neat. The above philosophers hold, or seem to hold, that moral rules are more than rules of thumb. In general the rightness of an action is *not* to be tested by evaluating its consequences but only by considering whether or not it falls under a certain rule. Whether the rule is to be considered an acceptable moral rule, is, however, to be decided by considering the consequences of adopting the rule. Broadly, then, actions are to be tested by rules and rules by consequences. The only cases in which we must test an individual action directly by its consequences are *(a)* when the action comes under two different rules, one of which enjoins it and one of which forbids it, and *(b)* when there is no rule whatever that governs the given case. I shall call this doctrine "restricted utilitarianism". . . .

The issue between extreme and restricted utilitarianism can be illustrated by considering the remark "But suppose everyone did the same". (Cf. A. K. Stout's article in *The Australasian Journal of Philosophy,* Vol.32, pp. 1–29.) Stout distinguishes two forms of the universalization principle, the causal form and the hypothetical form. To say that you ought not to do an action *A* because it would have bad results if everybody (or many people) did action *A* may be merely to point out that while the action *A* would otherwise be the optimific one, nevertheless when you take into account that doing *A* will probably cause other people to do *A* too, you can see that *A* is not, on a broad view, really optimific. If this causal influence could be avoided (as may happen in the case of a secret desert island promise) then we would disregard the universalization principle. This is the causal form of the principle. A person who accepted the universalisation principle in its hypothetical form would be one who was concerned only with what would happen *if* everyone did the action *A*: he would be totally unconcerned with the question of whether in fact everyone would do the action *A*. That is, he might say that it would be wrong not to vote because it would have bad results if everyone took this attitude, and he would be totally unmoved by arguments purporting to show that my refusing to vote has no effect whatever on other peoples' propensity to vote. Making use of Stout's distinction, we can say that an extreme utilitarian would apply the universalisation principle in the causal form, while a restricted utilitarian would apply it in the hypothetical form. . . .

For an extreme utilitarian moral rules are rules of thumb. In practice the extreme utilitarian will mostly guide his conduct by appealing to the rules ("do not lie", "do not break promises", etc.) of common sense morality. This is not because there is anything sacrosanct in the rules themselves but because he can argue that probably he will most often act in an extreme utilitarian way if he does not think as a utilitarian. For one thing, actions have frequently to be done in a hurry. Imagine a man seeing a person drowning. He jumps in and rescues him. There is no time to reason the matter out, but usually this will be the course of action which an extreme utilitarian would recommend if he did reason the matter out. If, however, the man drowning had been drowning in a river near Berchtesgaden in 1938, and if he had had the well known black forelock and moustache of Adolf Hitler, an extreme utilitarian would, if he had time, work out the probability of the man's being the villainous dictator, and if the probability were high enough he would, on extreme utilitarian grounds, leave him to drown. The rescuer, however, has not time. He trusts to his instincts and dives in and rescues the man. And this trusting to instincts and to moral rules can be justified on extreme utilitarian grounds. Furthermore, an extreme utilitarian who knew that the drowning man was Hitler would nevertheless praise the rescuer, not condemn him. For by praising the man he is strengthening a courageous and benevolent disposition of mind, and in general this disposition has great positive utility. (Next time, perhaps, it will be Winston Churchill that the man saves!) We must never forget that an extreme utilitarian may praise actions which he knows to be wrong. Saving Hitler was wrong, but it was a member of a class of actions which are generally right, and the motive to do actions of this class is in general an optimific one. In considering questions of praise and blame it is not the expediency of the praised or blamed action that is at issue, but the expediency of the praise. It can be expedient to praise an inexpedient action and inexpedient to praise an expedient one.

Lack of time is not the only reason why an extreme utilitarian may, on extreme utilitarian principles, trust to rules of common sense morality, He knows that in particular cases where his own interests are involved his calculations are likely to be biased in his own favor. Suppose that he is unhappily married and is deciding whether to get divorced. He will in all probability greatly exaggerate his own unhappiness (and possibly his wife's) and greatly underestimate the harm done to his children by the break up of the family. He will probably also underestimate the likely harm done by the weakening of the general faith in marriage vows. So probably he will come to the correct extreme utilitarian conclusion if he does not in this instance think as an extreme utilitarian but trusts to common sense morality. . . .

The restricted utilitarian regards moral rules as more than rules of thumb for short-circuiting calculations of consequences. Generally, he argues, consequences are not relevant at all when we are deciding what to do in a particular case. In general, they are relevant only to deciding what rules are good reasons for acting in a certain way in particular cases. This doctrine is possibly a good account of how the modern unreflective twentieth century Englishman often thinks about morality, but surely it is monstrous as an account of how it is most rational to think about morality.

Suppose that there is a rule R and that in 99% of cases the best possible results are obtained by acting in accordance with R. Then clearly R is a useful rule of thumb; if we have not time or are not impartial enough to assess the consequences of an action it is an extremely good bet that the thing to do is to act in accordance with R. But is it not monstrous to suppose that if we *have* worked out the consequences and if we have perfect faith in the impartiality of our calculations, and if we *know* that in this instance to break R will have better results than to keep it, we should nevertheless obey the rule? Is it not to erect R into a sort of idol if we keep it when breaking it will prevent, say, some avoidable misery? Is not this a form of superstitious rule-worship (easily explicable psychologically) and not the rational thought of a philosopher?. . .

Let us consider a much discussed sort of case in which the extreme utilitarian might go against the conventional moral rule. I have promised to a friend, dying on a desert island from which I am subsequently rescued, that I will see that his fortune (over which I have control) is given to a jockey club. However, when I am rescued I decide that it would be better to give the money to a hospital, which can do more good with it. It may be argued that I am wrong to give the money to the hospital. But why? *(a)* The hospital can do more good with the money than the jockey club can. *(b)* The present case is unlike most cases of promising in that no one except me knows about the promise. In breaking the promise I am doing so with complete secrecy and am doing nothing to weaken the general faith in promises. That is, a factor, which would normally keep the extreme utilitarian from promise breaking even in otherwise unoptomific cases, does not at present operate. *(c)* There is no doubt a slight weakening in my own character as an habitual promise keeper, and moreover psychological tensions will be set up in me every time I am asked what the man made me promise him to do. For clearly I shall have to say that he made me promise to give the money to the hospital, and, since I am an habitual truth teller, this will go very much against the grain with me. Indeed I am pretty sure that in practice I myself would keep the promise. But we are not discussing what my moral habits would probably make me do; we are discussing what I ought to do. Moreover, we must not forget that even if it would be most rational of me to give the money to the hospital it would also be most rational of you to punish or condemn me if you did, most improbably, find out the truth (e.g. by finding a note washed ashore in a bottle). Furthermore, I would agree that though it was most rational of me to give the money to the hospital it would be most rational of you to condemn me for it. We revert again to Sidgwick's distinction between the utility of the action and the utility of the praise of it.

Many such issues are discussed by A. K. Stout in the article to which I have already referred. I do not wish to go over the same ground again, especially as I think that Stout's arguments support my own point of view. It will be useful, however, to consider one other example that he gives. Suppose that during hot weather there is an edict that no water must be used for watering gardens. I have a garden and I reason that most people are sure to obey the edict, and that as the amount of water that I use will be by itself negligible no harm will be done if I use the water secretly. So I do use the water, thus producing some lovely flowers which give happiness to various people. Still, you may say, though the action was perhaps optimific, it was unfair and wrong.

There are several matters to consider. Certainly my action should be condemned. We revert once more to Sidgwick's distinction. A right action may be rationally condemned. Furthermore, this sort of offense is normally found out. If I have a wonderful garden when everybody else's is dry and brown there is only one explanation. So if I water my garden I am weakening my respect for law and order, and as this leads to bad results an extreme utilitarian would agree that I was wrong to water the garden. Suppose now that the case is altered and that I can keep the thing secret: there is a secluded part of the garden where I grow flowers which I give away anonymously to a home for old ladies. Are you still so sure that I did the wrong thing by watering my garden? However, this is still a weaker case than that of the hospital and the jockey club. There will be tensions set up within myself: my secret knowledge that I have broken the rule will make it hard for me to exhort others to keep the rule. These psychological ill effects in myself may be not inconsiderable: directly and indirectly they may lead to harm which is at least of the same order as the happiness that the old ladies get from the flowers. You can see that on an extreme utilitarian view there are two sides to the question.

So far I have been considering the duty of an extreme utilitarian in a predominately non-utilitarian society. The case is altered if we consider the extreme utilitarian who lives in a society every member, or most members, of which can be expected to reason as he does. Should he water his flowers now? (Granting, what is doubtful, that in the case already considered he would have been right to water his flowers.) As a first approximation the answer is that he should not do so. For since the situation is a completely symmetrical one, what is rational for him is rational for others. Hence by a *reductio ad absurdum* argument we see that it would be rational for none. Even without the edict, no one would water their flowers in a drought. (At least if the chance of doing so secretly were equal to all.) Notice that in this sort of case the extreme utilitarian in an extreme utilitarian society does not need edicts to keep him in order. . . .

I now pass on to a type of case which may be thought to be the trump card of restricted utilitarianism. Consider the rule of the road. It may be said that since all that matters is that everyone should do the same it is indifferent which rule we have, "go on the left hand side" or "go on the right hand side". Hence the only *reason* for going on the left hand side in British countries is that this is the rule. Here the rule does seem to be a reason, in itself, for acting in a certain way. I wish to argue against this. The rule in itself is not a reason for our actions. We would be perfectly justified in going on the right hand side if *(a)* we knew that the rule was to go on the left hand side, and *(b)* we were in a country peopled by superanarchists who always on principle did the opposite of what they were told. This shows that the rule does not give us a reason for acting so much as an indication of the probable actions of others, which helps us to find out what would be our own most rational course of action. If we are in a country not peopled by anarchists, but by non-anarchist extreme Utilitarians, we expect, other things being equal, that they will keep rules laid down for them. Knowledge of the rule enables us to predict their behavior and to harmonize our own actions with theirs. The rule "keep to the left hand side", then, is not a logical *reason* for action but an anthropological *datum* for planning actions.

I conclude that in every case if there is a rule R the keeping of which is in general optimific, but such that in a special sort of circumstances the optimific behavior is to break R, then in these circumstances we should break R. Of course we must consider all the less obvious effects of breaking R, such as reducing people's faith in the moral order, before coming to the conclusion that to break *R* is right: in fact we shall rarely come to such a conclusion. Moral rules, on the extreme utilitarian view, are rules of thumb only, but they are not bad rules of thumb. But if we *do* come to the conclusion that we should break the rule and if we have weighed in the balance our own fallibility and liability to personal bias, what good reason remains for keeping the rule? I can understand "it is optimific" as a reason for action, but why should "it is a member of a class of actions which are usually optimific" or "it is a member of a class of actions which as a class are more optimific than any alternative general class" be a good reason? You might as well say that a person ought to be picked to play for Australia just because all his brothers have been, or that the Australian team should be composed entirely of the Harvey family because this would be better than composing it entirely of any other family. The extreme utilitarian does not appeal to artificial feelings, but only to our feelings of benevolence, and what better feelings can there be to appeal to? Admittedly we can have a pro-attitude to anything, even to rules, but such artificially begotten pro-attitudes smack of superstition. Let us get down to realities, human happiness and misery, and make these the objects of our pro-attitudes and anti-attitudes.

The restricted utilitarian might say that he is talking only of *morality*, not of such things as rules of the road. I am not sure how far this objection, if valid, would affect my argument, but in any case I would reply that as a philosopher I conceive of ethics as the study of how it would be *most rational* to act. If my opponent wishes to restrict the word "morality" to a narrower use he can have the word. The fundamental question is the question of rationality of action *in general.* Similarly if the restricted utilitarian were to appeal to ordinary usage and say "it might be most rational to leave Hitler to drown but it would surely not be *wrong* to rescue him", I should again let him have the words "right" and "wrong" and should stick to "rational" and "irrational". We already saw that it would be rational to praise Hitler's rescuer, even though it would have been most rational not to have rescued Hitler. In ordinary language, no doubt, "right" and "wrong" have not only the meaning "most rational to do" and "not most rational to do" but also have the meaning "praiseworthy" and "not praiseworthy". Usually to the utility of an action corresponds utility of praise of it, but as we saw, this is not always so. Moral language could thus do with tidying up, for example by reserving "right" for "most rational" and "good" as an epithet of praise for the motive from which the action sprang. It would be more becoming in a philosopher to try to iron out illogicalities in moral language and to make suggestions for its reform than to use it as a court of appeal whereby to perpetuate confusions.

One last defence of restricted utilitarianism might be as follows. "Act optimifically" might be regarded as itself one of the rules of our system (though it would be odd to say that this rule was justified by its optimificality). According to Toulmin (*The Place of Reason in Ethics,* pp. 146–148) if "keep promises", say, conflicts with another rule we are allowed to argue the case on its merits, as if we were extreme utilitarians. If "act optimifically" is itself one of our rules then there will always be a conflict of rules whenever to keep a rule is not itself optimific. If this is so, restricted utilitarianism collapses into extreme utilitarianism. And no one could read Toulmin's book or Urmson's article on Mill without thinking that Toulmin and Urmson are of the opinion that they have thought of a doctrine which does *not* collapse into extreme utilitarianism, but which is, on the contrary, an improvement on it.

John Rawls

See earlier reading for biographical information on Professor Rawls.

A Theory of Justice (1971)*

Justice is the first virtue of social institutions, as truth is of systems of thought. A theory however elegant and economical must be rejected or revised if it is untrue; likewise laws and institutions no matter how efficient and well-arranged must be reformed or abolished if they are unjust. Each person possesses an inviolability founded on justice that even the welfare of society as a whole cannot override. For this reason justice denies that the loss of freedom for some is made right by a greater good shared by others. It does not allow that the sacrifices imposed on a few are outweighed by the larger sum of advantages enjoyed by many. Therefore in a just society the liberties of equal citizenship are taken as settled; the rights secured by justice are not subject to political bargaining or to the calculus of social interests. The only thing that permits us to acquiesce in an erroneous theory is the lack of a better one; analogously, an injustice is tolerable only when it is necessary to avoid an even great injustice. Being first virtues of human activities, truth and justice are uncompromising.

These propositions seem to express our intuitive conviction of the primacy of justice. No doubt they are expressed too strongly. In any event I wish to inquire whether these contentions or others similar to them are sound, and if so how they can be accounted for. To this end it is necessary to work out a theory of justice in the light of which these assertions can be interpreted and assessed. I shall begin by considering the role of the principles of justice. Let us assume, to fix ideas, that a society is a more or less self-sufficient association of persons who in their relations to one another recognize certain rules of conduct as binding and who for the most part act in accordance with them. Suppose further that these rules specify a system of cooperation designed to advance the good of those taking part in it. Then, although a society is a cooperative venture for mutual advantage, it is typically marked by a conflict as well as by an identity of interests. There is an identity of interests since social cooperation makes possible a better life for all than any would have if each

Excerpted by permission of the publishers from *A Theory of Justice*, by John Rawls, Cambridge, Mass.: The Belknap Press of Harvard University Press, and London: Oxford University Press, Copyright © 1971 by the President and Fellows of Harvard College.

were to live solely by his own efforts. There is a conflict of interests since persons are not indifferent as to how the greater benefits produced by their collaboration are distributed, for in order to pursue their ends they prefer a larger to a lesser share. A set of principles is required for choosing among the various social arrangements which determine this division of advantages and for underwriting an agreement on the proper distributive shares. These principles are the principles of social justice; they provide a way of assigning rights and duties in the basic institutions of society and they define the appropriate distribution of the benefits and burdens of social cooperation.

Now let us say that a society is well-ordered when it is not only designed to advance the good of its members but when it is also effectively regulated by a public conception of justice. That is, it is a society in which (1) everyone accepts and knows that the others accept the same principles of justice, and (2) the basic social institutions generally satisfy and are generally known to satisfy these principles. In this case while men may put forth excessive demands on one another, they nevertheless acknowledge a common point of view from which their claims may be adjudicated. If mens' inclination to self-interest makes their vigilance against one another necessary, their public sense of justice makes their secure association together possible. Among individuals with disparate aims and purposes a shared conception of justice establishes the bonds of civic friendship; the general desire for justice limits the pursuit of other ends. One may think of a public conception of justice as constituting the fundamental charter of a well-ordered human association. . . .

My aim is to present a conception of justice which generalizes and carries to a higher level of abstraction the familiar theory of the social contract as found, say, in Locke, Rousseau, and Kant. In order to do this we are not to think of the original contract as one to enter a particular society or to set up a particular form of government. Rather, the guiding idea is that the principles of justice for the basic structure of society are the object of the original agreement. They are the principles that free and rational persons concerned to further their own interests would accept in an initial position of equality as defining the fundamental terms of their association. These principles are to regulate all further agreements; they specify the kinds of social cooperation that can be entered into and the forms of government that can be established. This way of regarding the principles of justice I shall call justice as fairness.

Thus we are to imagine that those who engage in social cooperation choose together, in one joint act, the principles which are to assign basic rights and duties and to determine the division of social benefits. Men are to decide in advance how they are to regulate their claims against one another and what is to be the foundation charter of their society. Just as each person must decide by rational reflection what constitutes his good, that is, the system of ends which it is rational for him to pursue, so a group of persons must decide once and for all what is to count among them as just and unjust. The choice which rational men would make in this hypothetical situation of equal liberty, assuming for the present that this choice problem has a solution, determines the principles of justice.

In justice as fairness the original position of equality corresponds to the state of nature in the traditional theory of the social contract. This original position is not, of course, thought of as an actual historical state of affairs, much less as a primitive condition of culture. It is understood as a purely hypothetical situation characterized so as to lead to a certain conception of justice. Among the essential features of this situation is that no one knows his place in society, his class position or social status, nor does any one know his fortune in the distribution of natural assets and abilities, his intelligence, strength, and the like. I shall even assume that the parties do not know their conceptions of the good or their special psychological propensities. The principles of justice are chosen behind a veil of ignorance. This ensures that no one is advantaged or disadvantaged in the choice of principles by the outcome of natural chance or the contingency of social circumstances. Since all are similarly situated and no one is able to design principles to favor his particular condition, the principles of justice are the result of a fair agreement or bargain. For given the circumstances of the original position, the symmetry of everyone's relations to each other, this initial situation is fair between individuals as moral persons, that is, as rational beings with their own ends and capable, I shall assume, of a sense of justice. The original position is, one might say, the appropriate initial status quo, and thus the fundamental agreements reached in it are fair. This explains the propriety of the name "justice as fairness": it conveys the idea that the principles of justice are agreed to in an initial situation that is fair. The name does not mean that the concepts of justice and fairness are the same, any more than the phrase "poetry as metaphor" means that the concepts of poetry and metaphor are the same.

Justice as fairness begins, as I have said, with one of the most general of all choices which persons might make together, namely, with the choice of the first principles of a conception of justice which is to regulate all subsequent criticism and reform of institutions. Then, having chosen a conception of justice, we can suppose that they are to choose a constitution and a legislature to enact laws, and so on, all in accordance with the principles of justice initially agreed upon. Our social situation is just if it is such that by this sequence of hypothetical agreements we would have contracted into the general system of rules which defines it. Moreover, assuming that the original position does determine a set of principles (that is, that a particular conception of justice would be chosen), it will then be true that whenever social institutions satisfy these principles those engaged in them can say to one another that they are cooperating on terms to which they would agree if they were free and equal persons whose relations with respect to one another were fair. They could all view their arrangements as meeting the stipulations which they would acknowledge in an initial situation that embodies widely accepted and reasonable constraints on the choice of principles. The general recognition of this fact would provide the basis for a public acceptance of the corresponding principles of justice. No society can, of course, be a scheme of cooperation which men enter voluntarily in a literal sense; each person finds himself placed at birth in some particular position in some particular society, and the nature of this position materially affects his life prospects. Yet a society satisfying the principles of justice as fairness comes as close as a society can to being a voluntary scheme, for it meets the principles which free and equal persons would assent to under circumstances that are fair. In this sense its members are autonomous and the obligations they recognize self-imposed. . . .

I shall now state in a provisional form the two principles of justice that I believe would be chosen in the original position. In this section I wish to make only the most general comments, and therefore the first formulation of these principles is tentative. As we go on I shall run through several formulations and approximate step by step the final statement to be given much later. I believe that doing this allows the exposition to proceed in a natural way.

The first statement of the two principles reads as follows.

> First: each person is to have an equal right to the most extensive basic liberty compatible with a similar liberty for others.

> Second: social and economic inequalities are to be arranged so that they are both (a) reasonably expected to be to everyone's advantage, and (b) attached to positions and offices open to all.

There are two ambiguous phrases in the second principle, namely "every-ones's advantage" and "open to all." Determining their sense more exactly will lead to a second formulation of the principle in Ch. 13. The final version of the two principles is given in Ch. 46; Ch. 39 considers the rendering of the first principle.

By way of general comment, these principles primarily apply, as I have said, to the basic structure of society. They are to govern the assignment of rights and duties and to regulate the distribution of social and economic advantages. As their formulation suggests, these principles presuppose that the social structure can be divided into two more or less distinct parts, the first principle applying to the one, the second to the other. They distinguish between those aspects of the social system that define and secure the equal liberties of citizenship and those that specify and establish social and economic inequalities. The basic liberties of citizens are, roughly speaking, political liberty (the right to vote and to be eligible for public office) together with freedom of speech and assembly; liberty of conscience and freedom of thought; freedom of the person along with the right to hold (personal) property; and freedom from arbitrary arrest and seizure as defined by the concept of the rule of law. These liberties are all required to be equal by the first principle, since citizens of a just society are to have the same basic rights.

The second principle applies, in the first approximation, to the distribution of income and wealth and to the design of organizations that make use of differences in authority and responsibility, or chains of command. While the distribution of wealth and income need not be equal, it must to be everyone's advantage, and at the same time, positions of authority and offices of command must be accessible to all. One applies the second principle by holding positions open, and then, subject to this constraint, arranges social and economic inequalities so that everyone benefits.

These principles are to be arranged in a serial order with the first principle prior to the second. This ordering means that a departure from the institutions of equal liberty required by the first principle cannot be justified by, or compensated for, by greater social and economic advantages. The distribution of wealth and income, and the hierarchies of authority, must be consistent with both the liberties of equal citizenship and equality of opportunity.

It is clear that these principles are rather specific in their content, and their acceptance rests on certain assumptions that I must eventually try to explain and justify. A theory of justice depends upon a theory of society in ways that will become evident as we proceed. For the present, it should be observed that the two principles (and this holds for all formulations) are a special case of a more general conception of justice that can be expressed as follows.

All social values—liberty and opportunity, income and wealth, and the bases of self-respect—are to be distributed equally unless an unequal distribution of any, or all, of these values is to everyone's advantage.

Injustice, then, is simply inequalities that are not to the benefit of all. Of course, this conception is extremely vague and requires interpretation. As a first step, suppose that the basic structure of society distributes certain primary goods, that is, things that every rational man is presumed to want. These goods normally have a use whatever a person's rational plan of life. For simplicity, assume that the chief primary goods at the disposition of society are rights and liberties, powers and opportunities, income and wealth. (Later on in Part Three the primary good of self-respect has a central place.) These are the social primary goods. Other primary goods such as health and vigor, intelligence and imagination, are natural goods; although their possession is influenced by the basic structure, they are not so directly under its control. Imagine, then, a hypothetical initial arrangement in which all the social primary goods are equally distributed: everyone has similar rights and duties, and income and wealth are evenly shared. This state of affairs provides a benchmark for judging improvements. If certain inequalities of wealth and organizational powers would make everyone better off than in this hypothetical starting situation, they accord with the general conception.

Now it is possible, at least theoretically, that by giving up some of their fundamental liberties men are sufficiently compensated by the resulting social and economic gains. The general conception of justice imposes no restrictions on what sort of inequalities are permissible; it only requires that everyone's position be improved. We need not suppose anything so drastic as consenting to a condition of slavery. Imagine instead that men forego certain political rights when the economic returns are significant and their capacity to influence the course of policy by the exercise of these rights would be marginal in any case. It is this kind of exchange which the two principles as stated rule out; being arranged in serial order they do not permit exchanges between basic liberties and economic and social gains. The serial ordering of principles expresses an underlying preference among primary social goods. When this preference is rational so likewise is the choice of these principles in this order. . . .

The intuitive idea of justice as fairness is to think of the first principles of justice as themselves the object of an original agreement in a suitably defined initial situation. These principles are those which rational persons concerned to advance their interests would accept in this position of equality to settle the basic terms of their association. It must be shown, then, that the two principles of justice are the solution for the problem of choice presented by the original position. In order to do this, one must establish that, given the circumstances of the parties, and their knowledge, beliefs, and interests, an agreement on these principles is the best way for each person to secure his ends in view of the alternatives available.

Now obviously no one can obtain everything he wants; the mere existence of other persons prevents this. The absolutely best for any man is that everyone else should join with him in furthering his conception of the good whatever it turns out to be. Or failing this, that all others are required to act justly but that he is authorized to exempt himself as he pleases. Since other persons will never agree to such terms of association these forms of egoism would be rejected. The two principles of justice, however, seem to be a reasonable proposal. In fact, I should like to show that these principles are everyone's best reply, so to speak, to the corresponding demands of the others. In this sense, the choice of this conception of justice is the unique solution to the problem set by the original position. . . .

It will be recalled that the general conception of justice as fairness requires that all primary social goods be distributed equally unless an unequal distribution would be to everyone's's advantage. No restrictions are placed on exchanges of these goods and therefore a lesser liberty can be compensated for by greater social and economic benefits. Now looking at the situation from the standpoint of one person selected arbitrarily, there is no way for him to win special disadvantages for himself. Nor, on the other hand, are there grounds for his acquiescing in special disadvantages. Since it is not reasonable for him to expect more than an equal share in the division of social goods, and since it is not rational for him to agree to less, the sensible thing for him to do is to acknowledge as the first principle of justice one requiring an equal distribution. Indeed, this principle is so obvious that we would expect it to occur to anyone immediately.

Thus, the parties start with a principle establishing equal liberty for all, including equality of opportunity, as well as an equal distribution of income and wealth. But there is no reason why this acknowledgement should be final. If there are inequalities in the basic structure that work to make everyone better off in comparison with the benchmark of initial equality, why not permit them? The immediate gain which a greater equality might allow can be regarded as intelligently invested in view of its future return. If, for example, these inequalities set up various incentives which succeed in eliciting more productive efforts, a person in the original position may look upon them as necessary to cover the costs of training and to encourage effective performance. One might think that ideally individuals should want to serve one another. But since the parties are assumed not to take an interest in one another's interests, their acceptance of these inequalities is only the acceptance of the relations in which men stand in the circumstances of justice. They have no grounds for complaining of one another's motives. A person in the original position would, therefore, concede the justice of these inequalities. Indeed, it would be shortsighted of him not to do so. He would hesitate to agree to these regularities only if he would be dejected by the bare knowledge or perception that others were better situated; and I have assumed that the parties decide as if they are not moved by envy. In order to make the principle regulating inequalities determinate, one looks at the system from the standpoint of the least advantaged representative man. Inequalities are permissible when they maximize, or at least all contribute to, the long-term expectations of the least fortunate group in society.

Now this general conception imposes no constraints on what sorts of inequalities are allowed, whereas the special conception, by putting the two principles in serial order (with the necessary adjustments in meaning), forbids exchanges between basic liberties and economic and social benefits, I shall not try to justify this ordering here. From time to time in later chapters this problem will be considered (Chs. 39, 82). But roughly, the idea underlying this ordering is that if the parties assume that their basic liberties can be effectively exercised, they will not exchange a lesser liberty for an improvement in economic well-being. It is only when social conditions do not allow the effective establishment of these rights that one can concede their limitation; and these restrictions can be granted only to the extent that they are necessary to prepare the way for a free society. The denial of equal liberty can be defended only if it is necessary to raise the level of civilization so that in due course these freedoms can be enjoyed. Thus in adopting a serial order we are in effect making a special assumption in the original position, namely, that the parties know that the conditions of their society, whatever they are, admit the effective realization of the equal liberties. The serial ordering of the two principles of justice eventually comes to be reasonable if the general conception is consistently followed. This lexical ranking is the long-run tendency of the general view. For the most part I shall assume that the requisite circumstances for the serial order obtain.

It seems clear from these remarks that the two principles are at least a plausible conception of justice. . . .

I suppose the definition [of *good*] to have three stages as follows (for simplicity these stages are formulated using the concept of goodness rather than that of better than): (1) A is a good X if and only if A has the properties (to a higher degree than the average or standard X) which it is rational to want in an X, given what X's are used for, or expected to do, and the like (whichever rider is appropriate); (2) A is a good X for K (where K is some person) if and only if A has the properties which it is rational for K to want in an X, given K's circumstances, abilities, and plan of life (his system of aims), and therefore in view of what he intends to do with an X, or whatever; (3) the same as 2 but adding a clause to the effect that K's plan of life, or that part of it relevant in the present instance, is itself rational. What rationality means in the case of plans has yet to be determined and will be discussed later on. But according to the definition, once we establish that an object has the properties that it is rational for someone with a rational plan of life to want, then we have shown that it is good for him. And if certain sorts of things satisfy this condition for persons generally, then these things are human goods. Eventually we want to be assured that liberty and opportunity, and a sense of our own worth, fall into this category.

Now for a few comments on the first two stages of the definition. We tend to move from the first stage to the second whenever it is necessary to take into account the special features of a person's situation which the definition defines to be relevant. Typically these features are his interests, abilities, and circumstances. Although the principles of rational choice have not yet been set out, the everyday notion seems clear enough for the time being. In general, there is a reasonably precise sense in speaking simply of a good object of a certain kind, a sense explained by the first stage, provided that there is enough similarity of interests and circumstances among persons concerned with objects of this kind so that recognized standards can be established. When these conditions are met, saying that something is good conveys useful information. There is sufficient common experience with or knowledge of these things for us to have an understanding of the desired features exemplified by an average or standard object. Often there are conventional criteria founded upon commercial or other practice which define these properties. By taking up various examples we could no doubt see how these criteria evolve and the relevant standards determined. The essential point, however, is that these criteria depend upon the nature of the objects in question and upon our experience with them; and therefore we say that certain things are good without further elaboration only when a certain background is presupposed or some particular context is taken for granted. The basic value judgments are those made from the standpoint of persons, given their interests, abilities, and circumstances. Only insofar as a similarity of conditions permits can we safely abstract from anyone's special situation. In cases of any complexity, when the thing to be chosen should be adjusted to specific wants and situations, we move to the second stage of the definition. Our judgments of value are tailored to the agent in question as this stage requires. . . .

To this point I have discussed only the first stages of the definition of good in which no questions are raised about the rationality of the ends taken as given. A thing's being a good X for K is treated as equivalent to its having the properties which it is rational for K to want in an X in view of his interests and aims. Yet we often assess the rationality of a person's desires, and the definition must be extended to cover this fundamental case if it is to serve the purposes of the theory of justice. Now the basic idea at the third stage is to apply the definition of good to plans of life. The rational plan for a person determines his good. Here I adapt Royce's thought that a person may be regarded as a human life lived according to a plan. For Royce an individual says who he is by describing his purposes and causes, what he intends to do in his life. If this plan is a rational one, then I shall say that the person's conception of his good is likewise rational. In his case the real and the apparent good coincide. Similarly his interests and aims are rational, and it is appropriate to take them as stopping points in making judgments that correspond to the first two stages of the definition. These suggestions are quite straightforward but unfortunately setting out the details is somewhat tedious. In order to expedite matters I shall start off with a pair of definitions and then explain and comment on them over the next several sections.

These definitions read as follows: first, a person's plan of life is rational if, and only if, (1) it is one of the plans that is consistent with the principles of rational choice where these are applied to all the relevant features of his situation, and (2) it is that plan among those meeting this condition which would be chosen by him with full deliberative rationality, that is, with full awareness of the relevant facts and after a careful consideration of the consequences. (The notion of deliberative rationality is discussed in the next section.) Secondly, a person's interests and aims are rational if, and only if, they are to be encouraged and provided for by the plan that is rational for him. Note that in the first of these definitions I have implied that a rational plan is presumably but one of many possible plans that are consistent with the principles of rational choice. The reason for this complication is that these principles do not single out one plan as the best. We have instead a maximal class of plans: each member of this class is superior to all plans not included in it, but given any two plans in the class, neither is superior or inferior to the other. Thus to identify a person's rational plan, I suppose that it is that plan belonging to the maximal class which he would choose with full deliberative rationality. We criticize someone's plan, then, by showing either that it violates the principles of rational choice, or that it is not the plan that he would pursue were he to assess his prospects with care in the light of a full knowledge of his situation. . . .

I must now try to convey what is meant by the principles of rational choice. These principles are to be given by enumeration so that eventually they replace the concept of rationality. The relevant features of a person's situation are identified by these principles and the general conditions of human life to which plans must be adjusted. At this point I shall mention those aspects of rationality that are most familiar and seem least in dispute. And for the moment I shall assume that the choice situation relates to the short term. The question is how to fill in the more or less final details of a subplan to be executed over a relatively brief period of time, as when we make plans for a holiday. The larger system of desires may not be significantly affected, although of course some desires will be satisfied in this interval and others will not.

Now for the short-term questions anyway, certain principles seem perfectly straightforward and not in dispute. The first of these is that of effective means. Suppose that there is a particular objective that is wanted, and that all the alternatives are means to achieve it, while they are in other respects neutral. The principle holds that we are to adopt that alternative which realizes the end in the best way. More fully: given the objective, one is to achieve it with the least expenditure of means (whatever they are); or given the means, one is to fulfill the objective to the fullest possible extent. This principle is perhaps the most natural criterion of rational choice. Indeed, as we shall note later, there is some tendency to suppose that deliberation must always take this form, being regulated ultimately by a single final end (Ch. 83). Otherwise it is thought that there is no rational way to balance a plurality of aims against one another. But this question I leave aside for the present.

The second principle of rational choice is that one (short-term) plan is to be preferred to another if its execution would achieve all of the desired aims of the other plan and one or more further aims in addition. Perry refers to this criterion as the principle of inclusiveness and I shall do the same. Thus we are to follow the more inclusive plan if such a plan exists. To illustrate, suppose that we are planning a trip and we have to decide whether to go to Rome or Paris. It seems impossible to visit both. If on reflection it is clear that we can do everything in Paris that we want to do in Rome, and some other things as well, then we should go to Paris. Adopting this plan will realize a larger set of ends and nothing is left undone that might have been realized by the other plan. Often, however, neither plan is more inclusive than the other; each may achieve an aim which the other does not. We must invoke some other principle to make up our minds, or else subject our aims to further analysis (Ch. 83).

A third principle we may call that of the greater likelihood. Suppose that the aims which may be achieved by two plans are roughly the same. Then it may happen that some objectives have a greater chance of being realized by one plan than the other, yet at the same time none of the remaining aims are less likely to be attained. For example, although one can perhaps do everything one wants to do in both Rome and Paris, some of the things one wishes to do seem more likely to meet with success in Paris, and for the rest it is roughly the same. If so, the principle holds that one should go to Paris. A greater likelihood of success favors a plan just as the more inclusive end does. When these principles work together the choice is as obvious as can be. Suppose that we prefer a Titian to a Tintoretto, and that the first of two lottery tickets gives the larger chance to Titian while the second assigns it to the Tintoretto. Then one must prefer the first ticket,

So far we have been considering the application of the principles of rational choice to the short-term case. I now wish to examine the other extreme in which one has to adopt a long-term plan, even a plan of life, as when we have to choose a profession or occupation. It may be thought that having to make such a decision is a task imposed only by a particular form of culture. In another society this choice might not arise. But in fact the question of what to do with our life is always there, although some societies force it upon us more obviously than others and at a different time of life. The limit decision to have no plan at all, to let things come as they may, is still theoretically a plan that may or may not be rational. Accepting the idea of a long-term plan, then, it seems clear that such a scheme is to be assessed by what it will probably lead to in each future period of time. The principle of inclusiveness in this case, therefore, runs as follows: one long-term plan is better than another for any given period (or number of periods) if it allows for the encouragement and satisfaction of all the aims and interests of the other plan and for the encouragement and satisfaction of some further aim or interest in addition. The more inclusive plan, if there is one, is to be preferred: it comprehends all the ends of the first plan and at least one other end as well. If this principle is combined with that of effective means, then together they define rationality as preferring, other things equal, the greater means for realizing our aims, and the development of wider and more varied interests assuming that these aspirations can be carried through. The principle of greater likelihood supports this preference even in situations when we cannot be sure that the larger aims can be executed, provided that the chances of execution are as great as with the less comprehensive plan.

Alan Gewirth

Born in 1912 in Union City, New Jersey, Gewirth earned a bachelor's degree with honors from Columbia and studied as a Sage Fellow in Philosophy at Cornell and as a graduate assistant at the University of Chicago. He received his doctorate from Cornell in 1947 while a Rockefeller Foundation Fellow. Gewirth has taught at the University of Chicago since 1947 and was appointed Edward Carson Waller Distinguished Service Professor of Philosophy at Chicago in 1975. He has also held a number of visiting and distinguished lectureships at Harvard, Michigan, Johns Hopkins, Notre Dame, Padua (Italy), and elsewhere. A Fellow of the American Academy of Arts and Sciences, Gewirth is past president of the American Philosophical Association and of the American Society for Political and Legal Philosophy. He has received numerous academic awards, including the Woodbridge Prize and Nicholas Murray Butler Medal from Columbia University, the Gordon J. Laing Prize from the University of Chicago, and research and fellowship awards from the Rockefeller and Guggenheim Foundations and from the National Endowment for the Humanities. Gewirth's many publications include *Political Philosophy, Marsilius of Padua and Medieval Political Philosophy*, and *Social Justice*.

Reason and Morality (1978)*

Persons guide their lives in may different ways. Among the various goals, rules, habits, ideals, and institutions that figure more or less explicitly in such guidance, morality has a unique status. For it purports to set, for everyone's conduct, requirements that take precedence over all other modes of guiding action, including even the self-interest of the persons to whom it is addressed. What, if any, is the warrant for such a claim of precedence? Does the claim have a rational basis, or is it simply a product of superstition or societal conditioning? And even if the authoritative precedence of morality can in some way be justified, does this help to know which, if any, among the various competing moralities is itself first or justified?

As these questions suggest, from among the diverse meanings of "morality" and "moral" a certain core meaning may be elicited. According to this, a morality is a set of categorically obligatory requirements for action that are addressed at least in part to every actual or prospective agent, and that are concerned with furthering the interests, especially the most important interests, of persons or recipients other than or in addition to the agent or the speaker. The requirements are categorically obligatory in that compliance with them is mandatory for the conduct of every person to whom they are addressed regardless of whether he wants to accept them or their results, and regardless also of the requirements of any other institutions such as law or etiquette, whose obligatoriness may itself be doubtful or variable. Thus, although one moral requirement may be overridden by another, it may not be overridden by any nonmoral requirement, nor can its normative bindingness be escaped by shifting one's inclinations, opinions, or ideals. . . .

The main thesis of this book is that every agent, by the fact of engaging in action, is logically committed to accept a supreme moral principle having a certain determinate normative content. Because any agent who denies or violates this principle contradicts himself, the principle stands unchallenged as the criterion of moral rightness, and conformity with its requirements is categorically obligatory. . . .

In acting, the agent envisages more or less clearly some preferred outcome, some objective or goal he wants to achieve, where such wanting may be either intentional or inclinational. He regards his goal as worth aiming at or pursuing; for if he did not so regard it he would not unforcedly choose to move from quiescence or nonaction to action with a view to achieving the goal. This conception of worth constitutes a valuing on the part of the agent; he regards the object of his action as having at least sufficient value to merit his acting to attain it, according to whatever criteria are involved in his action. These criteria of value need not be moral or even hedonic; they run the full range of the purposes for which the agent acts, from the momentarily gratifying and the narrowly prudential to more extensive and long-range social goals. Now "value" in this broad sense is synonymous with "good" in a similarly broad sense encompassing a wide range of nonmoral as well as moral criteria. Hence, since the agent values, at least instrumentally, the purposes or objects for which he acts, it can also be said that he regards these objects as at least instrumentally good according to whatever criteria lead him to try to achieve his purpose. . . .

The agent's positive evaluation extends not only to his particular purpose but also a *fortiori* to the generic features that characterize all his actions. These features hence constitute, in his view, what I shall call *generic goods*. Since his action is a means of attaining something he regards as good, even if this is only the performance of the action itself, he regards as a necessary good the voluntariness or freedom that is an essential feature of his action, for without this he would not be able to act for any purpose or good at all. The freedom thus valued consists both in his controlling each of his particular behaviors by his unforced choice and in his longer-range ability to exercise such control. . . .

In addition to the voluntariness or freedom of his actions, the agent also values their generic purposiveness as a necessary good. Since he regards each of the particular purposes for which he acts as good, he regards as good in each case an increase in the level of purpose-fulfillment whereby he achieves the goal for which he acts. But viewed more extensively over the whole range of his actions, their generic purposiveness may be seen from the standpoint of the rational agent to encompass three kinds of goods. First, he regards as good those basic aspects of his well-being that are the proximate necessary preconditions of his performance of any and all of his actions. Second, he regards it as good that his level of purpose-fulfillment not be lowered by his losing something that seems to him to be good. Third, he regards it as good that his level of purpose-fulfillment be raised by his gaining something that seems to him to be good, namely, the goal or objective for which he acts. I shall refer to these three kinds of goods as *basic goods, nonsubtractive goods,* and *additive goods.* Each of these is necessarily involved in all purposive action as viewed by the rational agent, the first kind as its preconditions, the other two kinds as constitutive of his purposes. Each of the three kinds of good is hence also involved in the value-judgments that express his view of the goodness of the purposes for which he acts. . . .

The basic goods, which are the general necessary preconditions of action, comprise certain physical and psychological dispositions ranging from life and physical integrity (including such of their means as food, clothing, and shelter) to mental equilibrium and a feeling of confidence as to the general possibility of attaining one's goals. . . .

Besides basic goods, the agent also necessarily values what I have called nonsubtractive goods. These goods consist in his retaining and not losing whatever he already has that he regards as good. Hence, to lose a nonsubtractive good is to suffer a diminution of the goods one already has; it is to have one's level of purpose-fulfillment lowered. Now every agent, so far as he can, brings it about that his level of purpose-fulfillment is not decreased or lowered by his action, in that he does not lose something that seems to him to be good. The goods in question include the basic well-being of the first dimension of purposiveness, so that there is in this respect a continuum between basic and nonsubtractive goods. But nonsubtractive goods also include, more specifically, whatever else, before his acting, the agent has and regards as good. . . .

The third kind of good involved in the generic purposiveness of action is that which I have called "additive." In acting for a purpose, the agent intends to achieve the purpose for which he acts and hence to gain something that seems to him to be good. Such gain is an increase in his level of purpose-fulfillment, and he necessarily regards it as good, since it directly reflects the conative nature of his action, that for the sake of which he puts forth whatever effort enters into his action. . . .

The final ground for maintaining that the agent must hold that he has rights to the generic goods of freedom and well-being is that, unlike the particular goods or purposes for which he may act, the generic goods are the necessary conditions not merely of one particular action as against another but of all successful action in general. Right-claims are those essentially linked to action because, just as actions themselves are conative and evaluative, so right-claims are demands on the part of agents that the essential prerequisites of their actions at least not be interfered with. It was very likely for this reason that Jefferson included life, liberty, and the pursuit of happiness among the inalienable rights of man. If "happiness" is understood as well-being, these rights are inalienable because, being necessary to all action, no agent could waive them or be deprived of them and still remain an agent. . . .

[B]ecause of the agent's practical conative attachment to the generic features of his successful action, the ascriptions carry his practical advocacy or endorsement. In saying that freedom and well-being are necessary goods for him, the agent is not merely saying that if he is to act, he must have freedom and well-being; in addition, because of the goodness he attaches to all his purposive actions, he is opposed to whatever interferes with his having freedom and well-being and he advocates his having these features, so that his statement is prescriptive and not only descriptive. Similarly, in saying that because freedom and well-being are necessary goods for him it is necessary that other persons at least not interfere with his having these goods, he is not merely stating a "factual" connection between his having X and other persons' not interfering with his having X, or between its being necessary that he have X and its being necessary that other persons not interfere with his having X. In addition, he is setting forth a practical requirement he endorses, that other persons not interfere with his having freedom and well-being. . . .

Every right-claim or attribution of a right is made on behalf of some person or group under a certain description or for a certain reason that is held to justify the claim. This reason need not be set forth explicitly, but the person who upholds the right must at least have it implicitly in view as the justifying ground of his claim. Without such a reason, he would be making not a right-claim but only a peremptory demand akin to that voiced by a gunman. The reason given for the right-claim must ultimately be advanced as a sufficient reason, one that provides a sufficient justifying condition for the person's having the right. Just as, in general, "X is a sufficient condition of Y" means that if X occurs than Y must also occur, so "X is a sufficient justifying condition of Y" means that if X occurs then Y must be justified or established as correct. To take a tentative example, if "X" is that A has promised B to lend him ten dollars and if, given this promise, it must be justified or established as correct that B has a right to receive ten dollars from A, then A's promise is a sufficient justifying condition of B's having this right. . . .

A justificatory reason for a right-claim may or may not explicitly adduce, as the ground of the right, some description or descriptive characteristic of the person for whom the right is claimed. In either case, however, the reason implicitly refers to such a descriptive characteristic, and it can be reformulated, with no change of meaning, as giving such a description. Thus, in my example of the right derived from a promise, the justificatory reason does not explicitly adduce a description of B, the person who has the right; but implicitly it says that B has this right by virtue of having the description or descriptive characteristic that he is the person to whom A has made the promise.

Now whatever the description under which or the sufficient reason for which it is claimed that this person has some right, the claimant must admit, on pain of contradiction, that this right also belongs to any other person to whom that description or sufficient reason applies. This necessity is an exemplification of the formal principle of universalizability in its moral application, which says that whatever is right for one person must be right for any similar person in similar circumstances. But this formal moral principle, in turn, derives from a more general logical principle of universalizability: if some predicate P belongs to some subject S because S has the property Q (where the "because" is that of sufficient reason or condition), then P must also belong to all other subjects $S_1, S_2, \ldots, S_n$ that have Q. If one denies this implication in the case of some subject, such as S_1, that has Q, then one contradicts oneself. For in saying that P belongs to S because S has Q, one is saying that having

Q is a sufficient condition of having P; but in denying this in the case of S_1, one is saying that having Q is not a sufficient condition of having P. . . .

Since, then, to avoid contradicting himself the agent must claim he has the rights of freedom and well-being for the sufficient reason that he is a prospective agent who has purposes he wants to fulfill, he logically must accept the generalization that all prospective agents who have purposes they want to fulfill have the rights of freedom and well-being. This generalization is a direct application of the principle of universalizabiltiy, and if the agent denies the generalization, then, as we have seen, he contradicts himself. For on the one hand in holding, as he logically must, that he has the rights of freedom and well-being because he is a prospective purposive agent, he accepts that being a prospective purposive agent is a sufficient condition of having these rights; but if he denies the generalization, then he holds that being a prospective purposive agent is not a sufficient condition of having these rights. . . .

Morality. . . is primarily concerned with interpersonal actions, that is, with actions that affect persons other than their agents. . . . I shall refer to such actions as *transactions*, and to the persons affected by them as *recipients*. I shall also say that both the agent and his recipients *participate* in transactions, although the former does so actively and the latter passively, by undergoing or being affected by the agent's action toward him. . . .

Now the recipients of the agent's action are prospective purposive agents insofar as they can operate voluntarily and purposively, controlling their behavior by their unforced choice with a view to fulfillment of their purposes and having knowledge of relevant circumstances. When it is said that the recipients can operate in these ways, the "can" is a dispositional one, referring to the long-range abilities (whatever their hereditary and environmental sources) that enter into such modes of operation. It would hence be irrelevant for an agent to argue that because he has previously assaulted someone or otherwise made him unable to operate freely and with basic well-being, his victim is not a prospective purposive agent and does not have the rights referred to in the above generalization. The "ought"-judgment entailed by the generalization logically must be accepted by the agent as binding on all his conduct toward other prospective agents, so that in coercing or harming any of them he violates a requirement he is rationally obliged to accept. . . .

Since the recipients of the agent's action are prospective agents who have purposes they want to fulfill, the agent must acknowledge that the generalization to which we saw that he is logically committed applies to his recipients: they too have rights to freedom and well-being. Their right to freedom means that just as the agent holds that he has a right to control whether or not he will participate in transactions, so his recipients have the right to control whether or not they will participate. Hence, the agent ought to refrain from interfering with their freedom by coercing them: their participation in transactions must be subject to their own consent, to their own unforced choice. The recipient's right to well-being means that just as the agent holds that he has a right to maintain the conditions and abilities required for purposive action, so his recipients also have the right to maintain these. Hence, the agent ought at least to refrain from harming his recipients by interfering with their basic, nonsubtractive, and additive goods, especially when these are viewed generically-dispositionally. In certain circumstances, moreover, when his recipients' well-being cannot otherwise be maintained through their own efforts, their right to well-being entails that the agent ought to act positively to assist them to have these conditions or abilities.

It follows from these considerations that every agent logically must acknowledge certain generic obligations. Negatively, he ought to refrain from coercing and from harming his recipients; positively, he ought to assist them to have freedom and well-being whenever they cannot otherwise have these necessary goods and he can help them at no comparable cost to himself. The general principle of these obligations and rights may be expressed as the following precept addressed to every agent: *Act in accord with the generic rights of your recipients as well as of yourself.* I shall call this the *Principle of Generic Consistency (PGC),* since it combines the formal consideration of consistency with the material consideration of rights to the generic features or goods of action. The two components of the *PGC,* requiring action in accord with the recipients' generic rights of freedom and of well-being, I shall call the *generic rules.*

The *PGC* is a necessary principle in two ways. It is formally or logically necessary in that for any agent to deny or violate it is to contradict himself, since he would then be in the position of holding that rights he claims for himself by virtue of having certain qualities are not possessed by other persons who have those qualities. The principle is also materially necessary, or categorical, in that, unlike other principles, the obligations of the *PGC* cannot be escaped by any agent by shifting his inclinations, interest, or ideals. or by appealing to institutional rules whose contents are determined by convention. Since the generic features of action are involved in the necessary structure of agency, and since the agent must hold that he has rights to these features simply insofar as he is a prospective purposive agent, he rationally must accept that his recipients also have these rights insofar as they too are prospective purposive agents. In this regard, the *PGC* is unlike those moral principles whose contents are contingent and normatively escapable in that they reflect the variable desires or opinions of agents. . . .

The *PGC* is an egalitarian universalist moral principle since it requires an equal distribution of the most general rights of action. It says to every agent that just as, in acting, he necessarily manifests or embodies the generic features of action — voluntariness and purposiveness—and necessarily claims the generic goods as his rights, so he ought to accept that his recipients, too, should manifest or embody these same generic features and have these same generic goods as their rights. The agent must hence be impartial as between himself and other persons when the latter's freedom and well-being are at stake, so that he ought to respect their freedom and well-being as well as his own. He should therefore treat other persons as well as himself as persons and not as things or objects whose only relation to himself in transactions is that of facilitating his own purpose-fulfillment. To violate the *PGC* is to establish an inequality or disparity between oneself and one's recipients with regard to the generic features and rights of action and hence with regard to whatever purposes or goods are attainable by action. The equality required by the *PGC* runs in both directions. It does not require that an agent surrender his own freedom or well-being for the sake of his recipients. They have a right to a parity of generic goods with him but not to a disparity in their favor any more than in his own. . . .

The *PGC* is the supreme principle of morality, taking precedence over all other moral or practical principles of interpersonal conduct. For since its content is the generic features that necessarily enter into all action, the *PGC* bears on all actions or pursuits of purposes and hence of goods. Any other moral principles either are inconsistent with the *PGC*, in which case they involve contradictions and are morally wrong, or else are specifications of the *PGC*, dealing only with certain kinds of actions or purposive pursuits, so that its moral provisions are more extensive than theirs. Since their contents are related to the contents of the *PGC* as species to genus, the other principles must conform to the *PGC* if they are to be morally right. . . .

By way of brief summary: an agent is a person who initiates or controls his behavior through his unforced, informed choice with a view to achieving various purposes; since he wants to fulfill his purposes he regards his freedom and well-being, the necessary conditions of his successful pursuit of purposes, as necessary goods; hence he holds that he has rights to freedom and well-being; to avoid self-contradiction he must hold that he has these generic rights insofar as he is a prospective purposive agent; hence he must admit that all prospective purposive agents have the generic rights; thence he must acknowledge that he ought at least to refrain from interfering with his recipient's freedom and well-being, so that he ought to act in accord with their generic rights as well as his own.

Dorothy Emmet

Emmet was born in London, England, in 1904 and received her university education at Lady Margaret Hall, Oxford, and at Radcliffe College, where she studied with Alfred North Whitehead. After teaching for several years in the Worker's Education program in South Wales, Emmet studied and taught as a Commonwealth Fellow in the United States and as a Research Fellow at Somerville College, Oxford. She was appointed Lecturer in Philosophy at Newcastle-on-Tyne in 1932 and then taught at the University of Manchester from 1938 to 1966, where she was named Sir Samuel Hall Professor of Philosophy in 1946. An emeritus professor at Manchester since 1966, Emmet is also an Honorary Fellow at Lady Margaret Hall, Oxford, and an Emeritus Fellow at Lucy Cavendish College, Cambridge. Her writings include *The Nature of Metaphysical Thinking, Function, Purpose and Powers, Roles, Rules, and Relations,* and *The Effectiveness of Causes.*

The Moral Prism (1979)*

Morality indeed calls for powers of appreciation, to see what people are like in their passions, conflicts, achievements, and here the arts of the novelist and poet, sometimes too the painter, can enlarge understanding. But beyond understanding, morality is turned towards action, to principles which guide it and to purposes to be achieved, and to the clashes of principle and purpose, of principle and principle, and of purpose and purpose. There are diversities of claims, and priorities cannot be assumed.

Different types of theory may indeed give prominence to one feature rather than another, but a serious theory must, I believe, recognize that all have a place in any possible morality. . . .

There is nothing new in the notion of a diversity of types. James Martineau wrote *Types of Ethical Theory* in 1885, and C. D. Broad wrote *Five Types of Ethical Theory* in 1930, and their types are by no means exhaustive. Is this diversity limited by there being certain necessary conditions for any possible morality, even if no one is a sufficient defining condition?

One candidate has been Universalisability. To be moral is to accept that what would be right for you would be right for me if similarly placed. This goes with giving reasons for what may be right, since a reason, as distinct from an emotional reaction, must be more general than the immediate instance. Universalisability, however, cannot be a sufficient criterion of morality, since it only tells us to be consistent in the use of principles, not what principles to adopt. If we are prepared to say that anyone who applies his principles consistently is *ipso facto* moral, we can be confronted with what R. M. Hare calls "fanatics:" his example is the non-Jew who says that it is right to gas Jews because he sincerely maintains that he himself, were he a Jew, ought to be gassed. Hare thinks such people are logically unassailable. But he shows he is uneasy by calling them "fanatics." "Fanatics" is a term of opprobrium, and thus brings in an axiological factor. . . .

Indeed, if we look at the greatest moral theory which centered on the notion of principle, namely Kant's, we see that, while it says that one should act on a maxim which one can will to be a universal law, it says more than just "Be consistent," or even "Do not adopt self-defeating maxims such as that everyone should tell lies." Besides the dominant deontological factor that one should do one's duty according to principle, there is a latent axiological factor; some principles could not be *willed* because they would be conducive to a society of which one could not approve, such as one in which people acted on the principle of not bothering to improve their talents; although there need be nothing self-contradictory in adopting such a principle, Kant says one could not *will* this as a universal law.

Universalisability, as consistency in the application of principles, then, can be backed by approval of the principles to be applied and the purposes which they serve. Where do we look for criteria of approvals? One simple answer is the emotivist's; one need not look further than one's own feelings, expressed in one's "pro-" and "con-" attitudes. But a *judgement* of approval, if one acknowledges a need to justify it to others, or indeed to justify it to oneself, must be more than just expression of feeling. If justification is to be more than rationalising the feelings one already has, it will appeal for corroboration by others or by oneself in a cool hour, and it may be open to reconsideration.

One way of justifying or of revising approvals and deciding whether they are *moral* approvals was suggested by Adam Smith. The appeal is to the verdict of the character he called "the Impartial Spectator"; recent moralists have appealed to a more rarefied character called "the Ideal Observer". For Adam Smith, approval of the attitude of another person and the conduct stemming from it comes from sympathy, sympathy being "a fellow feeling with any passion of another whatsoever". ("Sympathy" in this use is concordance *with* the passions of another, not a feeling for another.) Though this feeling is at the root of moral sentiment, as a moral sentiment it must be combined with a sense of the *propriety* of the passion, particularly as being or not being in proportion to its cause. A passion of violent anger, for instance, might be disproportionate to the cause which excites it. "Propriety" brings in an element of judgement besides feeling, and it is the approval of the "Impartial Spectator" stemming from this which should be the court of appeal. Adam Smith's Impartial Spectator, "the man within the breast", stands for the capacity to distance oneself from one's own emotions and conduct; to see how they would look from another point of view, perhaps from what would nowadays be called a "reversal of roles", though the Impartial Spectator does not necessarily give the verdict from the reversed role. He gives his verdict impartially. . . .

When we come to actual moral judgements which we imagine might be made by Ideal Observers, these may well vary according to the moral surround in which they are passed. By this I do not just mean the empirical cultural moral surround. I mean rather the reactions of an Ideal Observer could be affected by the type of moral theory he is supposed to hold. The approvals of an Utilitarian Ideal Observer might not be the same as those of a Kantian one, or those of a more aesthetically-minded, whom I shall call a "Nietzschean", one. So while the appeal to an Ideal Observer fastens on the factor of approval guided by impartiality and knowledge of facts, these do not provide sufficient moral criteria, since "believing correctly all the facts" which would make a difference to his reaction, even if it could be known that he did so, would not in itself produce a unique moral reaction. Facts and their consequences have to be evaluated, and if he is to evaluate (let alone evaluate uniquely) the Ideal Observer will need some further qualifications. Brandt does indeed also give his Ideal Observer a strong and favourable sentiment towards all human beings, and this attitude of benevolence might evaluate facts in their bearing on people's welfare or happiness. Brandt's Ideal Observer, with disinterestedness, knowledge of facts and general benevolence, might be a universal utilitarian of the Sidgwick type, one who would consider consequences in their effect on people's welfare and happiness, and would also have a sense of fairness. There could still, however, be the question, for instance, of how an Ideal Observer would evaluate the priorities of someone striving for excellence in some particular attainment which may cut across concern for other people's welfare. There might also be a Kantian Ideal Observer, in whom the attitude of general benevolence gave place to one of respect for people's moral nature and moral freedom. Such a Kantian Ideal Observer need not take his stand on the notion of inviolate moral principles; there is a more liberal Kantian position, where the categorical imperative stands for confronting another person as a rational moral being. This Kantian Ideal Observer would not be concerned with the consequences for human welfare of a person's behaviour, but with seeing whether it expresses a good will. There might also be a Nietzschean Ideal Observer, who would approve of whatever led to someone doing something important, "important" standing, for instance, for some intellectual or aesthetic achievement, not necessarily just for the advancement of power. He could approve of other people being used for this, if the end was judged sufficiently important.

Here are three different types of Ideal Observer, registering approvals in the context of three different types of moral theory, and there could indeed be more. All Ideal Observers, however, share the quality of impartiality, and, in whatever moral surround they figure, they may all be taken to disapprove of callousness. By callousness, I mean indifference where care and thought could be taken. This is not the same as freedom from emotional involvement in circumstances where in fact there is nothing one can do. This—a form of Stoic *apatheia*— may indeed in some circumstances be a condition of moral and social survival.

Universalisability, then, as consistency of principle and impartiality in judgement, is by no means a sufficient moral criterion. Some Ideal Observer theorists put more flesh on these bones by adding a quality of general benevolence, but this is not incontestable. Moreover, are the original criteria of consistency and impartiality incontestable? If not sufficient criteria of moral judgements, are they even necessary ones? Consistency demands that what would be a reason in one situation would also be a reason in others like it. But Existentialists would say that there will never be anyone just like me, or any other situation just like this one. So I must make my unique decision, for which no reasons can be given, since reasons in the nature of the case are couched in general terms. This would cut out *thinking* about what one ought to do. A decision would be an individual response to a situation with no reasons by which one could back or justify it. Sometimes, no doubt, we may be reduced to these desperate straits, but I doubt whether they are prototypic of all serious moral decisions.

Nevertheless, there may well be situations where the moral decision has to be made not with an attitude of detached impartiality, but where one is, as the Existentialists would say, *engage*. One is committed, or one is passionately on someone's side; one might be in a towering rage, and the very strength of one's feelings might produce a more inspired judgement than might have come out of judicial detachment. Current Universalisability and Ideal Observer theories use forensic metaphors; the substantive virtues built into them are the judicial virtues. What is put forward as a piece of meta-ethics is in fact a part of a theory (or can appear as a part of various theories) which also has normative implications and whose generality over the whole range of moral judgements can be disputed.

Another suggested distinguishing characteristic of morality is that it is binding; the moral "ought," as distinct from the deliberative "ought" and as distinct from inclination, has binding force. If this is not just to be social pressure, it must be a pressure one puts on oneself. R. M. Hare puts this in an extreme way by saying that the force of "ought" is that of a command, and that "I ought to do this" is a command which I address to myself.

Small children are indeed sometimes found telling themselves to do and not to do things, probably because they are imitating what their elders say to them. But in adult life one does not usually so talk to oneself. In any case, why should an adult tell himself to do things unless he has some reason for doing so? And in communications to other people sheer command is hardly a basis for moral obedience, unless there is some context in which it is held that the person commanding is entitled to be obeyed.The morally prescriptive "ought" is, therefore, not just a command. I have suggested that its force may come from a commitment. Commitment is here being used widely, where there have been previous resolutions, or even where one has set oneself towards a way of living which will have implications for one's later actions. (I am not here thinking of intellectual commitments to particular views, except in so far as these have practical consequences.) Contracts are a paradigm case of commitments carrying obligations—so too are promises, but in the case of contracts the obligation is a mutual one. Some moralists have therefore tried to present the "obligation" aspect of morality in a contract model. . . .

The appeal of contract theories, especially where some putative social contract is made the basis of moral as well as political obligation, is that it seems unreasonable to say that one has obligations which one has in no sense undertaken; and, moreover, the mutual undertaking in the notion of a contract suggests a reason for making it—would an undertaking be mutual if it were not to the interest of both parties? In the case of moral obligations, how far can this notion of mutual undertaking be stretched metaphorically to cover cases where there is no explicit agreement between parties or means of enforcement? While a contract is a paradigm example of a commitment, I should want to use the notion of commitment more widely to cover not only mutual undertakings, but the taking on of courses of action or adoption of principles consequent on one's considered way of life. One can thus keep the element of responsible acceptance without having to imagine mutual undertakings. Particular obligations can then be consequential on this acceptance, rather than each one severally being taken account of *de novo* as something to be accepted or rejected. This need not mean, however, that we are just saddled with them.

Undoubtedly a good many of our "obligations" do seem to be things we just find ourselves saddled with: this may be because they are part of the *mores*—we are socialised into thinking we should so behave, and this, we have seen, is a source of the unanalysed feeling of "ought." Where the "ought" is what I have called a pressure we put on ourselves in virtue of a commitment, and where this commitment is not an explicit mutual undertaking, it can be seen more generally as consequent on one's considered decision to live in one way rather than another. So, though people are not responsible for having parents as they are for having children, they may, none the less, hold themselves to be committed to doing something about helping their parents in their old age. This is sometimes presented as a quasi-contractual return for services rendered in childhood. More likely, it is seen as part of a way of living in which one acquires concern for the needs of people with whom one has been intimately connected. This can be a concern which may not only be induced by social conditioning. It can become part of a responsibly adopted life-style. In making commitment, as distinct from unanalysed pressure, stand behind "ought", I am not saying that there need be no reasons for commitments, still less that to what one is committed does not matter so long as one is committed (which seems sometimes implied in the Existentalist notion of engagement), and that one does not have sometimes to disengage oneself.

Commitment, therefore, though a factor in morality, cannot stand as a sufficient one. The more we recognise different factors within morality, and do not allow that priorities can always be settled by applying one of them across the board, the more the weight in making decisions has to rest on *judgement*. If judgement is not just to be snap, it must be capable of improvement, of there being good judgement as well as poor judgement. How then is it cultivated? Partly, like any skill, by exercise; by seeing that situations present problems, and struggling with what one ought to do where there are no textbook answers. Partly also by taking responsibility for a decision when made, and, if it turns out badly, trying to see what one can learn from it. Knowledge of facts is obviously part of this; and also a moral quality of disinterestedness, which may be deeper than the quality of judicial impartiality which can be its appropriate form in some circumstances. This disinterestedness may be better designated as "liberty of spirit", or even as the "purity of heart" which Kierkegaard said was the condition for willing "the Good".

I have been speaking of "moral judgements". In the rest of this chapter I shall look at what it might mean for a moral judgement to be oriented towards "good". Is there a sense in which "good" has pride of place, standing over principle, purpose and approvals, which may be variably emphasised in any given applications of the essentially contestable concept of morality? Whichever factor is emphasised, is it still subject to the sovereignty of good, so that it is no accident that the great amoralists seek to go "beyond Good and Evil"?. . .

To speak *simpliciter* of Good registers a conviction that there are things which are admirable which we can learn to appreciate, whether or not they further our interests and purposes, and, most importantly, that there can be growth in appreciation. One would like to say that Good is a Regulative Ideal to which one can approximate in saying "*x* is better than *y* and *y* is better than *x*". But for something to function as a Regulative Ideal one must know in principle what it would be like to satisfy it, even if it never in fact is satisfied, otherwise how do we know that we are getting nearer to it and when we are deviating from it? Since Good *simpliciter* is not specifiable as to its content, can one call its sovereignty over particular judgements of "better and worse" a Regulative Ideal? I believe it has a function in standing for the belief that there can be growth in appreciation. To learn to appreciate is not just to register one's desires. It is to educate one's desires; to believe that judgements based on these at any given time can be improved; that one goes on learning, and that there is always likely to be a gap between what one appreciates here and now and what would be full appreciation. This would go for moral judgement as well as other kinds of appreciation such as aesthetic, and for our attempts to narrow the gap between what is subjectively right, as the best judgement one can now make, and what would indeed be the best judgement that could be made. Good, as what could command unqualified approval, is here used as a term with transcendental reference; we have met other such—"Objective Right","Will of God","verdict of an Ideal Observer"—and whether or not these have a metaphysical reference they function in affirming a belief that judgements are corrigible and there is indeed a difference between those which are better and those which are worse. "Better and worse" would then not only register preferences, but be grounds for preference.

Grounds for preference can of course, often be specifiable within a recognised purpose, or with references to already existing desires. Since one can normally take for granted that a person does not want to get typhoid, if he is in an unhealthy place he can judge that it is better to boil his water and not just drink it out of the tap. Such cases are easy to defend. One could also easily defend the cases where a person is told that he will very likely enjoy something more, for instance a certain kind of beer, if he takes the trouble to try it on a number of occasions and to acquire the taste. The more difficult cases are where growth in appreciation does not reach this kind of end state. I have suggested that one may educate one's desires as well as one's judgements with reference to an ideal which will not be a particular finite end state at which one stops, and I have called such ideal notions "transcendental". Transcendental notions, if they meant that unless one occupies the transcendental position (which of course one does not) one cannot get going in making judgements, would stultify morality. The reference to them should set a direction; one must be able to get going in making moral judgements from where one is and also be able to say that there are ways of making them which can lead to improvement. Yet this marks out a direction of improvement, not the prospect of an achieved adequacy. The reference to a transcendental notion can have this function of indicating openness to a possibility which cannot be fully satisfied. . . .

So our question is whether a person can come not only to change the things he desires, but whether he himself also is changed through changing the thing he desires, in more than the trivial sense in which A-desiring-*x* is different from A-desiring-*y*. And, most crucially, can he change from a person who desires things because he can use them for his own purposes to being a person who has come to appreciate things and adapt himself to his appreciation?

It is in these terms that I should want to see the distinction between "objectivity" and "subjectivity" in judgements where values as well as facts are involved. It is the distinction between what one happens to want and what one can come to appreciate—a change in orientation towards learning to appreciate, an orientation guided by the conviction that there is indeed something to be learnt, and that this includes ways of living, the life-styles to which we commit ourselves.

One might say that what is learnt is how better to follow one's chosen life-style, "better" and "worse" having an application within this context. Then if one's life-style is egoistic, promoting one's own interests and manipulating other people to serve one's purposes, one can learn to do this more skillfully and come to appreciate subtler methods. What of saying that there might be a better life-style? Here one must perforce make a first-person recommendation, hoping nevertheless that there are considerations by which it can be supported. I shall here only indicate some features in what might be such a life-style. I should put high any life-style which accepts the complexity of moral issues; the need to think about the worthiness of one's projects; the mutuality of relationships with other people; the need for courage in one's civic roles as well as generosity in one's more personal face-to-face dealings. I should also rank highly the capacity to see how proposed actions could threaten rather than strengthen mutual trust, since I see this trust as a condition for most of the enterprises and relationships which we find rewarding. All this will call on one to enlarge one's imagination in seeing the situations in which one acts; not only seeing single chains of cause and effect, but ramifications and repercussions. It will mean trying to see what one's proposed actions will be likely to do to other people, not only in external help or hurt, but in their effects on internal feelings. A person who sees proposed actions in terms of his own interests can simplify the issues by reducing them to one perspective; he may thereby make his own task of decision easier, but there will be aspects of the situation which he has not opened himself to appreciate. I maintain that a way of living in which such considerations are taken into account is one in which moral judgement is more likely to grow in capacity to face complex issues. It may be said that the considerations I have named are mainly factual, concerned with getting a more adequate grasp of situations. This is so, but I think that the attempt so to see situations is likely to be value-laden. Certain values, notably fairness and sympathy, will be congenial to the effort to detach our view from a weighting in favour of our own interests. Even if not natural features of situations fairness and sympathy can be, to use a medieval term, "connatural" to such a way of looking at the facts.

One has, I think, to decide to make the venture of believing that one can come to appreciate situations in greater depth, and this is a venture reinforced through following it rather than one whose correctness can be demonstrated at the start. The start is to change our orientation from preoccupation with our own interests to liberty of spirit to see things disinterestedly. This is what Iris Murdoch was saying, and I think she was right. Such growth in appreciation could, however, be aesthetic. In morality we speak of will and action as well as of vision and discernment, where discernment is not only of what is given, but in judging what to do. . . .

"What I ought to be doing now" is surely not just being moral. Morality is not so much an activity in itself as on the back of other activities, concerned with what one does in them, and how and when. The particular feature in morality dominant at any given time will be likely to be that most characteristically associated with whatever activity we are involved in. In acting politically, the feature of purpose will be dominant, in acting in a legal or administrative capacity the emphasis will be on principles to be applied impartially. But other factors within morality may become relevant both to the occasion and manner of what is done; there are times when a purpose in politics may be challenged for a principle, and times when sympathetic discretion will temper judicial impartiality, and times in personal relations when keen-edged criticism is more appropriate than tolerant acceptance. To judge morally calls for one to be alert to this complexity; to see that no activity can rightly be carried on by maintaining a form that can become a stereotype, still less by going by the book. There is also the complexity of what constitutes a "situation". The facts of situations in which one has to act and the likely consequences of one's actions are not just single events leading to other events in a single track; they are networks proliferating into other networks. Moreover, one may judge an action to be right because it fits a new emerging state of affairs, not just the alignment of the situation as it now is. One can never see more than a part of this complexity, but one can try to remove the blinkers which confine one's view. . . .

The full stringency of morality is realised when one sees both that one's judgement is problematic and that one must take responsibility for it. It may indeed be that morality can only be final if it is allowed to be problematic, not given in absolute principles. The transcendental reference in the sovereignty of Good can put a question-mark against the finality of any purpose, however imperious, and the universal applicability of any principle, however imperative. The person who sees the claims of some achievement as putting him "beyond good and evil" may be right in so far as he interprets these as the customs of some particular social morality. But if he cannot look towards a good beyond his "beyond good and evil", he forfeits a corrective against what may also become a blinkered vision. His purpose may be a noble one: to paint a great picture, or to liberate his country. But the moment may come when something else—perhaps something vitally affecting another person—may need to take precedence. Or perhaps it need not; but under the sovereignty of Good the possibility is not foreclosed.

Gilbert Harman

Born in East Orange, New Jersey, in 1938, Harman earned a bachelor's degree from Swarthmore College in 1960 and a doctorate from Harvard University in 1964. A member of the Department of Philosophy at Princeton University ever since, Harman was promoted to Professor of Philosophy in 1971. He has also directed summer institute and seminar programs sponsored by the National Endowment for the Humanities and has held visiting professorships at Berkeley, New York University, Rockefeller University, and Johns Hopkins. An editorial board member for several major journals, Harman has also held fellowships from the American Council of Learned Societies, the Guggenheim Foundation, and the National Endowment for the Humanities and has served on the Board of the Council for Philosophical Studies. He has authored a number of scholarly articles and has authored or coauthored such works as *The Nature of Morality*, *The Logic of Grammar*, and *Thought*.

Relativistic Ethics: Morality as Politics (1980)*

LET me begin by saying something about what I will call "the naive view" of morality. In this view, morality involves one or more basic moral demands that everyone accepts, or has reasons to accept, as demands on everyone on which all moral reasons to do things depend. This view has three parts. First, it says that there are certain basic moral demands that everyone accepts or at least has reasons to accept; let me refer to this as the claim that morality is "nonrelative." Second, these demands are supposed to be accepted as demands on everyone; they are to have universal application. I will refer to this as the claim that morality is "universal." Third, these demands are supposed to be the source of all moral reasons for agents to do things; I will refer to this as the claim that morality is "agent centered" or, sometimes, that it "takes the point of view of an agent" rather than a critic. In the naive view, then, morality is nonrelative, universal, and agent centered.

From Gilbert Harman, "Relativistic Ethics: Morality as Politics" in *Midwest Studies in Philosophy III*, ed. P.A. French, T.E. Uehling, and H.K. Wettstein (Morris: University of Minnesota, Morris), Copyright © 1978 by the University of Minnesota, Morris. Used with permission.

In this view, the basic moral demands are or ought to be accepted by *everyone,* as demands on *everyone,* providing reasons for *everyone.* Who is "everyone"? Kant included every rational being, not only human beings but also angels and rational inhabitants of other planets. A rational Martian would accept, or have reasons to accept, the basic demands of morality because, according to Kant, the basic moral demands are simply demands of rationality which follow from the nature of reason (which he took to be the same in all rational beings.)

We need not be so strict, however. Some people who accept what i am calling the naive view may not wish to commit themselves about Martians. They may see the source of moral demands in human nature, rather than in an absolutely universal reason. They may suppose, for example, that these demands derive from a natural human sympathy one feels for others or from some other presumed fact about "the human condition." They may therefore wish to restrict the range of "everyone," claiming only that every rational human being accepts or has reasons to accept the basic demands of morality. Some may even want to restrict the range of "everyone" even further to those who have been exposed to civilized morality, for they may not wish to claim that so-called ignorant savages have any reason to accept the basic demands of morality.

For my present purposes, it does not matter whether or not the range of "everyone" is restricted in one of these ways, for it seems to me highly probable that, whether or not the range of "everyone" is thus restricted, there are no substantive moral demands everyone has a reason to accept. I am inclined to believe that, for any such demand, someone might fail to accept it without being ignorant of relevant facts, without having miscalculated, without having failed to see the consequences of his or her opinions, and without being in any way irrational. You cannot always argue someone into being moral. Much depends on his or her antecedent interests and principles. If his or her principles and interests diverge sufficiently from yours, it may well happen that he or she has no reason to accept your morality.

Invaders from outer space who are unaffected by weapons we might use against them may have no reason to concern themselves with us. The fact that their actions are harmful to us may carry no weight at all with them, without their being in any way ignorant or irrational. Certain successful criminals seem to have no reason to be at all concerned about their victims; they simply do not care, seemingly without being irrational or ignorant in not caring. Cynical politicians who are interested only in acquiring and maintaining power will lie to the public without necessarily being uninformed, irrational, or stupid. In each of these cases someone would seem not to have reasons to accept moral demands most of us take to be important. Many other cases might also be cited, cases of commonplace amorality, other cases in which someone accepts a morality radically different from ours, and so forth.

Such cases obviously pose a problem for the naive view. Various responses are possible. Consider for example R. M. Hare's theory. Recall that, in the naive view, morality involves one or more basic demands that everyone accepts or ought to accept as demands on everyone on which all moral reasons to do things depend; morality is, in other words, nonrelative, universal, and agent centered. Hare is attracted to this naive position but, like many people today, he also believes that there are no substantive moral demands that everyone has a reason to accept. His response is to abandon nonrelativism, while attempting to retain universality and the point of view of the agent. In his view, then, each person accepts certain basic demands as demands on everyone on which all moral reasons to do things depend, but the demands in question may vary from one person to another.

This means that Hare takes himself to accept certain moral demands as demands on everyone even though he also agrees that some people have no reason at all to act in accordance with those demands; but that is puzzling. To accept a demand as a moral demand on George, among others, would seem to involve the thought that George ought to act in accordance with that demand—that there are moral reasons for him to do so. How then can Hare also suppose that George may, after all, have no reasons to act in accordance with that demand?

The answer is that, in Hare's view, one can accept a moral demand as a demand on everyone without supposing that everyone now has a reason to act in accordance with that demand. It is enough if one intends to try to get everyone else to accept that demand as a demand on him or herself.

There are, however, two things wrong with this. First, it does not provide a reasonable interpretation of universality. Hare is only pretending to accept certain demands as demands on everyone. Rather, he accepts them merely as demands on himself that he intends to try to get everyone else to accept. Second, the intention to try to get everyone else to accept a given demand is itself quite unusual. Few people ever have intentions of this sort. So it is unlikely that many people would ever accept moral demands in the way that Hare's theory says they should.

A related difficulty arises for Hare's analysis of the moral *ought*. In Hare's view, *George ought not to eat meat* is roughly equivalent to *George's not eating meat is in accordance with the general imperatives I hereby accept*. This allows a vegetarian to judge that George ought not to eat meat even if the vegetarian also believes that George (who is not a vegetarian) has no reason not to eat meat. But this is surely to misuse the moral *ought,* which is normally used to speak of things an agent has moral reasons to do.

Indeed, in each of its uses, the word *ought* is used to speak of things for which someone has reasons. The epistemic *ought,* for example, is used to speak of things that there are reasons to expect, as when we say that the train ought to be here soon. The evaluative *ought* is used to speak of what there are reasons to hope or wish for or take some other positive attitude towards, as when we say that there ought to be more love in the world or that a knife ought to be sharp. The simple *ought* of rationality is used to speak of something for which an agent has reasons of any sort to do, as when we say that a burglar ought to wear gloves. And the moral *ought* is used to speak of things an agent has moral reasons to do, as when we say that a burglar ought to reform and go straight.

In elaborating this connection between the moral *ought* and talk of reasons, I do not mean that the fact that an agent morally ought to do something is itself a moral reason to do it. That would be open to the objection that such a fact gives an agent a reason to do something only if he or she has some reason to care about what he or she ought morally to do. Actually, the issue here is whether the fact that an agent has a reason to do something is itself a reason for him or her to do that thing. Similarly, we can easily imagine a dispute as to whether the fact that the train ought to be here soon is a reason to expect the train to be here soon, which is to dispute whether the fact that there is a reason to expect the train to be here soon is itself a reason to expect the train to be here soon. This sort of technical issue is, however, not directly relevant to our present concerns, and I will not try to resolve it. . . .

Rather, we should say this: Two plausible ideas are in conflict, relativism and universality. It is difficult to believe in nonrelativism, because it is difficult to believe that there are substantive moral demands that everyone has reasons to accept. But, if relativism is true, then universality is false, and that is hard to believe, because it is hard to believe that basic moral principles do not apply to everyone.

More precisely, if relativism is true, as seems likely, the ordinary notion of morality is based on a false presupposition and we find ourselves in the position of those who thought morality was the law of God and then began to suspect there was no God. Relativism implies that morality as we ordinarily understand it is a delusion, a vain and chimerical notion.

Fortunately, there is a reasonable substitute. We can have relativism and a good approximation of morality as it is ordinarily conceived if we modify the naive view by relativising the range of "everyone" throughout to those who accept or have reasons to accept certain basic moral demands. In this relativistic view, there are various moralities, each involving different basic demands, demands which certain people accept or have reasons to accept as demands on those people—in other words on those people who accept or have reasons to accept those demands— demands on which depend all reasons arising from that morality for those people to do things.

This is a natural view of morality to take if one supposes that morality rests on a tacit agreement or convention among a group of people. Other things being equal, the existence of an agreement or convention gives someone a reason to act in accordance with it only if he or she accepts the agreement or has reasons to do so. Furthermore, the hypothesis that moral demands derive from conventions arrived at through implicit bargaining and mutual adjustment helps to account for the content of actual moralities. The fact that participants aim at provisions that are in their own interests helps to explain the rough utilitarian character of our own morality. The fact that compromises are necessary among people of different powers and resources accounts for the fact that the duty to avoid harm to others is much stronger in our morality than is the duty to help those who need help, even though these duties should have the same strength from a purely utilitarian point of view. Since everyone would benefit equally from a duty not to harm others, whereas the poor and weak would benefit much more from a duty of mutual aid than the rich and powerful would, the expected compromise is a fairly strong prohibition against harm and a weaker duty of mutual aid, which is what we have in our morality. It is difficult to see how else the distinction we make might be explained. . .

In my view, then, moral argument can involve not only argument over the consequences of basic demands but also bargaining over the basic demands themselves. Morality is therefore continuous with politics. Furthermore, a person may belong to a number of different groups with different moralities which may sometimes have conflicting implications. When that happens, a person must decide which side he or she is on.

As in Hare's analysis, a moral *ought* judgement will be made in relation to moral demands accepted by the person making the judgment. But, since such a judgment says that a certain agent has reasons to do something, the judgment presupposes that the agent also accepts the relevant moral demands or at least has reasons to accept them. *George morally ought not to eat meat* means, roughly, that George's not eating meat is in accordance with the moral demands that "we" accept, where "we" includes the speaker, George, and the intended audience, if any.

Moral *ought* judgments are therefore a species of what I call "inner judgments." Inner judgments are made only about those who are assumed to accept (or have reasons to accept) the moral demands on which the judgments are based. Inner moral judgments include not only moral *ought* judgments but also any other moral judgments that attribute moral reasons to someone — for example, the judgment that it was morally wrong of someone to have done a certain thing.

Although all moral judgments are, in this view, relative judgments made in relation to certain moral demands, not all moral judgments are inner judgments in this sense. One can judge that certain outsiders are good or bad or evil from the point of view of one's morality even if they do not share that morality, just as one can judge that outsiders are friends or enemies. Similarly, one can judge that certain situations are good or bad or right or wrong or that they ought or ought not to be the case, even if these situations involve agents that do not participate in the morality relative to which the judgement is made.

It is important to distinguish the moral *ought*, which is used to make inner moral judgments about agents, from the evaluative *ought*, which is used to make non-inner judgments about situations. The sentence *George ought not to eat meat* is ambiguous. It may be used to express an inner moral judgment of George, which presupposes that he accepts or has reasons to accept the relevant moral demands. It may also be used to express a favorable evaluation of the possible state of affairs in which George does not eat meat, an evaluation which does not imply or assume that George himself has any reason to avoid meat but implies only that we, with our standards, have a reason to hope or wish that George will not eat meat (and therefore perhaps a reason to try to bring it about that George does not eat meat). The first interpretation, as an inner judgment, is more natural if we say *George ought morally not to eat meat*. The second interpretation, as a non-inner evaluation, is more natural if we say *meat ought not to be eaten by George* or *it ought not to be the case that George eats meat*.

Now, philosophers commonly say that moral *ought* judgments are "universalizable," by which they mean in part this:

> If you judge of someone that he or she ought morally to do a particular thing, then you are committed to the further judgment that anyone else in similar circumstances ought morally to do the same thing.

This does not hold in the relativistic conception of morality I have been describing, however, since a moral *ought* judgment about someone who accepts or has reasons to accept the relevant moral demands has no implications about anyone who neither accepts nor has reasons to accept those demands. A useful special case does hold, however:

> If you judge of someone that he or she ought morally to do a particular thing, then you are committed to the further judgment that in similar circumstances you ought to do the same thing.

This means, in particular, that you cannot complain about him or her unless you agree that if the situation were reversed, you ought not to act as he or she is acting.

Moral *ought* judgments are also often said to be universalizable in another respect, which is supposed to rule out arbitrary discrimination:

> If you ought to treat someone in a particular way, you ought to treat any other person in the same way unless there is a morally relevant difference between them.

This principle can be counted trivially true, since any difference in the way you ought morally to treat people can be counted as a "morally relevant" difference. Still, the spirit of the principle can be violated in a relativistic conception of morality if the distinction between "us" and "them" is taken to be "morally relevant." In fact, many moralities afford less protection for outsiders than for the primary members of the group, without basing this distinction on any further ground. A morality is, of course, not forced to discriminate in the particular way, but I suspect that almost every morality does so at least to some extent.

Of course, a morality may rest on a tacit convention or agreement without participants realizing it. Participants may in fact accept the naive view, with its presupposition of nonrelativism. I do not wish to say that the relativistic theory I have been describing, morality as politics, captures everyone's conception of morality. I am inclined to believe, rather, that morality as conceived by the naive view does not exist, that the moralities that do exist are based on convention or tacit agreement, and that morality as politics is an acceptable substitute for the naive conception and indeed that it is the most acceptable substitute for that conception of morality.

Notice that in this conception of morality, which I am calling morality as politics, a morality is basically a group affair, depending on moral demands jointly accepted by several people after a certain amount of tacit bargaining and adjustment. We might allow also for a purely personal morality in which someone places demands only upon him or herself. But this is a special and limiting case. . . .

According to the conception of morality as politics, the principles that give you moral reasons to do things are the moral principles that you actually accept. You accept them as principles accepted by the members of some more or less well defined group. What makes a society your society is not, say, the proximity of its other members but rather that you accept the principles of that society as principles for you and other members of that society. You are indeed, in the relevant sense, a member of different groups with different principles: your family, friends, neighbors, colleagues at work, and so on. Since you accept all of the principles of all of these groups, all of the principles give you reasons to do things. This is not to say that once you accept certain principles you must blindly adhere to them ever after. Your acceptance of certain principles can give you reasons to give up or modify other principles you accept. Your other goals and interests can have the same effect.

The principles you accept may conflict—in that case there is typically no easy answer as to what you ought to do; you will have to choose—reasoning somewhat as in any other case in which prior goals, intentions, or principles conflict, making a minimal change in your antecedent principles, etc., that will promote the coherence of your resulting overall view. What reason do you have to follow the relevant principles? You accept them; and your acceptance of them gives you reason to follow them. What reasons did you have to accept the principles in the first place? Reasons of various sorts, for example reasons of self interest: for, if you accept certain principles as governing your dealings with others, they will tend to accept the principles as governing their dealings with you. And, as previously mentioned, once you accept certain moral principles, that may give you reasons to accept other principles.

I conclude that morality as politics provides the most reasonable substitute for the naive conception of morality. Recall that in what I am calling the naive view morality is based on certain moral demands that everyone accepts, or at least has reasons to accept, as demands on everyone and on which all moral reasons depend. Although this seems to capture essential aspects of many people's conception of morality, I have suggested that it must almost certainly be rejected on the grounds that there are no substantive moral demands satisfying those conditions. Morality as politics retains much of the content of the naive view but relativizes the references to "everyone" to the members of one or another group, all of whom accept certain moral demands as demands on themselves and other members of the group. I have argued that other conceptions of morality retain less of the content of the naive view and tend toward unrealistic accounts of what morality requires. Extremely agent centered theories, as in certain forms of existentialism, practically abandon morality as a social enterprise. This is also though less obviously true of extremely critic centered theories, like certain forms of emotivism and like Hare's theory, which are best seen as rejecting the moral *ought* in favor of the *ought* of evaluation. This is, I have suggested, why these theories can make some very unrealistic accounts of what morality requires seem plausible, such as one or another form of utilitarianism.

Alasdair MacIntyre

Alasdair Chalmers MacIntyre was born in Glasgow, Scotland, in 1929. After completing his education at Queen Mary College, The University of London, and Manchester University, MacIntyre taught at several British and American universities—including Manchester, Leeds, Nuffield College (Oxford), Princeton, Essex, and Brandeis—and he served as dean of the College of Liberal Arts at Boston University in 1972-1973. From 1980 to 1982 MacIntyre was Henry Luce Professor of Philosophy at Wellesley College. Since 1982, he has been W. Alton Jones Professor of Philosophy at Vanderbilt. He was awarded an honorary Doctorate of Humane Letters by Swarthmore College in 1983 and an honorary D. Litt. by Queen's University, Belfast, in 1988. MacIntyre was also named McMahon-Hank Professor of Philosophy at the University of Notre Dame in 1988. He is a past president of the American Philosophical Association, a Fellow of Queen Mary College and of the American Academy of Arts and Sciences, and has served on Great Britain's National Council of Diplomas in Art and Design and on its National Humanities Faculty. His publications include *Marxism and Christianity*, *The Unconscious*, and *Whose Justice? Which Rationality?*.

After Virtue (1984)*

By a "practice" I am going to mean any coherent and complex form of socially established cooperative human activity through which goods internal to that form of activity are realized in the course of trying to achieve those standards of excellence which are appropriate to, and partially definitive of, that form of activity, with the result that human powers to achieve excellence, and human conceptions of the ends and goods involved, are systematically extended. Tic-tac-toe is not an example of a practice in this sense, nor is throwing a football with skill; but the game of football is, and so is chess. Bricklaying is not a practice; architecture is. Planting turnips is not a practice; farming is. So are the enquiries of physics, chemistry and biology, and so is the work of the historian, and so are painting and music. In the ancient and medieval

From Alasdair MacIntyre, *After Virtue* (Notre Dame, Ind.: University of Notre Dame Press, 1981). Used with permission.

worlds the creation and sustaining of human communities—of households, cities, nations—is generally taken to be a practice in the sense in which I have defined it. Thus the range of practices is wide: arts, sciences, games, politics in the Aristotelian sense, the making and sustaining of family life, all fall under the concept. But the question of the precise range of practices is not at this stage of the first importance. Instead let me explain some of the key terms involved in my definition, beginning with the notion of goods internal to a practice.

Consider the example of a highly intelligent seven-year-old child whom I wish to teach to play chess, although the child has no particular desire to learn the game. The child does however have a very strong desire for candy and little chance ʾof obtaining it. I therefore tell the child that if the child will play chess with me once a week I will give the child 50 cents worth of candy; moreover I tell the child that I will always play in such a way that it will be difficult, but not impossible, for the child to win and that, if the child wins, the child will receive an extra 50 cents worth of candy. Thus motivated the child plays and plays to win. Notice however that, so long as it is the candy alone which provides the child with a good reason for playing chess, the child has no reason not to cheat and every reason to cheat, provided he or she can do so successfully. But, so we may hope, there will come a time when the child will find in those goods specific to chess, in the achievement of a certain highly particular kind of analytical skill, strategic imagination and competitive intensity, a new set of reasons, reasons now not just for winning on a particular occasion, but for trying to excel in whatever way the game of chess demands. Now if the child cheats, he or she will be defeating not me, but himself or herself.

There are thus two kinds of good possibly to be gained by playing chess. On the one hand there are those goods externally and contingently attached to chess-playing and to other practices by the accidents of social circumstances—in the case of the imaginary child candy, in the case of real adults such goods as prestige, status and money. There are always alternative ways for achieving such goods, and their achievement is never to be had *only* by engaging in some particular kind of practice. On the other hand there are the goods internal to the practice of chess which cannot be had in any way but by playing chess or some other game of that specific kind. We call them internal for two reasons: first, as I have already suggested, because we can only specify them in terms of chess or some other game of that specific kind and by means of examples from such games (otherwise the meagerness of our vocabulary for speaking of such goods forces us into such devices as my own resort to writing of "a certain highly particular kind of"); and secondly because they can only be identified and recognized by the experience of participating in the practice in question. Those who lack the relevant experiences are incompetent thereby as judges of internal goods. . . .

A practice involves standards of excellence and obedience to rules as well as the achievement of goods. To enter into a practice is to accept the authority of those standards and the inadequacy of my own performance as judged by them. It is to subject my own attitudes, choices, preferences and tastes to the standards which currently and partially define the practice. Practices of course, as I have just noticed, have a history: games, sciences and arts all have histories. Thus the standards are not themselves immune from criticism, but nonetheless we cannot be initiated into a practice without accepting the authority of the best standards realized so far. If, on starting to listen to music, I do not accept my own incapacity to judge correctly, I will never learn to hear, let alone to appreciate, Bartok's last quartets. If, on starting to play baseball, I do not accept that others know better than I when to throw a fast ball and when not, I will never learn to appreciate good pitching let alone to pitch. In the realm of practices the authority of both goods and standards operates in such a way as to rule out all subjectivist and emotivist analyses of judgment. De gustibus *est* disputandum.

We are now in a position to notice an important difference between what I have called internal and what I have called external goods. It is characteristic of what I have called external goods that when achieved they are always some individual's property and possession. Moreover characteristically they are such that the more someone has of them, the less there is for other people. This is sometimes necessarily the case, as with power and fame, and sometimes the case by reason of contingent circumstance as with money. External goods are therefore characteristically objects of competition in which there must be losers as well as winners. Internal goods are indeed the outcome of competition to excel, but it is characteristic of them that their achievement is a good for the whole community who participate in the practice. So when Turner transformed the seascape in painting or W.G. Grace advanced the art of batting in cricket in a quite new way their achievement enriched the whole relevant community.

But what does all or any of this have to do with the concept of the virtues? It turns out that we are now in a position to formulate a first, even if partial and tentative definition of virtue: *A virtue is an acquired human quality the possession and exercise of which tends to enable us to achieve those goods which are internal to practices and the lack of which effectively prevents us from achieving any such goods.* Later this definition will need amplification and amendment. But as a first approximation to an adequate definition it already illuminates the place of the virtues in human life. For it is not difficult to show for a whole range of key virtues that without them the goods internal to practices are barred to us, but not just barred to us generally, barred in a very particular way.

It belongs to the concept of a practice as I have outlined it—and as we are all familiar with it already in our actual lives, whether we are painters or physicists or quarterbacks or indeed just lovers of good painting or first-rate experiments or a well-thrown pass—that its goods can only be achieved by subordinating ourselves within the practice in our relationship to other practitioners. We have to learn to recognize what is due to whom; we have to be prepared to take whatever self-endangering risks are demanded along the way; and we have to listen carefully to what we are told about our own inadequacies and to reply with the same carefulness for the facts. In other words we have to accept as necessary components of any practice with internal goods and standards of excellence the virtues of justice, courage and honesty. For not to accept these, to be willing to cheat as our imagined child was willing to cheat in his or her early days at chess, so far bars us from achieving the standards of excellence or the goods internal to the practice that it renders the practice pointless except as a device for achieving external goods.

We can put the same point in another way. Every practice requires a certain kind of relationship between those who participate in it. Now the virtues are those goods by reference to which, whether we like it or not, we define our relationships to those other people with whom we share the kind of purposes and standards which inform practices. Consider an example of how reference to the virtues has to be made in certain kinds of human relationship.

A, B, C, and D are friends in that sense of friendship which Aristotle takes to be primary: they share in the pursuit of certain goods. In my terms they share in a practice. D dies in obscure circumstances, A discovers how D died and tells the truth about it to B while lying to C. C discovers the lie. What A cannot then intelligibly claim is that he stands in the same relationship of friendship to both B and C. By telling the truth to one and lying to the other he has partially defined a difference in the relationship. Of course it is open to A to explain this difference in a number of ways; perhaps he was trying to spare C pain or perhaps he is simply cheating C. But some difference in the relationship now exists as a result of the lie. For their allegiance to each other in the pursuit of common goods has been put in question.

Just as, so long as we share the standards and purposes characteristic of practices, we define our relationship to each other, whether we acknowledge it or not, by reference to standards of truthfulness and trust, so we define them too by reference to standards of justice and of courage. If A, a professor, gives B and C the grades that their papers deserve, but grades D because he is attracted by D's blue eyes or is repelled by D's dandruff, he has defined his relationship to D differently from his relationship to the other members of the class, whether he wishes it or not. Justice requires that we treat others in respect of merit or desert according to uniform and impersonal standards; to depart from the standards of justice in some particular instance defines our relationship with the relevant person as in some way special or distinctive.

The case with courage is a little different. We hold courage to be a virtue because the care and concern for individuals, communities and causes which is so crucial to so much in practices requires the existence of such a virtue. If someone says that he cares for some individual, community or cause, but is unwilling to risk harm or danger on his, her or its own behalf, he puts in question the genuineness of his care and concern. Courage, the capacity to risk harm or danger to oneself, has its role in human life because of this connection with care and concern. This is not to say that a man cannot genuinely care and also be a coward. It is in part to say that a man who genuinely cares and has not the capacity for risking harm or danger has to define himself, both to himself and to others, as a coward.

I take it then that from the standpoint of those types of relationship without which practices cannot be sustained truthfulness, justice and courage—and perhaps some others—are genuine excellences, are virtues in the light of which we have to characterize ourselves and others, whatever our private moral standpoint or our society's particular codes may be. For this recognition that we cannot escape the definition of our relationship in terms of such goods is perfectly compatible with the acknowledgment that different societies have and have had different codes of truthfulness, justice and courage. Lutheran pietists brought up their children to believe that one ought to tell the truth to everybody at all times, whatever the circumstances or consequences, and Kant was one of their children. Traditional Bantu parents brought up their children not to tell the truth to unknown strangers, since they believed that this could render the family vulnerable to witchcraft. In our culture many of us have been brought up not to tell the truth to elderly great-aunts who invite us to admire their new hats. But each of these codes embodies an acknowledgment of the virtue of truthfulness. So it is also with varying codes of justice and of courage.

Practices then might flourish in societies with very different codes; what they could not do is flourish in societies in which the virtues were not valued, although institutions and technical skills serving unified purposes might well continue to flourish. (I shall have more to say about the contrast between institutions and technical skills mobilized for a unified end, on the one hand, and practices on the other, in a moment.) For the kind of cooperation, the kind of recognition of authority and of achievement, the kind of respect for standards and the kind of risk-taking which are characteristically involved in practices demand for example fairness in judging oneself and others—the kind of fairness absent in my example of the professor, a ruthless truthfulness without which fairness cannot find application—the kind of truthfulness absent in my example of A, B, C, and D—and willingness to trust the judgments of those whose achievement in the practice give them an authority to judge which presupposes fairness and truthfulness in those judgments, and from time to time the taking of self-endangering and even achievement-endangering risks. It is no part of my thesis that great violinists cannot be vicious or great chess-players mean-spirited. Where the virtues are required, the vices also may flourish. It is just that the vicious and mean-spirited necessarily rely on the virtues of others for the practices in which they engage to flourish and also deny themselves the experience of achieving those internal goods which may reward even not very good chess-players and violinists.

To situate the virtues any further within practices it is necessary now to clarify a little further the nature of a practice by drawing two important contrasts. The discussion so far I hope makes it clear that a practice, in the sense intended, is never just a set of technical skills, even when directed towards some unified purpose and even if the exercise of those skills can on occasion be valued or enjoyed for their own sake. What is distinctive in a practice is in part the way in which conceptions of the relevant goods and ends which the technical skills serve—and every practice does require the exercise of technical skills—are transformed and enriched by these extensions of human powers and by that regard for its own internal goods which are partially definitive of each particular practice or type of practice. Practices never have a goal or goals fixed for all time—painting has no such goal nor has physics—but the goals themselves are transmuted by the history of the activity. It therefore turns out not to be accidental that every practice has its own history and a history which is more and other than that of the improvement of the relevant technical skills. This historical dimension is crucial in relation to the virtues.

To enter into a practice is to enter into a relationship not only with its contemporary practitioners, but also with those who have preceded us in the practice, particularly those whose achievements extended the reach of the practice to its present point. It is thus the achievement, and a fortiori the authority, of a tradition which I then confront and from which I have to learn. And for this learning and the relationship to the past which it embodies the virtues of justice, courage and truthfulness are prerequisite in precisely the same way and for precisely the same reasons as they are in sustaining present relationships within practices. . . .

Any contemporary attempt to envisage each human life as a whole, as a unity, whose character provides the virtues with an adequate *telos* encounters two different kinds of obstacle, one social and one philosophical. The social obstacles derive from the way in which modernity partitions each human life into a variety of segments, each with its own norms and modes of behavior. So work is divided from leisure, private life from public, the corporate from the personal. So both childhood and old age have been wrenched away from the rest of human life and made over into distinct realms. And all these separations have been achieved so that it is the distinctiveness of each and not the unity of the life of the individual who passes through those parts in terms of which we are taught to think and to feel.

The philosophical obstacles derive from two distinct tendencies, one chiefly, though not only, domesticated in analytical philosophy and one at home in both sociological theory and in existentialism. The former is the tendency to think atomistically about human action and to analyze complex actions and transactions in terms of simple components. Hence the recurrence in more than one context of the notion of "a basic action". That particular actions derive their character as parts of larger wholes is a point of view alien to our dominant ways of thinking and yet one which it is necessary at least to consider if we are to begin to understand how a life may be more than a sequence of individual actions and episodes.

Equally the unity of a human life becomes invisible to us when a sharp separation is made either between the individual and the roles that he or she plays— a separation characteristic not only of Sartre's existentialism, but also of the sociological theory of Ralf Dahrendorf—or between the different role—and quasi-role— enactments of an individual life so that life comes to appear as nothing but a series of unconnected episodes—a liquidation of the self characteristic, as I noticed earlier, of Goffman's sociological theory. I already also suggested in Chapter 3 that both the Sartrian and the Goffmanesque conceptions of selfhood are highly characteristic of the modes of thought and practice of modernity. It is perhaps therefore unsurprising to realize that the self as thus conceived cannot be envisaged as a bearer of the Aristotelian virtues.

For a self separated from its roles in the Sartrian mode loses that arena of social relationships in which the Aristotelian virtues function if they function at all. The patterns of a virtuous life would fall under those condemnations of conventionality which Sartre put into the mouth of Antoine Roquentin in *La Nausee* and which he uttered in his own person in *L'Etre et le neant*. Indeed the self's refusal of the inauthenticity of conventionalized social relationships becomes what integrity is diminished into in Sartre's account.

At the same time the liquidation of the self into a set of demarcated areas of role-playing allows no scope for the exercise of dispositions which could genuinely be accounted virtues in any sense remotely Aristotelian. For a virtue is not a disposition that makes for success only in some one particular type of situation. What are spoken of as the virtues of a good committee man or of a good administrator or of a gambler or a pool hustler are professional skills professionally deployed in those situations where they can be effective, not virtues. Someone who genuinely possesses a virtue can be expected to manifest it in very different types of situation, many of them situations where the practice of a virtue cannot be expected to be effective in the way that we expect a professional skill to be. Hector exhibited one and the same courage in his parting from Andromache and on the battlefield with Achilles; Eleanor Marx exhibited one and the same compassion in her relationship with her father, in her work with trade unionists and in her entanglement with Aveling. And the unity of a virtue in someone's life is intelligible only as a characteristic of a unitary life, a life that can be conceived and evaluated as a whole. Hence just as in the discussion of the changes in and fragmentation of morality which accompanied the rise of modernity in the earlier parts of this book, each stage in the emergence of the characteristically modern views of the moral judgement was accompanied by a corresponding stage in the emergence of the characteristically modern conceptions of selfhood; so now, in defining the particular pre-modern concept of the virtues with which I have been preoccupied, it has become necessary to say something of the concomitant concept of selfhood, a concept of a self whose unity resides in the unity of a narrative which links birth to life to death as narrative beginning to middle to end.

Such a conception of the self is perhaps less unfamiliar than it may appear at first sight. Just because it has played a key part in the cultures which are historically predecessors of our own, it would not be surprising if it turned out to be still an unacknowledged presence in many of our ways of thinking and acting. Hence it is not inappropriate to begin by scrutinizing some of our most taken-for-granted, but clearly correct conceptual insights about human actions and selfhood in order to show how natural it is to think of the self in a narrative mode.

It is a conceptual commonplace, both for philosophers and for ordinary agents, that one and the same segment of human behavior may be correctly characterized in a number of different ways. To the question "What is he doing?" the answers may with equal truth and appropriateness be "Digging", "Gardening", "Taking exercise", "Preparing for winter" or "Pleasing his wife". Some of these answers will characterize the agent's intentions, other unintended consequences of his actions, and of these unintended consequences some may be such that the agent is aware of them and others not. What is important to notice immediately is that any answer to the questions of how we are to understand or to explain a given segment of behavior will presuppose some prior answer to the question of how these different correct answers to the question "What is he doing?" are related to each other. For if someone's primary intention is to put the garden in order before the winter and it is only incidentally the case that in so doing he is taking exercise and pleasing his wife, we have one type of behavior to be explained; but if the agent's primary intention is to please his wife by taking exercise, we have quite another type of behavior to be explained and we will have to look in a different direction for understanding and explanation.

In the first place the episode has been situated in an annual cycle of domestic activity, and the behavior embodies an intention which presupposes a particular type of household-cum-garden setting with the peculiar narrative history of that setting in which this segment of behavior now becomes an episode. In the second instance the episode has been situated in the narrative history of a marriage, a very different, even if related, social setting. We cannot, that is to say, characterize behavior independently of intentions, and we cannot characterize intentions independently of the settings which make those intentions intelligible both to agents themselves and to others.

I use the word "setting" here as a relatively inclusive term. A social setting may be an institution, it may be what I have called a practice, or it may be a milieu of some other human kind. But it is central to the notion of a setting as I am going to understand it that a setting has a history, a history within which the histories of individual agents not only are, but have to be, situated, just because without the setting and its changes through time the history of the individual agent and his changes through time will be unintelligible. Of course one and the same piece of behavior may belong to more than one setting. . . .

Consider what the argument so far implies about the interrelationships of the intentional, the social and the historical. We identify a particular action only by invoking two kinds of context, implicitly if not explicitly. We place the agent's intentions, I have suggested, in causal and temporal order with reference to their role in his or her history; and we also place them with reference to their role in the history of the setting or settings to which they belong. In doing this, in determining what causal efficacy the agent's intentions had in one or more directions, and how his short-term intentions succeeded or failed to be constitutive of long-term intentions, we ourselves write a further part of these histories. Narrative history of a certain kind turns out to be the basic and essential genre for the characterization of human actions.

It is important to be clear how different the standpoint presupposed by the argument so far is from that of those analytical philosophers who have constructed accounts of human actions which make central the notion of "a" human action. A course of human events is then seen as a complex sequence of individual actions, and a natural question is: How do we individuate human actions? Now there are contexts in which such notions are at home. In the recipes of a cookery book for instance actions are individuated in just the way that some analytical philosophers have supposed to be possible of all actions. "Take six eggs. Then break them into a bowl. Add flour, salt, sugar, etc." But the point about such sequences is that each element in them is intelligible as an action only as a-possible-element-in-a-sequence. Moreover even such a sequence requires a context to be intelligible. If in the middle of my lecture on Kant's ethics I suddenly broke six eggs into a bowl and added flour and sugar, proceeding all the while with my Kantian exegesis, I have *not,* simply in virtue of the fact that I was following a sequence prescribed by Fanny Farmer, performed an intelligible action.

To this it might be retorted that I certainly performed an action or a set of actions, if not an intelligible action. But to this I want to reply that the concept of an intelligible action is a more fundamental concept than that of an action as such. Unintelligible actions are failed candidates for the status of intelligible action; and to lump unintelligible actions and intelligible actions together in a single class of actions and then to characterize action in terms of what items of both sets have in common is to make the mistake of ignoring this. It is also to neglect the central importance of the concept of intelligibility.

The importance of the concept of intelligibility is closely related to the fact that the most basic distinction of all embedded in our discourse and our practice in this area is that between human beings and other beings. Human beings can be held to account for that of which they are the authors; other beings cannot. To identify an occurrence as an action is in the paradigmatic instances to identify it under a type of description which enables us to see that occurrence as flowing intelligibly from a human agent's intentions, motives, passions and purposes. It is therefore to understand an action as something for which someone is accountable, about which it is always appropriate to ask the agent for an intelligible account. When an occurrence is apparently the intended action of a human agent, but nonetheless we cannot so identify it, we are both intellectually and practically baffled. We do not know how to respond; we do not know how to explain; we do not even know how to characterize minimally as an intelligible action; our distinction between the humanly accountable and the merely natural seems to have broken down. And this kind of bafflement does indeed occur in a number of different kinds of situation; when we enter alien cultures or even alien social structures within our own culture, in our encounters with certain types of neurotic or psychotic patient (it is indeed the unintelligibility of such patients' actions that leads to their being treated as patients; actions unintelligible to the agent as well as to everyone else are understood—rightly—as a kind of suffering), but also in everyday situations. . . .

It is now possible to return to the question from which this enquiry into the nature of human action and identity started: In what does the unity of an individual life consist? The answer is that its unity is the unity of a narrative embodied in a single life. To ask "What is the good for me?" is to ask how best I might live out that unity and bring it to completion. To ask "What is the good for man?" is to ask what all answers to the former question must have in common. But now it is important to emphasize that it is the systematic asking of these two questions and the attempt to answer them in deed as well as in word which provide the moral life with its unity. The unity of a human life is the unity of a narrative quest. Quests sometimes fail, are frustrated, abandoned or dissipated into distractions; and human lives may in all these ways also fail. But the only criteria for success or failure in a human life as a whole are the criteria of success or failure in a narrated or to-be-narrated quest. A quest for what?

Two key features of the medieval conception of a quest need to be recalled. The first is that without some at least partly determinate conception of the final *telos* there could not be any beginning to a quest. Some conception of the good for man is required. Whence is such a conception to be drawn? Precisely from those questions which led us to attempt to transcend that limited conception of the virtues which is available in and through practices. It is in looking for a conception of *the* good which will enable us to order other goods, for a conception of *the* good which will enable us to extend our understanding of the purpose and content of the virtues, for a conception of *the* good which will enable us to understand the place of integrity and constancy in life, that we initially define the kind of life which is a quest for the good. But secondly it is clear the medieval conception of a quest is not at all that of a search for something already adequately characterized, as miners search for gold or geologists for oil. It is in the course of the quest and only through encountering and coping with the various particular harms, dangers, temptations and distractions which provide any quest with its episodes and incidents that the goal of the quest is finally to be understood. A quest is always an education both as to the character of that which is sought and in self-knowledge.

The virtues therefore are to be understood as those dispositions which will not only sustain practices and enable us to achieve the goods internal to practices, but which will also sustain us in the relevant kind of quest for the good, by enabling us to overcome the harms, dangers, temptations and distractions which we encounter, and which will furnish us with increasing self-knowledge and increasing knowledge of the good. The catalogue of the virtues will therefore include the virtues required to sustain the kind of households and the kind of political communities in which men and women can seek for the good together and the virtues necessary for philosophical enquiry about the character of the good. We have then arrived at a provisional conclusion about the good life for man: the good life for man is the life spent in seeking for the good life for man, and the virtues necessary for the seeking are those which will enable us to understand what more and what else the good life for man is. We have also completed the second stage in our account of the virtues, by situating them in relation to the good life for man and not only in relation to practices. But our enquiry requires a third stage.

For I am never able to seek for the good or exercise the virtues only *qua* individual. This is partly because what it is to live the good life concretely varies from circumstance to circumstance even when it is one and the same conception of the good life and one and the same set of virtues which are being embodied in a human life. What the good life is for a fifth-century Athenian general will not be the same as what it was for a medieval nun or a seventeenth-century farmer. But it is not just that different individuals live in different social circumstances; it is also that we all approach our own circumstances as bearers of a particular social identity. I am someone's son or daughter, someone else's cousin or uncle; I am a citizen of this or that city, a member of this or that guild or profession; I belong to this clan, that tribe, this nation. Hence what is good for me has to be the good for one who inhabits these roles. As such, I inherit from the past of my family, my city, my tribe, my nation, a variety of debts, inheritances, rightful expectations and obligations. These constitute the given of my life, my moral starting point. This is in part what gives my life its own moral particularity.

This thought is likely to appear alien and even surprising from the standpoint of modern individualism. From the standpoint of individualism I am what I myself choose to be. I can always, if I wish to, put in question what are taken to be the merely contingent social features of my existence. I may biologically be my father's son; but I cannot be held responsible for what he did unless I choose implicitly or explicitly to assume such responsibility. I may legally be a citizen of a certain country; but I cannot be held responsible for what my country does or has done unless I choose implicitly or explicitly to assume such responsibility. Such individualism is expressed by those modern Americans who deny any responsibility for the effects of slavery upon black Americans, saying "I never owned any slaves". It is more subtly the standpoint of those other modern Americans who accept a nicely calculated responsibility for such effects measured precisely by the benefits they themselves as individuals have indirectly received from slavery. In both cases "being an American" is not in itself taken to be part of the moral identity of the individual. And of course there is nothing peculiar to modern Americans in this attitude: the Englishman who says, "*I* never did any wrong to Ireland; why bring up that old history as though it had something to do with *me*?" or the young German who believes that being born after 1945 means that what Nazis did to Jews had no moral relevance to his relationship to his Jewish contemporaries, exhibit the same attitude, that according to which the self is detachable from its social and historical roles and statuses. And the self so detached is of course a self very much at home in either Sartre's or Goffman's perspective, a self that can have no history. The contrast with the narrative view of the self is clear. For the story of my life is always embedded in the story of those communities from which I derive my identity. I am born with a past; and to try to cut myself off from that past, in the individualist mode, is to deform my present relationships. The procession of an historical identity and the possession of a social identity coincide. Notice that rebellion against my identity is always one possible mode of expressing it.

Notice also that the fact that the self has to find its moral identity in and through its membership in communities such as those of the family, the neighborhood, the city and the tribe does not entail that the self has to accept the moral *limitations* of the particularity of those forms of community. Without those moral particularities to begin from there would never be anywhere to begin; but it is in moving forward from such particularity that the search for the good, for the universal, consists. Yet particularity can never be simply left behind or obliterated. The notion of escaping from it into a realm of entirely universal maxims which belong to man as such, whether in its eighteenth-century Kantian form or in the presentation of some modern analytical moral philosophies, is an illusion and an illusion with painful consequences. When men and women identify what are in fact their partial and particular causes too easily and too completely with the cause of some universal principle, they usually behave worse than they would otherwise do.

What I am, therefore, is in key part what I inherit, a specific past that is present to some degree in my present. I find myself part of a history and that is generally to say, whether I like it or not, whether I recognize it or not, one of the bearers of a tradition. It was important when I characterized the concept of a practice to notice that practices always have histories and that at any given moment what a practice is depends on a mode of understanding it which has been transmitted often through many generations. And this, insofar as the virtues sustain the relationships required for practices, they have to sustain relationships to the past—and to the future—as well as in the present. But the traditions through which particular practices are transmitted and reshaped never exist in isolation for larger social traditions. . . .

A living tradition then is an historically extended, socially embodied argument, and an argument precisely in part about the goods which constitute that tradition. Within a tradition the pursuit of goods extends through generations, sometimes through many generations. Hence the individual's search for his or her good is generally and characteristically conducted within a context defined by those traditions of which the individual's life is a part, and this is true both of those goods which are internal to practices and of the goods of a single life. Once again the narrative phenomenon of embedding is crucial: the history of a practice in our time is generally and characteristically embedded in and made intelligible in terms of the larger and longer history of the tradition through which the practice in its present form was conveyed to us; the history of each of our lives is generally and characteristically embedded in and made intelligible in terms of the larger and longer histories of a number of traditions. I have to say "generally and characteristically" rather than "always", for traditions decay, disintegrate and disappear. What then sustains and strengthens traditions? What weakens and destroys them?

The answer in key part is: the exercise or the lack of exercise of the relevant virtues. The virtues find their point and purpose not only in sustaining those relationships necessary if the variety of goods internal to practices are to be achieved and not only in sustaining the form of an individual life in which that individual may seek out his or her good as the good of his or her whole life, but also in sustaining those traditions which provide both practices and individual lives with their necessary historical context. Lack of justice, lack of truthfulness, lack of courage, lack of the relevant intellectual virtues—these corrupt traditions, just as they do those institutions and practices which derive their life from the traditions of which they are the contemporary embodiments. To recognize this is of course also to recognize the existence of an additional virtue, one whose importance is perhaps most obvious when it is least present, the virtue of having an adequate sense of the traditions to which one belongs or which confront one. This virtue is not to be confused with any form of conservative antiquarianism; I am not praising those who choose the conventional conservative role of *laudator temporis acti*. It is rather the case that an adequate sense of tradition manifests itself in a grasp of those future possibilities which the past has made available to the present. Living traditions, just because they continue a not-yet-completed narrative, confront a future whose determinate and determinable character, so far as it possesses any, derives from the past.

STUDY/DISCUSSION ELEMENTS V

1. Terms

a. Impartiality
b. Ethical Statements
   (cf. Moral Judgments)
c. (The) Naive View of Morality
d. Good
e. Empirical Proposition
f. Right
g. Principle(s) of Social Justice
h. Injustice
i. Convention
j. (The) Virtue(s)
k. Internal Good
l. Pseudo-concept
m. Practice
n. (The) Judicial Virtue(s)
o. Restricted Utilitarianism
p. Simple Notion
q. Basic Liberties
r. (An) Agent
s. Moral Demand
t. Setting
u. Emotive
v. Universalizability
w. Justice
x. Standards of Excellence
y. Common Sense Morality
z. Descriptive Ethical Concept
aa. Social Contract
   (cf. Contract Theories)

bb. Generic Goods
   (cf. Primary Goods)
cc. Intelligible Action(s)
dd. (The) Summary View of
   Rules (cf. Rules of Thumb)
ee. Naturalistic Fallacy
ff. Verifiable
gg. Self-interest
hh. Transcendental Notion
ii. Generic Rules
jj. Narrative History
kk. Extreme Utilitarianism
ll. Fairness
mm. Retributive Justice
   (cf. Retributism)
nn. (The) Original Position
oo. Atomistic Thought
pp. Non-Relativism
qq. Plan of Life
rr. (Moral) Appreciation
ss. Duty (cf. Categorical Obligations)
tt. Rights (cf. Right-claim)
uu. (The) Veil of Ignorance
vv. Factual Content (cf. Meaning)
ww. Intrinsic Value
xx. Morality as Politics

2. Theses

a. Every agent regards his or her objectives and goals as good.
b. "Good" denotes an indefinable quality.
c. It is unreasonable to suppose that there are any moral demands which are moral demands on everyone (or on every rational being) whatsoever.
d. Statements of value are significant only when they are scientific statements; otherwise, they are emotive.
e. Every agent must logically accept that all prospective agents have rights to the generic goods of agency.
f. Rational parties to a social contract would agree first to a principle of equal liberty for all.

g. Practices are logically and evaluatively prior to particular actions specified by them.
h. Ethical statements are neither true nor false.
i. Practices and the achievement of internal goods depend upon the virtues (or, in particular, require justice, courage, and honesty).
j. Relativism and universality cannot both be true.
k. The good life for man is the life spent seeking the good life for man.
l. Generic consistency is formally and materially a necessary normative principle for every agent.
m. Goodness is a function of deliberative rationality.
n. We can never be sure whether any action is a moral duty.
o. Utilitarian considerations may be applied to a practice but not to actions falling under it, unless the practice admits of it.
p. The sovereignty of the Good makes moral growth, appreciation, and discernment possible.
q. Extreme utilitarianism uniquely specifies how it is most rational for us to act.
r. A just society will admit only inequalities which maximize the long-term expectations of the least fortunate group in society.
s. We should always obey the moral rules of common sense.
t. Neither universalizability, impartiality, nor commitment is a sufficient criterion for morality.
u. It may be rational to condemn a right action, or to praise a wrong action.
v. Competency to judge internal goods requires subordination within a practice.
w. Intuitionism implies that ethical statements are unverifiable.

Index